The Ethical Basis
of Economic Freedom

THE ETHICAL BASIS
OF ECONOMIC FREEDOM

Edited by Ivan Hill

Published by American Viewpoint, Inc.
University Square, Chapel Hill, N. C., 27514

Library of Congress Catalog Card Number: 76-5728
International Standard Book Number: 0-916152-02-2

Manufactured in the United States of America

Contents

Part Four

Part Five

Essay Reference Notes

Biographical Briefs
on Essayists

Jack N. Behrman, Ph.D., a former United States Assistant Secretary of Commerce (1961–64), is professor of International Business in the Graduate School of Business Administration at the University of North Carolina at Chapel Hill. He is engaged in research on the multinational enterprise and the role of foreign investment in economic development, and serves as an advisor to the National Academy of Science on problems of international industrial development. He has written and lectured widely in his field. Among his most recent publications (1974) are a study for the Department of State on *International Business-Government Communications* (Lexington Books) and monographs for the Council of the Americas, *Conflicting Constraints on the Multinational Enterprise*, and The Atlantic Institute (Paris), *Toward a New International Economic Order*.

John B. Condliffe, D.Sc. (Economics), was born in Australia, and educated in New Zealand and at Cambridge, England. Formerly professor of commerce at the London School of Economics, and visiting professor at the University of Michigan and Yale University, he taught at the University of

California at Berkeley from 1939–58. In 1972 he retired as Senior Economist at the Stanford Research Institute. During the 1930s, he was a member of the Secretariat of the League of Nations; in 1959–60, an advisor to the Indian National Council of Applied Economic Research in New Delhi. His publications include the first six World Economic Surveys written for the League of Nations and the widely quoted *The Commerce of Nations* (1950), for which he was awarded the Wendell L. Willkie Prize in 1960 by the American Political Science Association. His most recent publication, *Defunct Economists* (1974), is a collection of four lectures he delivered in March 1973 at the University of Canterbury, New Zealand, as part of its centennial.

Kenneth Fiester led the CIO delegation that created the Industrial Labor Press Association, AFL-CIO, and served in several offices including the presidency. Although he earned his B.S. in chemical engineering, his early years were spent primarily "newspapering," and for the past thirty years his writing has focused on labor matters. He has served as editor of *Textile Labor* (Textile Workers Union of America, CIO) and later as public relations director as well. In 1957 he was named publications director of the United Auto Workers and in that capacity was founding editor of *UAW Solidarity*, then a weekly. He subsequently served on the public relations staff of the AFL-CIO and as public relations director for the Industrial Union Department. Although much of what he has written has emerged under other bylines and from other lips, articles carrying his byline have appeared in the *Nation*, the *American Scholar*, *Worklife* (formerly *Manpower*) magazines and numerous union periodicals.

Wolfram Fischer, Ph.D., a native of Germany, is currently a member of the Institute for Advanced Study, Princeton, N.J., and professor of economic and social history at the Free University of Berlin. For the past twenty years, his teaching and research has focused on regional and comparative studies of the industrialization process, with special emphasis on sociocultural and sociopolitical variables. He has written widely in his field and is now editing a world economic history of the twentieth century and is writing the introductory volume.

Clifford E. Graese is a partner and member of the Executive Committee of Peat, Marwick, Mitchell & Co., the largest international certified public accounting firm. He is in charge of the firm's accounting and auditing activities. For the past three years he has served as chairman of the American Institute of Certified Public Accountant's (AICPA) Ethics Division's Executive Committee. He has also served as chairman of AICPA's committees on Independence and Code of Ethics Restatement, as well as chairman of the New York State Society of Certified Public Accountant's committee on Management Services.

Ivan Hill is the nonpaid, full-time president of American Viewpoint, Inc. and editor of this volume. After graduating from the University of California at Los Angeles, he worked for a newspaper and radio station, then entered the advertising agency business. He headed his own agency and served as executive vice president of one and senior vice president of another large national firm. His interests, however, have not been limited to advertising; he has also been president of a drug firm, a television-producing company, and a real estate firm. His editing of this volume on "The Ethical Basis of Economic Freedom" is part of his long, continuing effort to challenge America to relate honesty and ethics to the viability of our private enterprise economy.

Leon Jaworski, L.L.M., is senior partner of Fulbright & Jaworski, Houston, Texas. Notable for his role as Special Prosecutor, Watergate Special Prosecution Force (1973–74), he has also seen public service as Presidential Advisor (1964–69), United States Member, Permanent Court of Arbitration, The Hague (1965–69), Member, President's Commission on Law

Enforcement and Administration of Justice (1965–67), and Member, President's Commission on the Causes and Prevention of Violence (1968–69). He was president of the American Bar Association (ABA) in 1971–72 and was presented the ABA Medal, its highest award. He has also received the American College of Trial Lawyers Award for Courageous Advocacy. His articles and addresses have appeared in numerous professional journals and other publications.

Earl W. Kintner, J. D., former general counsel (1953–59) and chairman of the Federal Trade Commission (1959–61), is a senior partner in the Washington, D.C. firm of Arent, Fox, Kintner, Plotkin, and Kahn. One of the leading experts on antitrust and trade regulation law, he is the author of numerous legal articles and books, among them six classical textbooks on regulatory law: *An Antitrust Primer* (1964), *A Robinson-Patman Primer* (1970), *A Primer on the Law of Deceptive Practices* (1971), *Primer on the Law of Mergers* (1973), *An International Antitrust Primer* (coauthor, 1974), and *An Intellectual Property Law Primer* (coauthor, 1975). He served two terms as president of the Federal Bar Association (FBA), is currently president of the FBA Foundation, the Federal Bar Building Corporation, and the National Lawyers Club, and serves as general counsel, Washington counsel or special counsel to thirty-five national trade associations.

Andrew W. Kneier, M.A., is a member of the Issue Development staff at Common Cause, Washington, D.C. One of his special areas of concern is federal conflict of interest regulation and reform. Before joining Common Cause in 1972, he did graduate study in ethics and society at the University of Chicago. He has taught a graduate course on the politics of social change as well as high school courses on social ethics and theology. His writing, as well as his teaching, has dealt with social change and public policy issues from an evaluative perspective. Among his most recent articles are "After Thirty Years: Spotlight on the Lobbies" (*The Nation*, 21 June 1975), "Congress and the Public Interest" (*The Bulletin*, American Society for Information Science, April 1975) and

"Agency Reform and the Public Interest" (*Federal Bar Journal,* Fall 1975, coauthored with David Cohen, president of Common Cause).

Max H. Parrott, M.D., is president of the American Medical Association (1975–76). He has served continuously on AMA's Board of Trustees since 1966, including two terms as its chairman, and earlier as a member of AMA's policy-making House of Delegates and Council on Legislation. In his various AMA positions, he has devoted his major attention to continuing medical education, computer systems, and medical data banking. As president of the Oregon Medical Association in the early 1960s, he helped establish its Medical Political Action Committee, serving as the first chairman. In addition to his private practice in obstetrics and gynecology in Portland, Oregon, he is an assistant clinical professor at the University of Oregon Medical School.

James L. Peacock, Ph.D., is chairman of the Anthropology Department at the University of North Carolina at Chapel Hill. His teaching and research specialty is social anthropology —comparative behavior in various cultures—and he is an expert on Southeast Asian cultures. He is a member of the executive board of the American Anthropological Association, the National Institute of Mental Health's small grants review committee and the National Humanities Faculty, which involves serving as a consultant to secondary schools planning programs in the comparative study of cultures. He has authored or coauthored more than sixty articles and six books, one of which has been translated into other languages. His most recent book (1975) is *Consciousness and Change: Symbolic Anthropology in Evolutionary Perspective.*

Roy A. Rappaport, Ph.D. is chairman of the Department of Anthropology, University of Michigan, Ann Arbor. Much of his research and writing focus on system theory and cybernetics, with special emphasis on the structure of adaptive systems. He also has done considerable work in the anthropology of religion and application of general ecological theory to anthropological problems. As a specialist in Oceania, he has engaged in fieldwork in the Society Islands (archaeological) and New Guinea (ethnographic). He has authored or co-authored some forty monographs, articles, book chapters, and reviews including *Archeology on Mo'orea, French Polynesia* and *Pigs for the Ancestors*. His forthcoming book will explore the structure of ritual, the idea of the sacred, and the notion of the divine.

William E. Simon, United States Treasury Secretary since May 1974, is the nation's chief financial officer. He is chairman of both the Economic Policy Board and the East-West Foreign Trade Board, and is chief spokesman for the administration on economic issues. In December 1973, while Treasury's deputy secretary, he launched and administered the Federal Energy Administration at the height of the oil embargo. He continues on the president's Energy Resources Council with major responsibility for coordinating energy policy, both domestic and international. Prior to his government service, he was a senior partner in the Wall Street investment banking firm of Salomon Brothers, New York, where, as a member of its executive committee, he was responsible for the Government and Municipal Securities Department.

Introduction

In 1955 Dr. John Maurice Clark, John Bates Clark Professor Emeritus of Political Economy at Columbia University, presented two lectures on "The Ethical Basis of Economic Freedom." They were very ably reasoned and delivered with what was an obviously deep personal concern for ethics and freedom. One of the truly great political economists, he understood and emphasized the direct dependence of freedom on "truth and the feelings of common humanity."

Dr. Clark stated that the ethic of freedom "must somehow accommodate a multiplicity of personal ends, while still maintaining the essentials of orderly cooperation which any society must have if it is to survive. It is a commonplace that freedom unrestrained can destroy itself in the anarchy of conflicting purposes, of parasitic and predatory activities. These must be restrained. A free system is one that does this with a minimum of coercion and a maximum of reliance on voluntary action, including the voluntary assumption of the obligations that go with working together. Freedom will survive to just the extent that we learn that these obligations are a part of it; and take some trouble to find out what obligations our kind of society calls for, if it is to go on working." Dr. Clark's lectures inspired the title for this book.[1]

Free societies always have been faced with the problems described by Dr. Clark, but in recent years, here in the United States, we have had to cope with an accumulation of challenges. The extent to which this is true and the reasons why are subject to a variety of opinions. This nation has been experiencing a series of social earthquakes, part of a geological faulting in the continuity of contemporary civilization. Of course, all the world has felt the shocks, but we have been at its epicenter. Around us has been a rubble of discontent and uncertainty highlighting a lack of faith in one another and in our institutions.

We have an opportunity, however, to move upward to a new plateau of values, to a higher quality of life never reached by any other people. The key to our way up is the same that enabled man in the beginning to survive—cooperation and reciprocity. Our technology has not served to make the Golden Rule obsolete, but, instead, has made its application increasingly essential. This is no Sunday school class observation. In a highly complex, interdependent technological society, the tolerance for deviant behavior is narrower and shallower than in earlier times. One small bomb in a power plant can leave portions of a great city in darkness, close scores of manufacturing plants, disrupt airports, and spoil food in a hundred thousand home freezers. The few individuals who hijacked airplanes cost a vast public millions of dollars and much inconvenience. Sure, Jesse James robbed some trains in his day, but in doing so, he didn't affect the daily traveling habits of over a half million persons. The point is, as individuals and as a public, American citizens have got to be more responsible and ethical than our grandparents *needed* to be. We must understand this obligation if we hope to live in freedom.

The United States is a robust society and we have withstood a series of cataclysmic events in recent years. We need go back no further than the atomic bomb and Hiroshima. The next day, 7 August 1945, the world was different. During the mid-forties, another triumph of technology began to accelerate every change—the computer, probably the most notable technical development of this century. In quick succession we had the Korean War, then the Supreme Court decision on school segregation that awakened us to our ethical negligence. Soon the National Guard integrated a Little Rock high school and Martin Luther King, Jr. boycotted the buses in Montgomery. In 1957 the Soviets interrupted the peace of the Eisenhower years by launching Sputnik, prompting our educational system to rush deeper into science and to virtually discard the last small vestige of its concern for ethical values.

In May 1960, President Dwight D. Eisenhower forgot to tell the American public the truth about our U-2 flight over Russia. John F. Kennedy became president and didn't tell us much about the Bay of Pigs, but stood up to Khrushchev over Cuba. He was assassinated. The Vietnam War began to expand along with network color television. In living color the dead and dying were carried into the living rooms of American homes. Then followed the years of civil rights turmoil; the Civil Rights Act; the assassinations of Martin Luther King, Jr. and Robert F. Kennedy; the Chicago police and Democratic Convention confrontations; student riots; and Richard M. Nixon—who was elected to insure more law and order. Having survived the dishonest sixties, we entered the seventies to be greeted by Watergate and a recession. And all of these are just some of the things that happened to us. Even robust societies can be excessively strained.

During these decades, most educators in America, especially in the colleges and universities, failed in their human obligation to relate ethical values to the meaning and purpose of learning. Is it any wonder that so many Americans, especially those among the under-thirty majority of our total population, are uncertain and questioning in their compelling quest for human fulfillment? How can we get them to understand that the meaningful life they desire requires both freedom and material benefits? There is the never-ending need to feed body, mind, and soul. We have been enjoying, or rather experiencing, what some have called a "mature" industrial society. We must now move into a mature ethical society.

This volume is certainly not intended as the answer. But it is another step in the process of trying to get more Americans, especially the leaders in big business, in government, and in education to fully recognize that ethics is a very practical matter, that honesty directly relates to the efficiency and survival of open societies, of governments, and even to the sustainability of profits. Here we present viewpoints from authorities in differently oriented disciplines. The essayists have varied not only in their approaches, but in the extent to which they have addressed themselves to the subject of ethics and economic freedom.

We include in this book a major section on codes of ethics with commentaries on those codes by experienced professional and trade association leaders. There are three reasons we emphasize codes of ethics. First, we have received numerous requests from groups wanting help in developing a code. Second, we wish to encourage an alternative to regulation by statute. Third, we want to inspire a move toward self-regulation and more professionalization of all businesses at this stage of our increasingly service-oriented economy. This movement requires a stronger ethical base for business. It demands that professional and trade associations divest themselves of so-called codes of ethics designed for country club cartels. There are no ethics in codes that are economically restrictive and conspiratorial. Ethical practices should be not only within the law, but well above the law. Many associations have codes of ethics beneficial to their own members and to the public, but too many have failed in establishing effective codes because they lacked courageous leadership. Their members didn't have enough faith in one another, in their products, and in their services.

One thing we have learned from the news headlines is that ethics and honesty are no longer closet-hidden topics of conversation. What is not so readily perceived is that, paradoxical as it may seem, the public of America is more than ready, even eager, to learn that honesty is culturally "all right," that they will not be considered strange or stupid by peer groups if they opt for honesty. The corporation president and the United States senator are no less free from their own peer-group pressures than are teenagers. Business is generally honest, big business no less than small business. But in this transition period of our culture individuals are finding it difficult to develop the courage and faith to move from the pull of peer pressure to personal conviction, from the charisma of personality to the charisma of principle.

Almost any reader will find some of these essays of special

interest. There are statements in certain essays that some readers may condemn or consider unjustifiable. There are parts of some essays with which we certainly do not agree. But all of our essayists and commentators have made a serious effort to be informative and constructive. On the whole, we believe this book represents a substantial contribution to our efforts to extend economic and political freedom by strengthening the ethical underpinnings of our society.

The funds for all editorial costs in preparing this book were supplied by the Scaife Family Charitable Trusts, Pittsburgh, Pennsylvania. Funds for all production costs and the original first-run printing have been provided by the American Medical Association, Chicago, Illinois, and the David M. Milton Trust, New York City. We believe our readers will appreciate knowing that not one of these funding sources requested any kind of editorial influence. It is the policy of American Viewpoint, Inc. to accept no conditional or influencing funding from any source, but it is with special pride in American organizations that we note those who have supported our ethics programs have done so with impeccable ethics.

As to individuals outside our organization who made contributions of a different kind, Mr. Owen Frisby of Washington, D. C., has done more than any other person to foster the entire ethics program of American Viewpoint, Inc. In specific reference to this book, Joan Hill, the coordinating editor, not only greatly assisted in obtaining and editing the manuscripts, but, as my wife, helped me endure the frustrations of delayed manuscripts, production deadlines, and the innumerable details of editing to which this businessman is unaccustomed. Of course, as president of American Viewpoint, Inc. and as editor of this book, I am solely responsible for all its limitations. Therefore, all criticism and complaints should be directed at me and to me.

May 1976   IVAN HILL

Part One

Editor's Previews

Caution: Proceed slowly with anthropologist Roy Rappaport's essay, but keep on going. You'll gain new insights into group operations—very beneficial information to executives in any large bureaucracy, corporate or government. You'll even understand yourself better.

Currently the anthropologist is the social leader in the social sciences. You'll appreciate why when you read Dr. Peacock's fascinating review of gift giving and the developing principles of reciprocity. An economist might perceive something new about the historical basis of the profit concept.

The Meaning of Ethics and Freedom

Ivan Hill

In 1960 I spoke to a national conference of industrial and military leaders on the subject of ethics. At that time it was somewhat unusual for business conferences to schedule talks about ethics. As a businessman making such a speech, I was looked upon as a misplaced missionary. Today numerous speeches on ethics are presented by business and professional men and women to business and professional groups all over the country. Ethics has moved from the inside pages to the front pages of newspapers. The television networks have moved ethics from an item in the news to the main feature on documentary programs. Ethics is indeed a front-burner problem and getting hotter. Widespread bribery and thievery in business, even more than Watergate, have accelerated the attention given to ethics. And Watergate itself was a manifestation, the product, of the mores of the American society rather than a causal factor. But America is yearning for leadership in its struggle to remain a free society. And the problem of a weakening ethic, with its derivative product of increasing crime, is exactly that —a struggle in America to keep a free society.

For thousands of years philosophers have argued about values in life. Countless books have been written about ethics and morality. Although it is certainly reasonable to believe

3

that all these discussions and writings have been of enormous benefit to mankind, sometimes we may wonder, quite understandably, about the usefulness of systematic inquiries into various theories of philosophy and social sciences. Fortunately, my task here is not to philosophize. It is simply to focus on translating generalities into the daily coin of applied thinking and living.

The well educated and the less educated alike learn most of their ethics from living. From life itself, the simpleminded and the intellectual learn that one shouldn't lie, steal, or kill. Most humans agree on most things that are right or wrong; otherwise we could not maintain sufficient order to permit survival. Even in today's complex society, an individual does not have much difficulty in telling absolute wrong from absolute right. True, there is more to ethics than I have thus far allowed, but let's consider the elemental requirements first.

A definition of ethics that I believe will satisfy both the philosopher and the practitioner was given by Dr. Albert Schweitzer in a Paris speech in 1952. "In a general sense," Dr. Schweitzer said, "ethics is the name we give to our concern for good behavior. We feel an obligation to consider not only our own personal well-being, but also that of others and of human society as a whole." In this definition, Dr. Schweitzer had stated in another way the foundation principle of ethical behavior—the Golden Rule, which is the common denominator of all major religions. Men of many ages have considered the Golden Rule to be the fundamental moral imperative. Confucius once was asked, "Is there one word which may serve as a rule of practice for all one's life?" He answered, "Is not reciprocity such a word? What you do not want done to yourself, do not do to others." I wish Confucius had stated further that reciprocity should include as "others" people of all races, rich and poor, male and female.

Ethics precedes and leads to law. The ethics of an advancing society continues to generate new patterns of behavior that are ahead of and above the law. The ethic that is embodied into the law is usually based on the morality of the majority of a society. When the morality of the majority operates at a level lower than the law, such condition leads to a breakdown of the law and endangers the stability of a society. We now can see the symptoms of this process in our own country.

The late Earl Warren, former Chief Justice of the Supreme Court of the United States, made certain remarkably clear and profound statements on the relationship of law and ethics. Here are excerpts from a speech he made in November 1962:

> In civilized life, Law floats in a sea of Ethics. Each is indispensable to civilization. Without Law, we should be at the mercy of the least scrupulous; without Ethics, Law could not exist. Without ethical consciousness in most people, lawlessness would be rampant. Yet without Law, civilization could not exist, for there are always people who in the conflict of human interest, ignore their responsibility to their fellow man.
>
> We are sometimes painfully aware of the inability of Law to solve problems of Ethics . . . there are innumerable facets of our lives, with which the Law cannot possibly deal.
>
> Not everything which is wrong can be outlawed, although everything which is outlawed is, in our Western conception, wrong.
>
> One of the purposes of civilized society is to produce men capable of making righteous decisions and adhering to them. To compel obedience in all areas of life would be to reduce men to automata, incapable of making their own moral decisions and defeating the very purpose of civilization itself.
>
> If courts could compel love, there would never be divorce. If courts could compel friendship, there would hardly be any litigation. If courts could compel mercy, many of the evils of our life would cease to exist.
>
> Therefore, Society would come to grief without Ethics, which is unenforceable in the courts, and cannot be made part of Law. If there were no sense of love in families, if there were no sense of loyalty, if friendship meant nothing, if we all, or any large proportion of us, were motivated only by avarice and greed, Society would collapse almost as completely as though it lacked Law. Not only does Law in civilized society presuppose ethical commitment; it presupposes the existence of a broad area of human conduct controlled only by ethical norms and not subject to Law at all.
>
> There is thus a Law beyond the Law, as binding on those of us who cherish our institutions as the Law itself, although there is no human power to enforce it.

> In the Law beyond the Law, which calls upon us to be fair . . .
> each of us is necessarily his own Chief Justice. In fact, he is the
> whole Supreme Court from which there lies no appeal.[1]

The terms ethics and morality have long been used more or
less interchangeably. Both ethics and morality refer to rules or
standards of conduct. We can distinguish between the two by
stating that when the term morality is used in our society, it
is generally assumed that what is moral or immoral relates to
religious guidelines. Ethical standards, although common to
all major religions, need not be related to any transcendental or
religious source. But one may find it much more difficult to be
ethical than moral. Although there is no conflict between being ethical and being religious, having goodness is not nearly
so easy or so culturally acceptable as having religion. A businessman may be considered very moral, be a leader in his
church, sleep only with his own wife, and yet easily be less
than ethical. When good conduct is solely dependent on religion, one can often do bad acts because he has been taught,
and believes, that his God is so compassionate that he will be
forgiven. One whose ethical standards are high finds it more
difficult to be forgiving and forgetful of his own misconduct.
He cannot depend on the solace of Sunday for his sins of Saturday. Fortunate is the person who has both ethical and moral
guidelines.

How does honesty relate to ethics? Being ethical means more
than being honest, but honesty is the beginning point of all
ethical behavior—one cannot be ethical without being honest.
Honesty is a basic working social principle, not just a moral
guideline. Honesty must be affirmative. It is being forthright
and truthful, and the practice of honesty must begin with being honest with oneself. One cannot effectively communicate
with others, or even with one's own conscience, without being
honest. When you hear that a meeting broke up because of a
lack of communication, what is often meant is that the participants were not forthright and honest with each other.

Honesty, being integral to ethics, is part of the earliest survival principle for mankind—the concept of communicating,
cooperating, and sharing in order to survive. The predominance of honesty within a free society is essential to justice, to

equity, and to the effectiveness of law. Without an overwhelming pattern of honesty, a free society cannot function and becomes unmanageable. Without a high degree of honesty, government is expensive and inefficient. We can also see the effects of the law of the seesaw—when honesty and ethics sink down, centralized authority and coercive regulations rise up.

Hypocrisy is an insidious and pervasive form of dishonesty. When we leave honesty out of ethics we get hypocrisy. That's why so many so-called codes of ethics are ineffective. Hypocrisy is most harmful in the home. Children cannot understand or learn helpful value guidelines when the actions of parents contradict the teachings of parents. Citizens find the same disillusionment with politicians whose performances differ widely from their promises. Hypocrisy tends to thrive in any large bureaucratic structure—corporate, government, or academic. Many a good civil servant, young corporate executive, or assistant professor equates being ethical with being a nice fellow who won't report on his peers for fear they will quit playing golf with him or retaliate with unjustifiable criticism. In large organizations one often gains promotions by agreeing with all sides and tabling one's own convictions. The antidote for such hypocrisy is courage and confidence.

I have had many people tell me that they cannot hold a job, or even get a job, because they are honest. Some politicians have claimed they were not reelected because they were honest. It's possible those people may be right. But it has been surprising to me how many "honest" people are downright lazy. I can assure anyone that being honest and ethical is not a lazy person's game. Being honest is also no excuse for being stupid. Life is much more interesting, more fun, if you live it honestly according to your deepest convictions. Of course you may have to know a lot more than most people and work much harder, but the satisfaction gained is worth the effort.

Can we quantify honesty? Is a person simply honest or not honest? I do not believe any human being ever can achieve perfect honesty. I do believe, however, that a man or woman can live a lifetime in America without actually experiencing a situation that makes honest-to-goodness lying justifiable. In America, we don't have to lie to eat, to keep our jobs, to stay out of mental institutions and prisons, or to stay alive. You know, one can even get rich in America without being dishonest! Unfortunately, this is a fact too many of our young people refuse to believe. Today's sons and daughters know one fact quite well, however. They've observed it first-hand—the persistent greed for more and more money that makes so many nice parents evade and shade the truth.

Are we as honest as we used to be? Statistical evidence indicates rather dramatically that we are not nearly so honest as we were a few decades ago. Acts of crime against property reflect the changing mores and environment of a society. Take one example: burglaries per one hundred thousand population have increased almost 500 percent in America since 1940. Other statistics are equally alarming. Larceny has increased almost 400 percent per one hundred thousand population. Shoplifting is so rampant that in some communities family discount stores have difficulty surviving the high shrinkage of goods—from employees as well as from outside thefts. When opportunities to steal are easier and more numerous there is more stealing. That's why, historically, the virtue of the traveling salesman has been more open to question than that of the fellow who has to stay home all the time. A person may normally be honest and ethical, but an environment filled with opportunities and temptations may provoke an abnormal response.

Earlier in this essay, I referred to honesty as a beginning point for ethics. That would seem to be a goes-without-saying statement. It certainly cannot be so assumed. I have been studying numerous codes of ethics developed by various professional and trade associations. Some of these codes use the word honesty very sparingly or not at all. In reviewing conferences on ethics among business, professional, and academic groups, it appears the participants have a natural hesitancy, a psychological barrier, to using the word honest. They seem to prefer phrases such as unprofessional conduct, nonacceptable professional manner, divergent loyalties. Now I can understand this reluctance to use a simple word like honesty. It is much nicer, more gentlemanly, even less dangerous, to ask a man if he is being unethical rather than to ask him if he has been lying and stealing.

Although I have emphasized that honesty is essential to ethics, we must understand that being honest is not enough. There are no ethics without action. Even an honest man cannot do good by doing nothing. We do have, as Dr. Schweitzer stated, "an obligation to consider not only our personal well-being, but also that of others and of human society as a whole." There are two continuing obligations in ethics: to benefit others, to do no harm to others. Some philosophers believe that to be moral a person needs to know why he is acting morally, needs to have a reason to act morally, and needs to act with intentions to serve others. This is a reasonable view, but good begets good no matter what one's reason is for doing it. Each thing creates its kind. And no matter what good ends are claimed, bad means produce bad ends.

Without a strong base of ethics, law cannot be sustained. Without a sturdy framework of law, freedom cannot be sustained. We have a strong nation, but how long can any free society withstand a continuing erosion that attacks the full range of its traditional values? The *rate* of the increase in crime may go up and down, but crime continues to increase. Crime is bred in a bed of dishonesty. We should be asking: At what point on this ever-rising scale of social destruction does the balance tip toward not just the demand for, but the necessity for severe restrictions on our economic and personal freedoms? Historian Arnold Toynbee observed: "Freedom is expendable; stability is indispensable." We can talk about economic education until every citizen in America, young and old, knows about private enterprise, private property, profits, and economic models; but without a clear example of integrity and forthrightness by America's business and professional leaders, the public will continue doubting, and government will continue to increase the applications of its authority.

In January 1976 an unusual event made news in the business world, and it was not overlooked by the American public. It was good news about big business. In fact, it was an ethical cannon shot that was heard throughout the business world. The board of directors of a big business corporation, America's seventh largest corporation, a multinational oil corporation, divested itself of its chairman and two principal officers. A report in *The Wall Street Journal* stated that ". . . the board's tough stance in what some management experts are already calling a 'classic' case in corporate ethics has set a 'higher level of corporate responsibility.' " The men who were forced to resign were men of competence and were highly regarded by their peers. But professional regard and personal friendship among peers, business or professional, should yield to principle. These corporate officers had to go because the majority of directors apparently believed that their continued presence would weaken the ethical and, ultimately, the economic underpinnings of the company. This was a historically courageous and commendable action by the Gulf Oil Corporation.

The press, especially the business press, duly noted the importance of the Gulf decision. The Gulf action represents a breakthrough onto a higher plateau of business conduct. I hope all the leaders of American business, each director of every board of every major corporation, will be challenged to follow Gulf's leadership. This kind of decisive action, instead of equivocal testimony, is what the American public wants. This is the way to improve the image of big business—by constructive, foresighted action. If big business wishes to go up on the good image polls, it must replace public relations propaganda with ethics. The majority of American corporations already operate with a rather high sense of honor and responsibility, but now is the time for all of them to move in this direction.

In the professional areas, the American Medical Association, although it has not experienced the provocations that beset Gulf and many other multinational corporations, announced at its January 1976 National Leadership Conference an action that could represent a very significant move upward in professional leadership. It has initiated the formation of a National Advisory Committee on Ethics, a free-standing committee that will function externally to the AMA. An outstanding American businessman, one who has long championed a high level of ethics, has accepted the chairmanship of the committee.

There are noteworthy points about this committee. It represents a transdisciplinary body with membership to be selected from several professions—business, theology, law, and the academic community including graduate students as well as deans. Such cooperation among the different peer groups is an increasing necessity. Although the practice of any profession is the business of the particular profession involved, the problems are not confined to it alone. In considering the basic problems of economic freedom and the principle of voluntarism, no longer should professionals be prisoners of their own peer groups. It is urgent that one peer set cooperates to strengthen the base of other peer sets. To be truly productive and self-enforceable, codes of ethics must be covenants of peers and public.

Another important benefit that should result from a committee on ethics chaired by a businessman of broad practical experience is that the discussions and actions on ethics will not be relegated to scholarly groups parked on mountains or in deserts. We need to take ethics out of the linguistic closets. The time is here when philosophers must become practitioners, and even the most successful practitioners must take time out for philosophy. Those who concern themselves with ethics must develop a sense of reality, and those with perhaps too great a sense of reality must become far more concerned with ethics.

In recent years there has been an increasingly harsh criticism of big business and big businessmen. We can all list a number of reasons for this, and the current polls may include many more. None of these reasons include what I believe is the *main* reason, if I am to judge from thousands of letters I have received and my many years of activity in the field of ethics and in business. From the average citizen's standpoint, big business is more omnipresent than contemporary thoughts of God's own presence. Everyday, everywhere, the average citizen uses a big-business telephone, drives a big-business automobile, uses big-business gasoline to go to a big-business chain supermarket. He goes home and, while imbibing big-business beer, he watches big-business television give identity to big business by condemning the "personality" of big business. Now, all this is well known. Big-business leaders understand this and much more. There is one thing, however, they apparently do not comprehend. The head of a giant corporation simply (and rightly, of course) refuses to think of himself as any kind of a god. This man's power, however, and the omnipresence of that power which extends from his company to millions and millions of people, has forced upon him, like it or not, a spiritual responsibility as well as a secular one. He has become a god to the public, and when he commits bad acts he demoralizes a large segment of society. This is the source of much of society's so-called alienation. It is a prime cause of the public's disappointment with big business and free enterprise.

Of course, a large corporation is operated by many people in cooperation with thousands of others. To the religious person the manifestations of God are countless, too, but he identifies them all with one God. Therefore, when the board of directors and shareholders of any great corporation are considering a person to be its chief executive officer they not only should, but, as time passes, they *must* examine his spiritual and ethical qualifications as well as his managerial qualifications. Let us hope that no longer shall we see brought back to the head man's office the executive who made great profits in other countries by ignoring every ethical standard. He will do so in our country as well. In my 1960 speech to military and industrial leaders, mentioned at the beginning of this essay, I warned that notable group we should "always remember to export good ethics along with good products." They applauded agreement, but, as years passed, some apparently have suffered a loss of memory.

In recent years in America and in the West we have been hearing that "free enterprise is dead." Men of great business stature have made such statements, usually right after a trip to Washington. There are fewer such comments now because business and government leaders are finally becoming acutely aware that free enterprise can be severely crippled or destroyed. If free enterprise and the capitalist system in the United States does die out it will not be because a better system has been developed, but because this one became overburdened with dishonesty and laziness. All the leaders in business, government, and education must recognize that honesty, ethics, and forthrightness are not side issues, but are the central, core issues in keeping an open market economy functioning. The business community has dramatically suffered from the same peer-group pressure suffered by the kid in school who fears that if he doesn't cheat he won't get a passing grade. To the kid, his passing is his profit. Not all children cheat. They survive and learn, and many make all As and Bs. Not all businessmen cheat. They survive and make good profits. They are the ones to whom we owe the continuance of not only the free enterprise economy, but also the continuance of our personal liberties. Top business leaders in America must discard their robes of expediency and peer politeness. Indeed, they are now beginning to do what they should have been doing long before. They are summoning the courage and wisdom to openly condemn and reject those who cannot relate honesty, fairness, and ethics to the conduct of a business enterprise. They are beginning to attack the real destroyers of capitalism—those inside the top "fraternity" whose short-term methods erode the opportunities for the long-range viability of both their company and country. Such lovers of expediency are the agents who have been opening the doors to those who would kill off free enterprise. They have not cared about the freedom of those who must succeed them. They haven't had the courage or concern to correct their own mistakes; they simply leave that task for the next chairman or president of their company. Thank God that day is closing. A few great business leaders are now speaking and acting for ethics with the courage and conviction of contemporary Patrick Henrys. Let's hope they will be joined by a host of others from the top ranks of both big business and big labor.

Our society is, and must continue to be, committed to technology. No matter the nostalgia, we are also committed by necessity to the continuation of big business and big government. Historically, when the institutional leaders of a society are incompetent, or default in their duties, the alternative is the "knight on a white horse." In the contemporary world, that knight might well be a "knightess." I do not see dictatorship coming for America. What we have to guard against is a crowd of special-interest bureaucrats waiting in the wings. They could drag our nation gradually but inexorably into such a bothersome collectivism we might throw up our individual responsibilities in disgust and cry out for a dictator. I think we can avoid such a development. We are waking up and opening our eyes, minds, and souls.

Several times in this essay I have mentioned freedom. What do I mean by freedom? Freedom means to me just about the same, I believe, that it means to most of us. The minimum essentials include freedom of speech, the benefits of a free press, freedom to assemble and to associate with whom I wish, and to have a fair trial in a fair court. Freedom includes being able to change jobs, change places of residence, and to worship the God of my choice—or no God. The essence of freedom is to have the opportunity and courage to make almost unlimited choices, including all the big ones.

We sometimes forget that our rights, the rights of the people, extend far beyond those enumerated in the Bill of Rights and elsewhere in the Constitution. Government administrative agencies often forget how far the rights of citizens extend. Further, we should remember that the Constitution itself is only the framework for our freedoms. Without a strong ethical foundation and a cohesive ideology of common values, even our constitutional structure can crumble away. And above our Constitution there must remain, as was true at its creation, an inspired, endless faith in the nation.

In 1946 Winston Churchill outlined some tests he considered essential to freedom. Here are the questions that Churchill asked:

> Is there the right to free expression of opinion and of opposition and criticism of Government?
>
> Have people the right to turn out a Government of which they disapprove and are there constitutional means provided by which they can make their will apparent?
>
> Are there courts of justice free from violence by the Executive and free from threats of mob violence, and free of all association with particular political parties?
>
> Will these courts administer open and well-established laws which are associated in the human mind with the broad principles of decency and justice?
>
> Will there be fair play for the poor as well as for the rich, for private persons as well as Government officials?
>
> Will the rights of the individual, subject to his duties to the State, be maintained and asserted and exalted?
>
> Is the ordinary peasant or workman who is earning a living by daily toil and striving to bring up a family, free from the fear that some grim police organization under the control of a single

party . . . will tap him on the shoulder and pack him off without fair, open trial to bondage or ill treatment?

Today, when I think about Winston Churchill, I earnestly hope that our friends in Great Britain will soon find men and women as suitable to meeting their present leadership needs as Churchill was in World War II.

Recently I read a long essay on freedom written by a professor of philosophy in a large state university. He wrote about society crushing itself while at the same time building up institutions for the exercise of freedom. Then he said we should dispel the "mist" surrounding our classic democratic freedoms of speech, of assembly, and of the press so that the "actualities behind these ringing phrases are seen in a truer light." Reading further, I soon learned that the professor didn't think a totalitarian society is all that bad. He discounted the importance of freedom of choices in open societies. He pointed out that even slaves are free to choose out of a thousand possibilities. To sum up, he said that to act from one's inner self is what it means to be free. He implied that with this understanding one could be free in the Gulag Archipelago. My review does not do justice to the philosopher's comments. I am too biased. I want my inner self, my outer self, my whole self, and the body that goes with everything, to be free. I demand a better quality of choices than deciding which grain I shall select first from the thousand grains in my daily bowl of rice.

It may be that the professor was trying to tell us about the power and scope of our free will. This is the type of exercise not uncommon for some who have been provided with lots of learning at public expense, who live in relative affluence in a society that permits its participants to speak freely, to assemble, to read all the news, good and bad, supplied by a free press, watch television, and make love. Although Solzhenitsyn demonstrated the enduring strength of a determined human being, nowhere in *The Gulag Archipelago* did he indicate that life in a totalitarian society isn't bad, very bad. As in other disciplines, all philosophers do not think alike, and some reading what I have just reported may be as disappointed with the thinking of their colleague as I was. True, freedom is not limited to freedom of choice. It does include the freedom to express one's will, but how much "will" can one express in a closed society? Who can be happy with a yo-yo will that stretches only within the limits of a short rope?

Of course, some of us independent spirits who came up the hard way may not be as openminded and as compassionate as we should be. There are millions of American citizens who are not free to make all the big choices—the meaningful choices— such as moving to a better neighborhood, and eating better food. Although we criticize them for blaming their ills on society, they may be right in doing so—but not for the reasons either they or others believe. It could be that in the face of what they perceive as so much dishonesty and rottenness in business, including little neighborhood businesses that may enjoy ripping off their friends, their faith in their chances to move up and out may literally be killed off. So many of us who moved up from eating out of garbage cans to a position where we could make all the meaningful choices owe that movement out to the faith we had in the society around us. What our philosopher friend failed to understand is that without the "nominal" constitutional freedoms that have always existed in America, no citizen could ever achieve the meaningful freedom of choices about which critics seem to worry but do little. We must concern ourselves with what freedom *now* means to us or we'll not be free to sit around and wonder what it could mean.

It may seem paradoxical, considering the evidence, but I believe that the people of the United States are ready for a better quality life, a more genuine life. I believe that the old as well as the young are sick of hypocrisy and social irresponsibility. The vast majority of our citizens know that being more honest and responsible would be better for them as well as for their neighbors. They feel the pressures of insecurity, of discord, of inequities. But they do not wish to be looked at by their peers and made to feel they are not quite bright because they don't push, or cheat, or steal. They do not wish to be taken advantage of, or to be treated unfairly. Of course, they want their fair share. Most people, I believe, would be happy to settle for only their fair share of the rewards and responsibilities if they could feel "safe" in doing so—if others would do the same. That's why they are vulnerable to a move in either direction—toward more ethics and honesty, or toward more government authority. Underneath the crust of our current discontent is a powerful yearning for a quality of life no nation yet has achieved.

The first question the do-nothing, wiseacre skeptics may ask is: How do you change people? The quick answer is that people do not have to change. Except for continuing and scarcely discernible evolutionary changes that may occur back and forth in the biological substratum, man has not changed for thousands of years. Man has not been programmed for good or for evil, but only to survive (a few geneticists even credit him with a measure of genetic altruism). Man's environment has changed greatly. Most of these environmental changes he has effected himself, and some he will have to diseffect. Our behavior patterns can be changed. The quickest and the most effective way to change them is from the top. Everyone is implicated, but culture changes filter from the top.

One more point for the skeptics who doubt that we can become more honest. All we wish to do is to make being honest culturally "all right," smart, and maybe even the fashionable way to be. We wish to restigmatize dishonesty. We are not asking people to give up going to the church of their choice, to change political parties, or to move from the country to the city, or vice versa. We do not ask them to quit drinking, smoking, bowling, fishing, or watching television. We do not ask them to give up sex. In fact, we believe if people were more honest they would get more enjoyment from sex. In exchange for giving up none of the good things, they would receive a whole host of benefits. And everyone knows that our society already likes benefits.

So, what would happen to the United States if we "went" honest, if we truly ethicalized free enterprise? First, such a movement not only could serve to unite America, but it could lay the basis for a Western movement that Communist nations could not effectively fight. If Communists joined us in ethics, they would be helping to destroy their own system. If they didn't join us, then they would make it easier for the world to understand the basic cleavage between totalitarianism and democracy.

Within America, we could save billions of dollars by reducing the price we now pay for crime—stealing, embezzlement, shoplifting, and crookedness in almost every area of our economic life. Much of our inflation is directly attributable to dishonesty. The cost of government would go down. We do not realize how much government we have and how much added cost we pay for it due solely to institutionalized dishonesty. More welfare might go to those for whom it is intended. Indeed, more people might be honest and ethical enough to take care of their own welfare and assist their relatives as even our "primitive" ancestors did. Capital formation would be easier due to greatly increased confidence in business and government. Our neighborhood businesses might stop the petty rip-offs that they now engage in because the "big boys" have made it look smart. The professional people might become more objective and consider their client interests and the public interest if not first, at least along with their own.

If we were more ethical, perhaps our traffic problems would ease because people might get the idea a regard for other drivers would help them to survive, too. The discourtesies and go-to-hell attitude of people toward one another might decline. A surge of national honesty could attract a new kind of candidate into politics. Who knows what benefits a large dose of honesty could bring to America—to the free world? To those who denigrate the intangibles, I ask: Don't you know by now that attitudes determine all values, including the value of common stocks, the winners of political power, the survival of social systems? I agree with the late A. A. Berle who observed that idealism is long-range realism.

What shall we say to those who say they love mankind, but want to shoot you and me? To those who ask for an "alternative" system for which they have no known model? Or to the worthwhile and sincere people who believe that if they are going to be discriminated against anyway, they will pay less for government price-fixing than for private price-fixing, and might as well socialize democracy and let the government do it to them? They should know, however, that all things human and humanitarian do not have to be socialized. So while they wait for the perfect way and the perfect day, let's have their support, too.

Further, as to the socialists, they already know that "democracy in the productive process is the necessary condition for socialist development." Therefore, if a high degree of honesty is essential to democracy, a campaign to strengthen ethics and restigmatize dishonesty would be beneficial to a socialist as well as to a capitalist society. No political or economic system that is dishonestly operated will work for the benefit of the people!

To the economic and status egalitarians with the equal-sharing idea, my first admonition is to go back to the history books, travel around the world, and then honestly ask yourself: Has there ever been and can there ever be a social system of all equals with no incentives? Especially do I ask them to study the question: Should there be? The only time one wants equality is when it doesn't exist. There is evidence that disequilibrium is absolutely essential in nature at any level of life and in all social systems. If egalitarians acted on the platform of giving equality an "idiot's try," they would have to believe that there can be no way to achieve equality without honesty.

To the bureaucrat, if it were not for him and big government and big corporations, our technological society couldn't function. He should be proud of his task to the point that he resists the expediency that destroys individual ethics, resists the duress of team play that makes a farce out of the sacred tenet of loyalty. Incidentally, I know there are scores of thousands of female bureaucrats, too.

To the ardent free enterprisers I say: quit kidding yourself. Quit giving up a little more freedom for a little, or even for a lot, more short-term money. If you really believe in a competitive open-market economy, if you believe in the worth of your own product or service, then be honest. Drop the old working plan of first getting on, then getting honest, and finally hoping to get honor. Reverse the order of effort and you'll be happier than if you knew you were a rich thief with an honorary degree and a college building named for you.

All of us must understand there are no perfect social systems. The strengths and the desirability of a democracy rest on its imperfections. We already have had our revolution. Let's live up to its lasting challenges.

We need no new religions. We need no new ethics. We do not need to go back for anything. We do need to go forward to fulfill America's destiny, forward to the greater achievements possible in an ethical free enterprise system, to an ethical capitalism. We need no new system. We need to make honest the one we have. If we are to achieve more of our human potential, an upward movement possible only in an open society, ethics must be our bridge to the twenty-first century. We must strive for the fullest realization of the inspiration inherent in the Declaration of Independence and build on the laws that have given lasting substance to the Constitution of the United States. To meet this challenge we ask all the people of America: Shall we be honest and free, or dishonest and policed? I believe the citizens of this country will respond in favor of freedom, as they did in 1776.

Ethics, Economics, and Society in Evolutionary Perspective

James L. Peacock

The classical anthropological studies of economics treat pre-capitalistic systems. The study of capitalistic systems, whether in the new forms emerging in tribal societies and the Third World, or in the more familiar forms of highly industrialized societies, has hardly begun in anthropology. An advantage of anthropology, however, is that it endeavors to view the human condition in all of its varied aspects. Accordingly, I shall sketch a range of patterns extending across a wide spectrum of societies and, in this way, suggest a broad view of the role that ethics play in economic practice.

Let us begin with a generalization. A considerable amount of anthropological evidence supports the thesis that social cooperation has been at least as crucial for human evolution as has individual self-seeking.[1] The principle of natural selection operates on the species rather than the individual level: it is the species that becomes extinct when its mode of life adapts poorly to the environment. Likewise, what benefits the species does not necessarily benefit the individual member of the species. Accordingly, it is not necessarily the group of the most aggressive or strongest individuals that survives, but the group which attains a balance between the requirements of the group and those of its individual members. Survival re-

21

quires cooperation, which in turn requires control of individual behaviors by rules and, in the case of man, norms and ethics. Such rule-guided cooperation is found at levels ranging from the bands of baboons and packs of wolves to the societies of ants and of men.

Given the importance of the collective and normative element in human evolution generally, it is not surprising that this element is critical in economics specifically. Anthropologists have noted, for example, that labor is organized socially in all societies (even though in some societies, such as our own, the products of this labor are consumed privately). Recognizing the critical importance of the social framework of economic life, a number of social scientists have endeavored to bring social and economic analysis within a common framework. One may name three whose ideas guide the formulation proposed here: Emile Durkheim, Karl Marx, and Max Weber.

Durkheim's major contribution was to emphasize the social *consensus* that lay behind all manner of economic endeavor. He formulated this argument most sharply in his 1893 doctoral dissertation, *The Division of Labor*.[2] Here he opposed the utilitarian model of economic man as espoused by Herbert Spencer and others. Where utilitarianism argued that contracts (in the broad sense) were held by two parties because to do so served the self-interests of each, Durkheim insisted that a third party was also involved: it is society. Durkheim was able to show that contracts could hold not solely owing to the individual interests of each of the parties involved, but because of the social norms which they shared as a result of their membership in society. In the further development of his theories, he was able to argue that without this sharing of norms, economics and ultimately life itself would break down.

Marx's primary emphasis, on the other hand, was on conflict. He argued that the class structure of capitalist society and the exigencies of industrial technology provoked contradictions that ultimately limited the growth of capitalist-industrial systems. While this specific argument has received the most attention, broader contributions of Marx frequently are overlooked. He strove to create a unified framework for viewing both society and economy, a framework best exemplified in

Das Kapital.[3] By demonstrating the social basis of economics and the economic basis of society, Marx showed that the two were related in a more dialectical fashion than that suggested by Durkheim's heavy emphasis upon control of the social or normative aspects of human life.

Weber was an economist who became a sociologist, and he wedded the two disciplines in his tome *Wirtschaft und Gesellschaft* (Economy and Society).[4] Yet his distinctive contribution was to move beyond both systems in order to analyze the ethical and metaphysical basis that underlay them. Through his classical work, *The Protestant Ethic and the Spirit of Capitalism*, which was merely a chapter in a comparative work on the sociology of religion, he emphasized the ethical basis of modern capitalism. In his studies of India and China, he was able to show the other side of the coin, that without this ethical and metaphysical basis, modern capitalism did not emerge.

While recognizing the universal role of social norms in human behavior, including the economic, anthropologists have emphasized that these norms vary from culture to culture. Indeed, much of the early work in economic anthropology was designed to demonstrate this variation. Some anthropologists, such as Bronislaw Malinowski, attempted to prove that the proverbial "rational man" of classical economic theory did not exist in exotic societies.[5] Whether in Asia or the Pacific Islands, men were shown—or so it was thought—to be motivated by social and religious rather than sheerly economic motives. They would act "irrationally" in economic terms, sacrificing personal gain in order to achieve social prestige, maintain social solidarity, or appease the gods. As is typical of intellectual history, the excesses of this early view are met by opposing studies by, for example, Raymond Firth and D. W. Goodfellow.[6] They attempted to demonstrate, in contrast to Malinowski, that neoclassical economic theory could explain or at least help approximate economic behavior in precapitalist as well as capitalist societies. The two extremes continued well into the present as a debate between the rather Malinowskian "substantivists" (following Weber's notion of the economy as an institution dependent on the distinctive structure of each society) such as George

Dalton, Paul Bohannon, and Marshall Sahlins,[7] who have rejected the neoclassical economists in favor of the economic historian Karl Polanyi,[8] and the "formalists" (following Weber's alternative notion of the economic rationality as a universal aspect of behavior), such as Edward E. LeClair and Harold K. Schneider,[9] who hew more to neoclassical economic theory. Recent alternatives to the formalist/substantivist debate have been formulated by an emerging school of French Marxist anthropology, spearheaded by Maurice Godelier and Claude Meillassoux,[10] and the fundamental premises of economic anthropology now are being remodeled.[11]

Despite the flux in current thinking regarding economic anthropology, it is possible to hazard some generalizations based on "facts" currently at hand; these facts will of course change as theory changes, a situation which we are unable to do anything about. We are concerned to delineate certain relationships between economic systems and their social and ethical forms, in order to illustrate the central role that the latter play in the former. While the tracing of such covariation is a staggering task owing to the great variety of patterns, one may simplify by abstracting certain basic *types* of socio-economic-ethical systems. As in any typology, the following fits no single case perfectly, yet it helps highlight broad differences, similarities, and correlations.[12]

This typology is organized in a roughly evolutionary schema defining five types: "primitive," "archaic," "historic," "early modern," and "modern." This schema does not imply that every society, or even any society, evolves from the first type to the last in perfect sequence. It does, however, suggest that in the totality of world prehistory and history there has been an era when each type is dominant.[13] Thus the "primitive" type, though still existing today, was dominant at the time prior to the advent of urbanization (ca. 6000 B.C.). The "archaic" was the dominant and most rapidly spreading form after the origins of urbanization and is exemplified by the great kingdoms of Egypt, Mesopotamia, Peru (Inca), and Mexico (Aztec). The "historic" era came into prominence with the arrival of the great religions—Islam, Christianity, and Buddhism—during the first millenium before and after

Christ's birth. The "early modern" era began with the Industrial Revolution and the Protestant Reformation in the West, but appeared elsewhere, in varying forms, from Eastern Europe to Japan and China. The "modern" era, a type now emerging, is associated with the bureaucratization of the industrial state and its expansion to peripheral areas of the world system; it also involves the ideological reactions to these trends, including both radicalism and conservatism. In correspondence with the evolutionary principle of natural selection, one may argue that the emergence, spread and dominance of any given type is due to its adaptability to its social and natural environment during that particular epoch. Yet this broad pattern of the "general evolution" of culture on a worldwide scale has its counterpoint in the many variant adaptations of individual cultures, each following its own "specific evolution."[14] Today all of the types survive and flourish (even the so-called "primitive" type) at least for the moment, in particular environments peripheral to the main trends.

PRIMITIVE SOCIETIES

Primitive societies are defined as those that obtain their subsistence not from food production per se but from food finding by hunting and/or gathering, and are organized around kinship rather than more bureaucratic modes. We do not mean that there is no economy among primitives, but that kinship is both infrastructure *and* superstructure of society; for example, that both the material and nonmaterial bases of life are patterned around kinship. Thus, "economy" is not separate from "family" either organizationally or conceptually. Owing to the lack of both food production necessary to support a nonworking class and to the kinship rather than the bureaucratic ground of organization and thought, there is no basis in primitive society for the emergence of a sustained social hierarchy or a centralized power. Among the hundreds of examples of primitive societies are many, but not all, of the Indian bands of North America, the traditional aborigines of Australia (prior to their conversion to sheepherders, ranchers and other workmen after contact with Europeans), the hill tribes of Southeast Asia, certain of the Pacific islanders and many others.

In terms of the focus of this essay, the most outstanding trait of the primitive societies is the reciprocity among persons in social and economic transactions.[15] Although in primitive society a common standard for exchange purposes, such as money, is often lacking, anthropologists have noted the tendency to balance exchanges as a means of validating and revalidating social statuses, thereby maintaining some form of continuity between generations and among groups.

The most important early study of exchange in primitive society was *The Gift*, by Marcel Mauss,[16] who showed how the giving and receiving of a gift is a "total prestation" in the sense that it involves not only economic but also social, religious, political and familial aspects as well. Mauss argued that gift-giving involves a repetitive cycle of giving, receiving and repaying which, it may be noted, is similar to establishing a system of credit; an individual or group's network of alliances, sustained by reciprocal giving, helps insure against hardship in case of local loss or disaster. Mauss's analysis, like Malinowski's study of the Kula ring in the Trobriand Islands,[17] indicates that reciprocal exchange entails the emergence of self-sustaining alliances and forms of cultural expression that, while not in themselves "economic," do serve to underwrite the distribution of wealth in the society and to stimulate the search for and production of items for maintaining the economically crucial social alliances.

Inspired by Mauss's study of the exchange of objects, his successor, Claude Lévi-Strauss, undertook in *The Elementary Structures of Kinship* a vast analysis of exchange of persons.[18] Lévi-Strauss was concerned with several modes of marriage, one type of which was the so-called "circulating connubium" of the Southeast Asian hill tribes as well as other groups elsewhere in the world. In the circulating connubium, clan A gives wives to clan B, which in turn gives wives to C, which in turn gives them to A. As in the case of the Kula passing of objects around a circle of exchange partners, this passing of women is not dictated by the choice of the individual but by society, which in primitive society is manifested in the kinship norms. Thus the ideal mate for a man is his mother's brother's daughter. Should he marry a woman of this category, he receives his wife from the same clan as his father did. In this way, through the exchange of wives, the alliance between clans is maintained over many generations. But this is not all. In these tribes, the cosmos is conceived as being divided into halves such as left and right, male and female. Within any exchange, the wife-giving clan is conceptualized as male and thus is allied with that half of the cosmos, while the wife-receiving clan is conceptualized as female and is allied with the other half of the cosmos. Accordingly, a marriage unites not only clans but also the cosmos. Conversely, an erroneous exchange throws the cosmos into chaos and may (it is believed) have dire consequences for health, social order, and all of life. Again, as Mauss saw in the instance of the exchange of things, reciprocity for the primitive is a "total prestation," cementing relations at many levels of reality, from the economic to the spiritual.

Again, norms of kinship control the practice of exchange in primitive society as in dictating choice of one's exchange partner in the Kula ring and of one's mate in the circulating connubium. Yet these norms themselves have an economic basis. In a primitive society, such as precontact Australia, division of labor is rudimentary and technology is simple, while kinship is dominant both in organization and ideology. In such a system, subsistence is based on the simple labor power of group members rather than labor power multiplied by technology. Thus it is control of people, rather than technology or other material elements, that is crucial. Control of people implies control of the reproduction of people since it is through reproduction that new members of the work unit (the band, clan, or other kinship units) are recruited. This concern renders of utmost importance the norms that define who should marry whom and who is descended from whom (whether patrilineally, matrilineally, or in the numerous other patterns so distinctive of primitive society). In sum, at least a partial reason for the centrality of kinship norms in primitive society is the labor-based subsistence.[19]

From this brief summary of studies of the relationship between economic and social constraints in primitive societies, we may draw certain conclusions about the role of ethics in such societies. No event can be considered as merely economic nor as merely social, due to the all-encompassing function of kinship (some events, however, may appear superficially to be purely social in the most primitive of societies, due to the mythological elaboration of the acts to the point that their material bases are obscured). Economics and ethics are inseparable and indeed are *undifferentiated* from the total fabric of social and spiritual existence. Exchange agreements involving objects and wives are dictated by social norms that in turn are aspects of a richly mythologized spiritual culture that in its turn has a subsistence base. A wrong exchange is a great danger to the society and the cosmos, since all levels are entailed in any act. Only when kinship ceases to be the dominant mode of organization, as in the archaic and other stages discussed below, is there a differentiation of social and economic functions.

ARCHAIC SOCIETIES

Archaic societies differ from primitive societies in that the former's major source of subsistence is food production, rather than food finding (which may nonetheless continue as an aspect of subsistence), and their principal mode of social organization is not kinship but more bureaucratic modes, such as kingdoms. Examples of archaic societies range from the classical civilizations of the Old World in Egypt and Mesopotamia to those of the Aztecs and Incas in the New World, but also include the tribal kingships in Africa and Polynesia and the Hinduized kingdoms of ancient Southeast Asia.

Whereas primitive societies are relatively egalitarian, archaic ones are blatantly hierarchical. In the Kula ring and the exchange among Southeast Asian hill tribes, the parties are either roughly equal or ambiguously ranked (for example, among the hill tribes, while wife-givers outrank wife-takers in a given exchange, the wife-giver may outrank the wife-taker by other criteria, such as who the clan ancestor was). In addition, each party tries to reciprocate with material roughly equal to that of the other; thus for a necklace one gives a bracelet, while for a wife one gives an equivalent assortment of swords, clothes, and the like, to compensate for the services lost to the wife's family.

In archaic societies, by contrast, there is a class regarded as an elite at all times, in all circumstances, in every way. The pharaoh was not only the richest and most powerful man, but he was also spiritually superior to the masses; indeed, he was a god-king. The same is true of the Hinduized Southeast Asian god-king and the others. At more personal levels, the king-subject type of relationship holds between master and slave or servant. Under these circumstances, one may speak of exchange as involving unequal partners. All goods move ultimately upward and to the center, toward the elite and the leader. Receiving them, the leader at least partially redistributes them downward and outward.[20] Thus at a feast, his storehouses of food collected from the masses are opened to fill the stomachs of the crowd. Archaic religion is based on the same principle of "redistribution" that governs economics. The leader's spiritual essence distills powers of the multitude and, like food at the feast, is redistributed among the people, insuring magical safety.

Exchange, then, has moved from the horizontal to the vertical; instead of having as its dominant direction the linking of like units, it now links the high and low. That is, there emerges a hierarchy of structures manifested in the social norms that in turn seem to subsume the hierarchy, endowing it with legitimacy. The vertical economic transactions are richly spiritualized. In part, the power of the elite is their assumed ability to order the cosmos as well as the polity, and the proper subservience, coupled with pomp and pageantry, is believed to maintain the total socio-cosmic order.

Egalitarian exchange, of course, remains, but in one respect it has become de-sacralized. Sacrality has fled to the top and center, to be deposited in the leader and not the masses. Among the latter, therefore, incidental exchanges may in a certain sense occur more freely, without the constraints of the central social and cosmic rules. One thus sees the beginnings of market and money among the merchants, usually itinerant, who move around the periphery of these archaic civilizations. Within the traditional scale of values, the merchants typically are regarded as low and immoral. Whether in Hinduist India,

Confucianist China, or ancient Japan, it is the kings and priests who are ranked highest. Next are the farmers, who supply directly the material essence of the society. At the bottom are the merchants. Operating in a sphere bereft of wider social norms, their practices tend to echo the motto "caveat emptor" (let the buyer beware), and their low ranking is justified by their sharp practices with respect to all not bound to them by such particularistic ties as kinship or neighborhood.

We may remark how the hierarchy of norms and values in archaic societies mirrors the actual social hierarchy. These norms do not emphasize the role of each class (king, farmer, or merchant) in the production of subsistence, but in the process of distribution, which, of course, involves social rules regarding who gets what. Archaic societies are in essence two-class societies—elite and mass—with an emergent third class—merchants—that comes to dominate social and economic life in later stages. In the archaic merchant lies seeds for the development of the historic and modern stages. Later patterns are present in the archaic stage of social and economic evolution, a fact that suggests that evolution is propelled, as it were, in great part by forces internal to each formation; external forces merely condition the shape the emergent form takes.

HISTORIC AND EARLY MODERN SOCIETIES

Historic society differs from the primitive and the archaic not so much in social-structural innovations as in new ideological forms. In both primitive and archaic society, the sacred imbues the dominant social relationships of the society, and the sacred is felt to dwell in the world, embodied in the spirituality of the clan, the god-king and even the gods who characteristically reside in mountain or forest rather than on high.

But in historic society, a sharp distinction is made between this world and the other world. This dichotomy is seen with the rise of the world religions: Buddhism, Christianity, and Islam. In each of these religions, this world is seen as separate from, and, indeed, inferior to, the other, be it heaven or nirvana; and there is a tendency to imagine life in this world as short and leading, it is hoped, to the next life.

While one can trace significant economic trends in these societies that set the stage for the eventual emergence of capitalism in its early forms (for example, the expansion of Arabic and Indian traders with the rise of Islam), for the purposes of this analysis probably the most significant role of these historic ideas and their ethical conceptions comes with the rise of capitalism and industry in the early modern societies. By shifts of emphasis usually signaled by reformations, the historic ideas gave a new ethical basis for a scale of economic endeavor we now identify as emergent capitalism. The most familiar example is taken from Max Weber, in his analysis of the protestant ethic.

In Weber's analysis, Protestantism, especially of the Calvinist, Puritan-type, is built upon the historic distinction between this world and the next, making salvation the goal of the believer. The Calvinist believed God had predestined him for either eternal salvation or damnation, in heaven or hell, and his dominating motive was to assure himself that he was saved. Stripped of traditional modes of assurance, such as ceremony and the purchase of indulgences, he eventually fell back on the notion of working methodically at some calling to demonstrate his destiny for salvation. Weber, by training an eminent economist of his day, argued that this motivation found expression in a methodical, rational and dynamic capitalism. Thus, concluded Weber, Calvinism helped stimulate the rise of capitalism.[21]

What is often neglected in assessing Weber's analysis, however, is the *ethical* aspect of Calvinism and, indeed, of all the historic religions, especially as they were streamlined by reformations. This point may be illustrated by Weber's contrast between Calvinism and Confucianism.[22]

Confucianism exemplifies the archaic—but of course highly complex and sophisticated—world view in that it links its ethical precepts to specific and particular social relationships. Thus, in the five relationships characterized by Confucius, sons are told how to behave toward fathers, subjects toward rulers, but no rules are laid down for behavior toward *everybody*. Confucianism is particularistic; Calvinism is by contrast universalistic in that it proclaims that one is his brother's keeper, that one is beholden to observe certain ethical precepts universally, regardless of one's particular relationship to a specific individual involved. This simple difference, it can be argued, has had wide ramifications in economic life.

Thus, the ethical code of Confucianism would not legitimize holding to an agreement regardless of with *whom* the agreement was made, and, indeed, in traditional China and even today among the Chinese diaspora, merchants have a reputation for feeling ethically bound to keep agreements only when one is related to the client particularistically (for example, of the same clan). In modern Chinese centers, such as Hong Kong, universalistic laws of contract and the like have, of course, come into prominence, but the point is Confucianism as an ethic did not provide a legitimation or an ethical base for this type of practice. In Weber's analysis, Calvinism and, indeed, Christianity in general, did provide this base. Thus one could argue that the really quite incredible degree to which contracts are made and held with strangers in the modern world found its initial ethical base in the universalistic ethic of Christianity: Do unto others as you would have them do unto you—meaning *all* others. One can further argue that other aspects of Calvinistic doctrine, such as the covenant, the sect, and the rational calculation of efficiency (to assure carrying out the calling), gave a timely ethical basis for such modern business institutions as the contract, the corporation and cost-accounting. The notion of universal standards carried over into the practice of uniformity of product, so that if one sells a quart to one, he sells a quart to all, which in turn relates to mass production.

Certainly without sufficient trust in a contract, without sufficient consistency to maintain universal standards for a given product, and without the other features mentioned, modern business could not maintain its productivity, expansion, and distribution. One may cynically note the need for suits and other legal sanctions which make faith in a system more important than faith in a person and which serve to uphold the system, but these are meaningless without an understanding of the ethical code which *legitimizes* the legal structures. These

structures may exist independent of the indvidual's recognition of them, but it is in terms of this recognition that the
individuals act and, in so doing, perpetuate the same
structures. And one may feel strongly it was Christianity, at
least in the Western world and especially in its protestant
aspect, that originally provided a base for this ethic, that
persists in transmuted form today. The primitive notion of
reciprocity among particular, thickly bound persons was adequately rooted in primitive religion and notions of responsibility toward kin; the archaic notion of a kind of noblesse
oblige to partly redistribute the fruits of the masses, from the
elite back to the masses, was rooted in archaic notions of
sacred. Neither of these institutions could have existed without their corresponding ethical concomitants. Similarly, the
early modern, capitalistic system could not have existed—nor
for that matter originated, survived, and flourished—without
its ethical forms, derived most prominently, perhaps, from
Protestantism.

MODERN SOCIETIES

In the modern era, both ethical-cultural and socio-economic
institutions have become more complex than in earlier times,
and social institutions have become disarticulated, each seemingly obeying a distinct logic. The opinion is widepsread that
society has become more bureaucratized and depersonalized.
At the same time, there seems to be less opportunity for individual movement. The classical protestant ethic has gone into
decline. Along with the depersonalization which accompanies
bureaucratization, many have lost faith in any personal god—
for many God is dead. This means, for those who still believe in anything, that He becomes an abstract essence rather
than a moral super-parent. The charge toward salvation along
the straight and narrow has gone, together with the loss of
motivation and opportunity for individual achievement. As
the sacred has come increasingly to reside in the self, it is
believed that such categories as heaven or hell possess no objective essence but are merely projections, imaginations of the
self, and, further, since the sacred is imposed by the self,
anything may be believed to be sacred.[23] Similarly, in a more

secular vein, people seem to find less satisfaction in their daily work, a trend which implies the disappearance of even materialistic standards of ethics.

What do these developments imply? Does a breakdown of the ethical culture, most recently the protestant ethic, imply the breakdown of the economic system originally its partner? Has the remarkable path of economic development of the previous two centuries produced its own undoing, leaving the participants in that process without even a relatively objective ethical standard for confronting these changes? In the evolutionary process, we may discern a principle that helps us place these developments into context. We shall term the principle "transcendence." By transcendence is meant that with each step in socioeconomic complexity comes a correlated step in cultural-ethical generality. The principle can be illustrated by the types briefly surveyed in this chapter. With the shift from the primitive to archaic society, there is a shift in complexity from no classes, that is, all individuals and groups being more or less equal to two classes, an elite sharply and permanently differentiated from the masses. With early modern society, the two-class system gives way to a multi-faction system: social relationships become shifting multiple alliances and voluntary associations, not to mention individual endeavors. With the shift to modern society, this fluid situation continues but moves increasingly under the umbrella of a growing bureaucratization that adds a new layer to the whole.

Furthermore, with the shift from a situation of no classes to one of two classes, there can be discerned a cultural transcendence. From diverse, particular spirits and sacred objects linked to every individual clan, band, or household, one moves toward a unified pantheon of gods that are, however, still in the world, either personified in the god-king or on the mountaintop, or both. The cultural system thus becomes more general in response to changes in social and economic structures in order to legitimize and render meaningful the increasing socioeconomic complexity. Then, with the shift to the more fluid early-modern society, the pantheon of gods becomes unified into one God, and He now totally transcends the social order by assuming His residence in heaven.

The "God is dead" movement is only one of many that point to the emergence of a cultural base more transcendent than the protestant ethic. Here a personified God becomes an abstract, ill-defined essence, Tillich's "being," or something else. While this entity is in flux, it is difficult to derive from it the clear-cut ethical precepts of the old Protestantism. Yet it has the potential for a richer and broader basis for ethical definition. One point is certain. Socioeconomic institutions do not thrive independent of ethical systems: this is shown not only by general theory but also by the tracing of covariation between the two entities as they have evolved in tandem.

CONCLUSIONS

To this point in the discussion we have been satisfied to demonstrate the interrelatedness of socioeconomic formations and their ethical formulations through successive cultural evolutionary stages leading to the modern. In particular, we have pointed to the development of a broad-based ethical superstructure that transcends the limitations of the protestant ethic. We conclude with some further comments on what kind of world seems to be emerging in the second half of the 1970s and what role ethics will play in that world. These conclusions are necessarily speculative.

More than one person has referred to the emergent world order as "post-industrial society" or "post-modern society." To some, the recent deterioration of services such as telephone and train service, which had come to be taken for granted in this country, is an indication that what we have considered *other* countries' problems are now becoming ours. Perhaps the most startling expression of the recognition of this trend is what Richard J. Barnet and Ronald E. Müller call the "Latin Americanization of the U.S. economy."[24] The explicit recognition of the international scope of contemporary problems, which has long been a hallmark of anthropology, carries with it the realization that no simple ethical framework can deal with the large variety of conflicting and equally legitimate—and illegitimate—interests in the world.

The international perspective draws attention to an economic innovation of our times: the controversial multinational corporation. While some claim these gigantic and powerful corporations increase employment and raise general standards of living, others argue that a gain in one country signifies a loss in another. Regardless of the actual dynamics, the emergence of the multinational corporation highlights the problem of the relationship between ethics and economics: can a single economic institution, the corporation, flourish in a plurality of cultures, each with distinctive ethical traditions? As the experience of colonialism demonstrated long ago, the narrow protestant ethic that contributed to the rise of the distinctive type of capitalism in the early Modern West could not be transplanted easily, if at all, to the Asian, African, Near Eastern, or South, Middle, and native American cultures with radically different traditions. The broadening of the Western outlook reflected in such movements as the rise of Eastern religions in the West, together with other signs of a "counter-culture" following the postwar demise of colonialism, may contribute to some new world ethic. Such an ethic could enrich the ground for growth of such institutions as the multinational corporation as well as still mightier systems of international cooperation. This hope is plausible, if abstract and utopian. Meanwhile, the opposing interests of the different nations and cultures, and of the competing giant international corporations, reveal more ethical contradictions than ethical solutions.

To the anthropologist attuned to primitive society, certain tendencies in modern economic life suggest, interestingly, a rebirth of fundamental human patterns most apparent among the primitives. For example, with the explosion of electronic communications and rapid transport, international transactions become more personalized in the sense that the telephone call and the flying visit present the "person" more than does the letter or cable. As a result, personalized relations emerge which then require the kinds of norms embodied in the primitive concept of reciprocity—a key concept in international trade today. As a second example, the population explosion shifts emphasis from land as the resource of primary concern to labor, which is to say persons. This, too, is reminiscent of the primitive pattern and suggests that in its growing concern for dealing with its personnel as persons, business may again find insight in the time-tested primitive norms for guiding relations in personalized groups, such as reciprocity. However this may be, it stands to reason that the long primitive (and anthropological) experience of dealing with personalized groups will be informative to an economic system that revitalizes concern with person, cooperation, and community.

If this tracing of relationships between economic and ethical evolution has shown anything, it is that the economic is grounded in the ethical, and vice-versa. It follows, therefore, that the new levels of complexity achieved and promised in the sphere of economics will require a broadening and enrichment of ethical frameworks. This is necessary not only to motivate and justify productive work, but to preserve order and meaning in life.[25]

Adaptations and Maladaptations in Social Systems

Roy A. Rappaport

In this essay I shall first discuss adaptation and its disordering, maladaptation. I shall then consider some of the ways these concepts bear upon matters of freedom, ethics, and the place of free enterprise in contemporary society.

ADAPTATION

Adaptation and the related notion of adaptiveness are central to much biological and anthropological thought, but like a good number of other concepts claiming high degrees of generality, they are rather vague. In the most general possible terms, I take "adaptation" to refer to the processes through which living systems preserve themselves in the face of changing circumstances. Self-preservation may require reorganization, however. Therefore, it is useful to express the notion a little more technically. Adaptation refers to the processes through which living systems maintain homeostasis in the face of both short-term environmental fluctuations and, by transformations in their own structures, through long-term, nonreversing changes in their environments as well.

The term "environment" is meant to include not only natural phenomena—plants, animals, soil, and so on—but social phenomena as well, that is, the society that forms part of the environment of an organism or a local group, and the surrounding societies that form part of the environments of all but the most isolated societies of which history and anthropology inform us.

I have stipulated that adaptive processes are characteristic of living systems. If it were not for the existence of certain machines into which adaptive characteristics have been built it would, perhaps, be more accurate to define living systems as those which manifest adaptive characteristics. I take living systems to include organisms, single species assemblages or organisms, such as populations, clans, tribes, and states; and the multispecies associations of the interacting species forming ecosystemic communities, such as forests.

All living systems must maintain a dynamic internal equilibrium, or homeostasis, if they are to persist. Homeostasis may be given more or less specific, if not always very precise, meaning if it is conceived as a set of ranges of viability, or "goal ranges" on variables representing conditions crucial to the survival of the system. Any physiological, behavioral, or cultural process tending to keep the states of crucial variables (such as temperature, protein intake, population size, energy flux) within their goal ranges, or to return them to their goal ranges should they depart from them, may be taken, other things being equal, to be adaptive.

Our definition of adaptive systems as self-maintaining systems, systems maintaining themselves in homeostasis, implies, or even entails, that they are self-regulating. Self-regulating processes depend upon a limited family of mechanism. These include, first, immutability, in which a component of the system is held in what is apparently an absolutely invariant state. The clearest cases are those of religious propositions, such as creeds, which are taken to be eternally true. These have considerable importance in the self-regulation of human societies. Second, there are what Jean Piaget calls "operations."[1] Whereas operations may guide the considerations of human actors, the physical world does not yield easily or completely to logical operations, and operations in Piaget's sense are not by themselves of primary importance in the self-regulation of living systems. Third, there is time-dependent regulation, exemplified in organisms by such cyclical phenomena as circadian rhythms and in human affairs by ritual cycles, quadrennial elections, the use of traffic lights, and so on. In time-dependent regulation, corrective action is taken periodically regardless of the state of the regulated variable. (Traffic lights turn from red to green whether any automobile is waiting or not.) Finally, there is variable dependent, or cybernetic, regulation in which deviations of variables from desired reference values themselves initiate the processes correcting them. In response to signals of system-endangering changes in the states of a systemic component, or an aspect of the environment, actions tending to ameliorate the effects of those changes are initiated. Thermostatic regulation provides a familiar example. Cybernetic operation, it is probably safe to say, is the most fundamental, widespread, and important of the regulatory modes employed in the adaptive processes of living systems and will, accordingly, receive much more attention than the others.

Corrective cybernetic responses may take several forms. In some instances the stressor is eliminated. In others, compensatory adjustments are made within the existing structure of the system. In yet others, however, changes—genetic, constitutional, structural—of the organization of the system itself are made. The self-regulating processes through which living systems maintain themselves entail or subsume the self-organizing processes through which they transform themselves. These two classes of processes, self-regulation and self-organization, have generally been distinguished in the social sciences and have formed the foci of two distinct modes of analysis: "functional" on the one hand and "evolutionary" on the other. But the distinction has surely been overdrawn. In a changing universe, after all, the maintenance of organization is likely to demand its continual modification. The connecting generalization is what Charles Hockett and Robert Ascher called "Romer's Rule," after Alfred S. Romer, the zoologist who first enunciated it in a discussion of the emergence of the amphibia.[2] The lobe-finned fish, Romer argued, did not come onto dry land to take advantage of the terrestrial habitat. Rather, relatively minor modification of their fins and other subsystems made them better able to migrate from one drying up stream or pond to another still containing water during the intermittent periods of dessication presumed to have characterized the Devonian era. Such changes made it possible for these creatures to maintain their general aquatic organization during a period of marked environmental change. In slightly different terms, self-organizing or evolutionary changes in components of systems are functions of the self-regulatory process of the more inclusive systems of which they are parts. Thus, although structural or evolutionary changes, such as fin to leg, may be distinguished from "functional" changes or "system adjustments" on some grounds, they are not separated from them in the larger more inclusive scheme of adaptive process. Together they form ordered series of responses to perturbations of variables from their reference values. Perturbing factors may include opportunities as well as immediate threats. The two are not always radically distinct. An opportunity lost may result in future peril.

First, before discussing adaptive response sequences, it is worth making explicit (because there seems to be considerable confusion surrounding this matter) the view of adaptation of homeostasis and evolutionary change. Perhaps the most salient question to ask concerning any structural change is: What does this change maintain unchanged? Second, insofar as adaptive processes are cybernetic they are possessed of a characteristic structure because cybernetic systems have a characteristic structure, namely that of the closed causal loop. In a cybernetic system a deviation from a reference value itself initiates the process which attempts to correct it. Third, while adaptive processes may have cybernetic characteristics, all processes that are cybernetic are *not* adaptive in the sense that they maintain homeostasis in variables crucial to the persistence of the living systems in which they occur. In the most general terms, cybernetic systems attempt to maintain the truth value of propositions about themselves in the face of perturbations tending to falsify them.[3] In systems dominated by humans at least, the propositions so maintained (and the physical states represented by such propositions) may not correspond to, or may contradict, homeostasis biologically or even socially defined.

We may return now to adaptive response sequences. The anthropologist Gregory Bateson and the biologist Lawrence Slobodkin have argued that they have important general characteristics.[4] Sequence responses most quickly mobilized are likely to be energetically expensive, but they have the advantage of being easily reversible should the stress cease. They can hold the line, so to speak, until relieved by slower acting, less energetically expensive, but less easily reversible changes should the stress not cease. Thus responses to high altitudes start with panting and racing of the heart, which are immediate, and continue through a series of circulatory and other changes, until, after a year or so, irreversible changes in lung capacity and in the size of the heart's right ventricle.[5] The ultimate change in such sequences would be genetic, although this seems not to have been necessary in high altitude adaptation. Similarly, the initial response of a town to very heavy traffic loads during peak periods may be transitory redeployment of police. But if this response is inadequate, or itself causes an intolerable strain, a series of less reversible actions may be initiated—perhaps the construction of a highway bypass, a change which is virtually irreversible.

It is of note that the earlier responses deprive the system of immediate behavioral flexibility while they continue—the organism when it first moves to fifteen thousand feet can do little except aerate itself; the police force while it is taking care of peak traffic is not free to attend to emergencies. But while they continue, the structure of the system remains unchanged; thus, Bateson argues, the earlier responses conserve the long-run flexibility of the system. In contrast, while the later responses do alleviate the strain of the earlier, they are likely to reduce long-range flexibility. There is in such series a continual and graduated trade-off of adaptive flexibility for adapted efficiency. To the extent that the perturbations to which the system will be subjected in the future are unpredictable, it is good evolutionary strategy, Bateson and Slobodkin argue, to give up as little long-range flexibility as possible, and evolutionary wisdom seems to be intrinsic to the graduated structure of adaptive response sequences, at least in biological systems. Social systems, on the other hand, in which responses are self-conscious, can make mistakes of which biological systems may be incapable. This general argument suggests that evolution is likely to lead to collapse or even extinction, and it is well to keep in mind that many evolutionary lines that once flourished are no longer around.

Some qualification is in order. Evolutionary changes increasing flexibility do seem to occur. Any response which increases the range of conditions under which a system can maintain itself can be said to increase flexibility. The emergence of language and the control of fire in our own line may be cited as possible instances. Many of our advances, particularly technological advances, are much more problematic than language and fire (which themselves have set as well as solved problems for the species); however, we may ask of any evolutionary change what loss of flexibility it may have entailed. We may also meditate upon the likelihood that the long term survival chances of earthworms and blue green algae are probably better than those of men.

A second general point, related to the first, is that adaptive processes are not only cybernetic, sequential, and graduated. The adaptive structure of any living system is not merely a collection of more or less distinct feedback loops. Special adaptations must be related to each other in structured ways, and general adaptations, human or otherwise, biological or cultural, must take the form of enormously complex sets of interlocking correcting loops, roughly and generally hierarchically arranged, and including not only mechanisms regulating material variables, but regulators regulating relations between regulators and so on.[6] Adaptive structures are *structured sets of processes*, and regulatory hierarchies, whether they are embodied in particular organs or institutions or not, are found in *all* biological and social systems. It is important to issue a caveat here: to say that regulatory structure is hierarchical is not to say that it is centralized, nor does it imply stratification in social systems. For instance, among some egalitarian societies, components of regulatory hierarchies are embedded in ritual cycles; in others in segmentary kinship organization.[7]

Another aspect of the hierarchical organization of adaptation is the relationship of parts to wholes. This was implied in Romer's discussion of the emergence of the amphibia. Modifications in certain of the special purpose *subsystems* of the lobe-finned fish made it possible to maintain unchanged the general systemic characteristics of those organisms. Now whole living systems—organisms and assemblages of organisms—are what Gordon Park has called "general purpose systems,"[8] for they do not have special goals or outputs. Their only purpose or goal is that most general of purposes or goals (or, if you prefer, nonpurposes or nongoals): their own perpetuation. They are, as Lawrence Slobodkin has put it, "players of the existential game,"[9] one in which there are no payoffs external to the game because the player can't leave the table; one in which, therefore, the only reward for successful play is to be allowed to continue to play. But they are made up of subsystems that do have special goals or outputs valuable, presumably, to the larger systems of which they are parts. The increasing differentiation, in the course of evolution, of special purpose subsystems in organisms, societies, and ecosystems has been called "progressive segregation,"[10] and it is often accompanied in organisms and social systems, but not ecosystems, by increasing centralization of regulatory operation, or "progressive centralization." In organisms we note the elaboration of central nervous systems, in societies the development of administrative structures. This contrast between the development of ecological and other systems may rest upon their contrasting bases for order maintenance. The basis of orderliness in ecosystems seems to shift, in the course of their development from "pioneer" to "mature" stages, from a reliance upon the resilience on individual organisms to a reliance upon the increasing redundancy of matter and energy pathways resulting from increasing species diversity. These contrasting bases of order maintenance, in turn, reflect differences in the degrees of coherence these different classes of systems require and can tolerate. By "coherence" I refer to the extent to which a change in one system component affects changes in others. In a fully coherent system any change results in immediate and proportional changes in all components.[11] As no living system can be totally incoherent, neither could it be totally coherent, for in a fully coherent system disruptions anywhere would immediately spread everywhere. Whereas anthropologists traditionally have been concerned with the ways in which the various components of sociocultural systems are bound together—the jargon is "integrated"—they have generally ignored the ways in which the parts and processes of such systems are buffered from each other and each other's disruptions.

Organisms are, and in their nature must be, more coherent than social systems, and social systems are more coherent than ecosystems. As a rule of thumb, the more inclusive the system, the less coherent it is and must be. The less inclusive the system, the more its internal orderliness and the effectiveness of its activities depends upon the fine coordination of its parts. An organism requires and can tolerate closer coordination of the activities of its parts than societies, and societies more (at least from time to time) than ecosystems. Coordination depends upon centralization, hence progressive centralization in organisms and societies, but not ecosystems.

Living systems also differ in their relative autonomy. The relative autonomy of a system is a function of the degree to which the regulatory mechanisms upon which its persistence depends are intrinsic to itself. Thus, the relative autonomy of a politically independent village in New Guinea is greater than that of the city of New York. It is also a function of self-sufficiency. Again, the New Guinea village, which grows virtually all of its own food, is more autonomous than New York. "Relative autonomy" refers to the extent to which systems are themselves more or less distinct adaptive units. Organs, for instance, have very little autonomy, for they cannot function in the absence of the organisms of which they are are parts. Whole organisms have a much higher degree of relative autonomy; they are distinct adaptive units. It should be kept in mind, however, that no system less inclusive than the solar system is absolutely autonomous. In sum, whereas the adaptive structures of all living systems share certain fundamental features, they also differ in certain ways, probably related most importantly to differences in their coherence and in the relative autonomy of their subsystems.

THE STRUCTURE OF ADAPTIVE SYSTEMS

What are the salient features of orderly adaptive structure in societies and what are the ways in which they may be disrupted? Societies are, as I have noted, general purpose systems. It is important to keep in mind as we proceed, however, that the individuals composing societies and, in some cases, acting as regulating agencies, are themselves general purpose systems and they may, and frequently do, perceive their interests to be different from, or even at odds with, those of the societies of which they are parts.

For the sake of clarity the suggestions that follow will be expressed more certainly than they should be. Empirical research and further conceptualization are badly needed; what follows is to be taken as suggestive. I shall be concerned mainly with the hierarchical organization of adaptive structure, and shall follow the convention of referring to more inclusive systems and regulation as "higher order," less inclusive as "lower order." Certain of the features of orderly adaptive structures have already been implied, and some seem to be logically necessary, but it is well to make them explicit.

Level and Specificity. Lowest-order regulators are concerned with the regulation of specific material or behavioral variables. The regulation of, say, a garden is concerned with a complex of material variables—soil, moisture, weed density, insect infestation—that are likely to fluctuate or change in value very quickly and that require more or less constant attention. Lower-order regulators—like factory foremen or gardeners—operate more or less continuously, reacting very quickly to slight changes in conditions. The directives of low-order regulators are, typically, highly specific commands relating to immediate states of affairs. In sum, low-order regulation is concerned with specific operations in special-purpose subsystems. However, such operations are typically guided by goals or considerations established from "above," either by direction or by such mechanisms as demand in market economies. (The caveat of two paragraphs ago should be recalled here. Regulators in human societies are likely to be individuals, low-order regulators almost always are. As such they embody a multiplicity of values, all of which may not be consistent with the instrumental behavior demanded of them by the target objectives specified by the hierarchy.)

Reversibility. As a rule, the responses of lower-order regulators in social systems are more easily reversible than those of higher order. (They may differ in this regard from biological systems in which early response—such as easily reversible panting upon first entering high altitude—may mobilize much of the resources of the system as a whole, and which may radically effect the behavior of the system as a whole. This possible difference between biological and social systems is, perhaps, related to their differences in coherence, and in the ability of social systems to develop rather easily special purpose subsystems, like the Red Cross and the fire department, specifically for dealing with emergencies.) Moreover, being closer to possibly perturbing changes in the states of variables, and being in a position to take highly specific actions, or to issue highly specific commands very quickly, lower-order regulators are likely to respond more delicately to perturbations than are regulators of higher order.

The Regulation of Regulation. Higher-order regulators are, as a rule, not so much concerned with the correction of minor deviations in the states of particular variables as they are with regulating the relations among lower-order regulators and relations among the outputs, requirements, or special purposes of the several subsystems subordinate to them. In social systems this is likely to include, among other functions, the adjudication of disputes. Higher-order regulators often operate in terms of highly aggregated variables (such as monetary values), and they become directly concerned with affairs usually managed by lower-order regulators only when the lower-order regulators experience difficulty. Several comments should be made here.

First, it is clear that higher-order regulators do not "know," nor do they need to know, everything known by the lower-order regulators subordinate to them. In fact it is perhaps better that they don't, for economy of information processing capacity is an important aspect of regulatory hierarchies. Too much detailed information concerning the states of low-order variables could overload the capacities of higher-order regulators.

Second, in technologically simple and relatively undifferentiated societies in which a domestic mode of production prevails,[12] higher-order regulation is likely to be simpler and operate less continuously than that of low order. For instance, in the horticultural societies of New Guinea, the regulation of gardening is typically located in individual households and is continuous. The regulation of the dispersion of the population over land so that they *can* garden, a matter concerning relations among households, is "embedded" in the segmentary organization of more inclusive groups and, in some cases, in ritual cycles, and operates only occasionally.[13]

Third, whereas higher-order regulators do issue specific

commands, other sorts of directives are also likely to emanate from them. There are rules, which differ from commands in that they are not situation-specific. They specify what is to be done or not to be done under specified categories of circumstances. They are less specific, or more general, than commands. Yet higher-order regulation enunciates still more general directives that may be called policy statements or principles, such as "All men are entitled to life, liberty, and the pursuit of happiness." It is presumably to define the vague terms of such principles, and to fulfill them, that rules are encoded, and it is in conformity to rules that commands are issued. In sum, in descending from highest-order regulation (associated with the general purpose system as a whole) to lowest (associated with the operation of special-purpose subsystems), there is a progress from regulatory sentences high in generality and vagueness, to sentences high in specificity and concreteness.

Fourth, the hierarchical relations outlined here imply the inclusion of authority relations. Higher-order regulators are "higher authorities." It is important to note that higher-order authorities need not be discrete, living individuals. Highest authority may be, and in fact is almost always, vested in documents such as constitutions, in the conventions of ritual cycles, in immortal tradition, or in supernaturals.

Natural and Conventional Determination. In proceeding from lower to higher order, the degree to which regulatory operation is directly determined by environmental or other material factors seems to diminish. That is, high-order regulation may be more affected by conventional considerations than regulation of lower order. For instance, the ways in which a particular inventory of crops may be grown in a particular region may be rather narrowly determined by soil conditions and climate. The ways in which the harvests are distributed, a function of a higher-order system, "an economic system," of which "the agricultural system" is only a part, are probably not as narrowly determined. There are likely to be, therefore, more ways to distribute the crop than to grow it. To put this into a different terminology, relations of production are less determined by natural environmental factors than are means of production.

Level, Value, and Sanctity. Possibly correlated with the increasingly conventional character of higher-order regulation is the increase in the value-laden terms surrounding it. For example, the discourse concerning both Soviet and American wheat farming is highly concrete and instrumental. It is concerned with such things as seed, soil, water, tractors, fuel, and auto parts. The fundamental agricultural assumptions of a Soviet wheat farmer would probably be acceptable to his American counterpart. Differences of opinion would be, for the most part, slight and technical. But when economics are discussed, phrases like "free enterprise" and "from each what he can give, to each what he needs" begin to appear. The difference between the connotations of these phrases is not technical but ideological: both are taken by those subscribing to them to be highly moral. Yet higher-order regulation is bolstered by such notions as honor, righteousness, and patriotism. At the highest levels of regulation divinity is likely to be invoked. This was patent in such archaic states as Egypt, in which the pharaoh was the living Horus, and remains even in modern societies in which there is an ostensible separation of church and state. The United States takes itself to be "one nation under God."

The higher order the regulator, the more support it is likely to receive from sanctification, or even from the ultimately sacred: God Himself. The increasingly sanctified character of higher and higher order regulation seems to be related to its conventional nature. We note here a curious sleight-of-hand. To say that regulation is "conventional" rather than "natural" is to say that it is the invention of human minds no different in their general capacities from the minds of those subordinated to the regulation. This implies further that at least some people are capable of grasping the conventional nature of the regulatory modes prevailing and of imagining alternative modes that might be more to their liking. To sanctify conventions, however, is to hide their conventional nature behind supernatural veils. Thus, for the ancient Mesopotamians the conventions of kingship descended from heaven, and even for the English, Elizabeth is queen by the grace of God. Moreover, since the gods who ordained the conventions are also the gods who ordained the physical world, the distinction between the conventional and the natural becomes indistinct. To sanctify the conventional (and perhaps even the arbitrary) is to transform it into the natural (and perhaps even the necessary).

It is also important to point out that it is not only the discourse *surrounding* high-order regulation that is value laden. Regulation at the highest levels is likely to be concerned with the maintenance of what the society takes to be its basic values. We find, for instance, in the second sentence of the founding document of the United States "that all men are created equal, that they are endowed by their Creator with certain inalienable Rights, that among these are Life, Liberty and the pursuit of Happiness." These rights are explicitly proclaimed to be self-evident, God-given, and natural, and, as such, unassailable and unchangeable (an instance of the immutability alluded to in the first section of this essay).

Lower-order regulatory mechanisms are taken to be no more than instruments for the fulfillment of these basic values: "That to secure these Rights, Governments are instituted among Men. . . ." It follows that the yet more particular organizational arrangements established or franchised by governments or other higher-order regulators to meet specific goals or needs —military or educational organizations, economic institutions, and laws—are to be regarded as instruments of yet lower order: their particular goals are not basic but instrumental goals. For instance, large military establishments, college educations for all, high gross national products, and even efficient governments, are not in themselves to be valued as fundamental. Their values are to be assessed, finally, only in terms of the extent to which they contribute to the achievement, in the United States, of "Life, Liberty and the pursuit of Happiness" for the members of the society. The vagueness of fundamental values makes assessment difficult, of course, but this vagueness is simply a fact of life and, moreover, it is not a simple weakness of organization (although a certain problem, to which we shall return in the next section, is intrinsic to it). Vagueness is an adaptive characteristic of basic values, for it allows instrumental values and the institutions responsible for maintaining them to be changed in response to the continuing interpretation required to relate ever-changing historical circumstances to fundamental values. The overspecification of the fundamental would impede the reinterpretive process. We note an interesting association of the vague and the immutable in the fundamental. Adaptive process requires that the immutable be vague.

Regulatory hierarchies are, in sum, hierarchies of values as well as hierarchies of mechanisms. The highest are very general, and properly vague, but taken to be fundamental and immutable. The lower are more variable, more specific, less fundamental, and more instrumental. The lower are justified only in relation to the higher and more fundamental, for it is the higher that set the goals of the lower in terms of the logic and assumptions of the higher. The relationship between values at different levels of the hierarchy is one of logical typing. Whereas the lower-order instrumental can be derived from higher-order fundamental, the reverse is not the case. Instrumental values derive their meaning and utility only by reference to the ends which they serve, and these are established at higher systemic levels. Conversely, ends and meaning cannot be derived from the means for achieving or discovering them.

To return to a matter raised earlier, the possible disparity between the goals and interests individuals perceive for themselves and those specified for them by their positions in societies, we may note that it is at the highest levels of regulation that the interests of societies and the interests of individuals are supposed to coincide, even in absolutist societies. It is to the maintenance of the basic values, and not to the instruments that in fact may or may not serve the basic values, that individuals are, in the expectations of democratic systems at any rate, supposed to give their support.

Systemic Transformation. The general structure of adaptive processes outlined here implies there are included in the repertories of higher-order regulators rules and procedures for modifying or changing the goals of lower-order regulators, or even replacing both them and the special-purpose subsystems over which they preside with others. Thus, adaptive structures may transform themselves in more or less orderly ways in response to changes in environmental or historical circumstances. As noted earlier, the maintenance of general purpose systems may require their more or less continual modification in response to nonreversing environmental changes as well as in response to reversible environmental fluctuations.

It should not, however, be imagined that all structural

change emanates from the higher reaches of regulatory hierarchies. Self-organizing changes continually take place within relatively autonomous subsystems as well. In systems that are not overly coherent, but are, rather, "loosely coupled," to use Herbert Simon's term,[14] these do not always have much of an effect upon the society as a whole. We shall return to instances in which they do in the next section.

It is also important to note, although history makes it obvious, that fundamental changes in societies are likely to originate not in the highest levels of the structure, but among men in subordinate positions. We may profitably return once again to the Declaration of Independence to note an ultimate cybernetic mechanism: ". . . Governments are instituted among Men, deriving their just powers from the consent of the governed—That whenever any form of Government becomes destructive of these ends it is the Right of the People to alter or abolish it, and to institute a new Government, laying its foundations on such principles and organizing its powers in such form, as to them shall seem most likely to effect their Safety and Happiness."

A virtue of the Declaration of Independence is that it explicitly vests in the governed the right to overthrow governments that violate the basic values of the society. In fact, the recognition of such a right is widespread. While the basic values of societies differ, the violation of basic values by authorities has always been taken to be grounds for removing them. Among the ancient Germans it was a religious duty to depose bad kings, as it was in many African societies, and the prophets inveighed against the inequities of monarchs. It is not surprising that revolutionary movements have often taken religious form, for they are reactions against what are taken to be violations of that which is highly sanctified.

Time. Throughout this account certain temporal relations between levels have been noted in passing or merely implied. These temporal relations may themselves imply qualities other than temporal, and it would be well to make them explicit.

First, it was suggested the response times of low-order regulators are faster than those of higher order. It may be suggested their rapidity is correlated with their reversibility, and also with their position in what Simon calls "nearly decomposable systems."[15] A qualification is, however, necessary here. In the face of strong perturbation from outside the system—for instance, in response to imminent attack—higher-order regulators may respond more quickly than those of lower order. Complex systems include mechanisms for calibrating the level of response to the strength and pervasiveness of perturbation.

Second, that a typical relationship of longevity prevails between systems and their subsystems or components was also implied by the observation that among programs of higher-order regulators are included programs for changing or even replacing lower-order regulators or subsystems. This suggests that as a rule general purpose systems are more enduring than their subsystems or components. I refer here to particular living systems located in time and space and *not* to principles of organization. For instance, clans are longer lived than any of the conjugal families of which they are composed. Tribes endure through the extinction and replacement of their clans. However, the conjugal family as a mode of organization was operative before clanship appeared and it survives in societies, organized as states, from which clanship has disappeared.

Third, there also seem to be differences in the temporal qualities of the sentences concerned with regulation at different levels. The sentences typical of low-order regulation—commands—are situation specific and thus ephemeral. Rules, which are typical of middle-range regulation, are more or less enduring, and the principles characteristic of highest-order regulation may be conceived to reflect timeless aspects of nature. Indeed, highest-order regulation is likely to be associated with propositions concerning gods conceived to be outside of time altogether. We move from the quick to the eternal. These relations of duration seem to correspond to the continuum from the specific, concrete, pragmatic, and materially determined to the conventionally determined, value-laden, general, vague, and sacred.

Regulatory Hierarchies and Administrative Structures. It is well to reiterate here that terms like "higher" and "lower order," "systems" and "subsystems," and "hierarchy" should not be taken to indicate that adaptive structure in human societies is necessarily incorporated in discrete bureaucracies, well-defined administrative structures, or special-purpose subsystems to which special personnel are assigned. Regulatory hierarchies are sets of responses to perturbation ordered along axes of specificity, concreteness, reversibility, authority, time, sanctity and, perhaps, other dimensions as well. While in some societies administrative structures are clearly defined, in others, notably the small, technologically simple and relatively undifferentiated societies that form the subject matter of traditional anthropological studies, adaptive structure is intrinsic to segmentary organization, exchange relations, ritual cycles, and other aspects of the general social organization. The emergence of well-defined administrative structures with special offices and officers is an aspect of progressive centralization, a process that seems to be characteristic of evolution generally. In the evolution of human societies, a high degree of centralization is found only in some state-organized societies.

However, it should not be assumed that even in modern state societies adaptive structure is completely embedded in administrative structure. Individuals, private firms and voluntary organizations, "grass roots movements," and revitalistic cults may also participate in the cybernetics of social and ecological correction, and thus are also to be included in any account of adaptive structure. There is a dialectic, so to speak, between formal organization and "spontaneous" adaptive responses, the latter modifying the former and even, perhaps, redefining systemic boundaries from time to time. Indeed, as we have already suggested, it is at least as correct to say adaptive processes define, discriminate, or establish living systems and their limits as it is to say they "inhere in" living systems. We should not be bemused by the apparently immutable boundaries of the living systems most easily observed, namely organisms, or the enduring frontiers of some societies, into taking living systems to be "things" when they are better regarded as dynamic processes organizing matter, energy, and information.

MALADAPTATION

The adaptive structures of living systems of different classes (ecosystems, societies, organisms) surely differ in important respects, possibly related to differences in the coherence they require and can tolerate. There are also, surely, important differences to be discerned among the adaptive structures of members of the same class, such as different human societies. I have suggested, however, orderly adaptive structure has certain universal characteristics, and orderly adaptive human social structures share additional characteristics, particularly an order of sanctification. We may, therefore, expect to find important structural similarities underlying apparently great differences. Orderly adaptive structure, I have argued, is both cybernetic and hierarchical, and I have made some suggestions —they are no more than that—concerning features or dimensions that may be organized hierarchically. These suggestions may be of some use in guiding investigations leading to more refined formulations. For now they may serve as the basis for further suggestions concerning the nature of maladaptation.

If adaptive processes are those tending to maintain homeostasis in crucial variables in the face of perturbation, maladaptations are factors internal to systems inferfering with their homeostatic responses. They reduce the survival chances of a system not, in the first instance, by subjecting the system to stress, but by impeding the effectiveness of its responses to stress. Maladaptations are not to be confused with stressors, or perturbing factors, although they themselves can produce stress. This view of maladaptation, it may be noted, is similar to the concept of disease (dis-ease) proposed by I. J. Young and W. F. Rowley.[16]

If the maintenance of homeostasis depends upon hierarchically ordered sequences of adaptive responses, it should be possible to describe maladaptation structurally. That is, maladaptations may be conceived as anomalies in the hierarchical and cybernetic features we have taken to be characteristics of orderly adaptive structure.

Cybernetic Problems. If the feedback of information to regulators concerning the states of systemic variables and the effects of their operations upon those variables is faulty, trouble is likely to ensue. The simplest forms of maladaptation are such cybernetic difficulties as impedence to the detection of deviation of variables from crucial ranges, breaks in feedback loops, or even excessive delay of information transmissions concerning variable states to system regulators, loss or distortion of information in transit, and the failure of regulators to understand the signals they are receiving. These and other difficulties to which we shall attend are exacerbated by size. For instance, the more nodes through which it must pass, the more subject information is to distortion or loss. Other things equal, the higher the administrator the less accurate and adequate his information is likely to be, and the more diverse the subsystems he is regulating the more likely he is to misunderstand the signals upon which he must act. Loss, distortion, and misunderstanding of information are likely to result in erroneous or inappropriate regulatory responses. We have heard much of the economies of scale. The diseconomies of scale also require attention.

This may seem an inconsistency in argument, but it is rather, I think, a problem in the real world. It was suggested earlier that high-order regulators do not need to "know," indeed, cannot affort to "know," all that the lower-order regulators subordinate to them "know." Now it is claimed that distortion or even simple loss of information can lead high-order regulators into error. Complex living systems, especially human social systems, are faced with the problem, perhaps never fully resolved, of balancing comprehensiveness of information against information-processing efficiency. Intrinsic to the reduction of information required by limited information-processing facilities is the danger of faulty, distorting, or self-serving editing. There is perhaps no way for such a danger to be avoided completely, but it can perhaps be minimized by maximizing the autonomy of low-order regulators, thus reducing the amount of information that must be processed by those of higher order.

Much more remains to be said about cybernetic problems per se, but they are relatively well known and in the interest of brevity we may turn now to hierarchical anomalies. Their likelihood, too, is increased with scale, and some of them are closely related to the cybernetic disorders we have been discussing.

Time Aberrations. The deeper the regulatory hierarchy the more likely are time aberrations. Excessive time lag between the onset of a perturbation and response to it may sometimes be a problem, but so may the opposite—too rapid a response by a high-order regulator. Excessively fast response by high-order regulators may destroy those of lower order by continuously overriding them. The destruction of the lower-order regulator may then throw an additional burden upon that which overrode it, with error and possibly breakdown resulting. The likelihood of excessively rapid high-order response—let us call it "premature override"—is increased of course, by high-speed communications, which may put information concerning perturbations into the hands of higher authorities as quickly as it informs the lower.

Over-response. "Over-response" is related to, and may even be entailed by, premature override. The responses of higher-order regulators are not likely to be as delicate or as reversible as those of lower order, and if they are initiated too quickly they may be more massive than required. Since they may not be easily reversible, they commit the system's future more than necessary. That is to say, they reduce its evolutionary flexibility. Over-response, it may be suggested, is impossible, or at least highly unlikely, in biological systems, for in strictly biological processes the sequencing of adaptive responses to perturbation is ordered not by conscious purpose but by nonconscious somatic and genetic organization. Over-response may be a product of intelligence, particularly human intelligence with its great powers of foresight and imagination. It becomes more serious, of course, as that intelligence comes to control ever more powerful means for effecting its ends.

Over-segregation and Over-centralization. We are led here to several more general interrelated trends that seem to be common aspects of the increased scale of social systems. First there is what may be called "over-segregation," the extreme differentiation of special-purpose subsystems. Over-segregation may be expressed geographically, with serious ecological and social consequences. Increasingly large areas become increasingly specialized. Whole regions are turned into wheat fields, whole countries into sugar plantations. But with increasing regional specialization there is decreasing ecological stability, for monocrop fields, particularly those planted in high-yield varieties, are among the most delicate ecosystems ever to have appeared on the face of the earth. Part of this decrease in ecological stability is an aspect of the reduction of self-sufficiency, for modern monocrop agriculture depends upon fuel, machinery, pesticides, and herbicides that usually travel through far-flung and complicated networks, and distant disruptions in such networks, as well as local problems, can disrupt local activities. With loss of local self-sufficiency there is also loss of local regulatory autonomy, and the homeostatic capacity lost from the local system is not adequately replaced by increasingly remote centralized regulators responding to increasingly aggregated and simplified variables (like the dollar values of crops) through operations increasingly subject to simple cybernetic impedences and time aberrations, to say nothing of the self-interest of those in whose hands regulation lies. The net result is the ecological, economic, and political impoverishment of local systems—sometimes entire Third World countries—and the enrichment of the industrialized powers, or rather elite groups within them. It is a mystification or even falsehood to refer to this process as "economic development."

Hypercoherence. The regulatory responses of distant regulators are often to factors extraneous to some of the local systems they effect. For instance, the effect of market response to increased vanilla production in Madagascar may be decreased cash in Tahiti. We recognize here a consequence of over-segregation and "over-centralization" that has elsewhere been called "hyper-coherence" or "hyper-integration."[17] The coherence of the world system increases to dangerous levels as the self-sufficiency of local systems is reduced and their autonomy destroyed. Disruptions occurring anywhere may now spread everywhere. A local war in the Middle East disrupts the economies of the West and results in increased starvation in India, for India relies upon Japanese fertilizer, which requires Middle Eastern oil for its manufacture. As Geoffrey Vickers has put it, "the trouble is not that we are not one world, but that we are."[18]

Hierarchical Maldistribution of Organization. Over-segregation and over-centralization taken together are complementary aspects of a more general structural anomaly that I have mentioned elsewhere, and which may be called the "hierarchical maldistribution of organization."[19] "Organization" is notoriously difficult to define; I take the term to refer to complexity and the means for maintaining order within it, and have been suggesting that organization at more inclusive levels seems to be increasing at the expense of organization at local levels. Increasing organization at the world level is based upon decreasingly organized local, regional, and even national social and ecological systems. It seems doubtful that a worldwide human organization can persist and elaborate itself indefinitely at the expense of its local infrastructures, and it may be suggested that the ability of the world system to withstand perturbation would be increased by returning to its local subsystems some of the autonomy and diversity they have lost, as China may be doing. This is not to advocate fracturing the world system into smaller, autonomous, self-sufficient systems, a program as undesirable as it would be impossible to achieve. It is to suggest that redistribution of organization among the levels of the world system, with somewhat greater autonomy and self-sufficiency vested in localities, regions, and even nations than presently is the case, would serve well the world system as a whole. This is also, and very emphatically, not to suggest the stability of the world system would be well served by increasing the autonomy of entities in their nature narrowly defined by special purposes, such as manufacturing firms. The very opposite is, in fact, indicated.

Usurpation. There is another general class of maladaptations, combining with those discussed so far in complex evolutionary sequences. The basic form has elsewhere been called "usurpation," "escalation," and "overspecification."[20] I speak here of special-purpose subsystems coming to dominate the larger, general-purpose systems of which they are parts. When particular individuals become identified with special-purpose systems they tend to identify the special purposes of those subsystems with their own general purposes, that is, with their own survival and betterment. Their own general purposes become highly specialized, and they attempt to promote these purposes to positions of predominance in the larger systems of which they are parts. As they become increasingly powerful, they are increasingly able to succeed. Needless to say, power is not equally distributed among the various components of highly differentiated "developed" societies such as our own, but is, rather, concentrated in their industrial and financial sectors. These sectors are frequently able to dominate the agencies charged with regulating them, and the logical end is for the interests of groups of industrial firms, financial institutions, and related military establishments to come to dominate the societies of which they are merely specialized parts. This eventuality is nicely summed up in the phrase "What's good for General Motors is good for America." But no matter how public spirited or benign General Motors might be, what is good for it cannot in the long run be good for America. For a society like the United States to commit itself to what may be good for one of its special-purpose subsystems, such as General Motors, or even the entire set of industries devoted to the manufacture, maintenance, and operation of automobiles, is for it to overspecify or narrow the range of conditions under which it can persist—that is, it reduces its evolutionary flexibility.

While loss of evolutionary flexibility is disguised by what seems to be the characteristics of progress, and is therefore difficult to discern, other concommitments of the elevation of low-order goals and values to positions of predominance in higher-order systems related to loss of flexibility, but having other implications as well, are rather obvious. First, as industrial subsystems become increasingly large and powerful, the quality or utility of their products, or both, are likely to deteriorate. For the subsystem's contribution to the society becomes less its product and more its mere operation, providing wages to some, profits to others, and a market for yet others. Arms, which are both expensive and immediately obsolete, and automobiles into which obsolescence is built, are ideal products. There is nothing wrong with products that serve no useful purpose whatsoever. The product tends to become a by- or even waste-product of what might be called the "industrial metabolism" which is, ultimately, simply the operation of machines. Neither competition nor an independently established demand serves to regulate or limit "industrial metabolism" effectively because large industries are usually not very competitive and they can exercise considerable control over the demand to which they are supposed to be subject.[21]

Second and more serious, with the escalation of low-order goals to dominating positions in society, it becomes increasingly possible for ancient and complex systems, particularly ecological systems, to be disrupted by ever smaller groups with ever more narrowly-defined interests.

For instance, there is some evidence to support the contention that certain fluorocarbons used in propellants in spray cans dispensing shaving cream, deodorants, and the like are destroying atmospheric ozone that shields life from lethal intensities of ultraviolet radiation. Yet these aerosols are still manufactured and sold. That the putative effects of these chemicals upon the atmosphere have not yet been "proven" hardly justifies their continued use, given the trivial nature of their advantages and the catastrophic nature of the risks their use may entail. A rudimentary sense of self-preservation, let alone any altruistic ethical sense, would seem to suggest even to the manufacturers that they suspend production until there is a very high degree of assurance these compounds are proven harmless.

We note in this instance and in many others the violations of orderly time relations and relations between the instrumental and fundamental—violations such as the clear-cutting of forests in areas in which they are unlikely to regenerate, offshore drilling in unstable geological zones, the dumping of undegradable poisons into fresh waters. Short-run narrow and instrumental interests subordinate long-run, general, and fundamental needs. But these instances suggest that the facilitation of disruption for the sake of narrowly defined special interests is not the whole of the ecological or indeed human problem following from the promotion of the low-order goals of industrialized subsystems to predominant positions in societies. The ultimate consequence is not merely that the short-run interests of a few powerful men or institutions come to·prevail, but that the "interests" of machines—which even powerful men serve—become dominant. Needless to say, the interests of machines and organisms do not coincide. They do not have the same needs for pure air or water, and being blind and deaf, machines have no need for quiet or for landscapes that refresh the eye. Whereas organisms have need of uncounted numbers of subtle compounds the needs of machines are few, simple, and voracious.

The Degradation of the Sacred. There is one further concomitant of the maladaptive form we are calling overspecification or usurpation that we should mention here. It is likely to lead to aberrations of sanctification. It is important to note that ultimate sacred propositions about gods and the like are typically without material terms. As such they themselves specify no particular social arrangements of institutions. Being low in specificity, they are well suited to be associated with the general goal of societies, namely their own perpetuation, for they can sanctify changing social arrangements while they themselves, remaining inviolate and unchanged, provide continuity through change.

The typically cryptic nature of ultimate sacred propositions is also of importance. The association of mysterious propositions concerning ultimate reality with the immediate reality of contemporary institutions and events is a matter of interpretation. That which is a matter of interpretation allows or even demands reinterpretation, but reinterpretation does not challenge ultimate sacred propositions themselves. It merely challenges previous interpretations of them. Thus, if any proposition is to be taken to be unquestionable, it is important that no one understand it. The very qualities of such propositions that lead positivists to take them to be without sense or even to be nonsense—devoid of logical necessity or empirical reference—are those that make them adaptively valid.

Sanctification, however, can become maladaptive through the process we are calling usurpation. As the specific material goals of lower-order systems usurp the places of those of higher-order systems, they may lay claim to their sanctity. To use a crude example, if the United States is "one nation under God," and if, as Coolidge said, "the business of America is business," then business becomes highly sanctified. What is highly sanctified is resistant to change; thus to oversanctify the specific and material is to reduce evolutionary flexibility. It is of interest that the theologian Paul Tillich used the term "idolatry" to refer to the "absolutizing of the relative" and the "relativizing of the absolute."[22] What he took to be a form of evil we may take to be a form of maladaptation.

The social effects of what we, following Tillich, may call "idolatry" are not limited to the reduction of adaptive flexibility. At least as serious, and perhaps closer to the concerns of this volume, is the degradation of basic values. The instrumental and derivative are confused with, and usurp the place of, basic values. The "pursuit of happiness" comes to be little more than the accumulation of goods; "liberty" comes to mean self-service. Materialism and selfishness are thus honored as highest ideals. We need not dwell upon the unacceptable demands upon the general ecological system that the sanctification of these degraded values encourages, for they are obvious. We may, however, consider our recent history in this light. Given the degradation of values this society has suffered, the complex corruption of Watergate was hardly surprising. Perhaps most significant, the public statements of many of those involved, including some of the president's men, some corporate executives guilty of attempting to buy favor, and even the former president himself, indicate that they did not understand, and perhaps still do not understand, that anything they did was wrong. This is to say that for them there had been no violation of basic values, perhaps because for them the place of basic values had been usurped by values of a lower order. Governance had become nothing more than politics; liberty had been reduced to the untrammeled right to power, wealth, and self-aggrandizement. As the sworn defenders of basic values, those who participated in Watergate did not simply violate the basic values of the society. They came close to destroying them. They did not conspire to overthrow them openly, of course. The words remained the same. They conspired to turn them into lies—not ordinary lies, but what Denis de Rougemont many years ago called "diabolical lies," in honor of the devil's putative proclivity for claiming to be what he is not.[23] Diabolical lies are not simply transmissions of information known by the transmitter to be false, but lies which tamper with the very canons of truth. The most insidious aspect of the general corruption of Watergate was that it was corrupting, for its effects are lasting. The basic values of this society, and the hope of reestablishing them, remain the dubious objects of widespread cynicism.

CONTINGENCY, CAUSE, AND CORRECTION

We have been led beyond structural anomaly to substantive problems, and we may return here to a question raised, but not answered, earlier. What are the variables to be maintained in homeostasis if a living system is to be adaptive? Some, after all, may be maintained at the expense of others. It has been suggested, for instance, that when highest-order regulation is directed toward economic goals, it may impede the maintenance of biological variables—organic, demographic, and ecosystemic—within their ranges of viability. We may ask whether this may be properly regarded as adaptive, even if the cybernetics of the system seem to be in good order.

If the goal of general purpose systems is simply persistence, and if persistence entails survival, then the question of what is ultimately to be maintained in homeostasis is reduced to the question of what the term "survival" minimally implies. Here we may be reminded that the term "adaptation" is basically a biological term, and that the systems with which we are concerned have living components. "Survival," although difficult to specify, has, minimally, a biological meaning, and the adaptiveness of aspects of culture may ultimately be assessed in terms of their effects upon the biological components of the systems in which they occur. As we noted earlier when distinguishing adaptive processes from cybernetic processes in general, what is called "cultural adaptation," the processes through which social structures or institutions maintain themselves in the face of perturbation, may contradict or defeat the general or biological adaptation of which culture in its emergence must have been a part. But, since survival is nothing if not biological, evolutionary changes perpetuating economic or political institutions at the expense of the biological well-being of man, societies, and ecosystems may be considered maladaptive. This assertion is not arbitrary for it reflects the way contingency is structured. There are no particular institutions with which a society could not dispense; but, obviously, if man perished culture would cease to exist.

There are problems, however, with biological criteria. For one thing, given the "counter-intuitive" nature of complex systems, it is difficult or impossible to assess the long-run effects of any aspect of culture on particular biological variables. For a second, it does not seem possible to specify any particular feature of biological structure or function that will always contribute to survival chances.[24] Although particular variables are, and must be, maintained within ranges of viability at particular times, these ranges, and even the systemic components of which they are states, may be changed by evolution. Thus, adaptiveness is not to be identified with particular variables, even biological variables, but with the maintenance of a general homeostasis in living systems, systems with biological components.

The notion of a general homeostasis is not fully operational, but neither is it mystical. One of the implications of the argument presented here is that it is intrinsic to adaptive structure, to a certain ordering of processes and the systemic components in which they may occur, with respect to time, reversibility, specificity, sanctity, and contingency. If such an order is maintained, general homeostasis, it is suggested, prevails. This is to claim that the *formal* or *structural* characteristics of adaptive processes have *substantive* implications. The primacy of biological considerations is intrinsic to the structure, for the escalation of nonbiological variables to positions of predominance violates adaptive order with respect to specificity, contingency, and possibly sanctity as well. We noted earlier that societies differ with respect to the values they take to be basic, but all which are to survive, even those holding life after death in high esteem, must include "life" among them, implicitly if not explicitly.

In light of possible contradictions between cultural and biological adaptation it seems reasonable to search for the factors impelling maladaptive trends among those that have been taken to be advances in cultural evolution. In the world of events, cause is seldom simple, and in complex systems causes and consequences are not always distinct. The discussion which follows implicates certain factors but could have brought in others. It is illustrative rather than exhaustive and does not presume to represent a general theory. It is intended to do no more than suggest, briefly and tentatively, a few of the many factors that could be adduced.

Some suggestions have already been made about energy capture in this regard. It is important to remember, however, that energy capture has sometimes been taken to be the metric of cultural evolution. A quarter of a century ago Leslie White, following Wilhelm Ostwald, proclaimed what he called "The Basic Law of Cultural Evolution" as follows: "Other factors remaining constant, culture evolves as the amount of energy harnessed per capita per year is increased, or as the efficiency of the instrumental means of putting energy to work is increased."[25]

There can be no denying the first clause of this formulation. Large technologically developed states appearing late in history surely do harness more energy per capita per day or year than do the small "primitive" societies which appeared earlier. One recent estimate would place daily per capita energy consumption in contemporary United States at 230 thousand kilocalories, and in hunting and gathering societies at two to three thousand.[26]

Contemporary United States has a population of 214 million people; bushmen bands seldom include more than a score or two of people, and increases in energy capture have made possible much larger and more sedentary social systems. But some, if not all, of the maladaptive trends we have noted here are related to increased scale. Moreover, high energy technology itself frees those operating in local ecosystems from the limits imposed upon them by the need to derive energy from the contemporary biological processes of those systems themselves. Gasoline, pipelines, bulldozers, and high voltage electrical transmission permit virtually unlimited amounts of energy to be focused upon very small systems, and the ecological disruption of those systems can be tolerated—at least for a time—because of the increased specialization of other local systems. I have argued, however, that in the long run the increasing specialization of larger and larger regions—made possible by a technology that provides means for moving even bulky commodities long distances inexpensively, and for transmitting information long distances instantaneously—is unstable.

The increasing specialization of increasingly large geographical regions is simply one aspect of increasing internal differentiation of social systems. Progressive segregation and progressive centralization, were, of course, encouraged by the emergence of plant and animal cultivation ten thousand or so years ago, for plant and animal cultivation provided significant opportunities for full-time division of labor. By 4000 B.C., if not earlier, subsistence, craft, religious, and administrative specialization was well developed. But the emergence of high energy technology based upon fossil fuels has accelerated and exaggerated this trend and the maladaptations associated with it. These include not only over-segregation and over-centralization, with their concomitants of ecological instability and hypercoherence. High energy technology is differentially distributed among the subsystems of societies, and it permits or encourages the promotion of the special purposes of the more powerful to positions of dominance in systems of higher order than their degree of specialization warrants.

Perhaps less obviously, the differentiation of societies into increasingly specialized subsystems has had implications for the ways in which men conceive the world and their place in it. Since action is guided by understanding, peoples' understandings of the structures of the world may impede or impel maladaptive trends, and it is useful to spend a little time in comparing so-called "primitive" to modern societies in this regard.

In small "tribal" societies internal differentiation is rudimentary. The division of labor follows lines of age and sex, in the main, with everyone doing pretty much what everyone else in his or her age and sex category is doing. Even chiefs, where they exist, are likely to work in their own gardens. Not only is everyone engaged in the same general activities, but what they are all engaged in, of course, is food production. Producers, usually both men and women, are aware from firsthand experience of their place in the circular structure of ecological processes and behave accordingly. It is true, of course, that in the absence of exotic energy sources the ability of tribal peoples to abuse the ecosystems in which they participate is limited by those ecosystems because it is only from them that energy for work can be extracted. Among such people, however, abuses need seldom be revenged by declining yields because trouble is likely to be signaled sooner by subtler signs of environmental degradation. Effective ecological regulation— the maintenance of the circular structure of ecosystems— depends in systems dominated by men on effective information feedback from the environment to those operating upon it (the flow of information through ecosystems, like the flow of materials through the same systems, must be circular). Information feedback from the environment is sensitive and rapid in small autonomous ecological systems in which everyone is directly engaged in food production. While there are surely conflicts of interest in such societies, there are no special interests, for there are no special purpose subsystems with which full-time specialized personnel are associated. It is thus clear to all those living in such systems that their survival is contingent upon the maintenance, rather than the mere *exploitation* of the encompassing ecological community of which they know themselves to be only parts. It is not surprising that tribal peoples often, if not indeed, generally, express in religious terms their relationship to the ecosystems upon which they depend. For the Maring, a group of New Guinea horticulturalists among whom I have lived, the cosmos is conceived as a set of cyclical processes having both spiritual and material aspects. The relations of people to these processes, and in some degree these processes themselves, are regulated by protracted cycles of rituals.[27] The forest within which the hunting and gathering Ituri pygmies live is both personified and sanctified by them as *Ndura*.[28] *Ndura* is both God and forest, or forest as God, "mother and father to us all." The pygmies say that no harm will befall *Ndura*'s children (themselves) as long as the Forest-God is kept happy. *Ndura*'s happiness is secured through entertainment—song and dance—and through respect for *Ndura*'s person, which includes trees, animals, and even streams and rocks. The pygmies explicitly establish with the ecosystem what the modern Jewish theologian Martin Buber calls an "I-Thou" relationship (a relationship in which the other is treated as an equivalent of ego, in contrast to an "I-It" relationship, in which the other is considered to be no more than an object to be exploited).[29] The pygmy religious conception is also reminiscent of the theology of Paul Tillich, who took what he called "the ground of one's being" to be continuous with "the ground of all being."[30]

We may smile at the naivete of people who sanctify a world which we take to be perfectly natural. Yet it seems to become more apparent each day that there is no simple direct relationship between the amount of empirical knowledge contained within the world view of a people and the appropriateness of the behavior elected by it. It is by no means certain that the representations of nature provided us by science are more adaptive than those of the pygmies and the Maring, replete as the latter may be with supernaturals. Indeed, they may be less so, for to veil nature in the supernatural is to provide her with some protection against human parochialism and destructiveness, a parochialism that may be encouraged by a natural view of nature.

The ecological circularities apparent to the Maring horticulturalist, and possibly to the pygmy hunter and gatherer, are masked from men in state-organized societies by the sheer scale and complexity of these societies. Because of each man's specialization, no man has immediate experience of the circularities of nature that are grasped by all Maring, because all Maring are aware that they are grasped by them. Each man experiencing for himself only a short arc on such circles is likely to lose sight of the circles in their wholeness. And even where some ecological awareness is present, this awareness is likely to be less compelling in the decisions of increasingly specialized men than are their own immediate and increasingly specialized interests. Nor do the religious conceptions of contemporary societies serve to protect the integrity of ecosystems against the voracity of its human participants. For one thing, to become universal the great contemporary religions had to separate themselves from the ecological particulars of the localities in which they emerged, and to remain separate from all ecosystems. They are oriented toward the next world rather than this one. For another, contemporary religions are generally very weak. Not only do they not protect ecosystems from exploitation, they don't provide much protection for society's weak from exploitation by its strong.

Thus it comes to be that ecological, or systemic "rationality" —a rationality that is concerned to maintain the circular wholeness of ecological systems, a rationality that may not be ashamed to invoke mystical conceptions and feelings—is replaced by "economic rationality"—the application of scarce means to the attainment of differentially graded ends for purposes of the maximization of narrowly defined interests. Ecosystems are now conceived in a way entirely different from the way they are conceived in the tribal society. Contemporary societies are seldom encompassed by particular ecological association, as the highly autonomous local groups of tribal societies frequently are. Instead, they are likely to span a range, frequently a great range, of distinct environmental zones. In such a setting an ecosystem such as a forest is no longer likely to be conceived as a generalized, autonomous, encompassing ecological system, but as simply one element or subsystem in a larger socioeconomic system. It is no longer "mother and father to us all," as it is to the pygmies, or an indispensable link in the circle of life and death as it is for the Maring. It is now a resource, an "it" to be exploited. While it is true contemporary man does not depend as utterly upon any local ecological system as do tribal peoples, he depends no less than man ever did upon the integrity of ecological processes in general. The increasing scale and differentiation of society, however, has increased the likelihood of the subordination of ecological processes to the purposes of men whose understanding becomes ever narrower and shorter in term.

Consideration of changes in man's view of the world and his place in it leads us to consider the ways in which knowledge may be organized, and the implications for maladaptive trends. Generalizations are dangerous, but I think it possible to claim that cultural evolution has been characterized by what might be called an inversion in the order of knowledge.

Among tribal peoples, in the ancient civilizations and perhaps remaining in the form of religious thought, what might be called ultimate knowledge was sacred knowledge. That is, knowledge of ultimate sacred propositions, propositions concerning gods and the like, in their nature mysterious and, although neither verifiable nor falsifiable, taken to be unquestionable, were regarded as that which is most fundamental. These propositions sanctified others expressing social values, and they also often sanctified systems of classification applying to broad ranges of phenomena that would seem to the outsider to be disparate. The Maring, for instance, classify plants, animals, land, diseases, persons, activities, states of society, spirits, and spiritual states as "hot" or "cold." The result is that the world is not only laden with agreed upon values, but it is generally full of meaning. If meaning is to be derived from the perception of deep similarity underlying apparent difference, and if many things are, as it were, icons of each other (since, for example, they might all be composed of oppositions between hot and cold: man/woman, high gardens/low gardens, war/peace, marsupials/eels, headache/stomachache, and so forth) then meaning is to be found everywhere. Finally, there is knowledge of ordinary material fact. As such knowledge is well developed in our own society, so it is in tribal societies. The Maring are very much aware of the special characteristics of each of the many varieties of taro and sweet potato that they plant, and the pygmies know where they are likely to find the species which are their prey. Such knowledge is considered to be obvious, however, and while important, hardly fundamental or ultimate. Of greater interest is the subsumption of material facts by such classificatory devices as totemic systems, in which they are ordered into "logics of the concrete."[31] In such logics, material facts become tokens in elaborate and embracing systems of meanings supported finally through the operations of myth and ritual, by the ultimate, mysterious sacred.

In contemporary Western society, in contrast, material fact is ultimate knowledge. Facts are ordered, within limited domains, by subsumption under more or less specific scientific laws that are always subject to overthrow by the discovery of new facts. Attempts to apply general ordering principles to disparate domains are often regarded as improper, and knowledge becomes fragmented. Nothing is any longer an icon of anything else. If meaning lies in the perception of deep similarities underlying apparent differences then, paradoxically, meaning is diminished as empirical information is increased. The position of that which in earlier times was taken to be ultimate knowledge—unquestionable religious propositions and the values they sanctify—becomes anomalous in a world of empirical fact. The empirical and logical rationality that discovers and applies facts and that defines knowledge as knowledge of fact is not hospitable to sanctity or value. Ultimate sacred propositions are no longer counted as knowledge, but "mere belief"; basic values become matters of taste or, to become apparently compatible with the rationality of fact, they are reduced to idolatrous terms. In either event, values which men agree to be self-evident, natural, or God-given are either dissolved or degraded by an ever-narrowing rationality. It is a rationality reduced to that of the syllogism, the experiment, and the dicta of the economists. It has no room for the insights of art, religion, fantasy, or dream. The evaluational capacities of such a rationality are, of course, very limited.

Our increasing concern with fact, then, has fragmented the world, depriving us of meaning, and has degraded values to the status of preference. It is of interest to consider the semantics of money—money as meaning or a substitute for meaning —in this light. Meaning arises, I have argued, from the discovery of similarities shared by apparently distinct phenomena. Money does not provide a means for discovering such similarities among distinctive things. Rather, it dissolves what is distinctive among all of the things to which it applies by providing a common metric against which all things can be assessed. As such it reduces *qualitative* distinctions to mere unidimensional *quantitative* differences. The most compelling answer to such a question as "What is the difference between a forest and a shopping center?" becomes "So many dollars per acre." Answers concerning differences in species diversity, cover for wild life, transpiration rates, recreational possibilities, and aesthetics are less likely to figure in decision making.

But this is error. That the world upon which the simple metric of money is imposed is not as simple as this metric is obvious. What seems to be less obvious is that it *must not* be. Living systems—plants, animals, societies, ecosystems—while displaying similarities of organization, are each in some considerable degree unique, and each requires a great variety of particular materials to remain healthy. Monetization forces the great range of unique and distinct materials and processes that sustain or even constitute life into an arbitrary and specious equivalence, and decisions informed by monetary considerations are likely to simplify, that is to say to degrade and disrupt the ecological systems in which they operate.

We have moved from the general question of the semantics of money to the more specific problem of money as value. With this in mind, we approach the part that capitalism may be playing in the maladaptive trends discussed in the last section. It should be clear these trends cannot be accounted for entirely by private enterprise, and other factors have been explicitly noted. It should be equally clear that private enterprise is deeply implicated. Large, privately owned firms, or associations of them, have been able to elevate their own specialized goals to positions of predominance in the societies of which they are parts and in the development of their domination they have contributed significantly to the destruction of ecological systems, to the subordination of men to machines, to the debasement of values and even to the degradation of the sacred. Moreover, multinational corporations preside over processes commenced under earlier colonial forms. They encourage geographical over-segregation, which entails diminishment of local, regional, and even national autonomy. Their operations increase world coherence to levels that may be approaching the lethal. They contribute to the general hierarchical maldistribution of organization characterizing the contemporary world. In less formal terms, global business organizations have exploited and impoverished the countries they claim, or even intend, to be developing as often as they have assisted them.

It will do no good for the business community to deny its contribution to maladaptive trends, nor for it to treat the problem as one of public relations. It should be kept in mind by those interested in preserving private enterprise that human groups, unlike associations of other species, are governed by conventions rather than by genetically established patterns of behavior. Humans have the ability to change the regulatory modes under which they have been living, or even to abolish them. In our own society, as we have seen, the Declaration of Independence transforms this ability into a right that may be legitimately exercised if existing modes of governance violate basic social values. If private enterprise is to survive its ills, businessmen must recognize the contribution they make to the social, political, and ecological problems of the world. Recognition is the first step toward cure.

The problem of cure is extraordinarily difficult because we are without a comprehensive theory of correction of systemic disorder. The hard-headed "problem-solving approach" so favored by men who like to think of themselves as practical causes as many problems as it solves when it is brought to bear in systems so complex as to be beyond our capacity to comprehend them completely, and thus to predict the comprehensive outcome of the actions we take in them. Fundamental to any theory of correction, however, is the notion that few, if any, important problems can be isolated for solutions independent of their systemic contexts. A theory of correction, therefore, would have as its aim not the solution of particular problems, but the establishment of principles from which could be derived actions aiming to restore orderly function to malfunctioning systems. The goal of such actions is not the establishment of some static problem-free utopia, but of systems that could continually reorganize themselves in response to the problems inevitably arising out of continually changing historical circumstances.

The notions of adaptation and maladaptation developed earlier in this chapter at least point in the direction of a possible theory. Maladaptations are disorders of adaptive structure. They are defined as deformations of a postulated adaptive *order*, a set of relations among the components of living systems organized hierarchically with respect to time, reversibility, specificity, instrumentality, sanctity, contingency, and perhaps other characteristics as well. In this view there is nothing "wrong" with, let us say, high-energy technology. What is wrong is the domination of a human system by a technology that should be serving it. There is nothing wrong with money per se, if it does not come to usurp the position of ultimate value. Similar assertions can be made of private enterprise and other problem-generating components of contemporary society. High-energy technology, money, and private enterprise all have their places in society. The problem is to "keep them in their places," or, more accurately in view of the state of the contemporary world, to "put them in their places" in the larger systems of which they are only instrumental parts.

Putting things in places defined by a theory of adaptive structure as proper for them is no easy task in a world full of vested special interests. Some degree of acquiescence from those with such interests is perhaps necessary if there is to be accord with the democratic principles espoused by the society, and it is certainly necessary if progress is to be made. We may consider in this light the proposal advanced by the editor of this volume that business firms, trade associations, and profes-

sional groups adopt rigorous codes of ethics. Aside from stipulating appropriate particulars, these codes of ethics would
enshrine such social values as honesty and service to society.

It should be kept in mind, of course, that codes of ethics can
become self-serving or mere public relations devices. They
must be serious. They not only must say "the right things,"
they must do the right things. This is to say that they must be
enforced. It may be suggested in this regard that their proper
locus is more often in associations than individual firms, for it
is more likely to be in the immediate interests of associations
than firms to enforce them.

There can be no objection to such codes if more is not asked
of them than they can accomplish. For one thing, their mere
enunciation may clarify the ethical principles obtaining in
areas otherwise remaining ambiguous. For another, the acceptance of an ethical code, which may be entailed for a person
by his entrance into the firm or association espousing that
code, is tantamount to an obligation to abide by its terms.
That is, whether a man abides by such rules or not, his free
acceptance of them has obligated him to do so. If he does not,
he has violated an obligation that *he himself has freely avowed.*
The assertion here is similar to that of the philosopher John
Searle who has argued that:

> . . . when one enters an institutional activity by invoking the
> rules of the institution one necessarily commits himself in such
> and such ways, regardless of whether one approves or disap-
> proves of the institution. In the case of linguistic institutions
> like promising [or accepting] the serious utterances of the
> words commit one in ways which are determined by the
> meaning of the words. In certain first person utterances the
> utterance is the undertaking of an obligation.[32]

Searle later notes that the notion of obligation is closely related to the notions of accepting, acknowledging, recognizing.
There is no obligation without acceptance. The acceptance of
codes of ethics, then, both clarifies ethical principles and
obliges those accepting to abide by them. To make them more
effective, I would suggest that acceptance not be regarded as
simply a tacit concomitant of entrance into the firm or association espousing the code. Acceptance should be made a memo-
rable public act, in which the acceptor is himself required to

articulate his acceptance in a manner sensible both to himself and to others, as in oath-taking.

Ethical codes are useful, and their adoption is to be encouraged. Yet it is to be doubted that they alone would be sufficient to hold businesses in their proper places in the adaptive structure of society. To ask too much of ethical codes would be to discredit them for failing to do what they cannot do. While ethical codes can explicitly espouse an ideal of service to society, it would be unrealistic to imagine that business firms will ever place the public interest above their own. They are in their nature profit-seeking and oriented toward growth, and it would not be reasonable to expect them to make themselves over into something other than they are. Conversely, as it would be unreasonable for society to expect business firms to transform themselves into charitable institutions, so would it be unreasonable for the business community to expect society to refrain from regulating it. The society at large has, after all, interests of its own in the operations of business, particularly when these operations exploit natural resources on public lands, as in the case of much oil-drilling and lumbering, and when the industry is so basic that it sets the conditions of life, as in the case of energy production.

It continues to be, as it has been, a function of society as a whole to establish the place of business firms in the complex processes of the social system. In the past, when business firms were smaller, less far-flung, and less powerful, social regulation may have been effected through the informal operations of the market, or so it was believed. In our day it is quite clear that the regulatory functions of the market are very limited. This leaves government.

One of the concerns of this volume is with freedom, and we could ask whether governmental regulation of business constitutes ipso facto an odious abridgment of freedom. Phrased in this way the question is naive. All societies have always imposed limits upon the actions of their members. There is, however, a less obvious question to be asked: What sorts of entities can properly claim rights to life, liberty, and the pursuit of happiness? Our general argument has raised the problem of probable contradiction between what might be called "economic freedom" on the one hand, human and social freedom on the other. That is, the freedom of societies to maintain and transform themselves in the face of ever-changing circumstances, and the right of individuals to life, liberty, and the pursuit of happiness may be jeopardized by the freedom of economically defined entities, such as large and powerful business firms, to seek their own goals.

It seems clear to me that individual humans and societies are the proper loci of freedom. Business firms, despite the fact that most of them (virtually all of the larger and more powerful ones) are legal individuals, are not human. Nor are they to be regarded as general-purpose systems, as are societies, clans, and families, for their purposes are narrow. They can be kept in their appropriate places in adaptive orders only if they are regarded as, and treated as, instruments whose special outputs make a contribution to social and human values more basic than their own perpetuation.

It may be objected that most individuals are associated in one way or another with business firms and that restrictions upon the prerogatives of business firms are therefore abridgments of personal freedom. I do not take this to be the case. Corporations are entities distinct from those who are employed by them, and even from those who share in their ownership. Moreover, the identity of a person is not exhausted by what he owns or who employs him, or even by the rational thought processes he uses on the job. He is surely more complete and complex than the abilities exercised in his work, and as such he is both distinct from and transcends the terms of his employment.

To argue that individuals and societies are the proper subjects of freedom and to argue for the necessity of governmental regulation of business is not to advocate the abrogation of management's prerogatives to seek its own goals. The question which remains concerns the nature of the regulation to which government should subject business. I am unqualified to discuss this matter in any detail, but some general suggestions have been implicit in the outline of adaptive structure and maladaptive forms developed earlier. Certain points, however, may be emphasized here. First, regulation should, by and large, be proscriptive rather than prescriptive. Proscriptive regulation is less cumbersome than prescriptive, and it preserves the prerogatives of business firms while setting limits on their operations. Second, it may be that limits do need to be placed on the size of firms, for inordinate power and influence are intrinsic to inordinate size. Third, the restrictiveness of regulation should be correlated with the size and power of the firms regulated, and with the degree to which their operations can affect the conditions of life. The oil industry, for example, needs to be regulated much more tightly than the ladies garment industry.

In fact, business has never been free of governmental regulation. It is fantasy to imagine that it ever will be, and most businessmen would probably agree that it should not be. Businessmen are not, after all, only businessmen. They are members of society. They and their children ultimately suffer, as do others, from the disorders afflicting the societies in which they participate and from which they, no more than others, can separate themselves. In an interdependent world Buber's principle of I-Thou is both an ethical dictum and an imperative of survival. It is therefore not unrealistic to expect businessmen to join with others in seeking to restore adaptive order to a deformed system. It is in their own ultimate interest, even if it may sometimes seem to them to be to their immediate disadvantage.

Part Two

Editor's Previews

In an engagingly personal essay, Professor Condliffe blends first-hand experience as a government advisor with a wealth of economic and historical scholarship. If you have been too busy practicing economics to read about it, his essay will bring you up to date.

Economic historian Wolfram Fischer gives us a fresh slant on relations between the big industrialized nations and the less-developed ones. His views on international trade add something new and substantial to the discussions.

International codes of ethics are topics of discussion in board rooms across the nation. In this comprehensive study, Dr. Behrman, one of the noted authorities in the field, presents new insights on what impact the adoption of such codes might have on transnational enterprises.

Capitalist Enterprise and Bureaucracy

J. B. Condliffe

This essay is written primarily to emphasize the basic principles on which the market system of capitalist enterprise is built.

Honesty and freedom are fundamental. Peace, stable money, and the rule of law administered by settled governments are also basic.

Honesty is a very old word, inseparably connected with honor. As economic activity became more complex, the word and the idea came to be identified with monetary transactions; but initially it meant behavior that earned respect. Its antonym originally was disgrace. Now it is more commonly fraud. Always honesty has connoted trustworthiness.

Freedom, and its synonym, liberty, are also very old words originally connected with the privileges and responsibilities of group membership.[1] Freedom of enterprise, therefore, carries with it the responsibilities of good citizenship and is not to be confused with individual license.

Capitalist enterprise has always been associated with trade and with peaceful exchanges, ignoring tribal or national boundaries. It works within the law. Indeed, traders developed and administered the definitions and rules of fair dealing that became the codes of commercial law by which ancient, medieval and modern governments have regulated trade. More than general principles were established by the medieval law merchant which was "a body of rules laid down by merchants for regulating their conduct one with another. *Economical definitions of exchange and juristic definitions of contract are derived from these rules, not vice-versa. In all the great matters relating to commerce, legislators have copied, not dictated.*"[2]

Moreover, the medieval merchants set up their own tribunals in important trading centers and at the great medieval fairs, to settle disputes and enforce standards of fair dealing. These Piepowder Courts (courts of the dusty feet) were presided over by consuls who were officials of the merchant bodies. The decisions of the consular courts developed into important codes, for example, of maritime law. Not until the consolidation of nation-states in the sixteenth century was the title "consul" appropriated by national representatives commissioned to reside in a foreign land to protect their nationals and to assist in all matters pertaining to the commercial relations between the two countries.

Capital enterprise needs peace, settled government, stable money, and the rule of law. At the moment of writing, Beirut, which was the commercial and financial capital of the Middle East, has lost its enterprises and agencies to more distant centers—Athens, Vienna, Geneva, the Hague, and London.

The lack of effective government was the reason European merchants from the sixteenth century onward pressed their own governments to impose colonial rule on many peoples. In the late nineteenth century most of Africa and a large part of Asia was partitioned. The distrust of capitalist enterprise by the former colonial peoples, now become independent nations, dates from this period of colonial expansion. It is renewed and strengthened by every case of bribery, unfair dealing, and interference in national affairs by unscrupulous business enterprisers.

In our own time, farsighted merchants, aware of these facts, have led efforts to establish codes of equal treatment and fair dealing. The International Chamber of Commerce, for example, was the driving force behind the World Economic Conference convened in 1927.[3] Founded in 1920 to apply the principles of private business to current issues of economic policy, it followed the precedent of the law merchant. Agreements were worked out on specific issues such as double taxation, commercial arbitration, Customs formalities, river communication, bills of lading, and the interpretation of most-favored-nation treatment (equality of trading opportunity). The 1927 World Economic Conference reached a large measure of agreement on such issues. Much of these specific agreements was incorporated into later trade treaties negotiated under the auspices of GATT (General Agreement on Tariffs and Trade). But the major recommendations of the 1927 conference for freer trade were overtaken by the collapse of the New York stock market in 1929, followed by the Hawley-Smoot Tariff of 1930, and the world economic depression which reached its nadir in mid-1932.

What was to have been a second world economic conference was convened by the League of Nations as the Monetary and Economic Conference of 1933. It followed the Lausanne Agreement of 1932 that brought to an end the futile attempts to collect war reparations from Germany—attempts that had bedeviled international economic relations throughout the 1920s.

It should be noted that these reparation demands, incorporated in the Treaty of Versailles that ended World War I, were purely political and devoid of economic reality. They were, in fact, never paid and could never have been paid; but like the White Knight's recipe of blotting paper, gunpowder and sealing wax, they were "a very clever pudding to invent."

By chance, on an Atlantic voyage, I encountered Mr. David Lloyd George. He asked me if I was related to Lord Cunliffe who had been governor of the Bank of England and chairman of the Reparations Committee when he was prime minister of the United Kingdom. I disclaimed any relationship, whereupon he told me he had asked Lord Cunliffe how he had arrived at the amount of reparations to be exacted from Germany: "Twenty thousand million pounds, 80 thousand million marks, 100 thousand million dollars, a magnificent figure, I won an election on it!" Lord Cunliffe replied that he had thought of it in his bath. Allowance must perhaps be made for Mr. Lloyd George's exuberance; but I later had the opportunity to verify the fact that the figure was quite arbitrary and there were no statistical calculations or economic analyses behind the demands made on Germany.

J. M. Keynes made his reputation by his attack on these preposterous demands in his best-selling book, *The Economic Consequences of the Peace,* and the issues were debated at length in the economic and political literature of the 1920s. Finally, in 1932, an agreement was made at Lausanne, Switzerland between Britain, France, and Germany to write off the reparation demands. The United States did not participate in the Lausanne-Ouchy conversations that led to this agreement, and its diplomats were forbidden to go within ten miles of the meeting place; but a meeting between the United States ambassador and some of the conference principals outside the ten-mile limit led to the perhaps wishful belief the United States would respond to the cancellation of reparations by cancelling the war debts owed by the European allies. Instructions were then sent to the League of Nations (of which the United States was not a member) to convene what was intended to be a second World Economic Conference.

The Monetary and Economic Conference was formally opened by the King of England on 12 June 1933. The League secretariat had convened committees of international experts to prepare its agenda. When the committees first met in November 1932 little could be done, but at a second meeting in February 1933, after Franklin Roosevelt had beaten Herbert Hoover in a fateful presidential election, an agenda was quickly agreed upon. What emerged from these meetings, which included eminent American economists, was a workable bargain in which the pound sterling would be stabilized, war debt obligations would be written off, and effective procedures would be instituted to reduce the barriers to international trade. The pivot of the agreement was the fact that the U.S. dollar was still maintained at its prewar parity with gold.

On 18 April 1933, while the British prime minister, Ramsay MacDonald, convenor of the conference, was visiting the United States, President Roosevelt devalued the dollar. This destroyed the basic assumption on which the agenda had been worked out. No opportunity was given to revise it. There was still a glimmer of hope that an agreement might be reached. As the conference opened, a group of American monetary experts was meeting with the Bank of England and Treasury officials. And the new secretary of state, Cordell Hull, was known to be a convinced advocate of freer trade.

The conference opened on schedule. Its bureau set up committees, one of which was chaired by Senator Key Pittman from Nevada, who was also chairman of the Foreign Relations Committee of the United States Senate. This committee achieved the only conference recommendation—to raise the price of silver.

The United States representative on the committee for a permanent international monetary standard (to which I was posted as secretary) did not appear for several meetings; however, the committee began its discussions on what was thought to be an official United States proposal. The fifty-six members of the committee included central bank governors, ministers of finance, and eminent economic experts. When the United States representative finally appeared, he was asked some elementary questions on the technical operative aspects of his proposal, to which, in fact, subsequent experience has shown that there are practical answers. He replied, "Perhaps we haven't thought this quite through," and withdrew the document. This document turned out to represent the ideas of a group of "new dealers" lacking official approval. Soon afterwards, a cable from President Roosevelt, referring to "so-called international bankers," brought the conference to a sudden end.

If these details seem bizarre, readers may be referred to a published report of the discussions within the United States delegation, including the extracurricular activities of some of its members.[4] These incidents have been recorded only to indicate that it was political bumbling that nullified business and expert efforts to take effective action against the Great Depression and the political deterioration that led inevitably to World War II. President Roosevelt summed up the causes of failure when he said, "The blame for the danger to world peace lies not in the world population, but in the political leaders of that population."[5]

The International Chamber of Commerce met at Copenhagen in June 1939 for a last effort. As rapporteur-general, I was privileged to deliver the opening speech on the agenda. The leader of the German delegation defended the trade regulations and planned economy of Hitlerite Germany as superior to the outmoded notions of free trade. But, on a personal visit to the Danish foreign minister, who had not long before signed a trade agreement with Germany, the reality was made clear to me. At the foot of his garden, he pointed a trembling finger across the sound and told me a great German air base and ferry terminus, Warnemunde, was only a few minutes' flying time across the water.

During the 1930s, a new mercantilism had begun to develop—quotas, exchange controls, floating currencies, and many varieties of indirect trade restrictions. The volume and value of world trade fell steadily. From January 1930 to June 1933, its value each month was less than in the corresponding month of the previous year.[6] A large literature sprang up justifying what was described as national economic planning. An even larger flood of planning regulations began to accumulate, rivalling the "paper pyramids" of Soviet planning. After Hitler assumed power in 1933, planning was clearly directed to war purposes.[7]

It is obvious that those in the United States who once more advocate national economic planning as necessary to solve our present economic problems do not advocate it for war purposes. There are new devices of economic calculation: input-output, which is a modern development of the eighteenth century Tableau Economique developed by Quesnay; linear programming; and national income accounts. They can be informative though it is difficult to encompass all the qualitative factors of economic activity within numerical calculations. But they must be interpreted and acted upon if they are to be more than suggestive. In a highly organized business corporation, decision-making, though more dispersed than is often realized, is finally concentrated in some person or group with responsibility and power to act. In an authoritarian state, the power of decision is centralized. In a war economy, there is an overriding objective to be achieved and all decisions are dominated by it. But, in a democracy at peace, there is always confusion of purpose. Capitalist enterprise, pursuing its competitive endeavors to maximize profit, is more likely than any planning system to meet the needs and desires of most people.[8] That it does not do so at the present time is clear enough from the statistics of unemployment and poverty in our midst and in the world as a whole, but the fault does not lie with business enterprise. It lies with the hampering bureaucracy that stifles enterprise.

The preceding account, written from personal observation, surely offers sufficient evidence that our present dilemmas have not been caused by defects in the economic system, but by ill-judged political interference with it. The sketch of historical development that follows is intended to outline and illustrate the conflict between political and economic motivations that has persisted over the centuries. To do so in detail is not possible in a short space, but the lesson is clear. Government attempts to regulate the competitive system and eliminate cheating and fraud have had a dubious record. The most successful attempts have been firmly based on the experience of practical traders. Pushed to extremes, they create opportunities for cheating and fraud (as, for example, in periods of monetary inflation) beyond the capacity of individuals to achieve. And, only too often, they have resulted in the loss of personal freedom and even in war. Always, they create a nonproductive bureaucracy "dressed in a little brief authority."

MONEY AND TRADE

The origins of the capitalist form of competitive enterprise cannot be precisely dated. It has gone through many phases and has never been completely competitive or free of regulation. There were primitive uses of capital, such as storing of supplies, even in barter trade.

From about the middle of the fifteenth century the increasing use of money as liquid capital created new problems. Improved and safer transport had increased the traffic along the European roads and rivers. Great fairs sprang up at crossroads and ports. Overland trade with Asia also increased when the Mongol emperors made the routes safe. When this Asian trade was interrupted, exploration around the coast of Africa and across the Atlantic revealed a new world. To profit from its resources entailed heavy capital investment. Merchants created the essential practices of capitalist enterprise and international monetary transactions. The essential condition of trade is division of labor which is based on credit—the ability to rely on the good faith and honesty of those from whom one buys or to whom one sells.

Attempts by individuals and groups to promote their own self-interest are as old as mankind. They were as common in primitive as they are in civilized communities. But there have always been benevolent as well as selfish motives prompting individual action. Cooperation as well as competition finds a place in every society. Both depend on good faith. Traders learned very early that cheating may yield a quick profit but destroys the basis for continuing trade. The biggest cheats have been governments who debase their currencies. Merchants learned to weigh the coins offered to them and scholars who noted this developed the first "laws" of political economy.

NATIONALISM

As long as individuals lived in small groups, selfishness was checked by mutual affection and by the authority of custom enforced by community elders. As tribes developed from extended families, patriarchal (and sometimes matriarchal) rule persisted through the tribal to the early stages of national organization.

Nationalism developed contemporaneously with money and trade. It could rely on the loyalties that originally were necessary for group survival. These loyalties rested on tradition and were reinforced by religious belief. As numbers grew, loyalty was transferred to ruling families claiming descent from ancestral leaders who were often deified and thereby acquired divine authority.

The inevitable consequence was the emergence of a ruling class and subordination of the ordinary folk. Among his many insights, Adam Smith pointed out that, while the founders of royal and aristocratic families may have possessed superior qualities of leadership, "antiquity of family means everywhere antiquity either of wealth, or of that greatness which is either founded upon wealth, or accompanied with it." Since "all families are equally ancient" what enabled ruling groups to perpetuate their power was the accumulation and inheritance of wealth originally entrusted to them for common purposes such as defense of the realm, administration of justice, and large public undertakings.

THE EXPANDING WORLD

The sixteenth century was a period of fundamental social change. A new world was born, literally and figuratively. In Europe a prolonged struggle for freedom of thought led to the schism that split Christendom and ultimately destroyed the temporal power of the universal church. The flowering of Renaissance art and literature, renewed contact with the ancient civilizations of Asia, and reinterpretation of the European classic literature, were accompanied by the first gropings of modern science.

The European scholars of the Middle Ages had been churchmen. They had answers for every human question, sanctioned and enforced by ecclesiastical authority. But the new age questioned everything. A French student of English literature has summarized the spirit of the Renaissance, which was truly a rebirth of human aspirations: "Former solutions of great problems are no longer accepted. Everything must be probed, every saying sifted. Did Aristotle say so? Did Ptolemy? Did St. Paul? Do the Decretals? No matter: we must verify, ourselves, on the spot, by independent studies and personal journeyings. The word End at the last page of the Book of Science has no meaning; nothing is ever ended. . . ."[9]

STATE SUPPLANTS CITY

It was in this exciting era of inquiry, experiment, and adventure that merchants opened new channels of trade and governments created new institutions to regulate them. The city governments that had flourished in the later Middle Ages fell into decline. In the freer trading countries their functions were taken over by nation-states. The city states of northern Italy—Genoa, Milan, Pisa, Florence, and Venice—had fought among themselves to dominate the Mediterranean trade routes to Asia. As in the Greek cities earlier, war destroyed their oligarchic democracy. Venice had controlled the eastern Mediterranean and held "the gorgeous East in fee"; but in the fifteenth century, the irruption of the Turks into southeast Europe and the Middle East put an end to its empire. Neither in Italy nor in Germany, however, were the city-states and small principalities consolidated into nations before the nineteenth century.

The northern cities in Germany, Scandinavia, and the Low Countries built their riches largely on herrings, salt, and the forest products of the Baltic shores. At the height of its power, their Hanseatic League, founded in 1370, was widely spread. It was courted not only by German princes and Scandinavian monarchs but by the Spanish king. The English explorer, Sir Richard Chancellor, struck a blow at the League's monopoly of Russian trade when in 1553 he discovered the Arctic route to Archangel. English seamen destroyed the trade with Spain, and the Merchant Adventurers were increasingly hostile to the Hanseatic Steelyard in London. In 1601 its trading privileges were revoked and the secretary of the merchant adventurers reported that "most of their teeth have fallen out, and the rest sit but loosely in their head."[10]

The death blow to the Hanseatic League was delivered by the chaos of the Thirty Years War (1618–48). It was never able to function effectively during, or after, that catastrophic struggle and its merchant princes became mere shopkeepers struggling for survival. Lubeck was finally absorbed into the German Zollverein in 1867, but Hamburg and Bremen resisted Bismarck's pressure and remained free ports until 1888. These were the last vestiges of the efforts made by the merchant cities to maintain their independence against the nation-state. Effectively they had lost the battle in the sixteenth and seventeenth centuries.

THE PURITAN INFLUENCE

It has been argued that Calvinism created the moral and political conditions that favored the growth of capitalist enterprise. This thesis, propounded by Max Weber in 1920, has some truth but can be exaggerated. As R. H. Tawney has pointed out, Weber wrote of economic thought rather than of economic fact:

> There was plenty of the "capitalist spirit" in fifteenth century Venice and Florence, or in South Germany and Flanders, for the simple reason that these areas were the greatest commercial and financial centres of the age, though all were, at least nominally, Catholic. The development of capitalism in Holland and England in the sixteenth and seventeenth centuries was due not to the fact that they were Protestant powers, but to large economic movements, in particular the Discoveries and the results which flowed from them. Of course material and psychological changes went together, and of course the second reacted on the first. *But it seems a little artificial to talk as though capitalist enterprise could not appear till religious changes had produced a capitalist spirit.* It would be equally true, and equally one-sided, to say that the religious changes were purely the result of economic movements.

Professor Tawney went on to point out that the political thought of Machiavelli and the speculations of business men on money, prices, and the foreign exchanges also "contributed to the temper of single-minded concentration on pecuniary gain." Moreover "Both the 'capitalist spirit' and 'Protestant ethics' were a good deal more complex than Weber seems to imply."[11]

It is obvious that the Puritan virtues were favorable to the accumulation of riches. Wherever the Reformation succeeded, particularly in Holland and the United Kingdom, the middle-class city merchants were its major defenders against the land-owning aristocracy. Their colonial offshoots were led by middle class gentry and city merchants—Catholic (in Maryland) as well as Protestant—seeking liberty to pursue their own religious observances. But they also sought freedom from the oppressive economic regulations to which they were subjected by the rulers from whom they had fled. To them, religious liberty and economic freedom were equal and mutually reinforcing principles.

Puritan "emphasis on the moral duty of untiring activity, on work as an end in itself, on the evils of luxury and extravagance, on foresight and thrift, on moderation and self-discipline and rational calculation . . . created an ideal of Christian conduct which canonized as an ethical principle the efficiency which economic theorists were preaching as a specific for social disorders."[12]

SPANISH TREASURE

While capitalist enterprise has older and deeper roots in the trade that developed between western Europe and Asia, the discovery of the Americas presented governments with unprecedented economic problems. Not least among them was the disruption of values caused by the flood of gold and silver that poured into Spain from its American empire. Spain tried to protect its treasure and at the same time to prevent inflation from ruining its artisans and merchants; but this attempt, by hoarding and autarky, to prevent other peoples from sharing in the New World cornucopia was futile. Traders found ways to bleed Spain of its treasure. Their methods and those of their governments ranged from smuggling and what would now be called covert operations to piracy and war.

The more literate merchants and officials wrote books and pamphlets to justify their operations. They rested on the principle enunciated by Thomas Mun in a famous work: "The ordinary means therefore to increase our wealth and treasure is by foreign trade, wherein we must ever observe this rule; to sell more to strangers yearly than we consume of theirs in value."[13]

Economic ideas on value, price formation, foreign exchange, taxation, inflation, and national wealth evolved rapidly in this mercantilist period. The Greek philosophers had touched on some of these questions in relation to ethics. The medieval schoolmen had fixed ascetic notions based on their interpretation of the scriptures. But in the seventeenth century the first schools of political economy appeared. They were offshoots of political philosophy concerned primarily with what would now be called public finance and with economic wealth and social welfare primarily as they affected the national revenue. It was the monarch and his realm whose prosperity was the main concern of political arithmeticians or mercantilists in England and the cameralists in Germany. After Adam Smith dissected their protectionist doctrines, however, they were discredited by economists until J. M. Keynes in 1936 dealt sympathetically with some aspects of them.[14]

ADAM SMITH

Adam Smith's systematic treatise—*An Inquiry into the Nature and Causes of the Wealth of Nations,* published in 1776, set forth the advantages of division of labor and of the free competitive exchange of goods and services. He did this largely by criticizing the mercantilist doctrines. The United States of America was to become the outstanding example of a society that thrived on capitalist enterprise. Adam Smith drew many illustrations from the old colonial system that in his day was throttling the development of colonial resources. He also favored the emancipation of the American colonies.[15] Political, religious, and economic liberty are, all three, essential aspects of the struggle for human dignity.

Like many famous books, *The Wealth of Nations* is more quoted (and misquoted) than read. Adam Smith was the child of his age and took for granted much that we should now deplore. His book should not be read as holy writ. Many of his judgments on particular issues proved to be wrong; but this is true of all economists, even Keynes. The only comment Adam Smith made regarding the bondage into which many Scottish coal miners had sold themselves—and their children—was that slave labor was more expensive than free labor. There is no evidence that he contrived the Stamp Act and other colonial levies that ultimately drove the American colonists to rebellion. A document does exist that indicates he believed that the colonies would become independent. And he was the advisor in London on taxation to Charles Townshend, the chancellor of the exchequer in 1766–67. As Jacob Viner has pointed out, he believed that if the empire was to continue, every province must contribute to its support. He was particularly emphatic that India should contribute heavily to the imperial revenues.[16]

Adam Smith perceived and articulated the truth—as valid

today as ever it was—that free competition *among equals* in the market place promoted the public interest. There is a much-quoted passage that has often been represented as implying that competition was divinely ordained. A merchant, striving for his own advantage, Smith wrote, "intends only his own gain, and he is in this, as in many other cases, led by an invisible hand to promote an end which was no part of his intention. . . . By pursuing his own interest he frequently promotes that of the society more effectually than when he really intends to promote it."[17]

Adam Smith was a Deist and believed that there was natural law in the universe; but he did not capitalize the invisible hand. His argument does not depend on a mystical belief in a divinely ordained order. It is based on observation of human frailties and buttressed by historical examples. In a passage that immediately follows the invisible hand metaphor, he states the argument from the opposite angle.

"The statesman who should direct private people in what manner they ought to employ their capitals would not only load himself with a most unnecessary protection, but assume an authority which could safely be trusted, not only to no single person, but to no council or senate whatever, and would nowhere be so dangerous as in the hands of a man who had folly and presumption enough to fancy himself fit to exercise it."[18]

THE FRENCH CONNECTION

Among the philosophers who influenced Adam Smith were his own Scottish contemporaries, Hutcheson and Hume; but both he and they were greatly influenced by the French intellectuals who called themselves Les Economistes, but became better known as the Physiocrats. Adam Smith lived in France for several years in contact with the small but highly placed group of liberals who were moved by the poverty and distress of the regimented peasants and urban workers. Like Thomas Jefferson, he was an intellectual child of the Enlightenment, the Age of Reason. He was impressed by the phrase coined by Gournay—"laissez faire, laissez passer" (let them act, let them go)—which was a plea not for rich merchants but for the poor and oppressed peasants and city workers subjected to rigorous government regulation. But he rejected the Physiocratic ideal of an agricultural society and applied the plea for freedom to the wider area of trade and manufactures.

MERCANTILIST BUREAUCRACY

The seventeenth and eighteenth century attempts to grapple with questions of public finance and money in the newly developing nation-states provided the material that Adam Smith used as a target to illustrate his thesis that trade should be allowed to flow freely. Primarily, his attack was on the bureaucratic efforts to regulate monetary and trade transactions so as to enrich the nation-state and on the corruption that permeated the mercantilist system. He was as shocked as the American colonists by the privileges and immorality of a corrupt aristocracy, as well as by the restrictive devices they used.

These bureaucratic devices, primarily designed to establish monopolies and restrict enterprise, should be distinguished from the practices of the merchants out of which the Law Merchant had earlier developed and which later formed the basis of commercial law. Essentially, the law merchant grew out of *voluntary* agreements to ensure good faith in trading transactions. It was designed to outlaw the cheats and to establish standards and tribunals by which departures from honest trading might be judged and punished.

What Edwin Cannan described as really the text of the polemical portion of *The Wealth of Nations* was Adam Smith's conviction that: "The natural effort of every individual to better his own condition, when suffered to exert itself with freedom and security, is so powerful a principle that it is alone, and without any assistance, not only capable of carrying on the society to wealth and prosperity, but of surmounting a hundred impertinent obstructions with which the folly of human laws too often incumbers its operations."[19]

This conviction was not based on illusions of intervention by an anthropomorphic deity or on the perfectibility of human nature. Adam Smith was a philosopher, but he was also a man of the world, a commissioner of Customs, and in close touch with the business world of his day. The first draft of *The Wealth of Nations* was begun in France; but he was not a believer in Rousseau's notions of innate human goodness. On the contrary, there are many passages where he makes very plain his belief that: "People of the same trade seldom meet together, even for merriment and diversion, but the conversation ends in a conspiracy against the public, or in some contrivance to raise prices."[20]

In stating the case for laissez faire, Adam Smith concentrated on the inefficient and corrupt administrative procedures of his day. In his pragmatic view no weakness of laissez faire could be as bad as the specific abuses of the government controls and monopoly practices at which his attack was directed. There are passages in *The Wealth of Nations* upon which it would be possible to make a case for state intervention to ensure defense, to control investment through the usury laws, to use taxation as a means of social reform, to ensure economic justice, and to promote public works, public health, education, and even commercial enterprises, if they do not entail a burden upon the public finances. His book was an attack on specific evils of his day, not a defense of economic anarchy in later and vastly different circumstances.

EARLY NINETEENTH CENTURY EVILS

In the hands of his successors, and the thrusting entrepreneurs of the early stages of the industrial revolution, his argument for economic freedom was used to justify exploitation of the weaker members of society who were unable to compete effectively in a market that was far from free.

The classical economists of the early nineteenth century, including David Ricardo, were not opposed to the protection of women and children by factory legislation or to the repeal of the harsh Combination Acts that were used to repress the first attempts to organize trade unions. Ricardo voted in Parliament for repeal. It was the popularizers of laissez faire who argued against "the meddling legislators" of the Factory Acts and urged governments "to leave to workers in factories, as to other workers, the care of their own lives and limbs."

The economists, it is true, were concerned primarily with

general principles. For the sake of logical simplicity they often worked out their theories "on the tacit assumption that the world was made up of city men" fully aware of and able to cope with changing circumstances. Moreover they wrote largely in abstract terms that were capable of misapplication.[21]

Karl Marx was later to use the reports of successive Factory Commissions to elaborate his condemnation of capitalism and there is no denying that the misery of the urban poor was largely ignored by the early nineteenth century economists. They were more concerned, however, with the distress of the rural poor and their hopeless destitution. The harsh administration of the Poor Laws brought indignant protest from popular writers such as Thomas Carlyle and Charles Dickens. But this distress was caused by land enclosures from which rural tenant farmers and small craftsmen fled to the crowded tenements of the industrial cities. It could not be cured, but was in fact worsened, by indiscriminate charity. A large segment of the rural population was pauperized and degraded by relief doles. Those who fled to the cities (as they still do in many countries today) found it almost impossible to secure employment or housing. Unscrupulous employers exploited the labor of women and children.

THE TRIUMPH OF FREE TRADE

Ultimately, after prolonged suffering, the combined efforts of far-sighted employers and social reformers brought increased productivity and eliminated the worst forms of exploitation. Even though population increased rapidly and urban concentrations became denser, working hours were reduced, wages increased, and living levels were raised. It is not easy to quantify these improvements, but it has been estimated (by J. M. Keynes) that by the end of the nineteenth century, the British population had quadrupled, and its living levels had been improved by the same fourfold factor. The struggle for equality continued, but it was more and more a struggle for recognition and opportunity rather than for mere existence.[22]

No small part of the raising of living standards came from cheap food made possible by free trade. The Corn Laws, that maintained high prices in the interest of landowners, were abolished, and Britain drew on the resources of the world to feed its increasing population and cheapen the production of its manufactured exports.

It should be noted that the effects of free trade on the overseas countries that supplied Europe's needs for raw materials and foodstuffs differed in the independent former colonies and self-governing dominions from those in the less developed dependent colonies. The independent countries grew and flourished because their producers were able to bargain on equal terms. They also were able to borrow the capital and technology to build ports, roads, railroads, and bridges to open new land. The costs of transport by land and sea fell as steam power developed so that producers' prices rose while consumers' prices fell.

COLONIAL EXPLOITATION

The less developed countries lacked this competitive strength. Most of them had been carved up into colonies governed by Europeans. Investment in tea, sugar, jute and rubber plantations, mines, and export processing factories was managed in the interests of foreign consumers. The citizens of the producing countries lacked the capital, technology, and bargaining power to create the transport and manufacturing industries necessary for national development. They also lacked the political power to secure a fair return from the increased production of foodstuffs and raw materials.

Colonialism was not all bad. In most colonies the population gained from the cessation of civil conflict and the detached government that replaced the arbitrary rule of local rulers. New avenues of employment were opened. Increasing population proves that the limits of subsistence were raised. But the traditional crafts were largely destroyed and there was little but token preparation for self-government and economic independence.

EVOLVING CAPITALISM

In the early stages of industrialization Karl Marx formulated the "iron law of wages," the thesis that the reward for labor could never for long exceed the minimum necessary for subsistence. Marx argued that labor was the sole source of value and the profit of employers was "surplus value"—the difference between the market price of a product and its labor cost. Belief was widespread, influenced by Malthus's population theory, that the number of workers would always increase to the point where subsistence became inadequate so that the condition of the laboring classes could never be greatly improved.

The nineteenth century experience disproved these dismal theories. The condition of the workers in the industrial countries steadily improved. One reason was that legislation to control the worst abuses of the early factory system, and to enable them to bargain collectively, increased their bargaining power. Even more important in the long run were better living levels and universal education which, combined with a changing structure of industry, increased both the demand for and the supply of skilled labor and progressively eliminated the need for heavy manual labor.

In recent years, in most industrial countries the wheel has come full circle and highly organized trade unions, buttressed by legislative protection, exercise considerable economic power. A recent statement by a New Zealand economist could be paralleled from the experience of many other countries:

> The most prevalent form of monopoly in the country today is the trade union. The powerful trade union—like the corporate monopoly—typically supplies a product or a service which the community needs for its very survival, and for which it can find no ready substitute: transport, fuel, electricity, rubbish disposal, export income and so on. The trade union in New Zealand today has an additional advantage not enjoyed by the corporate monopoly: it knows that, however rapacious its demands, its workers are ensured of full employment, or substantial comprehension for being unemployed.[23]

Parallel with more complicated and more automatic mechanisms, came changes in management structure. The modern corporation is very different from those Adam Smith described as incompetent to handle anything but routine business. In the early industrial era small entrepreneurs, usually emerging from the crafts, formed companies of which they were both owners and technicians. Improved transport and communication facilities, and the introduction of limited liability which tapped wider sources of capital, enlarged markets and produced larger-scale enterprises. The original inventor-owner-organizer was forced to rely increasingly on technicians, many of whom became expert in the new skills of marketing and advertising. Gradually, not only marketing but production decisions passed into the hands of what Galbraith has described as the "technostructure."[24]

THE TECHNOLOGICAL REVOLUTION

These changes in corporation structure, and, generally, in the organization of business transactions were overtaken by a technological revolution reminiscent in many respects of the sixteenth century expansion of horizons. Not, alas, in its literary or artistic or moral quests, but in material and scientific exploration. The chief instruments of this technological revolution are devices to improve and quicken calculation and communication.

The conquest of space has not revealed a new world in the sense that the concept can be applied to the sixteenth century discoveries. Rather it is shrinking the proportions of the known world and revealing its problems. The intellectual excitement of the space age is largely confined to the technologists. Outside their circle there is doubt, trouble, and fear, and much confusion of purpose as the inadequacy of political institutions to cope with change becomes apparent.

As in the sixteenth century, a new world economy is being created which existing governments cannot deal with effectively. We begin to glimpse the twilight of the nation-state and the development of a new mercantilism operating through inefficient international institutions. The shrinking of time and distance has gone far to destroy the insulation of national communities. Civil wars in remote areas as well as the unceasing conflicts of diplomacy become immediate visual realities rather than far-off events and battles long ago. The stark contrast between affluence and starvation penetrates every living room. In a different sense from Wordsworth's, "the world is too much with us."

TRADE EXPANSION

The statistics of world trade, even corrected for monetary inflation, showed unprecedented rates of increase in the period following World War II until 1975, when depression and increasing trade restrictions caused a decline of about 5 percent.[25] This vast and long-continued increase in both volume and value of trade was mainly between the industrially developed countries and was largely the work of multinational corporations. In part it was caused by monetary inflation, but it also reflected a series of tariff reductions on manufactured goods. The principle of equality of trading opportunity (most-favored-nation treatment) spread the tariff reductions beyond the immediate signatories to successive multilateral agreements negotiated under the auspices of GATT (General Agreement on Tariffs and Trade).

In recent years the industrially developed countries have been pressured by the less-developed countries which have used the United Nations as a sounding board for their demands for preferential treatment. Since 1970, the western European countries, Canada, Australia, New Zealand, Japan and, finally, the United States have granted preferential tariff treatment to ninety-eight countries and thirty-nine dependencies. As of 1 January 1976 the principle of equality of trading opportunity (MFN) has been abandoned. Curiously, little publicity was given to this momentous policy change. Neither those who fought for and defended the principle of equality of trading opportunity, nor their protectionist opponents appeared to be interested. The press and the media largely ignored the change, which was represented to be a generous gesture to the poorer countries of the world, but is in fact the beginning of a new regime of trade regulation managed by politicians and bureaucrats.

THE NEW MERCANTILISM

The executive order issued by President Gerald Ford on 24 November 1975, "Implementing the Generalized System of Preferences," was authorized by the Trade Act of 1974. It occupies eight pages of the Federal Register, half of which are devoted to a listing of tariff items in regard to specific imports from particular countries that are not entitled to duty-free treatment.[26] It is a curious list of over two hundred items and thirty-one countries and provides an interesting example of the new mercantilism rapidly taking shape.

Before the executive order was published, the United States Customs Service issued a briefing of twenty-one pages intended to elucidate the operation of the system.[27] Certificates of Origin, drawn up by the United Nations and signed by designated government authorities in the exporting countries, must attest that at least 35 percent or in some cases 50 percent of the final appraised value of the article was produced in the exporting country. There is an eligibility ceiling (quota) on the total value of any one product or tariff group shipped from any one country—$25 million in a calendar year or 50 percent of total United States imports of the article. The $25 million limit is calculated with reference to the Unitd States Gross National Product and is therefore a token figure. Beyond these limits the country will not receive beneficiary (duty-free) treatment.

It is obvious that administration of such a complicated system lends itself to manipulation and fraud.

It also adds a new dimension to mercantilism. The format of Form A has been internationally negotiated under the aegis of UNCTAD, a subsidiary of the United Nations. The weight and quality of the paper used, its dimensions, and overprinting with "a green guilloche pattern background" are prescribed, and each certificate must bear a serial number. A new tier of bureaucracy will be required at the international level as well as in the exporting and importing countries. This raised difficulties for countries, for example Taiwan, that are not members of the United Nations, but these have been overcome.

It does not require much imagination to visualize the evasive devices and the bargaining that will develop in the administration of the quotas (euphemistically called eligibility ceilings) and the denial of free entry to specific commodities (sea-shell ornaments, for example) as well as the certificates of origin. Before the system actually came into force on 1 January 1976, importers and exporters were devising means of arranging nominal compliance. Production and trade will be directed less by price comparisons and more by political bargaining. In the United States, decisions will be made by a special agency in the White House, although several departments—State, Commerce, Labor, Agiculture and Treasury—will be involved. Trade again will tend to become an instrument of diplomacy, serving the purposes of government rather than consumers.

In justice to those who negotiated for the United States, it should be said that they resisted the idea of reverse preferences. United States' policy always opposed the British preferential system negotiated at the Ottawa Conference in 1932. Its opposition was not without cause since the United Kingdom proceeded to negotiate a series of bilateral trade treaties with Denmark, Norway, Argentina, Iceland, Sweden, Latvia, Estonia, Finland, and the USSR. This created a preferential bloc. Tariffs and quotas for British goods, supplemented by agreements to purchase definite quantities of particular products, were reciprocated by agreed import quotas and the promise of stability of duties and quotas. Britain was using its import market to negotiate an area of assured exports. The so-called sterling area (which did not include Canada) included a large number of countries both in and out of the British Empire. In 1939, exchange control was introduced, and the exchange reserves of the sterling area were pooled in London.

That the possibility of similar trading blocs developing still exists was evidenced in a speech made to the British Commonwealth Conference in May 1975 by the prime minister of the United Kingdom. Mr. Wilson envisaged a complicated system of intergovernmental agreements designed "to redistribute the wealth of the world in favor of the poverty-stricken." These agreements would be "centered around [sic] a proposed general agreement on commodities," as extensions of the present limited network of commodity agreements and buffer stocks. These would complement the Lomé convention between the European Economic Community and forty-six African, Caribbean, and Pacific states (countries).[28]

The United States has so far been able to prevent the development of new closed trading blocs and even to have those negotiated under the Lomé convention withdrawn.

THE SIGNIFICANCE OF HONEST TRADE

Within any country, the dishonest trader destroys confidence in the principles on which society is based. The United States is dedicated to individual liberty—political, religious, and economic. Every abuse of that liberty, small or large, betrays the trust on which the country was founded and continues to function. Whether this abuse is criminal or simply sharp practice, exploitation of a weak or too-trusting neighbor, or breach of a public trust—by individuals or trade unions or business enterprise or public servants—overt or concealed—it diminishes the commonwealth.

It is, of course, obvious that since "the heart of man is deceitful and desperately wicked," no society is ever free from cheats. As John Milton wrote on the first page of his plan for a free press: "That no grievance ever should arise in the Commonwealth, that let no man in this World expect; but when complaints are freely heard, deeply consider'd and speedily reformed, then is the utmost bound of civil liberty attained."[29]

That every society contains dishonest members who abuse the trust reposed in them in order to seek their own gain is not a sufficient argument for restriction by authority. There is "a dark side to the marketplace"[30] in authoritarian as well as in liberal societies; but in the authoritarian regimes it is hidden. In a democracy its best antidote is publicity.

Liberty can be abused; it can also be lost in the effort to restrain and punish those who abuse it. It is an illusion that it can be promoted by the proliferation of legislation and bureaucratic administration. It is not easy to cope with the increasing powers of an overgrown bureaucracy. In our own time the injustice done to ordinary people from the monetary inflation caused by political and bureaucratic decisions is far greater than any private pilfering of the public or private purse—or of funds that belong to stockholders.

On the international scale, the struggle for freer trade is a large part of the struggle for peace. It is also an aspect of the struggle for individual liberty, not least against arbitrary interference by governments with the rights of corporate enterprise.

THE MULTINATIONAL CORPORATION

It is not possible in a brief essay to analyze the complex recent changes in corporate structure and procedures. But, it is obvious that, once again, capitalist enterprise has been forehanded in using the new means of communication to leapfrog political restraints. Governments remain national, but business operates in a world setting. Governments are cautious, secretive, and suspicious, but enterprise ventures boldly into new areas of operation, modifying its activities as necessary to achieve its purposes.

The new political instruments of international discussion and cooperation were conceived within national limits. Some are necessary for the smooth operation of the new communication facilities—air travel, radio operation, health controls—but they too must operate within the political restraints imposed by jealous nationalisms. This is still truer of the monetary and financial agencies and of those concerned with trade regulation. The major international institutions dealing with the momentous issues of war and peace are frankly nationalistic and therefore largely ineffective.

In this situation, the conduct of business operations on a world scale raises new issues of business ethics. Who in the technostructure that directs a multinational corporation makes the decisions that involve moral issues? It can be argued that the chief executive officer is in fact largely the mouthpiece of a ramifying committee structure. Even if he must take responsibility for the final decision, it may have been largely predetermined by exploratory discussions and presentations at lower levels in the hierarchy. What factors enter into his judgment?

It is often said that in dealing with individuals and governments, business must accept local custom and not attempt to impose higher moral standards than are customary. It is obvious that newcomers to a very different civilization are wise to listen to advice from those familiar with it. The barriers of language, religion, and social custom are not easily overcome. The confidence and trust of those with whom one is dealing must usually be won over time. Often, however, it is difficult to know with whom one is dealing. Governments fall and their personnel and policies change. Agents make impressive claims of influence in high places that cannot easily be verified.

In the many recent cases of apparent bribery in attempts to gain lucrative contracts, apart altogether from the legality or morality of the transaction, what is clearly at issue is the business judgment of those concerned and particularly the ability to judge men, which is a highly-regarded attribute of business leadership.

The transfer not just of technology, but of the capacity to handle it, is imperative if the poorer countries of the world are to cope with the relentless pressure of population on their limited resources. Monetary loans enable them to buy the mechanisms of industry, but the ability to use these mechanisms can be achieved only by practical training over a long period. The best way to learn is by doing. The multinational firm has proved successful in training workers at all levels of operation, from manual labor to management. It is unlikely that the less developed countries can transform their economies without such practical help.

It is, therefore, pitiful to find that the attack on multilateral corporations is provided with ammunition by dishonest, or at least questionable, actions by a minority of business leaders in search of quick profit. Those who accept, and indeed solicit, the bribes are at least as culpable as those who give them. The critics, in the developed and the less-developed countries, who exaggerate the extent of such practices are more concerned with the political than the economic aspects of international business. But it should be remembered that the livelihood of hundreds of millions of poverty-stricken people, and the development of a peaceful world, depend on honest and purposeful effort not only to equip the less-developed countries, but to train their peoples to industrial productivity.

Economic aid and technical assistance, despite much devoted service and some successes have largely failed to equip the less-developed peoples with the training necessary for modern industry. Where aid programs have been successful, there has usually been a combination of local skill with imported technology.

The abuses that have attended capitalist enterprise as distinct from government aid have occurred where corrupt governments have been willing to sell their national endowment for personal gain. It is deplorable that some industrial leaders in the developed countries have shown poor business judgment by using corporate funds to finance such practices.

That the majority have not done so is evidenced by the fact that most of the foreign investment and expanded trade that has been so marked a feature of recent decades has been among the developed countries themselves. There have been few instances of graft in this tremendous expansion of multinational enterprise. There have been, and continue to be, conflicts between their branches and the host governments, especially when strict business practice is faced with the planning and welfare policies of socialist government.

The fact is investment and trade have been diverted from the areas where they are most needed to those where settled and responsible government gives assurance of fair and continuing contractual relations. Capital is scarce and investors are cautious. They are not encouraged by arbitrary actions in the host country. There is little prospect that they will be attracted to invest in countries dominated by dogmatic political leaders inexperienced in the technological operations of world trade.

The powerful multinational corporations are inevitably confronted with suspicion and nationalist hostility. Yet they are more capable of bringing to the poorer people of the world the means of lifting themselves out of their misery than any form of government aid yet devised. Sharing wealth or markets can do little. The need is to expand them by creating more productivity. Part of the attack leveled against them is politically motivated, part springs from an attempt to blame them for the failures of the governments in whose area they operate. But some is caused also by ill-judged efforts on the part of a relatively few of their managements to interfere with the rights of peoples to govern themselves and make their own mistakes. A high price could be paid for this poor business judgment—nothing less than the reversion of large parts of the Third World to the misery of authoritarian rule.

Ethics and the Law in Dealings between Unequals

Wolfram Fischer

It is a basic fact of life that men are not equal. Biological strains and the life cycles, individual characteristics, natural environment and climate, cultural heritage, language and religion, the diversity of historical experiences that created a great variety of social structures amongst the people of the world—all contribute to men's unequality. Males and females, elderly, grown-ups, adolescents, and infants are different, even in very homogeneous societies. But most societies are not homogeneous; they consist of people of different ethnic, linguistic, religious, or social origin. Educational opportunity, professional competence, individual drive, health, or luck continue to create new inequalities, even if the same factors contribute to reduce some of the inherited inequalities. However we may maintain that man is created equal, in real life we deal mainly with unequals, with men more or less experienced or advanced in life, with stronger or weaker personalities, with higher or lower intelligence, income, social status or prestige, and in more or less powerful positions.

Some inequalities matter more than others because they are inequalities in substance rather than in degree. The inequality between a slave-holder and a slave, a prison warden and an inmate, certainly is deeper than that between a man with a

111

greater income and one with a more modest income in the same profession. Societies have developed very different value systems and laws to deal with such inequalities. While most of the ancient cultures seem to have used them as a means of reinforcing inequalities, modern societies generally try to lessen them.

In the course of the European expansion over the world, societies of utterly different backgrounds, experiences, and value systems have been confronted, brought closer to each other and, by sheer physical contact, finally have become one universal human society that depends for its survival on the possibility that its members, different as they may be in outlook and ideology, cultural heritage and social structure, economic or military strength, or in the way they arrive at political decisions, manage to get along with each other.

This essay deals with the problem of whether the Western business ethics and commercial law, as it was carried into other parts of the world by European settlers, merchants, administrators, and judges as part of their sociocultural heritage, contributed to the establishment of durable relations with cultures of different heritages, and how it can continue to do so in a constructive and meaningful way in the future.

Intercultural contacts have a long history. They seem to have been most frequent in those parts of the world often referred to as the "cradle of civilization" and now known as the Middle and Near East. East Asia and northern Europe, on the other hand, and more so the indigenous cultures of Africa and the New Worlds of America and Oceania, seem to have been more isolated although contacts also existed between ancient China and southeast and northern Asia. In all these contacts trade played an important part. Business habits developed that very early were cast into legal rules expressing certain codes of behavior, which the merchant class probably developed and which legislators copied rather than dictated.[1] Business dealings wherever they occurred, needed some basic ethics. Partners in an exchange of goods or services have to rely on each other, a given promise has to be fulfilled, be it the delivery of commodities, the payment for them, the repayment of a credit, or the disposition of means of transport or of shelter. Most of the different cultures of the ancient world knew several forms of contract and had means to enforce them.

The Mediterranean was the main thoroughfare in the medieval world. It was bordered by different cultures that most of the time stood in close contact, exchanged goods and services and developed habits and codes of behavior very much the same irrespective of whether they adhered to the Islamic, Jewish, or Christian faith, or remained outside of the "religions of the book."[2] "The Mediterranean merchant, as he appears in the records, was interested in the acquisition of wealth and cultivation of thrift. He relied upon his own intelligence, but was careful to enlist the support of superior authorities. He was respectful of legal regulations and yet determined to evade them whenever necessary. He was enterprising and adventurous but also cautious and conservative. He invoked the protection of his deity for each of his transactions, but he was bent upon pursuing predominantly worldly purposes. He was loyal to his native country but itinerant in his thoughts and actions, always seeking to expand his field of operations. And while he was ever ready to outwit his competitors from abroad, he was yet acutely conscious of the fact that a certain degree of international cooperation was indispensible for the success of most of his ventures."[3] Did he differ significantly from a modern businessman engaged in internal or international transactions?

The early modern western European merchants, when they administered their particular law merchant, first at merchants' courts in the centers of international commerce and then with the assistance of learned judges and lawyers throughout the Western countries, relied heavily on traditional customs as passed on to them mainly by the Mediterranean commercial cities: "The courts enforced the custom of merchants and the customs made the law."[4] The two great distinctive elements in the merchants' law were good faith and dispatch, for speed and honesty were indispensable, and the procedures of the ordinary courts often prevented one or both of these elements, common law even more than the civil law of the continent. The special law merchant was, therefore, retained even when England became the center of world commerce. English judges, mainly those of the Courts of Admiralty that administered the law of the sea (part of the law merchant), through their decisions, integrated this general European customary law into the law of England.

In a similar fashion, the modern continental codes like the *Code de Commerce* in France of 1808, or the German Commercial Code (*Handelsgesetzbuch*) of 1900, preserved basic institutes and rules of the common European commercial law. The German code particularly made ample use of such elastic provisions originating from an inherited ethical code of business behavior. "It is less rigid than some other civil law systems, and has achieved that elasticity by granting the courts a free exercise of a sense of equity. There are more provisions utilizing the terms 'good faith' and 'good morals' than were customary in preceding codes."[5] At the international conference on private law, in The Hague in 1912, it served as the basis for a draft of a universal law on negotiable instruments.

Certain features in the law merchant demonstrate that a particular code of business ethics was taken for granted throughout Europe: vocal evidence was admitted to contradict a written document, a notarial document did not take general precedence over one under the sign manual, and a merchant's journal and ledger were admissable as evidence on proper proof of regularity in favor of his owner's claim. W. A. Bewes, the historian of the law merchant, comments on this fact: "That a statement in his own handwriting could be any evidence at all in his favor when adduced by himself against an opponent, who was not a party to the entry being made, is remarkable, and a tribute to the general good faith of merchants."[6]

If one takes these seemingly universal features of business ethics into account, it may be asked if scholars like Karl Marx, Anton Troeltsch, Max Weber, Werner Sombart, and Richard H. Tawney, who attributed a new and "revolutionary" attitude to the capitalist, or protestant businessman in northwestern Europe in early modern times, did full justice to the role of ongoing traditions in the process of transformation of the Western countries into industrial societies. Perhaps the peculiar attitudes they observed in Dutch, Swiss,

English, and American entrepreneurs were only pronounced features of quite universal attitudes in specific classes devoted to international commerce. Max Weber asserted in his famous treatise *The Protestant Ethic and the Spirit of Capitalism* that the protestant interpretation of Christian beliefs favored stricter business morals and, in its Calvinist form, also a devotion to worldly duties, since economic success demonstrated conspicuously that a man was elected for a place in heaven.[7]

We know today that the "innerworldly askesis" which many western European and early American businessmen displayed, particularly in the seventeenth and eighteenth centuries, did not necessarily derive from religious beliefs, but could also be influenced by other factors, for example, the minority position in a particular society or an immense drive to lay the foundations for a lasting family fortune. But the fact remains that many of the most outstanding men in business, politics, or the sciences in the Western world were deeply imbued by these values that guided them in the pursuit of their business or profession as well as in their general moral outlook and judgment. Well-known Americans such as Benjamin Franklin or Cotton Mather are often quoted as examples of this weltanschauung, and America as the society most deeply influenced by it. But we can find the same attitude of restless work and moral righteousness also in a Swiss mechanic of modest social origin and standing who, while pursuing mechanical inventions of the utmost importance, questioned his virtues and prayed to God for help when he wrote in his diary: "Give me in your infinite mercy, O Lord, the strength to strive for a wise division of my time between the claims of soul and body and temporal and eternal matters, and by means of this struggle to improve as well my inner self as my secular affairs. Let no minute of my life pass unutilized or—worse—lost to me altogether. How often, indeed, does men's fortune and salvation, their misfortune and perdition depend on a single minute; and yet how carelessly we tend to this most precious of our possessions. Let me be mindful of the brevity of human life and of the nearness of the time when I must give an account of myself, remembering what awaits me should I fail to employ according to your will the talents you have granted me."[8]

Men of such a character made the Industrial Revolution in Europe. The Swiss mechanic by the name of Bodmer left his native Switzerland first for Germany, then for England, where he worked as one of the most ingenious inventors of the early nineteenth century and helped thereby to secure the technological, economic, and military superiority of the West over the rest of the world. Men like him also put their stamp on the attitudes and values of their countries when they transformed them from the more leisurely old days to what nowadays is being called the "achieving society."

But these men were not the foremost amongst the Europeans who rushed into foreign continents to seek there adventure, or riches, or both. It is true, they were not lacking when Europe established the contact with the East that had been lost for all but some Italian merchants, itinerant scholars or occasional envoys in the later Middle Ages. Explorers and missionaries, Jesuit scholars, merchants and sea captains, and later the administrators and judges who came to represent the West in the East and in the South, varied a lot in respect to their motives and habits. Not all were arrogant and ruthless, but the majority seems to have felt that Western values and laws they would have respected at home did not, or not fully, apply to countries outside the Christian and European tradition. International judges and lawyers put these attitudes in the form of doctrines of the law of nations. Sir William Scott, judge at the High Court of Admiralty, which decided many cases in which Europeans and non-Europeans were involved, held in 1801 that the law of nations should not be applied to territories outside Europe "in its full vigour." He stated in *The Hurtige Hane*, "It would be extremely hard on persons residing in the kingdom of Morocco, if they should be held bound by all the rules of the law of nations, as it is practiced among European states. On many accounts, undoubtedly they are not to be strictly considered on the same footing as European merchants." And in a similar case one year later he maintained that the inhabitants of the Ottoman Empire "are not professors of exactly the same law of nations with ourselves" and that the court, therefore, would be inclined "not to hold them bound to the utmost rigor of that system of public laws, on which European states have so long acted, in their intercourse with one another."[9]

What was expressed here in a seemingly benevolent manner, otherwise often turned into a naive and arrogant display of superiority of the West. This display could take many forms, for example, that of a legal doctrine that non-Christian territories could be treated as *res nullius*, nobody's land, and were a mere object, not a subject of international law, or the belief that non-Christian countries by definition were "uncivilized" and "barbarous." The irreproachable Sir Henry Jenkyns, for many decades legal advisor to British governments and the parliament, describes at the end of his life the institution of a protectorate in which the native ruler is barred from entering into foreign relations with any power except his protector. He states matter-of-factly, "This is the exact condition of the native princes of India; and states of this kind are at the present moment rising in all of the more barbarous portions of the world . . . however, there has not been any case of a civilized, or one should rather say a Christian, state under British protection." And, nearly astonished, he adds in a footnote: "Recent treaties with Japan . . . seem to place Japan in the same position as Christian states."[10]

Nowhere has this Western arrogance created more misunderstandings and harm as in Western relations with China, since China displayed in its own way the same arrogance against the West and was made to feel, therefore, those claims were supported by material force. Sino-Western relations in the nineteenth century became the classic example of dealings between unequals. China was accustomed to think in terms of the unequality of rulers, rather than of a family of nations, since it regarded itself as the center of the world and exercised, however loosely and nominally, suzerainty over surrounding territories like Korea, Annam, Laos, Siam, Sulu, or Burma. When Western missionaries and traders arrived, the Chinese authorities treated them like other aliens, tolerantly but expecting them to subject themselves to Chinese laws, customs, and suzerainty. Misunderstandings about rights and wrongs seem to have arisen at an early stage of Sino-Western contacts. Traders in China formed the lowest class and contempt for trade was extended to the foreign merchants as well. Probably the attitudes of European traders reinforced this view. Later Western observers, sympathetic to China, maintained that "a want of regard for Chinese laws characterized the foreigners who went to China in the seventeenth and eighteenth centuries . . . they were either adventurers or desperate characters and with the exception of a few missionaries, they were all animated by the sole desire to seek fortunes in a new land."[11] More important, however, was the totally different notion about international trade. While China did allow it on a modest scale and under government control—it always had Indian, Arab, or Persian traders in its ports and sometimes had entertained overland routes to western Asia into Europe for the trade of silk—it did not seek it and particularly did not know of any "natural right" of strangers to be admitted to do business on Chinese soil. This, however, was exactly what the Westerners assumed, and in the nineteenth century Western governments supported this claim of their merchants with military and political pressure. Westerners also expected to find business regulations similar to their own, a civil or merchant law and courts at which private claims could be enforced. China, however, did not possess such a law. China's merchants managed their own affairs avoiding government courts, which administered mainly penal law and were not used to treat litigant parties as both seeking their right with the court making the decisions. At their best they used arbitration-like methods, at their worst they exacted penalties from those seeking justice. Westerners were convinced, therefore, that inter alia Western norms of law had to be introduced into China to open it for Western commerce. The British government particularly served "as the hand-maiden of commerce, the civilizing benefit of which was deemed obtainable only through the establishment of the rule of Anglo-Saxon law. The energies of the British consuls were bent for a generation toward the creation of a framework of legal regulation within which foreign trade might prosper and Sino-foreign relations remain tranquil."[12] When the Chinese refused to allow such a framework to be developed, it was forced upon them by the unequal treaties. They superimposed the "privileges" of Western law to the treaty ports where they were extended also to the Chinese living under Western jurisdiction. By the end of the century, an American visitor noted that the Chinese merchant class, so long suppressed by its low status, crowded into the territories held by foreign nations, such as Hong Kong and the international settlement of Shanghai. This illustrated to him "the desire of the Chinese merchants for settled legal conditions" under which "they may enjoy the advantages of impartial courts and consistent rules of law which they so highly appreciate."[13] The same visitor also observed that the Chinese merchant class—measured on Western standards—was undoubtedly honest and capable and that Japanese houses "generally employ Chinamen in positions of trust."[14] He regarded them as one of two great assets of China—the other being abundant natural resources.

If his observations are correct, an intriguing question arises: How could the "public values" of China and the West differ so markedly and yet the ethics of business life be so similar? Considering what has been said about the common value system in Mediterranean trade, perhaps the answer can be found in the requirements of business dealings throughout history and amongst most different cultures: the necessities to rely on each other's promises and basic honesty (while seeking one's own advantage). If Chinese merchants in centuries of self-reliance, as far as the enforcement of rules of behavior in business dealings was concerned, developed norms so similar to Western ones, the cultural, social, or historical variable in it might after all not be as wide as often is supposed. And when they managed to maintain them in the midst of a decaying empire with a corrupt and petty bureaucracy that wielded considerable power over them, the inherent value of such a code of business ethics, so it can be concluded, must be of particular strength.

It would be premature, however, to derive from such observations that the business community should be left alone in working out its particular ethics because its common interest will force it to adhere to commonly acceptable rules like "fair play" and "good faith." The merchants of ancient, medieval, and early modern times, when they developed their codes of "good behavior" relying on "good faith" and "good morals," created rules between equals. As long as no member of an international community can hope easily to outdo the rest, these rules may work sufficiently, as their long endurance testifies. They are not without merit in a wider world which is composed of many unequals. In order to continue to serve their purpose they have to be supplemented; however, Adam Smith knew this already. He deeply distrusted "the mean rapacity, the monopolizing spirit of merchants and manufacturers" whose interest it was "to secure themselves the monopoly of the home market."[15] Since monopolies gave one market partner an enormous strength, they created unequals. Merchants and traders, being only few, could easily arrange understandings on prices or wages and had an advantage over consumers and laborers who, because they were many, could not unite so easily for their common interest. For Adam Smith, the best way to prevent, or at least reduce, such unequalities in market power was the enforcement of competition. The more people would act independently of each other the more the common good would be furthered by an "invisible hand."[16] This belief in the benefits of a self-regulating competitive economy is by no means common to all cultures. Most traditional societies—to use this somewhat vague term—seem on the contrary to have preferred to rely on government supervision, public monopolies, corporate cooperation, or clan-relations in much of their economic activity. Even in western Europe, guilds and regulations were time-honored devices that, in the minds of most contemporaries of Smith, were a necessary condition for a sound economy. When the liberal economists came to question this belief, they argued on several lines. First there was the observation that those sectors of the economy working on a higher degree of competition, like international trade outside the colonial companies, was more efficient, tended to lower the prices and gave more room to individual initiative and enterprise. From this observation it could be concluded that if all sectors would behave that way, the whole economy would function better and the total wealth of nations would grow faster. Moreover, they argued that free enterprise would tend to strengthen the liberty and independence of individuals and allow them to lead a more dignified life. Adam Smith and

John Stuart Mill were, after all, moral philosophers. They believed that an economy of free and independent men once set up would be guided by an "invisible hand" to the common good of all, but we know today that it often needs a very visible hand, clear and enforceable rules preventing not only the collusions of some against the rest of the society, but also the overpowering of the weaker through the stronger ones.

For about a century, Western countries have tried to find solutions to this problem. New fields of law such as antitrust and labor law have been developed; government agencies and, in some countries, particular courts have been established to administer them. But, even within the industrialized Western countries, law and its enforcement alone can scarcely prevent unequalness to grow in such a way as to endanger the very values a liberal economy, based on freedom of enterprise, is supposed to serve. Ethical codes that stress "fair play" of the stronger against the weaker, and self-restraint where necessary, have to be added.

If this is true for fairly homogeneous, industrialized societies, it applies even more to the international economy of today and the future. Because of huge differences between countries—size, wealth, resources, technology, efficiency of available labor, and capital—and the minimal effectiveness of worldwide rules of law and courts, only the self-restraint of the first-world nations and their large business corporations, the voluntary obedience to rules of "fair play," "good faith" and "good conscience" that have been implanted into the ethics of businessmen for centuries, can prevent utter injustice being done to those who, by whatever reasons, cannot hope to meet Western businesses on equal footing.

It may be helpful here to recall the damage done to the lives of many non-Western people and the Western nations' reputation when Europeans first swarmed around the earth and encountered people they did not regard as equals—and thus did not treat according to their "home" standards. Whether the Portuguese and Dutch in Southeast Asia, or the Spaniards in South America, or the English and French in North America, India, and Australia, or all of them together including the Belgian, German, Italian, and American newcomers to the final "scramble for Africa" and the Pacific

Ocean—all violated rules they had developed in their own international relations. It is true, in the beginning, when they met nearly equals in the East, they generally would subject themselves to the rules of the host country,[17] but with the growing unequalness between the West and East following the Industrial Revolution, Westerners tended to exclude non-Westerners from the "privileges" of Western laws. Only when Western conscience was publicly awakened, when reform and abolition movements spread in England and elsewhere, only then did Western governments also begin to enforce their rules of law in non-Western countries, even applying it against their own countrymen. In the later eighteenth century English judges were sent to India to administer law in the territories of the East India Company and their immediate surroundings. They were instrumental in restricting arbitrary company rule and bad business behavior of individual employees by forcing them, for example, to keep contracts they had privately concluded. They added a new element to British rule in India. As one Indian student of the introduction of English law into India has observed: "The Mughal system of government which the English Company had adopted in Bengal, was dictatorial, arbitrary, and coercive. It served the commercial and colonial purposes of the English, but it was contrary to English law. Thus, the conflict which ensued between the Supreme Court and the Supreme Council was in fact a conflict between a rule of law and arbitrary methods of government."[18]

In a similar way England had to extend colonial government in South Africa later in the nineteenth century, Germany had to establish orderly administration in her east and southeast African colonies and the Belgian government had to assume responsibility for the Congo in order to restrain adventurous and ruthless Europeans who exploited these regions without regard to any law or ethical principles, even if they did so in the names of their countries or of "civilization." The expansion of European law and its institution into non-European areas served thus not only as an instrument for European domination as is often assumed, but also as means to restrain the arbitrary exercise of power. It served to establish legal concepts and rules throughout the world that are now being used by indigenous governments to ascertain their sovereignty and equality in relations with former colonial masters and other nations. Equality before the law now has been achieved in international affairs nearly universally, but equality before the law does not, as we know from the experience within our societies, in itself guarantee social and economic justice or equality. To advance them, additional rules may have to be devised for the conduct of international affairs, as they are being devised within societies which strive for more social justice—not in a dictatorial or doctrinaire way, but by balancing the interest of different groups of individuals. This historical survey has shown that as far as the formulation of business codices for the conduct of affairs beyond national boundaries is concerned, some basic ethical principles are available which have served mankind for centuries and could guide them also in the future.

Codes for Transnational Enterprises

Jack N. Behrman

The increasingly significant roles of transnational enterprises in the international economy have given rise to widespread demands for imposition of codes of conduct which would alter their behavior towards that desired by governments and other interested groups. The gestation of these codes has been slow and is even now fraught with numerous conflicts among the parties involved—the companies, governments of the host countries, governments of the parent companies (home governments), and various labor and community-oriented groups. By examining the issues and conflicts, this essay seeks to determine the usefulness of codes. If their usefulness is less than expected by various parties, their promulgation will create another frustration on the international scene. On the other hand, if the limited value of codes is recognized, they can be useful in setting the stage. At present, much more is claimed for and apparently expected of them than seems reasonable.

CONCERNS OVER TNEs

The primary concern which arises from the spread of the transnational enterprises (TNEs) is that of dependence—both economic and political. The fear of dependence arises not only from the large size of the companies and their tendency to dominate activities in whatever sector they operate, but also from the fact that companies tend to be headquartered in the old colonial powers, within which the United States and Japan are included, despite the absence of significant colonies in their history. Since the TNE headquarters make a large number of the significant decisions concerning the activities of affiliates in other countries, the host countries feel that their own interests will not be taken sufficiently into account. Consequently, dominance exists even if it is not sought by the parent company or its home government. Dominance through decision making is reinforced by the fact that many of the TNEs operate in key economic sectors—banking, high technology manufacturing, and extraction. Their technological dominance arises from control over the origins and flows of technology. The ability of the parent company to determine not only the types of products and services provided the host country, but also the type and level of employment in particular sectors, as well as the technology employed, makes the host countries feel subservient and therefore incapable of achieving prestige in the international community.

The fear of economic dependence is increased by a concern over *interference* in the economic, political, and social life of the host country by both the enterprises and their home governments. Thus, United States antitrust law, tax law, and controls over capital flows have been extended into activities of U.S. affiliates abroad, whether or not such extension violated or controverted the laws of the host country. Some companies have themselves attempted to interfere in the elections of host countries and have attempted to alter the application of law through political and sometimes corrupting pressures. Finally, interference is perceived by the host countries in their own economic plan and social welfare objectives when TNEs have the capability of pursuing their own goals, regardless of the goals of the host government.

For countries that have not developed in the Western traditions, there is a fear of *cultural* change through the spread of Western life styles, values, goods, and familial relationships.

Managerial styles which emphasize rapid hiring and firing of individuals, so as to maximize profits or minimize costs, are not always acceptable. And values which emphasize gadgets or a multiplicity of goods which are only marginally different will sometimes seem to cause a waste of resources, especially when the masses lack basic goods and services. The idea that income and the market should determine what goods are produced is also not universally accepted by host countries. The desire to retain cultural differences is tied up with the concept of self-identity: the billboards in Peru encouraging citizens to "Be proud to be Peruvian" and the bumper stickers in Brazil asserting "Brazil: love it or leave it." This drive to retain the cultural identity raises an apparent conflict with economic progress, which seems to be attainable only by following Western modes of industrialization. Since the TNEs are carriers of this mode, they are both welcomed and rejected—the frequently noted love-hate syndrome.

Still another concern arises over an *inequitable distribution* of the benefits of economic growth at the hands of the TNEs. Serious questions are raised about the percentage return to capital invested by the foreigner, the direction and volume of trade, the cost of imports from the parent company to the affiliate, and the charges for technology and headquarters expenses. The TNE is seen as looking after its own financial interest first, leaving in the host country only that which is necessary to continue operations. Whether this is the fact or not, it is the *perception*, creating a demand for codes of conduct.

The accumulation of these impacts on the host country gives rise to a feeling that the TNEs have considerable *power*—political, economic, and social—causing unwanted changes. Not all of the TNEs have the same kinds of impact nor the same power, even though they may be perceived to have similar power. These differences are significant and need to be taken into account in assessing the application of any code of conduct. But public debate seems not to focus on such differences, frequently aggregating quite diverse types of activities and impacts under a single indictment.

What is sought among all countries is a means of legitimizing (and reducing?) the power which the foreigner wields in the host country. The justification of power, on the basis that it comes from the consent of the governed, reinforces the demand that TNEs conduct themselves in a manner "acceptable" to those affected. This acceptability is the only basis for the legitimacy of the TNEs. The codes simply are a means of spelling out what is acceptable action.

The host governments are not the parties that are concerned over the relationships created by the spread of the TNEs. These enterprises are themselves concerned about the reactions of the host governments and what they may mean for the successful conduct of their operations around the world. Although companies will operate under almost any set of conditions imposed by host governments—if they are imposed equally for all and leave an opportunity for successful ventures—there are some conditions that are more conducive to their activities than others. Causes of concern to TNEs include political or economic instability, governmental violation of contractual obligations, inadequate protection against expropriation or inadequate compensation when expropriation does take place, interference in daily operations through inflexible laws and regulations, and discrimination against them in comparison with national enterprises. These concerns have given rise to demands from the TNEs that governments themselves adopt a code of conduct which is suitable to their own operations around the world.

Finally, various interest groups are concerned about the conduct of the transnational enterprises and the way in which they affect their particular areas. Labor unions of diverse orientations—national and international—have indicated that they wish to require given types of conduct from the TNEs concerning collective bargaining, working conditions, fair labor standards, and so forth. Consumer groups have shown an interest in the marketing activities of the transnational enterprises. And a number of church-related groups have expressed strong concerns over transnational enterprises' treatment of minority groups and women around the world. Each of these feels that they should have an appropriate input into any code of conduct to be promulgated.

OBJECTIVES OF THE CODES

The primary objectives of the proposed codes are to change the policies and operations of TNEs and to alter their behavior and orientation. These two objectives need to be distinguished quite clearly in any analysis of codes. To change policies and practices of companies means specific acts of the companies that give rise to the concerns noted above would be proscribed and desired actions would be prescribed. Any company which undertook the former or failed to undertake the latter would be considered in violation of the code. Alteration of behavior or changes in orientations have to do with attitudes and loyalties of decision-makers and concern their ethical guidelines. Even if a given act is not proscribed under the code, the host governments would like to think the foreign investor will take into consideration the interests of the host governments before they yield to pressures from outside that country. They would also like to think that the companies will act under concepts of equality and justice higher than the law, in order to provide an equitable distribution of benefits to all parties.

The avoidance of proscribed action, fulfillment of prescribed acts, and the acceptance of host-government loyalties and orientations would assure an "appropriate" approach on the part of the TNEs and therefore gain them legitimacy in the host countries. The proposed international codes, therefore, are substitutes for both national legislation and company ethical guidelines. They are also a substitute for international treaties, which become the law of the land of the signatory countries.

But why are codes deemed more desirable than legislation in proscribing particular actions on the part of the trans-national enterprises? To legislate such proscriptions would require either the unification of national laws or their harmonization. Once the debate were thrown into the national parliaments, questions would be raised as to the applicability of the legislation to all domestic business. The differences between foreign and domestic enterprises, as well as within each group, would readily become apparent. It seems impossible to harmonize legislation even among a few countries in areas as desirable as transport regulations, social security, unemployment compensation, and patent law. We are quite some distance from such harmonization of national laws and still further from creation of international law. Several groups proposing codes would like to see them imposed in a mandatory fashion, implicitly creating international law which would supercede national law, but there is a fundamental conflict here among several governments. One governmental objection to passage of laws is that they would place mandatory requirements on national as well as foreign-owned companies.

It is to avoid these problems that many of the proposed international codes are projected to be voluntary. TNEs would then comply only if they considered it desirable to do so. The voluntary approach also avoids problems of penalties and reduces the need for surveillance of company operations. Most of the host governments that have imposed national codes have done so in a mandatory fashion (making them the law of the land), and most of the governments of parent companies considering codes have proposed them to be voluntary. The code being considered by the Organization for Economic Cooperation and Development (OECD), the organization of industrialized countries, is to be voluntary, while those proposed by the Organization of American States and the Group of 77 (made up of developing countries) are projected to be mandatory. The code proposed by the TNEs themselves would also be voluntary.

One objective of an international code, therefore, is to move towards an agreed set of rules without going as far as international law or the harmonization of national law. Whether the codes are then seen as an unwarranted interference or as a too timid step towards international law depends on the predilections of the analyst. The fact that there are a number of sources proposing codes signals there will be numerous conflicts over the orientations of the codes, their provisions, mechanisms for enforcement, and means of settling disputes.

FORMATION OF CODES

A variety of private groups have proposed codes for international investment and the behavior of transnational enterprises. Several governments have promulgated their own, and at least three regional groups of countries have agreed upon or are considering codes for international investment and for technology transfers by TNEs. The provisions of these codes differ considerably, reflecting the divergent interests of each of the parties concerned.

Code Signatories

The signers or participants in any code set its objectives and provisions and determine its applicability. The four different sources of codes—some proposed, some in existence—appeal to different sets of potential signatories. The interests of these four groups are divergent, and there are conflicting interests even within each group.

The first of the entities to promulgate a code on investment and technology transfer was a national government—Japan—that set the terms of reference for foreign investors and companies wishing to license Japanese companies. The Japanese code had the force of law, although not all of its provisions were backed by statutory regulations. Rather, the Ministry of International Trade and Industry (MITI) simply made determinations relative to any application by a TNE as to whether the proposal fit the national interest of Japan.

The success of this code has attracted the attention of many other governments. Several things need to be noted, however, about this unique success. First, it was applied early in the development of the TNE and at a time when Japan was already more technically advanced than present developing countries. Second, there was a considerable attraction in the Japanese economy for foreign companies who saw the growing market there as one they would like to enter even under severe constraints. Third, the conditions of the code applied almost wholly to entry negotiations, not to the behavior of the companies after they had been approved for entry. Fourth, the code applied to policies, not to questions of ethical behavior. The Japanese code, therefore, was simple.

The next code promulgated by a national government was that of Canada. It was directed not at the conditions of entry into Canada, but at the behavior of the companies after they were already established in the country. The code was prompted by ostensible interference in the activities of the American-owned affiliates by the United States government through its controls over foreign direct investment in the late 1960s. The U.S. government sought to reduce the outflow of capital and to increase the return of earnings to ease its balance-of-payments deficits. To reduce Canadian criticism of this and other interferences by the United States government through the international companies, the minister of Trade and Commerce issued a set of "Guidelines for Good Corporate Behavior" for foreign companies.[1] There were no statutes or regulations issued requiring the companies to fulfill any one of the conditions, but the companies were asked to report quarterly as to their fulfillment of these terms. Compliance is, therefore, essentially voluntary, although nearly all of the companies can readily assert they are doing what was asked—as long as they are not required to prove it in every specific decision. Contrary to the Japanese code, the Canadian guidelines on behavior are voluntary and raise no serious problems of surveillance and compliance.

Later dissatisfaction with the code's not applying to continued entry of foreigners led to passage of a law concerning new foreign investment requiring governmental screening of proposals—particularly those which would acquire existing Canadian companies. Since the Canadian market has considerable attractiveness and the regulations relate only to Canada, international companies have learned to live with them fairly readily.

Mexico, Argentina, and a number of other countries have imposed extensive and detailed codes on foreign investment and technology transfers in their countries that set the terms of reference for entry and subsequent behavior of affiliates. The codes have raised a considerable number of complaints from international companies not only because of their scope, but also, their specificity, leaving little flexibility to negotiate different arrangements suitable for different types of companies. These countries are less attractive to international investors than are Japan and Canada so the codes are expected to reduce the volume of investment, damaging the prospects of economic growth. The Mexican government has itself become sufficiently concerned to request an independent study of the impact of its technology code on these transfers into the country. Since these codes are mandatory, having not only the full force of law but also significant penalties for non-compliance, the international companies are justifiably wary. The codes not only cover specific policies and practices, but also require that the international companies take into account "the national interest" of the host country in broad management decisions and that they protect the culture of the host country, without specifying what this would mean in any given situation.

Several national governments have agreed on codes concerning practices and behavior within a given region, setting guidelines for investment and technology transfers occurring within any of the signatory countries. The nations west of the Andes in South America have formed the Andean Pact, within which they have agreed on such codes, and the Association of South East Asian Nations (ASEAN) have also adopted similar guidelines. The OECD, the Group of 77, the Organization of American States (OAS) and the United Nations are in the process of promulgating their codes. The Andean and ASEAN codes differ in several respects, although both apply to a group of countries that are members of a regional association. The orientation of each is to attempt to set the terms of entry for foreign investors within any of the countries of the region, but the ASEAN code seeks more to achieve harmonization of incentives and inducements among the members while the Andean code seeks to harmonize constraints.[2] Since promulgation of their code, the ASEAN countries have become more restrictive while, contrarily, the Andean countries have found it necessary to relax some of their constraints with reference to specific investment or technology proposals. Both of these codes are exceedingly detailed and require negotiations with international companies and continuing surveillance. Experience under these codes is not yet sufficient to assess their impact fully, but the attractiveness of investing in these regions is not strong enough to overcome numerous companies' reluctance to undertake activities under the conditions required.

The Organization of American States, comprising the countries of North and South America, has been working on a code of conduct for its members. The Group of 77 (whose membership has risen from seventy-seven to over one hundred countries) is composed of developing countries; the purpose of its proposed code is to set guidelines to remove dependence on the international companies and the industrialized countries and to redistribute the benefits of economic progress toward the host countries.[3]

OECD is made up of a group of industrialized countries of North America, Europe and Japan. It is considering a code on foreign investment that would deal essentially with investment among the advanced countries, but that would also set terms the developing countries might follow. Given the expressed interest of the developing countries, however, it appears that the conflicts of interest are such that the two groups are not likely to reach agreement.

The United Nations has set up a Center on Transnational Corporations and has given it the responsibility for developing a code of conduct for those companies. So far it has recommended to member states that they establish national codes somewhat similar to those of Mexico and Argentina and has offered assistance to the various countries in promulgating and implementing them.

As a counter to and yet in line with governmental codes, the transnational enterprises, through the International Chamber of Commerce, have proposed a code on international investment which would apply not only to the investors, but also to the host countries, the governments of parent companies and labor. All would have responsibilities to abide by the code, which, however, is voluntary.[4] The orientation of this code is largely to make certain that conditions around the world will be conducive to the spread of international investment and technology transfers, thereby removing the concerns, noted earlier, of the international companies. Although this code has been debated for some years, there seems to be little willingness on the part of governments to undertake the responsibilities specified therein. Concerns of governments are recognized and provisions are stipulated to relieve some of these fears, but the fact that the company responses are voluntary reduces the attractiveness of this code to the less-developed countries.

An attempt to develop a code that would be acceptable to both companies and governments was made by the Pugwash Conference (composed of officials of companies and governments acting in their own personal capacities).[5] It shows a similarity to other codes and would be voluntary. Although this code has also been debated for several years, it has not been the subject of formal discussions aiming at agreement by governments.

Finally, some companies have decided it would be advisable to publish their own code of conduct concerning international activities to publicize the company's policy orientations and the way it would intend to behave. One such code is that adopted by the Caterpillar Company.[6] It is a mixture of policy prescriptions and ethical rules of conduct, but lacks any mechanism for surveillance or proof that, in fact, officials have operated as intended. Such surveillance would have to be set up between the company and the host country if it were to exist, and it is not clear what penalties would be imposed within the company for misbehavior on the part of any company official.

Code Provisions

There are basically three types of provisions included in the existing and proposed codes on foreign investment and technology transfer. One set deals with alternations of policies, the second with changes in behavior or in attitudes and orientations, and the third with the disclosure of sufficient information to determine whether the provisions have been fulfilled.

The *policy shifts* requested by host countries include at least the following:

    a. Foreign investment should not displace nationally-owned investment of a similar sort.

   b. Foreign investment should be complementary to nationally-owned investment, supporting the development of the latter.

   c. Foreign-owned affiliates should not be wholly-owned by the foreigner, but a majority of shares should be held by local nationals.

   d. Extractive investments should occur only in unexploited areas of the host economy.

   e. Maximum effort should be made to export the foreign-owned affiliate.

   f. Preferences should be given to the hiring of local personnel, and minority groups should not be discriminated against.

   g. Local technicians should be trained and put in high-level positions.

   h. Support should be given for local technical and educational centers.

   i. Imports of materials and semi-finished goods for processing by the affiliates should be reduced to a minimum.

   j. The foreign investor should make a maximum contribution to the balance of payments of the host country.

   k. The foreign investor or licensor should not employ restrictive business practices (some twenty or more specific practices are prohibited).

   l. Foreign investors should not acquire existing companies in the host country.

   m. The foreign investor should reduce local borrowing to a minimum.

   n. The foreign investor should not attempt to avoid or evade taxes in the host country.

   o. The foreign investor should seek to reinvest a maximum percentage of earnings in the host country.

Although this is but a partial listing of the types of provisions found in the proposed codes, one can readily see their relationship to the concerns discussed earlier. There are several seeking to remove the dependence on the foreigner, others to redress what is considered to be a maldistribution of benefits, and others to remove control from the foreigner.

The specific nature of the provisions covering the above points differs according to whether the code is promulgated by a national government, a regional association, or an international group. And, certainly no code proposed by the TNEs themselves, or promulgated by a single company, would be as binding as these provisions would appear to be.

A second set of provisions relates to *behavior* in general, including such items as:

  a. Foreign enterprises should abide by the laws of the host country.
  b. The foreign investor should not interfere in local politics.
  c. The parent government of the foreign investor should not use the international company to interfere in the host country.
  d. The foreign investor should not rely on his own government for representation with the host government.
  e. Foreign enterprises should, in accordance with relevant laws, promote free labor unions, bargain collectively with them, and seek to increase benefits to the workers.
  f. Foreign enterprises should not upset the cultural patterns of the host country.

In its official position on such codes of conduct, the United States government has stated that any code of conduct concerning transnational enterprises should set forth "general principles of good business practice applicable, where relevant, to all enterprises, whether multinational or national, whether owned privately, by the state, or by a mixture of the two. It should indicate that multinational enterprises have an obligation to comply with local law and that they should take account of public policy and national development priorities; at the same time, it should confirm the obligation of governments to treat these enterprises equitably and in accordance with international law. Any code should also indicate the necessity for both enterprises and governments to respect contractual obligations freely undertaken by them."

This statement of policy was made in partial response to a resolution of the Permanent Council of the Organization of American States (10 July 1975) which stated that a "necessary respect . . . must be maintained for the sovereignty and laws of the countries in which transnational enterprises operate. . . ." And that "the activities of transnational enterprises should contribute to achievement of the goals of national policies on economic and social development and on the development of natural resources of the countries where they operate, and abide by their laws. . . ." In this same resolution, the Permanent Council resolved "To condemn in the most emphatic terms any act of bribery, illegal payment or offer of payment by any transnational enterprise; any demand for or acceptance of improper payments by any public or private person, as well as any act contrary to ethics and legal procedures."

The principal orientation of provisions relating to behavior is to reorient the loyalties and interests of the companies towards those of the host government and to insist on acceptance of national laws and regulations—rather than adhere to foreign laws (of the parent government) or to international law. The U.S. government, on the other hand, has continued to insist on adherence also to international law, thereby restraining to some extent the application of national law. Few of the provisions get to the level of strictly ethical behavior, although some so proscribe discriminatory treatment of minorities—even in Third World countries such as South Africa— even though the country may not be a signatory of the code and its laws may not require the same behavior.

Provisions relating to *disclosure of information* have two purposes: one is to provide adequate surveillance of company activities to make certain they are following code provisions; the other is to obtain more information about what companies are doing to see if the provisions are appropriate or likely to achieve the objectives sought by the signatories to the code. The latter provisions are a type of fishing expedition, while the former have to do with possible penalties. The lack of information is reflected in the basic request under the proposed OECD code that international companies publicly disclose information on "the composition, location and nature of the multinational enterprise, showing the parent company, all subsidiary companies together with the relevant shareholdings, all associated companies together with the nature of the association and indicating all significant activities carried on and their geographical location." The OECD code would also request information on profits, number of employees, sales, wage and salary bills—this in reference to the multinational enterprise as a whole and, where practicable, for each country where any significant activity was undertaken. It also would like the companies to make public policies regarding intra-enterprise pricing and financing. In addition, it requests the accounting policies of the company be made public to permit reconciliation of the accounts in comparison with other companies. Some of the other codes are less (and others more) precise regarding information to be disclosed. Some national codes require certain data to be presented before the arrangement will be considered valid in the host country. In this case, an agency of the host government is to receive the data within particular time periods, otherwise penalties will be imposed.

Host countries seek especially to obtain information on a worldwide basis, rather than only within their own country. They seek to have comparative information in order to know whether they are being treated equitably in comparison with other countries. Besides the problem of comparability, which would require harmonization of accounting practices, there are several other unresolved conflicts over provisions. There is, for example, considerable difference between public disclosure and disclosure to a government agency; between information to determine fulfillment of provisions and that merely to raise additional questions for further investigation; information required of international companies but not required of domestic enterprises; and between data relating to a single country and that relating to total worldwide operations of an international company.

The divergent interests potential code signatories have in the promulgation of codes show up in the specific provisions and in the ways they would be implemented. A comparative study shows the provision proposed by different developing countries have a considerably greater similarity than they do to those proposed by advanced countries.[7] Similarly, the provisions proposed by members of the OECD show a greater degree of agreement than there is between these provisions and those proposed by the less developed countries (LDCs). What is likely to be accepted as a code among advanced countries is not likely to be accepted by the LDCs.

There is even some disagreement among the developing countries because certain ones wish to be considerably more restrictive on foreign investment and technology transfers than others. For example, South Korea is quite eager to obtain foreign investment as is Taiwan and as Malaysia has been, but many of the Latin American countries wish to impose numerous constraints. Consequently, there is considerable disagreement about precisely what provisions the code should include. To obtain agreement, the provisions are made more and more general, and therefore more and more difficult to implement—or at least to know whether they have been fulfilled. It is this generality and uncertainty that makes international companies concerned over the proposed codes. But if there is considerable difficulty in achieving agreement on the provisions themselves, there are even greater problems of code implementation.

PROBLEMS OF IMPLEMENTATION

At least five difficult problems face authorities who would be responsible for application of the codes: the determination of the appropriate administrative mechanism; the determination of which provisions will be voluntary and which mandatory; surveillance and the necessary information disclosure; the penalties imposed for nonfulfillment of the code provisions; and the settlement of disputes over nonfulfillment and appropriate penalties (which would arise not only between international companies and governments but among governments).

Administrative Mechanisms

The administrative mechanisms likely to be used to implement nationally promulgated codes will, of course, be quite different from those used to implement regional or international codes. It can readily be recognized that creation of appropriate mechanisms at regional or international levels will be difficult, but it is also difficult to form the appropriate mechanisms even at the national level.

Since foreign investment and the transfers of technology affect a wide range of national interests, no single ministry brackets all the policy issues or impacts that need to be assessed. If the responsibility for implementation of the codes is given to a single ministry, its own concerns and interests are more likely to be given high priority, compared to the interest of others. If the Ministry of Finance is in charge, the concerns over the impact of financial flows and of changes in the balance of payments are likely to be emphasized over employment levels and types of technology employed. The latter concerns would be given a higher priority by the Ministry of Industry or that of Labor. Nationally-based codes, therefore, tend to be implemented by an independent commission, or by an inter-agency committee. Either mechanism has difficult problems in dealing with the bureaucracy. Despite the success of the Japanese code, which was the primary responsibility of the Ministry of International Trade and Industry (MITI), there were frequent disputes between MITI and the Ministry of Finance and sometimes with the Ministry of Foreign Affairs, both of which might have been more willing to open the country to foreign investment in order to assuage criticism of foreign governments.

If a code is regionally based, such as the Andean Pact, a separate regional commission is formed to oversee the implementation of the code. Day-to-day implementation in the Andean countries, however, rests with national governments. Each of the governments has seen the code somewhat differently and has applied its provisions differently. For example, some have argued that the regional code sets the maximum of restriction that can be applied against foreign investment and technology transfers; others have considered the code as the minimum restraint that had to be applied by a national government. More stringent restraints would be acceptable in the view of the latter. Where provisions permit some flexibility of interpretation and action, members obviously will see their own national interest differently.

The difficulty of erecting acceptable administrative mechanisms at the international level may be one of the primary reasons why most of the codes proposed at this level are projected to be voluntary. Voluntarism avoids the necessity for precise administrative mechanisms.

Voluntary vs Mandatory Codes

The OECD projected code would be voluntary for the international enterprises. But the report of the secretary general of the United Nations on the "Impact of Multinational Corporations on the Development Process and on International Relations" (14 June 1974) provides that the new Center on Transnational Corporations is responsible to "evolve a set of recommendations which, taken together, would represent a code of conduct for governments and multinational corporations to be considered and adopted by the Economic and Social Council, and review in the light of experience the effective application and continuing applicability of such recommendations"; and also to "explore the possibility of concluding a general agreement on multinational corporations, enforceable by appropriate machinery, to which participating countries would adhere by means of an international treaty."

Although the United States Government would like a voluntary code, the Latin American countries are seeking a mandatory code. Neither appears wholly satisfactory from the standpoint of objective analysis. A voluntary code raises the question of discrimination among the transnational enterprises simply because of the differing perceptions of each as to what would be required to fulfill the code provisions. Or, some of the companies might comply fully, while others complied only partially or not at all. This differential compliance would introduce a kind of discrimination.

Since a voluntary code would not provide for sufficient surveillance mechanisms, the question of honesty is raised, simply because no one would be sure of the accuracy of the report by a company that it was in compliance. If surveillance mechanisms were established, the worst of both worlds would exist—companies would be permitted to make their own interpretations of compliance, but some third agency would be looking over their shoulder to see if, in fact, they "did it right." Thus, the voluntary nature of the codes is removed. Yet, one would not know precisely what action would fulfill the code provisions, nor what hidden penalties might be imposed for noncompliance. The most likely consequence would be that the code would be made mandatory, with surveillance mechanisms being set up formally.

Mandatory provisions have their own difficulties, however, because they would require a precise definition of the acts which would fulfill the guidelines, and most of the provisions so far proposed are vague for the reason that it is impossible to obtain agreement on specifics. Mandatory provisions, without specific agreement on the activities which would fulfill them, would lead to a considerable number of disputes and require a mechanism of dispute settlement. As will be seen below, this aspect raises still more difficulties.

Surveillance and Information Disclosure

It is highly unlikely that voluntary codes would be acceptable even among advanced countries. If data on company operations is made public, questions will arise over whether the provisions are being fulfilled. Even if formal surveillance machinery is not set up, increased calls for information are likely to permit determination of whether the guidelines are being met.

The problem of surveillance is essentially that of information disclosure unless the governments are going to put inspectors in each of the international companies to ferret out what is being done and the impact of particular activities. Without such internal and official inspection, surveillance relies on disclosure of information by the companies—whether that disclosure is voluntary or under governmental requirements.

There are multiple problems surrounding the process of information disclosure. Not the least of them is the scope of the demand for information and data concerning the operations and impact of the TNEs. From an examination of the various codes and the rationale given for them, the following array of the types of information demanded can be constructed:

Statistical Data	Company Practices	Impact on Host Countries
1. Balance of payments flows	1. Nature of operations	1. Political interference
2. Sources and uses of funds	2. Organization structure	2. Community development
3. Purchases, by source	3. Location of activities	3. Cultural identity
4. Sales, by product	4. Product lines	4. Employment
5. Profits	5. Ownership and shareholdings	—training
6. Wages and total wage bill	6. Control channels	—elevation
7. Employment, total and by skills	—management contract	5. Environmental protection
8. Exports by destination	—licenses	6. Participation in industry associations
9. Imports by sources	7. Transfer pricing	7. Communication with government
10. Remittances	8. Taxes paid to different jurisdictions	8. Location and control of technology and R & D
—by type	9. Acquisitions, mergers, takeovers	9. Social responsibility
—by source	10. Restrictive business practices	10. Pursuit of host-country economic and social objectives
11. Value of investment	11. Market concentration	11. Obedience to local laws and regulations
—book	12. Local financial operations	12. Interference by home government—directly or through TNE
—going concern	13. Collective bargaining	13. Preferential treatment of TNE by host governments
12. Capital movements		—incentives
—long		—subsidies
—short		
13. Accounting reconciliation		

This array demonstrates that there are three quite distinct types of information wanted by governments; the final column on social, political, and economic impact is the most significant in terms of policy objectives. Yet, it is this last type of information which is most difficult to come by. Because of the penchant for statistical data, most of the requests for information focus on the first column, which will not necessarily provide information useful in assessing the impacts noted in the last column and certainly not data for the second.

Even the statistical data raise a number of issues. First, will the data be presented in an aggregated form in order to prevent undesirable competitive disclosure of information on a particular company? United States government practice is to present only aggregated data, thereby hiding activities of particular companies. Second, will this data be gathered for all companies—national, international, private, and state-owned? Third, will such statistical data be gathered only on a national basis—that is, relating to the activities of each affiliate in a particular country—or will data be demanded for the entire worldwide operations of a company? Fourth, will national governments process the information, or will this responsibility devolve on a regional or international agency? And, if the latter, will companies deal directly with such a nonnational agency, bypassing the government of the host or home country? Finally, how will such data be made comparable among companies and among countries? Differing accounting practices make it virtually impossible to compare data among companies that are based in different countries. It is even difficult to reconcile the accounts of foreign affiliates of the same international company. Before such comparability may be obtained, it may be necessary to harmonize international accounting practices. Given the difficulty of doing this even within a single country, it would appear that the reliability of statistical data gathered from affiliates of the international companies may not be very high.

In fact, discussions with many of the international companies indicate that they simply may not be able to develop the types of information demanded. They certainly are unable to determine the impact of some of their activities. It is widely assumed that these international companies have a vast information-gathering network and a precise method of collating and assessing the information—not only concerning their own operations but also concerning the environment within which they operate. This assumption is inaccurate, for there are significant gaps in the accounting records of the company and slippage exists between what is actually happening within various affiliates and what is recorded back in the parent company concerning these operations.[8] Given the varying accounting practices around the world, it is likely that many affiliate managers do not have a complete picture themselves—at least in the detail that is requested under proposed codes. It would be quite feasible, therefore, for parent companies to provide information which they deem to be accurate but which, in fact, is not.

To achieve the degree of accuracy which most policy makers would like to have—including the international companies and governments—would raise the cost of information gathering to levels which the governments themselves would not wish to bear. The cost of information-gathering is itself not a subject of negotiation among companies and governments because the promulgators of the various codes assume that the cost will be borne by the companies (substitute "consumer"). If one looks at the amount of information demanded and notes that data would have to be gathered for sometimes as many as a hundred or more affiliates around the world, collated, rationalized and justified, checked again for accuracy, and then presented in appropriate forms, one could readily estimate that direct costs of such additional information gathering would run into the tens of millions of dollars if not hundreds of millions for some of the giant companies. Although $100 million is only a fraction of 1 percent of total sales of General Motors, it is still a substantial cost for the company to bear unless the objective can be fully justified. And if the average cost per TNE were only two million dollars for one thousand such companies, the total would reach two billion dollars per year.

Each requester should have to determine the justification for specific information gathering. This can only be done by giving a priority to each of the issues and then determining the desirability of expending time and money to gather the appropriate information. Even the gathering of published information for analysis—such as is being developed under the United Nations Center on Transnational Corporations—will require a substantial outlay, with some thirty or forty professionals to analyze the information. Given the variety of data banks which exist (the United States Department of Commerce, the United States Treasury Department, the Securities and Exchange Commission, Dun and Bradstreet, and a variety of university and private consulting groups) there will be a substantial problem even of reconciling the data available publicly.

Questioning the justification of the cost of information gathering and disclosure raises the further question of the "right to know" on the part of any group to be given the information. Demands that information be provided to the public do not appear to be as justifiable as demands by governments for specific information on precise questions. Although governments can probably justify any demand for information, it is unlikely that regional or intergovernmental agencies would be accorded the same right to know.

It will be up to the member government to determine the extent to which the international agencies have a "right to know." The governments will always to able to stand between the international agencies and the companies which are incorporated within their boundaries. This does not mean that no national government can demand extensive information from a corporation operating within its boundaries. However, there are limits to the information which Mexico can demand of a TNE concerning its worldwide activities. These limitations do not arise from any legal constraint on the Mexican government, but simply on the unwillingness of the TNE to comply and the tradeoffs which will arise if the Mexican government tried to impose mandatory requirements for information on worldwide activities. If these demands became onerous or threatened the ability of the company to maintain confidentiality, it might decide to give up, or at least lessen substantially, its operations in Mexico.

A further question concerning information disclosure is that concerning the relevance of the data gathered. There is a large volume of what might be called "promiscuous data," which is gathered merely because it can be obtained. For example, much of the data in columns one and two of the array presented earlier are not relevant to the basic issues listed in column three. Much greater care will be required to make certain that the issues being examined are, in fact, significant and that the data being gathered are relevant to those issues. Relevance includes also the absence of excess data; great volumes of data can readily be produced by companies, virtually snowing the investigators so that they cannot focus on the specific data needed.

These problems raise sufficient question about the ability

of governments to carry out surveillance of the companies and even to know enough about what is going on to write realistic guidelines. The process of gaining understanding and obtaining control is likely to be a long term one because it is a micro- rather than macro-process and will not yield useful results simply through admonitions or enunciation of broad guidelines.

Penalties

Very little discussion has taken place to date concerning possible penalties for noncompliance. This reflects the fact that most of the codes are considered to be voluntary, except those which have been promulgated by national governments. Penalties have been provided for, at the national levels, including the removal of the right of incorporating or registration from a noncomplying company. Such a penalty would not, of course, be available to an international or regional agency, since incorporation occurs within the host country. Without penalties, however, it is unlikely that mandatory provisions will have any bite. With penalties, especially at the regional or international level, disputes will undoubtedly arise among governments and between them and international companies as to the applicability or reasonableness of particular penalties.

Dispute Settlement

Given the virtual inevitability of a movement toward mandatory codes, the necessity of surveillance, and the imposition of penalties, disputes are inevitable—not only as to the interpretation of the provisions but also as to the compliance of companies and the application of particular penalties. Again, however, there is very little discussion of the codes which focuses on the mechanism for the settlement of disputes. For nationally promulgated codes (Mexican and Argentinian), the national courts are the locus of dispute settlement. This would not be acceptable, however, under regional or international codes. But an international agency also seems unacceptable given the history of the International Center for the Settlement of Investment Disputes (ICSID) under the World Bank, which was rejected by the Latin American governments. It was set up largely to handle disputes over expropriation and could readily be used for disputes under codes. However, with only a few of the countries accepting that mechanism, and there being no other, this area of implementation would seem to raise a series of further problems not as yet even grasped by government officials.

USEFULNESS OF CODES

We have excluded from our discussion codes which would require governments to behave in a manner facilitating the spread and operations of TNEs. It is worth mentioning the rationale behind such codes, however, because it points up some of the problems with codes affecting the TNEs themselves. The official position of the United States government is that codes constraining the transnational enterprises should be matched by governmental agreements to constrain their own interferences with these companies. The rationale behind this position is that economic growth is best achieved at the hands of private enterprise and that TNEs represent this concept at the international level and will, if permitted, bind the international economy together in the most efficient manner. Therefore, not only should the TNEs be permitted to exist, but governments should facilitate their operations by providing a "favorable climate" for their operations.

This rationale extends, historically, back to the "Development Decade" of the 1960s and still further back to the recovery period of the 1950s and the immediate post-World War II period. United States Government policies with the same orientations were enunciated also in the 1920s after World War I, but without much success. United States foreign economic policy from 1945 to date has relied significantly on the initiative and activities of the private sector to spread capital around the world, bind the international economy, and increase trade in order to stimulate economic growth. After some years of disappointment in the fifties and sixties over the success of foreign governmental aid, still greater emphasis has been placed on the role of the private sector in accelerating economic development abroad.

Contrary to the United States government's view, a number of the host governments have begun to question whether the TNEs should exist at all. Some have argued that, if they are to exist, they must be radically altered so they operate in a more acceptable manner. From this standpoint, the codes are directed at resetting the nature, structure, and orientations of the TNEs (potentially even breaking them up) and altering their behavior—both as to policies and as to ethical criteria.

Given these differences of view, it is highly unlikely governments will accept any code which restricts their ability to alter the structure, operations, or loyalties of the TNEs. These differences of approach also prevent agreement on codes directed at TNEs.

To assess the usefulness of the codes requires an understanding of the objectives sought through the codes by the signatory governments against which the effects of the provisions can be measured; or, it requires an independent assessment of what is likely to be achieved, regardless of the objectives sought. Other worthwhile objectives may be achieved, even though they were not initially the ones sought by the signatory governments.

For example, there may be some playacting among the governments negotiating these codes. It is quite conceivable that one of the objectives of the codes (unstated) is to remove the pressure for further action against the TNEs. If the signatory governments can appear to be taking strong and positive action to constrain the enterprises, calls for further constraints of a mandatory or legislated nature may subside. The enterprises could then move rather readily within the voluntary guidelines laid down without much fear of further interference. The objective, then, would be to provide the enterprises with considerable freedom by diverting the complaints over their behavior or impact. One has the impression this is at least partly the purpose of the OECD code: to demonstrate to the developing countries that the behavior of the enterprises can be altered marginally, yet adequately, for the purposes of the host governments, without destroying their usefulness in terms of efficiency and economic growth. The success of this approach depends on the degree to which the host governments feel threatened by the concerns enumerated earlier and consider that the only remedy is to break up or seriously constrain the activities of the TNEs.

Information Gathering

Before governments can be effective in guiding or altering the behavior of the enterprises, they need to know the effects of their constraints on company decisions. Constraints which do not produce the result desired, but an alternative and potentially undesired result, are of course counterproductive. Such a constraint would be one which attempted to guide technology transfers, but in fact merely set up obstacles preventing the transfers from being made. Another example relates to information disclosure, for however necessary information is for policy formation, it appears that codes are likely to be inefficient and ineffective for the purpose of obtaining information. Voluntary codes are not likely to produce useful information unless extensive bureaucracies are set up to gather and interpret the information. In addition, questions of discrimination between national and international companies are raised that are likely to lead to interminable debates over the scope of the codes.

It would be much better to draft national laws, harmonized among countries, to produce within each country the similar sorts of information needed to make appropriate decisions. Immediately it would be evident the type of information that the Ivory Coast, Taiwan, or South Korea wants would differ somewhat from that which is wanted by Mexico, Argentina, or Peru. The national laws would, in fact, be quite different, and exchanges of information among the states would not produce what each of them wanted in terms of the worldwide operations of the enterprises. It will be found even that specific countries, such as Canada and Germany, would have considerable difficulty passing national laws requiring domestic companies to produce the detailed information wanted from the foreign-owned enterprises. Pushing the discussion into the arena of domestic legislation points out the very serious problems which underlie the calls for information disclosure through codes. Codes are, therefore, an effort to sidestep or circumvent the serious difficulties raised by the legislative approach.

Regarding the usefulness of codes in obtaining information on company activities, we may conclude that *national* codes, having the force of law, *can* produce the information desired at least as to the activities inside of the host country, but it is doubtful that they can force disclosure of worldwide data. An international code also will run into substantial difficulties in obtaining appropriate and useful information.

Achieving Specific Results

The usefulness of codes in achieving specific results or re-quiring specific activities on the part of the companies also varies according to the source of the codes. A nationally-based code which requires exports by the foreign-owned affiliate can be implemented through a negotiation with the company or through statutory regulations, specifying precisely the volume of production that must be exported. And an adequate sur-veillance procedure can be constructed to make certain the provision is fulfilled. However, at the international level, the vague provisions that "the balance of payments position of the host government must be taken into account in decisions by the foreign-owned affiliate" or that "exports should be promoted to the maximum extent feasible" are likely to be nothing more than an entrée for subsequent discussions between the companies and each host government. A com-pany may "take the balance of payment situation into account" and still do nothing constructive about it. Conversely, it cannot promote exports "to the maximum extent feasible" for each host country; it will have to make trade-offs among them, likely seen as *non*-maximizing by one or more of them.

Therefore, most of the provisions in the international codes urging a specific company act or performance are without useful content. Similarly, the provision of an international code urging "the promotion of collective bargaining, under the laws of the host government" is hortatory. It does little more than open the door for subsequent discussions. The existence of the national laws is what is operative, not an international code provision urging operations that coincide with national laws. Code provisions urging "compliance with the laws and regulations of the host countries" are also nonoperative, and imply that the enterprises are not presently so complying. In fact, this type of provision is aimed not at the companies, who can be made to abide by national law through the power of the national government or courts in the host country, but at the home government; it emphasizes that host-country law supersedes and cautions against extraterritorial interference. Such a provision is nothing more than an invitation to negotiate among the two governments. Such negotiation can take place without a code; however, the existence of the code may predispose the home-country government to enter such negotiations and to be more compromising.

Preventing Specific Acts

Also, code provisions directed at preventing specific company acts are achieved better through national laws and enforcement mechanisms. For example, the extensive code provisions covering restrictive business practices are quite suitable to national codes, where they can be followed up through surveillance and enforcement mechanisms. To try to achieve international agreement on the specific restrictive practices has proven impossible over the past thirty years; they were first attempted under the old International Trade Organization Charter. Efforts within the United Nations have not succeeded either, and efforts to harmonize antitrust laws hardly have gotten off the ground. Even where statutory law appears similar (the United States, Japan, and Germany), the interpretation of permissible acts of companies is quite different. If there were agreement regarding the nature of the acts to be prohibited, implementation of the prohibition under an international code would require an extensive bureaucracy because of the substantial powers of sovereignty by the signatory governments.

Provisions aimed at prohibiting acts of corruption and bribery are also best handled at the national level. There is no reason why the government of either the host country or the home country cannot make such acts illegal, and legislation of that type would be much more forceful than an international code abjuring such activity. All an international code could do in this area would be to encourage national governments to apply their own laws and to pass such laws where they did not exist. This alone might be useful, but it certainly would not be successful by itself. Provisions of this sort in international codes, therefore, are neither necessary nor sufficient conditions to achieve the goal desired.

Code provisions directed at acts in third countries are even more tenuous in their effect. For example, an international code that prevents discrimination against minority groups, when such discrimination remains not only permissible but is practiced within a given host country, is unlikely to be effective in that particular country. Under the United Nations' concept of prohibiting interference in domestic affairs, it is probably inappropriate for an international code to proscribe discrimination in hiring based on sex, race, or creed. Despite the offense to human sensibilities, such discrimination does exist and is not prohibited in all countries of the world.

In the area of preventing specific acts by companies, the best an international code can do is to focus attention on particularly undesirable activities and therefore hope to obtain correction at the national level—that is, through national legislation or regulation.

Setting Orientations and Expectations

We come then to the kernel of the usefulness of international codes: they can focus the attention of both governments and transnational enterprises on emerging problems, preparing both for subsequent legislation and regulation *and*, it is hoped, raise the expectations of all parties for a higher level of ethical conduct on the part of the companies and government officials. Although the code provisions are unlikely to be specific enough to require precise ethical behavior on the part of any company or government official, they can focus on the issue. The code provisions, therefore, provide an ethical setting within which the game is to be played. It is this purpose that company-promulgated codes serve best. Thus, the Caterpillar code does not specify particular acts for its officials, but enunciates an orientation, putting them on notice that this orientation is held by top management and should be reflected in all company activities. Such a public announcement alters the setting of negotiation with host governments when the company seeks to enter a particular country or to negotiate a change in its operating conditions. The company code states not only that the company will judge itself by high standards, but that the host government should also judge it by the same high standards. This should put the negotiations on quite a different footing from that of adversary proceedings. Similarly, a nationally promulgated code would put all companies on notice that they will be judged by the same standards and that none will be given a favored position through significant differences in negotiation results.

A code of behavior signed by the international companies for themselves would state, in effect, that the signatories would expect to be judged by the high standards of the code and that they would be prepared to justify any deviation from these standards. Whether all TNEs could bring themselves to such an agreement is another question. But an international code they could sign among themselves would certainly alter the nature of the discussions concerning the issues raised by their growth and spread around the world.

Since specific acts should be enumerated or prohibited by law, if they are desired of all enterprises, no code agreed to by companies should seek to alter *specific* activities or policies. Rather, it should set forth agreement on those necessary ethical orientations essential to the maintenance of freedom and continuation of corporate decision-making. These include honesty, truth, equity, and community responsibility. The institution of private enterprise, operating in a market, requires (a) the passage of truthful (relevant) information among buyers and sellers (and to regulators), (b) the fulfillment of promises, a part of *any* capitalistic system of production, and which requires honesty, (c) the adjustment of contractual relationships under changed circumstances to achieve equity and (d) demonstration of a sense of belonging in and continuing responsibility to the community.

All of these assurances place the conduct of the signatories at a level higher than required by law, though no higher than required for the protection and maintenance of a free society.

If the TNEs expect to be treated as *world* citizens, they must act like *citizens*, accepting full responsibility and setting the highest examples. And they must be willing to call to account members of their group who violate the *spirit* of the code. If TNEs required such conduct internally and demonstrated such a code externally, much of the concern over their power would be dissipated. And the dialogues which remained would be set in a much more cooperative atmosphere.

Similarly, and finally, an intergovernmental code of behavior signed among either the developing countries or among the major members of the United Nations would be essentially a stage-setting exercise. It would indicate the basic expectations of governments concerning the development of the TNEs. In order to set such a stage, however, a fundamental problem would have to be resolved—that of the basic role of the TNEs in the international economy: is it one largely determined by the companies themselves or basically determined by governments in line with their objectives of efficiency, equity, participation, creativity, and autonomy?[9] If the former, codes are probably desirable in setting the ethical limits of the decisions taken by the companies. If the latter, codes are basically unnecessary, although they may be desirable in setting the ethical framework. Unless these limitations on the nature and effectiveness of codes is recognized, their promulgation is likely to lead to unfulfilled expectations and further frustration, directed at the companies and undeservedly so.

In sum, the promulgation of codes is an ineffective surrogate for coming to grips with the fundamental question of the role the TNEs should play in the new international economy. This role must be determined, and it can be determined only in the light of the specific areas in which the TNEs can be useful. These areas include those of energy, food, nutrition and hunger, industrialization, development of the world's resources, environmental protection, equitable distribution to the benefits of economic growth, means of developing self-identity and national pride, provision of mass-consumption goods and services, rising educational and health levels, and so forth. Merely to turn the transnational enterprises loose does not necessarily direct them towards the solution of these problems. Nor will a code of conduct alter their direction or impact significantly in relation to these particular problems. Of much greater importance is an effort to utilize the capabilities and resources of the TNEs to meet developmental goals in an equitable and creative manner.

While this effort is already begun at the national levels, it needs to be accelerated at regional and international levels, taking into account the necessity to redeploy industry around the world and to relocate research and development activities in order to provide all countries at least some role in industrial creativity. Task-oriented and system-oriented efforts would be required to direct the TNEs to the problems of regional development, agribusiness growth, creation of complex transportation systems, urban-industrial development, international complementation arrangements, resource development, and so forth.

The present rejection of the approach of using the TNEs in solving these worldwide problems stems not only from the lack of information about the operations and capabilities of these enterprises, but also from a general rejection of the dominant position they have achieved within the world economy. Both the lack of understanding and this dominant position can be rectified, but only if there is closer government-business cooperation in understanding the problems and the alternative solutions available.

Once the mystery of business operations and government objectives is removed, cooperative efforts can be mounted. With such cooperation, the need for codes is largely removed, and the same results will be achieved within the specific task assignments undertaken by the transnational enterprises. However, codes, having the limited objective of raising expectations and focusing on issues that will eventually have to be met in other ways, are not undesirable. What is undesirable is to expect concrete results to come from the mere enunciation of codes. It is likely, therefore, that the small results that can be expected from codes are not worth all the negotiating effort that has been going into them. Quite appropriate guidelines for stage setting can be agreed on without requiring accord on specifics at the international level. Specific requirements still are best left to national regulation affecting behavior within the national economy. Only within (and after creation of) a new international economic order can an international code become specific as to policies and operations of TNEs. In the meantime, promulgation of detailed governmental codes can be avoided only by TNEs adopting high levels of ethical behavior, enunciated either through company or international industry codes, and demonstrated by appropriate actions.

Part Three

Editor's Previews

Dr. Max Parrott, president of the American Medical Association, gives us an inside look at the ethical decisions doctors must make every day. He tells it like it really is—from the vantage point of a truly great doctor.

Leon Jaworski invokes his own vast experience and great names in history to buttress his argument that the lawyer's position at the focal point of American justice demands adherence to exemplary professional ethics.

However well you may understand the role of certified public accountants in our economy, you will gain a new insight into the respective responsibilities of client, government, and accountant by reading Clifford Graese's essay. If you are a CPA, you'll read it with pride, too.

Conflicts of interest in government service are detailed and documented by Andrew Kneier, who maintains that regulations prohibiting favors often do not provide adequate means for enforcement.

In his incisive historical overview of labor union ethics, Kenneth Fiester details how unions have used stringent codes of ethics to deal with the abuses and corruption that have been a part of the union movement.

Honesty and Professional Ethics: Focus on Medicine

Max H. Parrott, M.D.

University of Connecticut researchers conducted an opinion poll a few years ago in which respondents were asked to rate twenty professions in terms of truthfulness, competence, and altruism. People were inclined to rank physicians in the number-one spot for truthfulness and competence, the researchers found, and second only to clergymen for altruism.

Subsequent polls by other organizations have tended to confirm the same basic finding: most people consider their physician to be highly ethical.

Ethics is one of those words that defies precise definition. Whole volumes have been written on the subject seldom arriving at a simple, yet comprehensive definition of the word. For our purposes let us just agree that we are talking about the proper or improper behavior of individuals or groups within the framework of society.

A physician's relationships within society encompass more than his relationship to his patient. Also to be taken into account are his relationships to other physicians, to his profession as a whole, and, perhaps most important of all, his relationship to himself.

A physician's pride, his proficiency, his relationship with himself, all have profound effect upon his intellectual honesty

161

—the inner turmoil of honest judgment. In his everyday practice, he must honestly gather facts, properly weigh those facts, make allowances for applicable variables, come to a proper and honest diagnostic conclusion, and appropriately prescribe treatment or a referral.

Thus the code of physician-to-self and physician-to-physician consultant is complicated and, in turn, the covenant with the profession itself—the teaching debt, the educative payback, and other professional obligations—are not without complexities. The contract with the patient has been put under severe stress from extrinsic forces. The means, methods, and modes of compensation have been forced into new and untried molds with effect and affect on professional behavior. This is not to mention the spectre of retrospective critical and punitive review in the form of peer standards, if not the form of professional liability. However, for the sake of simplicity, one cannot separate the ethic of honesty in medicine into intellectual and economic compartments. They hold as one.

Honesty, by definition, must be a positive ethic, a freestanding, worthy end-point, but when placed in certain contexts or environments, can it, does it, show more than one face? I will explore this with the focus on medicine and on medical practice.

Thought in medical practice is substantially a unified process. There is usually only one brain held responsible for coordinating the care and treatment of any given medical problem. Committees cannot practice medicine efficiently. Let's start then with one physician in various processes of fact finding, diagnosis, and treatment.

He ought not to undertake a case with some preconceived notion based upon an impression, style, or fancy, although that is frequently done. A recent rash of cases of hypoglycemia (low blood sugar), diagnosed from a variety of symptom patterns, may be an example. The frequent diagnosis of hypoglycemia almost seems like an epidemic. The upsurge in the incidence of such cases cannot be justified wholly on scientific grounds because scientific methodology hasn't changed. Rather, it seems to stem from a patient-pressure situation which demands an answer—any answer—to a complex of symptoms that satisfies a certain pseudo-scientific aura.

The practice is intellectually dishonest but, fortunately, it usually doesn't balloon into a major ethical problem because it is normally recognized by only one mind (the physician's) and often results in a certain amount of patient satisfaction.

Another obstacle to honest thought processes behind a diagnosis is what the Romans called *post hoc ergo propter hoc* ("after this, therefore because of this"). It's an error in logic that is as old as mankind, devoid of the scientific method, and related to a sort of faith mysticism. It is a fallacious method of reasoning, a denial of the hard fact cause-and-effect relationship. It is not only a dishonest approach, it can have disastrous consequences.

Sound thinking behind a diagnosis must be founded not only upon a solid base of scientific knowledge, but also upon true facts of happenstance—facts tempered by judgment based upon experience. This is the nature of intellectual honesty in diagnosis. Anything less would be deemed dishonest, negligent, and most emphatically unethical.

The same sort of sound thinking—in which the patient's well-being comes first—ought to be carried over into the areas of treatment and referrals to other physicians for consultation. In actual practice, unfortunately, it doesn't always work that way. When it comes to choosing a consulting physician, for example, such things as pride and economic considerations may affect sound, ethical judgment. Pride comes into play when a physician establishes a large referral base among his colleagues, perhaps to enhance his status, perhaps to bolster his own self-esteem. Economic considerations enter when a physician comes to an understanding with a colleague that "I'll refer my patients to you, if you'll refer yours to me." It's the old I'll-scratch-your-back-if-you'll-scratch-mine syndrome, with no compensating consideration of excellence.

Either way, the patient and his problem become secondary considerations. Judgments based upon pride or economic considerations, if observed by a physician's peers, would be deemed unethical behavior, and condemned as such. But these things allow a lot of room for rationalization, so the practice has become fairly widespread.

A large extrinsic problem in this area of appropriateness of referrals is the recent tendency of physicians to be herded—or to herd themselves—into closed groups, such as so-called health maintenance organizations, in which the referral base that can be compensated for is narrowly limited. This tendency could be laced with an unethical flavor, were it not for the fact that it is actively favored by the government and widely accepted by society.

The covenant with the profession and obligation thereto has in itself some sticky problems of ethics. It is true that we were taught and should teach in return. But to what extent ought our teaching obligation impinge upon the care of our patients? Take an everyday example: I have an implied contract with my patient to provide his medical care or to supervise those who provide his care. But as soon as he, or she, is hospitalized in, let us say, a community hospital with university teaching affiliations, the so-called "cluster" system takes over. In effect, the care of my patient is removed from my control to that of the resident staff, for "benefit of teaching."

This is unethical because it is predicated upon a deception. It takes an exceedingly strong, stubborn attending physician to buck this type of system; and his efforts are likely to achieve only limited success. A lesser man might retreat into the non-teaching environment; but then he is lost as a teacher and his patient is lost to the clinical base of teaching.

Another example is in the field of surgery within a teaching setting. The deception here may be extreme or it may be very little at all. The extreme would be an absolute taking over by the resident staff; but there are many in-between degrees of takeover. A first-year resident as a first assistant, or as an operator assisted by the attending physician, slows any surgical procedure considerably. This may or may not be bad, but if time in surgery is accounted on an economic sliding scale, it represents an unethical exploitation of the patient. What balance, then, are we to strike between code and covenant?

There are two ethical aspects related to doctors and patients that have been in the forefront of recent days: patient solicitation and patient exploitation. These come under the general category of patient-doctor relationship or what, in this discussion, we call the contract or the implied contract between the physician and the patient. Other problems within this same category are confidentiality, full disclosure, identity, and communications. There is a twist of honesty and ethics in all of these categories also.

Solicitation of patients through advertising was deemed unacceptable professional behavior by the American Medical Association as long ago as 1847, when the association was founded. The action was taken to avoid the implicit warranty associated with blatant advertising—the sort that used to be associated with peddling of snake root oil and other "miraculous" cures. So complex is the human mechanism that any such offer of warranty is in itself a lie, and unethical. Other means of communication were deemed by the AMA to be dignified, in keeping with true professionalism, and therefore acceptable.

Recently, however, the Federal Trade Commission has brought suit to annul the provision in the AMA Code of Ethics that prohibits solicitation of patients through advertising. It may be some years before the issue is finally resolved.

As to the other current ethical issue in the news, exploitation (meaning compensation for medical care based upon deception), it is by definition unethical. Even so, it shows up in medical practice in many, often subtle, ways. An example is the so-called "unnecessary" surgical procedure.

If a given procedure is indeed unnecessary, then there is no question it is dishonest and unethical. But the whole concept of unnecessary surgery hinges upon a definition of what is, or is not, necessary. A universally acceptable definition of "necessary" or "unnecessary" surgery has yet to be devised.

The process by which an intellectually honest physician decides whether a given procedure is necessary often includes a number of factors that probably never are considered by critics of the medical profession. The needs and wants of the patient are entered by the physician into his judgmental equation, along with whatever pathology is involved. The equation seeks to balance the worth of the outcome procedure against the risk of an unfavorable outcome. Oftentimes the necessity of a procedure stems not so much from the patient's biological circumstances as from the necessity of the patient to be able to support himself financially, or to have his quality of life improved. A perfectly honest physician might decide to go ahead with the procedure while another physician, equally honest, would decide the procedure is unnecessary.

Risk-taking in medicine is almost constant, particularly in this litigious age of malpractice suits. But this again has more than one facet as far as honesty and ethics are concerned. And these facets are not always back to back, as in the case of the traditional other-side-of-the-coin illustration. Granted, the physician and surgeon are always at risk. This is a way of life and a part of their built-in responsibility to the patient on a one-on-one basis.

The question is: Just how much of that risk should the physician cover and still be fair to the patient? Consider the doctor who takes a super defensive posture. He may call for a battery of tests and procedures, aimed more at protecting himself than the welfare of his patient. A point can be reached when his attitude of leave-no-stone-unturned-for-my-own-protection becomes an unconscionable burden on the patient, in the form of an adverse benefit-to-cost ratio. It then amounts to an economic rip-off of the patient, wholly unethical.

Continuing with the above example, we need to consider the economic factors that inevitably taint such cases. Is the doctor being defensive only, or is he just coining the patient's dough? The one extreme becomes an exercise in cowardice on the physician's part, while the other is a study in greed—neither of which could we equate with honesty or ethical behavior.

It is felt on balance that some risk must be taken. It is the nature of the game. Disclosure to the patient is the offset. Whether that disclosure is full or complete or understood by the patient can only be assumed by the professional judgment of the attending physician. The fact that the prospective nature of that judgment may become subject to retrospective legal review will depend upon how firmly the patient believes in his doctor's honesty. If the doctor's judgment was, in fact, honest and the patient believes it, there is no problem. And what could be more ethical?

Two important concepts are involved here: identity and communication. Identity refers to the physician's ability to deal with his patient as a person, rather than as an abstract medical problem to be solved. Communication refers to the physician's ability to present the patient with the facts in his case: the diagnosis, the implications of that diagnosis, the treatment required, and the potential risks.

Now all this sounds simple enough on paper; but for a physician to put it in practice is quite another matter. It is actually the toughest part of medical practice. "The practice of technically excellent medicine is easy," goes an old cliché, "it's only the people who are difficult." This includes not only the patient, but the personality behind the patient, and the family behind that personality.

This often has an effect on the physician through a mechanism known as "patient pressure" which, in turn, creates overtones in the field of ethics and honesty. And it also has profound effect on the physician in his role of advocate for his patient in the world of medical institutionalization; that is, in an adversary relationship with the hospital, the third parties, and government agencies. The pressure imposed by this advocacy can have a bizarre, inside-outside effect on the physician who is basically ethical and honest.

For instance, a patient will frequently request, or even insist upon, treatment that is not in his own best interest—such as "shots" of penicillin for upper respiratory infections. Or the patient may demand that the physician "doctor" the facts so that he will be eligible for a job to make some insurance plan applicable. Or, he may demand time and attention of the physician that could more wisely be used for someone more seriously ill.

Conversely, hospitals and third-party payers have been known to rip-off the patient, and in a variety of ways. It is not exactly a secret that hospitals now charge for what they used to give away as a service. The price of drugs in a hospital is apt to be a lot higher than at the pharmacy around the corner. And the hucksterism of some insurance companies, peddling health policies that scarcely are worth the paper they're printed on, is legendary.

In all of this the doctor is right in the middle. And, being in the middle, he sometimes finds himself condemned by the patient as unfeeling or lacking in compassion on the one hand; and, if he takes the patient's advocacy role too strongly, damned by the institution as a troublemaker on the other hand. Even so, it is the physician's uncomfortable responsibility to stand for the patient against the institution to protect the quality of his patient's care and to assure a fair price for the goods and services rendered. This is a part of his contract and responsibility to the patient and must be a part of his advocacy for the patient. This advocacy must be honest, and, if so, it is an intrinsic part of the ethic of the physician's professionalism.

Although understanding and human compassion are among the attributes of most medical practitioners, medicine cannot and should not be practiced by shrinking violets. The decisions to be made are too tough and too complex for vacillation, particularly if the whole exercise is to be held within the intellectual and material framework of ethics and honesty.

Another factor that falls within the concept of the doctor-patient contract, or relationship, is the maintenance of confidentiality from the patient's point of view. This is a basic canon of medical ethics, but one that is becoming increasingly difficult to hold clearly and not compromise. The numbers of nonprofessional people required in doctors' offices to help process claims, the demands of government agencies, and an unbelievable variety of governmental regulations are making a shambles of whatever privacy the patient thinks he has, or thinks he is entitled to.

Most patients are simply not aware that they have signed away much of their privacy in their application for reimbursement from an insurance company or a government health program. The crux of the problem is: How much information is it essential to reveal, and who is to determine what information is to be supplied in any given circumstance?

In my view, the physician, and only the physician, is entitled to make these determinations. After all, who else has access to the whole story? Who else had the patient's confidence within the doctor-patient relationship to obtain the whole story? And, who else is in a position to violate or protect that confidence?

Physicians are confronted with this kind of problem almost every day. Consider, for example, the case of a woman patient who (a) has recovered from an operation performed partially to relieve a psychosomatic condition involving pain, and (b) decides she now wants to receive further disability payments from her insurance carrier because of that condition.

In such a case the physician must try to answer some questions: Is the patient's psychosomatic condition honest and genuinely disabling? (It must have been so in the first place, or it would not have warranted surgery.) Is the continuing disability honest on the part of the patient, or is it merely a gimmick for added disability compensation?

If it's just subterfuge, what ought the physician report to the carrier? Does he have permission to report it? Does the carrier cover the patient to this extent? And so on. In many such cases, questions of relative honesty and dishonesty could be avoided if the physician would only sit the patient down and explain to him his rights of privacy, and the extent to which that privacy would be diminished if compensation by a third-party carrier were insisted upon.

Depending upon the circumstances of the patient's case, the physician might have to explain the stigma and the societal price that may go with such disclosure. He would need to spell out the third party's contractual responsibility to the patient, and the patient's to the third party.

Often such conversations between the doctor and his patient do not take place, or if they do are not done well because they are time consuming and difficult. But they really ought to occur more often if the ethic of doctor-patient confidentiality is to be maintained. The problem is: Who but the attending physician is in a position to initiate that conversation if, in fact, confidentiality is to be maintained? Who but the physician has the ethical responsibility to do so? This has honesty as an ethical device written all over it, but still falls back on the human judgment of the attending physician.

Another gray area of doctor-patient confidentiality involves certain instances in which the patient's state of health is a matter of interest or concern to society. It is always the patient's prerogative to order his records disclosed. President Gerald R. Ford recently ordered his physician to make his medical records available to the public. But what of the airline pilot, whose work involves flying passengers? Ought his entire medical record be made an open book, or only those pages that could affect his work and the safety of his passengers?

Should the record be kept entirely private within the doctrine of doctor-patient confidentiality?

We can apply those same questions to other patients—the teenager with a case of VD, or the Army veteran who clearly has homicidal, suicidal, or other antisocial tendencies.

Only the attending physician is in a position to make the final decision in such questions. And his judgment must be based on the protection of all parties involved.

Proper compensation of the medical practitioner is a subject that encompasses many ethical problems. Solving them is not made any easier by the sheer complexity of various payment mechanisms, complicated further by various sorts of government interference, regulations, and controls. In such circumstances it should surprise no one that nearly everyone involved—physicians, hospital administrators, insurance-company people, government people—sooner or later becomes befuddled by it all. Mistakes and misunderstandings are inevitable.

The complexity of payment mechanisms leads to occasional fraud, too. But the available evidence indicates that fraud by physicians is not nearly so widespread as press reports might lead one to believe.

In 1974, for example, the Social Security Administration ran a computer check to identify those physicians who were receiving more than $25 thousand a year in Medicare reimbursements and whose patterns of practice differed sufficiently from their peers as to suggest that investigation would be in order. The computers spotted 1,329 physicians—about six-tenths of 1 percent of all physicians who treat Medicare patients—whose patterns met the above description. Their cases were turned over to Medicare's insurance carriers to determine whether the services provided by those physicians were medically necessary.

Investigations by the carriers indicated that 174 of the physicians—slightly over one in ten of those spotted by the computer—had received overpayments from Medicare. But in only forty-two instances did the cases seem to warrant further investigation for possible fraud.

In the news recently have been reports of mass-produced medical care, largely to Medicare and Medicaid patients, involving such things as unnecessary lab tests and kickbacks to cooperating physicians by the laboratories. I believe no one knows for sure how widespread these practices are. But they are clearly fraudulent, dishonest, and unethical.

Even if such laboratories are honestly run and produce quality work—and in some cases that appears to be open to question—the charges for their work must be passed on to the patient.

For his part, the practicing physician is entitled to nothing beyond his own costs in these transactions, plus whatever part the results of ethical lab tests play in his overall judgment. Anything more is exploitation of the patient. The room for rationalization and mental gymnastics in many of these situations is fantastic, and again it comes down to intellectual honesty as an ethical device, and its effect on the ways and means of compensations. Thus, economics and intellectual exercise are inseparable within the field of ethics.

The manner in which a physician charges for his services need not involve fraud or rationalization to have unethical overtones. Whether he charges interest on past-due accounts, for example, depends, or at least ought to depend, upon what information the physician gave the patient at the time the service was provided. Traditionally, physicians have considered charging interest on past-due accounts to be unethical. Recent thinking is that any problem of ethics is offset by full disclosure at the time of the service.

Finally, a few words about professionalism in medicine: what it is, how to keep it. As I mentioned earlier, Americans tend to see their physician as a man or woman who is unusually truthful, competent, and altruistic. By all odds, we ought to be all those things, and more. To be deemed a "professional" by reason of an M.D. degree, and then to be licensed to practice medicine, carries with it implicit obligations of acquired knowledge, emotional stability, intellectual capacity, ability to communicate, understanding, and compassion. But a professional also must have the ability to make hard, honest judgments tempered by all the forgoing characteristics. This is an ideal of professionalism seldom achieved by the average physician, but worth shooting for. It's an ideal that salvages the professionalism needed to achieve the best ethical standards.

If the physicians' public image is false—if we allow ignorance, stupidity, self-indulgence, arrogance, negligence and/or incompetence to take any part in the way we ply our practice—then our professionalism is a sham. We have all heard the "horror stories" about physicians who had a favorite surgical procedure or a pet potion they treated all comers with, whether the patient needed it or not. Although they are the exceptions, it would behoove the 99.9 percent of us who are not that sort of physician to help winnow out those exceptions from the practice of medicine.

The place to start is with the selection committee at the medical school. The ethics of honesty begin directly at the point of selection and continue through medical school, advanced training, continued education, and into the way the practitioner practices.

The selection process cannot be so perfect as to never let a student leave without a degree. This is the old pass-through-no-matter-what syndrome and it is more flagrant now than it has ever been. But the selection process ought to include parameters beyond those of grade-point averages alone.

It is really quite obvious that those in the learned professions, as well as in the business community, have suffered greatly from a lack of unbiased training in ethical and philosophical studies during their student years. What they have had has been largely distorted by the preconceived attitudes of others and a variety of mystical approbations.

American education should be overhauled to include solid, unbiased philosophical training in its curricula, preferably beginning at the elementary school level. It is our failure to teach honest philosophic values that has brought this country to the brink of some kind of behavioral disaster.

The scientific method must be brought back into good grace. It must be used honestly and applied rationally to social problems. In the full human equation, there is no middle ground to honest facts, honestly gathered, honestly considered, which result in honest conclusions and honest human action. If the areas are gray and complex, then honest judgments must be made by a professionalism that strives to maintain the highest standard of honesty in the performance of its duties within the total ethical framework of society.

Principles of
Medical Ethics

American Medical Association

Preamble These principles are intended to aid physicians individually and collectively in maintaining a high level of ethical conduct. They are not laws but standards by which a physician may determine the propriety of his conduct in his relationship with patients, with colleagues, with members of allied professions, and with the public.

Section 1 The principal objective of the medical profession is to render service to humanity with full respect for the dignity of man. Physicians should merit the confidence of patients entrusted to their care, rendering to each a full measure of service and devotion.

Section 2 Physicians should strive continually to improve medical knowledge and skill, and should make available to their patients and colleagues the benefits of their professional attainments.

Section 3 A physician should practice a method of healing founded on a scientific basis; and he should not voluntarily associate professionally with anyone who violates this principle.

Section 4 The medical profession should safeguard the public and itself against physicians deficient in moral character or professional competence. Physicians should observe all laws, uphold the dignity and honor of the profession and accept its self-imposed disciplines. They should expose, without hesitation, illegal or unethical conduct of fellow members of the profession.

Section 5   A physician may choose whom he will serve. In an emergency, however, he should render service to the best of his ability. Having undertaken the care of a patient, he may not neglect him; and unless he has been discharged he may discontinue his services only after giving adequate notice. He should not solicit patients.

Section 6   A physician should not dispose of his services under terms or conditions which tend to interfere with or impair the free and complete exercise of his medical judgment and skill or tend to cause a deterioration of the quality of medical care.

Section 7   In the practice of medicine a physician should limit the source of his professional income to medical services actually rendered by him, or under his supervision, to his patients. His fee should be commensurate with the services rendered and the patient's ability to pay. He should neither pay nor receive a commission for referral of patients. Drugs, remedies or appliances may be dispensed or supplied by the physician provided it is in the best interests of the patient.

Section 8   A physician should seek consultation upon request; in doubtful or difficult cases; or whenever it appears that the quality of medical service may be enhanced thereby.

Section 9   A physician may not reveal the confidences entrusted to him in the course of medical attendance, or the deficiencies he may observe in the character of patients, unless he is required to do so by law or unless it becomes necessary in order to protect the welfare of the individual or of the community.

Section 10   The honored ideals of the medical profession imply that the responsibilities of the physician extend not only to the individual, but also to society where these responsibilities deserve his interest and participation in activities which have the purpose of improving both the health and the well-being of the individual and the community.

Honesty and Professional Ethics: Focus on Law

Leon Jaworski, Esq.

Writing about legal ethics at this point in American history has its hazards. We have seen more change in the makeup of the legal profession and the rules governing lawyers' conduct within the past dozen years than ever before in our history, and the near future rather clearly holds more major developments in store. And, unfortunately, we are without the perspective of history—the clear eye that comes with distance from events—that would be of such immeasurable value in attempting to describe the current state of legal ethics in the United States.

Even without the advantage of detachment in time we can, nevertheless, describe some of the significant events of the last few years and tentatively assess the importance of these occurrences to the legal profession and its ethics.

Of greatest short-term importance to the legal profession has been the adoption in all states of the revised Code of Professional Responsibility. The code was approved by the American Bar Association in 1969, to become effective 1 January 1970, after more than five years of study and debate. The select committee that drafted the Code of Professional Responsibility was given the awesome task of presenting a modern, coherent set of rules that preserved, explained, and identified principles basic to the functioning of the legal profession in a modern society. Their product was an entirely new approach to the problems inherent in defining standards prescribing the conduct of as large and diverse a group as is found in the American legal profession. We shall say more about this code, looking closely at its treatment of lawyers' ethics.

Almost equally important to lawyers was the recognition by the Supreme Court of the United States that legal services are constitutionally required in many circumstances and that lay organizations may play a role in furnishing such services even though legal ethics are violated. The Supreme Court's involvement in these issues began in 1963, when the court held in the famous case of *Gideon* v. *Wainwright* that the due process clause of the United States Constitution required that indigent persons accused of felony crimes should be furnished legal counsel for their defense. In the same year the Supreme Court in *NAACP* v. *Button* held that a Virginia statute prohibiting the NAACP, a lay organization, from soliciting business for its attorneys was unconstitutional because it abridged First Amendment rights of expression and association. Prior to *Button*, state statutes that prohibited direct or indirect solicitations by attorneys or their agents had been uniformly upheld. The case created for the first time a constitutional justification for furnishing legal services through a group arrangement. The two cases opened a Pandora's box of possibilities that has not been exhausted today, and indeed appears to be barely tapped. Developments traceable to these cases and their progeny will also be examined more fully.

Constitutional doctrine on furnishing legal services and the permissible vehicles for delivery of these services was not the only significant force at work on legal ethics in the 1960s. A third catalyst for change was the "war on poverty," which in the Economic Opportunity Act of 1964 had as one of its programs legal services grants to community action programs. The Legal Services Program became a separate division of the Office of Economic Opportunity in 1965 and over the following years became the means of furnishing lawyers to millions of clients who had never before received legal assistance. The success of the scheme was evident to all, even though traditional canons of ethics were often violated in the administration of the offices. A result was the general recognition by enlightened lawyers and legislators that some forms of group legal services that departed from tradition offered significant advantages to the public and required some ethical reorientation.

A further pervasive impact on the legal profession and its ethics resulted from the increasing application of other federal laws to lawyers' ethics. Once the public demand for legal services became obvious, and the need was identified, both Congress and the executive branch (through the attorney general and various administrative agencies) began to bring pressure for change in the legal profession's principles. When *Goldfarb* v. *Virginia* was decided by the Supreme Court in 1975, its holding that antitrust laws prevented lawyers' controlling fees through controlling minimum fee schedules struck a blow to a practice that some members of the profession had defended for many years.

Running through all these developments was the theme that the public interest required a reexamination of practices that have become indefensible and unacceptable in a society that had needs which were constantly shifting and being redefined. Lawyers were both in the vanguard and wake of this reform movement, often quarreling among themselves about policy and direction and tone, but always debating the issues and taking sides.

It was this sort of associational activity that set in motion the fifth great shift in ethics. Lawyers were surprisingly responsive to public outcries that the profession protected itself and its members at the expense of the public and embarked on a study of the enforcement of discipline and its deficiencies. The Clark Committee, headed by retired Justice Tom C. Clark of the United States Supreme Court, began its 1970 report with this bold statement:

> After three years of studying lawyer discipline throughout the country, this Committee must report the existence of a scandalous situation that requires the immediate attention of the profession. With few exceptions, the prevailing attitude of lawyers toward disciplinary enforcement ranges from apathy to outright hostility. Disciplinary action is practically nonexistent in many jurisdictions. . . .

This forthright opening was followed by chapter and verse documentation of the ills besetting self-regulation of lawyers including concrete recommendations for curing those ills.

Sixth and last, as a result of Watergate, which saw the forced resignation of a president who was a lawyer and the trial and conviction of numerous of his advisors who were lawyers, the profession began to rethink the rules of ethics that govern its conduct. Never before in American history had members of the legal profession been participants in such a conspiracy; the public outcry that followed forced the profession to look anew at its educational, licensing, and disciplinary processes.

PROFESSIONAL RESPONSIBILITY AND THE CODE

Everyone in the legal profession agrees that lawyers must assume the "ethical" and "public" responsibilities of membership in the legal profession. Surprisingly, there is even a semblance of agreement about what those responsibilities are. Dean Howard Sacks, while director of the National Council of Legal Clinics, listed three elements of professional responsibility: 1) legal ethics, 2) the lawyers' special obligation to use those talents peculiar to the lawyer-professional for the betterment of the society in which they function, and 3) competent performance of client counseling. In the landmark speech that has continued to influence professional thinking since its delivery in 1934, Chief Justice Harlan Stone pointed out that the lawyer was particularly qualified to solve the problems of a "sorely stricken social order" because he was "specially trained in the field of law and government, invested with the unique privileges of his office, experienced in the world of affairs, and versed in the problems of business organization and administration." Stone questioned "whether the professional school has done well to neglect completely the inculcation of some knowledge of the social responsibility which rests upon a public profession [without doubting] the power of [professional schools] . . . to impart a truer understanding of the functions" of the legal profession. In the Fuller-Randall Report on the 1958 Conference in Professional Responsibility, held in Boulder, Colorado, the lawyer's public responsibility was said to include "an affirmative duty to help shape the growth and development of public attitudes toward fair procedures and due process"; "a clear moral obligation" to make legal services available to all who need them and to furnish competent counsel to men with unpopular causes, and a "special obligation . . . to interest himself actively in the improvement of the law" and to use his special insights about problems of implementation "to improve public discussion of political and economic issues."

In both the Stone speech and the Fuller-Randall report the canons of ethics were regarded as only the starting point for an analysis of lawyers' professional responsibility. Chief Justice Stone deprecated the canons, describing them as "generalizations of an earlier era" that were largely concerned with "petty details of form and manners." More generously, the Fuller-Randall Report dismissed them with the brief observation that "a letter-bound observance of the canons is not equivalent to the practice of professional responsibility."

Even granting that "traditional" lawyers' ethics are narrow in their demands, it is nevertheless the lowest common denominator of professional duty. The canons, in whatever form, state a minimum standard or level of ethical norms for the regulation of lawyers. When one goes beyond them to questions of "broader" responsibility, it becomes increasingly important to recognize that the term used is "responsibility," which connotes something quite different from "duty." As the standard shifts from conduct prohibited to conduct hoped for (for example, from prohibiting subornation of perjury to exhorting representation of unpopular causes), the difficulties of ethical enforcement increase geometrically. In the peripheral areas of professional responsibility lawyers' attitudes and values are often the determinants of their behavior and, whether the behavior is considered desirable or undesirable, may be a subjective judgment of the observer.

Critics of the ABA's Canons of Professional Responsibility began to be heard soon after the adoption of the original thirty-two canons in 1908. In 1928, 1933, and 1937 special committees of the association returned reports recommending overall revision of the canons, and in 1954 a distinguished committee of the American Bar Foundation made a similar recommendation. It was not until 1964 that the association's

House of Delegates created the Special Committee on Evaluation of Ethical Standards at the request of then-President
Lewis F. Powell, Jr., who now serves as an associate justice of
the United States Supreme Court. That committee recommended an entire new code, rather than amendments to the
old canons, because: "The present Canons are not an effective
teaching instrument and they fail to give guidance to young
lawyers beyond the language of the Canons themselves. There
is no organized interrelationship of the Canons and they often
overlap. They are not cast in language designed for disciplinary enforcement and many abound with quaint expres-
sions of the past."

In addition to the structural flaws and substantive omissions
and errors, the committee also noted the impact of Supreme
Court decisions affecting traditional ethical rules concerning
group legal services, admission to the bar, and discipline of
lawyers.

The objectives of revision were stated by Professor John F.
Sutton, Jr. of the University of Texas School of Law, who
served as reporter to the committee, as requiring success in
four areas:

> (1) A proper code of ethics must appeal to the reason and
> understanding of the lawyer, and yet it must also serve as a
> basis for discipline. (2) A proper code of professional responsi-
> bility must identify, explain and preserve those principles that
> are basic to the proper functioning of the legal profession in
> modern society. (3) A proper code of professional responsi-
> bility must provide the lawyer serving as advocate with spe-
> cific, authoritative standards. (4) A proper code of professional
> responsibility must be in harmony with proper, modern
> methods of marketing legal services.

Viewed from another perspective, a code that attempts to set
standards for protection of the public welfare by regulating
lawyers' conduct must balance several competing claims. To
serve the public interest the bar must satisfactorily achieve a
balance of rules that affect a lawyer's relationship with other
lawyers, his relationship with those whom he represents, and
his relationship with the government that franchises him. For
example, the code must resolve, however imperfectly, the inevitable conflict arising when the lawyer, on the basis of the

information given him because he has entered into an attorney-client relationship, must decide whether to preserve a client's confidences or reveal that the client has committed a crime or perpetrated a fraud.

The issues are not easily resolved, and the difficulty is increased by the peculiar role and function of our courts and lawyers in the American system of government. The judiciary is one of the three branches of government and is charged with peculiar duties to review and avenge acts of the other two branches, the executive and legislative. Commenting on this, the Supreme Court of Utah said in 1943:

> The present status of the attorney in our judicial system has been a result of historical development which dates back for some seven centuries. Regardless of what may have happened in some jurisdictions to the rights and privileges of attorneys, the right to practice before the court as an officer of the court, still remains. While doctors, plumbers, electricians, barbers, etc. may sell their time and skill to the public by virtue of their license from the state, the attorney alone has the right to set the judicial machinery in motion in behalf of another and to thus participate as an officer of the court in a judicial proceeding. This right springs from his status as an officer of the court. To properly function it is necessary that courts retain control of their officers. The attorney's part has developed until he now is a necessary and essential part of our judicial machinery.

In the same vein the American Assembly on "Law and a Changing Society II" held at Stanford Law School in 1975 noted that its recommendations for change and reform required the legal profession's cooperation.

> Our legal system depends upon the legal profession for implementation. Lawyers and the organized bar have a special obligation for the proper functioning of that system, for its improvement and for assuring that its benefits are extended equitably to all citizens. Each of the recommendations previously set forth carries with it the implicit corollary that lawyers should undertake its accomplishment in appropriate forums and through appropriate mechanisms. If, for example, the public interest demands, as it does, that legal services be provided for the poor or that certain business of the bar be eliminated through changes and simplification in substantive and

procedural law, the legal profession has the primary responsibility to see to it that these objectives are carried out.

Implicit in such statements as these is that lawyers must respond to public needs even if personal sacrifice is required. Denying self-interest lies at the heart of legal professionalism.

Also built into the inherent difficulty of framing a code of ethics for lawyers is the system, known as the adversary system, of finding truth. Few Anglo-American institutions are as revered by lawyers as this device for adjudicating disputes. But in framing ethical prescriptions for seeking truth through its instrumentality, certain limitations must be noted. Chief among these is an acceptance of a certain relativism in truth. Judge Simon Rifkind, a distinguished former jurist serving as United States District Judge for the Southern District of New York and president-elect of the American College of Trial Lawyers, related a trial to the search for truth by concluding that "the object of a trial is not the ascertainment of [absolute or objective] truth but the resolution of a controversy by the principled application of the rules of the game." For better or worse, attorneys accept this compromise; the possibilities of improper resolution of a dispute pervade law practice, whether the practice is one of trying lawsuits or counseling individuals. This eternal uncertainty of result, and unpredictability, is of course a part of our humanness, but its existence means that the fallibility of human judgment and its testing by a courtroom proceeding make peculiar demands on the person who attempts to impose standards on others.

Lawyers' responsibilities to their clients, their profession, and their community may be stated with different orders of priority, depending on time and circumstances and depending as well on the individual. These possibilities were recognized in the ABA's Code of Professional Responsibility. Nine "principles that are basic to the functioning of the legal profession in modern society" are stated as "Canons." Under each canon are detailed, relatively precise "Ethical Considerations" and "Disciplinary Rules." The ethical considerations are "aspirational in character, and represent the objectives toward which every member of the profession should strive." They guide a lawyer in areas in which he is free to follow his own conscience without external compulsion. Disciplinary rules, on the other hand, are "mandatory in character [and] . . . state the minimum level of conduct below which no lawyer can fall without being subject to disciplinary action." Describing the code in detail would require several volumes, as it is a distillation and abstraction of thousands of opinions of ethics committees and courts. The Canons, however, can give at least the general thrust of the principles:

Canon 1. A lawyer should assist in maintaining the integrity and competence of the legal profession.

Canon 2. A lawyer should assist the legal profession in fulfilling its duty to make legal counsel available.

Canon 3. A lawyer should assist in preventing the unauthorized practice of law.

Canon 4. A lawyer should preserve the confidences and secrets of a client.

Canon 5. A lawyer should exercise independent professional judgment on behalf of a client.

Canon 6. A lawyer should represent a client competently.

Canon 7. A lawyer should represent a client zealously within the bounds of the law.

Canon 8. A lawyer should insist in improving the legal system.

Canon 9. A lawyer should avoid even the appearance of professional impropriety.

Although the approval of the new Code of Professional Responsibility by the ABA and all the state enforcement agencies is the event of single greatest importance in the area of ethics to American lawyers in the last decade, it is quite possible that the matters surrounding delivery of legal services will ultimately be of greater significance. *NAACP* v. *Button*, decided by the Supreme Court in 1963, involved solicitation by the NAACP of clients who were willing to engage in desegregation suits. The NAACP was soliciting legal business and stirring up litigation, and was a lay organization exercising control over lawyers in their employ, all in violation of the canons of professional responsibility. But the Supreme Court found that solicitation in these circumstances was a form of political expression constitutionally protected against either state or federal encroachment. Although Virginia had an interest in regulating solicitation and the unauthorized practice of law, thus limiting first amendment freedoms, the state "failed to advance any substantial regulatory interest, in the form of substantive evils flowing from petitioner's activities, which can justify the broad prohibitions which it has imposed."

Button marked the first incursion into the state's power to regulate aspects of the practice of law on ethical grounds, but it was merely the precursor of cases to come. One year later, in *Brotherhood of Railroad Trainmen* v. *Virginia, Button*—and the First and Fourteenth Amendments—was extended to protect the Brotherhood's practice of recommending attorneys to its members who were injured in railway accidents. The Brotherhood selected these attorneys on the basis of skill and honesty and actively solicited cases for them. Further, the Brotherhood provided investigators for use by the attorneys. The clear result of the plan was to channel legal business to those lawyers in violation of ethical rules. Virginia's rules against solicitation of legal business and aiding the unauthorized practice of law were clearly violated. Nevertheless, the Supreme Court found that the activity was constitutionally protected against those state restrictions:

> The First Amendment's guarantees of free speech, petition and assembly give railroad workers the right to gather together for the lawful purpose of helping and advising one another in asserting the rights Congress gave them in the Safety Appliance Act and the Federal Employers Liability Act (FELA). . . . The right of members to consult with each other in a fraternal organization necessarily includes the right to select a spokesman from their number who could be expected to give the wisest counsel. That is the role played by the members who carry out the legal aid program. And the right of workers personally or through a special department of their Brotherhood to advise concerning the need for legal assistance—and, most importantly, what lawyer a member could confidently rely on—is an inseparable part of this constitutionally guaranteed right to assist and advise each other.

To those who had urged that *Button* was simply based upon the kinds of rights that were protected by the NAACP, the *Brotherhood* decision came as a surprise. The only interests at issue were the common economic interests of the union members in securing full FELA benefits.

The third case in the triumvirate is *UMW* v. *Illinois State Bar Association*. In that case the union employed a full-time attorney to handle workmen's compensation claims of members and their dependents. The attorney's salary was paid by the UMW, and he received no fees for representing injured employees. The union provided injured members with report forms and advised them to complete the forms and forward them to the union's legal department. Secretaries prepared claims, and the attorney then conferred with the employer and prepared his case from the file without consulting the employee. If agreement was reached between the union lawyer and the employer on the amount, the attorney notified the employee, who accepted or rejected the offer.

After the Supreme Court of Illinois affirmed a trial court injunction prohibiting the union from engaging in the unauthorized practice of law, the Supreme Court reversed and held that "the freedom of speech, assembly, and petition guaranteed by the First and Fourteenth Amendments [gave the union] . . . the right to hire attorneys on a salary basis to assist its members in the assertion of their legal rights." The court again conceded to the states the power to regulate the practice of law, but, nevertheless, held that the power was qualified by the first amendment rights of association. "Broad rules framed to protect the public and to preserve respect for the administration of justice can in their actual operation significantly impair the value of associational freedoms." Dangers to the public that Canons 27, 28, 35, and 47 were designed to prevent were too speculative to justify the broad limitation of the union members' rights of association.

Running through these cases is the theme that a group's right of association under the First and Fourteenth Amendments requires that a state show real danger to the public from legal service plans before it can impose restrictions on their activities by ethical regulations.

The controversy begun by these cases has continued unabated. Canon 2, regulating group legal services and the related matters of advertising and solicitation, has been amended three times since 1969, and more change is inevitable. Further, *Button, Brotherhood* and *UMW* opened the door to other kinds of related litigation that questions the organized bar's traditional precepts. This questioning and criticism from within and without the profession has already produced responses by the bar on a national and local level, each directed to improving the delivery of legal services to the American public. Group legal services, prepaid legal services plans, specialization by lawyers, increased use of paralegal assistants, compulsory continuing education, and increasing acceptance of nonlawyers services are all part of the bar's attempt to furnish more and better legal aid to a larger segment of American society. Each change requires a change in legal ethics.

While the bar associations have moved forward to implement a wide range of programs of this nature, they have also devoted increasing attention to improving enforcement procedures. One of the commonly accepted hallmarks of a "profession" is its self-regulation, the maintenance of standards through internal rather than external controls. Because lawyers operate under a state-approved monopoly. over furnishing legal services, they have a correspondingly high duty to justify that authority through exclusion of the incompetent and dishonest. In this area the Clark Committee report catalogued the defects in existing disciplinary machinery and offered solutions to the problems. As a result of that report the American Bar Association in 1973 established the Center for Professional Discipline (under the aegis of the Standing Committee on Professional Discipline) that performs the following services for bar disciplinary agencies throughout the United States:

1. Furnishes advice on disciplinary questions and consults with bar disciplinary agencies and courts.

2. Maintains a Disciplinary Brief Bank of significant disciplinary decisions, periodically distributes a Disciplinary Case Index and makes copies of briefs, pleadings, and materials from the Brief Bank available upon request.

3. Prepares educational materials for disciplinary counsel, disciplinary board members, respondent's counsel, and the judiciary, and arranges for periodic Disciplinary Workshops.

4. Supervises the operation of the National Discipline Data Bank, a central record-keeping source for information on attorneys who have been publicly disciplined by court action or

who have resigned from the bar while their conduct was under active investigation. The Data Bank receives information on attorney discipline from reporting authorities (usually either a disciplinary agency or court clerk) of the highest courts of the states and some federal courts. (When an attorney is publicly disciplined, the reporting authority in that jurisdiction fills out a "Report of Attorney Discipline" form and sends it to the Data Bank. These reports are computerized and quarterly and annual reports of the discipline imposed are prepared and sent to the reporting authorities. This enables a reporting authority to learn when a member of that bar has been disciplined in another jurisdiction so disciplinary proceedings can be initiated based on that disciplinary action.)

5. Supports the Standing Committee in arranging for and conducting conferences for the judiciary and the bar to promote stronger discipline.

6. Distributes, at the request of disciplinary agencies, copies of the "Clark Committee" report entitled "Problems and Recommendations in Disciplinary Enforcement."

7. Compiles and maintains a Grievance Referral List and a library of current disciplinary rules from state, district, federal, special court, and administrative agency jurisdictions.

8. Assists the Standing Committee in drafting and distributes upon request informational pamphlets on ethics.

All of the above activities do little more than illustrate the involvement of lawyers with ethics. In an era that has found lawyers in public disrepute as never before, the irony of the fact that no other profession has shown more concern over its ethics, or done as much to change them, is not lost on the bar. Lawyers have long accepted the theme of this volume—that freedom from governmental control is earned by reason of adherence to ethical norms. Codes of ethics are not properly used as means to protect privilege.

THE FOUNDATIONS OF ETHICS

In 1831 Alexis de Tocqueville, a young man from France, only twenty-six years old but already accomplished in scholarship, philosophy, and statesmanship, was sent by the French government to our country primarily to examine prisons and penitentiaries. He became intrigued by our system of government and its institutions, and therefore devoted considerable time to analyzing life in America. On his return he wrote his classic *Democracy in America*, first published in 1835. This volume represented a wide-ranging study of the political and social institutions of the United States as viewed in 1830. Scholars have commented that the result of de Tocqueville's visit to America and the writings that followed brought forth not only "the greatest book ever written on America, but probably the greatest on any national polity and culture."

Perhaps one of the most significant conclusions he reached relates to the legal profession as it manifested itself in the day of his study. He wrote: "In visiting the Americans and studying their laws, we perceive that the authority they have entrusted to members of the legal profession, and the influence that these individuals exercise in the government, are the most powerful existing security against the excesses of democracy."

Perhaps even more striking was this statement: "The profession of the law is the only aristocratic element that can be amalgamated without violence with the natural elements of democracy and be advantageously and permanently combined with them. I am not ignorant of the defects inherent in the character of this body of men; but without this admixture of lawyer-like sobriety with the democratic principle, I question whether democratic institutions could long be maintained; and I cannot believe that a republic could hope to exist at the present time if the influence of lawyers in public business did not increase in proportion to the power of the people."

And finally he concluded: "The lawyers of the United States form a party which is but little feared and scarcely perceived, which has no badge peculiar to itself, which adapts itself with great flexibility to the exigencies of the time and accommodates itself without resistance to all the movements of the social body. But this party extends over the whole community and penetrates into all the classes which compose it; it acts upon the country imperceptibly, but finally fashions it to suit its own purposes."

Now, let us reexamine the lawyer's role in the American society in more recent years. When my friend E. Smythe Gambrell was president of the American Bar Association, there emerged a most worthy volume entitled *The Lawyer's*

Treasury. President Gambrell wrote the foreword on 13 July 1956. Following is one of the paragraphs of that foreword:

The lawyer exists to serve the public. He is a priest in the Temple of Justice and, as Daniel Webster so aptly said, "Justice is the great interest of man on earth." We must train the finest men for the law, men who will pursue the law in a high spirit of public service. Over the years lawyers have not been tradesmen in the market place. As professional men both in England and America they have lived by their own high code of ethics and their own moral and educational standards. They may well be proud of their record as architects and builders of our free society.

I read this volume of classic gems several years ago and again recently. I found it of special interest to contrast the comments and observations of two decades or more ago with the challenges the legal profession faces today, and I found them to be largely the same. The stark fact that rises above all others, is whether complexities of society in contemporary times are causing us to be neglectful of the obligations and responsibilities lawyers have recognized in days past as belonging peculiarly to their profession.

I also found in this volume a thought-provoking article by Reginald Heber Smith, an eminent Boston attorney. His concern was not only with the great vista of opportunity but also with the concomitant responsibility that, as he put it, "lie ahead for legal education in America." Mr. Smith had long taken a deep interest in legal aid—in fact, he was one of the pioneers in this cause when he served as counsel to the Boston Legal Aid Society from 1914 to 1918 and as chairman of the American Bar Association's Committee on Legal Aid from 1921 to 1936. He observed: "If the Bar, therefore, is to state quite honestly the measure of its participation in public life, it must admit that law-trained persons maintain a complete monopoly over one branch of government and considerable control over the other two."

Quoting a staff member of the director of the Bureau of the Budget, he wrote: "The attorney [in government service] should be a trustworthy source of legal counsel. More distinctively, he should have a sure touch in the fine art of human and institutional relationships. And finally he should be what is best described as a clearheaded philosopher of democratic governance, quietly effective within the institutional framework of public administration."

And finally, referring to Dr. Esther Lucille Brown's book on *Lawyers, Law Schools, and the Public Service* he concluded: "The Bar is responsible in no small measure for determining the future of our society and, as a consequence, its own future. From this responsibility it cannot escape except by relinquishing, or being forced to relinquish, a considerable part of its intervention in public affairs."

The I came across another great contribution to legal lore— a treatise entitled *Abraham Lincoln . . . Profession, A Lawyer.*

What caught my eye in particular was the statement by the author, William L. Ransom, president of the American Bar Association in the years of 1935 to 1936, that described Lincoln as a man who "was ever at war with those lawyers who stirred up litigation and strife, for their own gain. He said, in language apt today: 'A moral tone ought to be infused into the profession which should drive such men out of it.' "

Speaking further of Lincoln, Mr. Ransom adopted the words of Chief Justice John D. Caton of Illinois, saying: "His great reputation for integrity was well deserved. The most punctilious honor ever marked his professional and private life. He seemed entirely ignorant of the art of deception or of dissimulation. . . . I venture the assertion that no one ever accused him of taking an underhanded or unfair advantage in the whole course of his professional career."

Every now and then I hear a great sermon. I heard such a sermon last year when the pastor of The First Presbyterian Church in Philadelphia filled the pulpit in The New York Avenue Presbyterian Church in Washington. His sermon was on the subject of seeking a city. He took his text from Hebrews 11:10: "For he looked for a city which hath foundations, whose builder and maker is God." When in his sermon this preacher laid out the elements of a city "which hath foundations," he said: "Seek the Law, Seek the Word. Seek to do good. The old truth remains, you see, that you cannot achieve good by evil means. Apparently nothing is so difficult to understand in our present society. The tired old excuse is still that the end justifies the means. It has always been wrong. It is wrong still."

What this minister was driving home is the word from Holy Writ that there is no way that a nation or a state or a community—or a profession, if you please—can blossom and flourish into greatness unless it has foundations of truth and integrity.

It is basic that as good citizens the older generation as well as the younger generation must concern themselves, and deeply, with the problems of government, both international and domestic, with peace, with economic soundness, and with social gains. But this is not enough; more is needed. As these challenges are faced, we must ever hold before us the pronouncement of Thomas Jefferson at the time he was drafting the Declaration of Independence: "The whole art of government," he said, "consists in the art of being honest." And if you consider this comment to be an oversimplification of the art of government, then let me express to you my firm belief that Jefferson's premise at least must serve as the foundation of government, and if the honesty of which he speaks is absent, sooner or later the affairs of government are sure to fail.

This is a very timely topic. It pertains not only to law students and lawyers, but to students in business schools and other institutions of higher learning as well. Note with me, if you please, Howard Flieger's comments on the Editor's Page of *U.S. News & World Report,* 29 September 1975:

> If moral education is about to make a comeback, there are those who are convinced it is just in the nick of time. They trace rising crime, political chicanery, even inflation, the federal deficit and setbacks in foreign policy to a nationwide decline in moral and ethical values that have been eroding at an accelerated pace for years.
>
> The world is littered with the ruins of societies destroyed by irresponsibility. We cannot succeed by trying to treat the symptoms—crime, anger, hostility, poverty and war. We must seek the root causes and deal with them.
>
> Any signal of increasing interest in the study of morals and ethics can be taken as an indicator that today's young people do, indeed, care about such things.

In 1974 the American Assembly, in its Forty-eighth Annual Report, criticized the advocacy system as one that often "conceals and distorts the truth." This is a sad commentary indeed, for the objective should be just the opposite—a search for the truth. In the following year, the American Assembly and the American Bar Association met jointly at Stanford Law School. Again these conclusions were reached: "The legal profession should . . . formulate ethical prescriptions embracing a higher professional duty to seek the truth." This comment followed: "Lawyers are administrators of justice as well as advocates of clients. Lawyers and those training for the practice of law have an affirmative responsibility to nurture justice and truth."

One of the great tragedies of Watergate, looming quite large, was the involvement of an inordinate number of lawyers who engaged in immoral conniving, conspiratorial scheming, and just plain unprincipled conduct. Time and again the truth was shunned and falsehoods were embraced. The people of America, whose trust they held, were lied to. The very individuals who as government officials should have set exemplary standards, prostituted their obligations and responsibilities. This is a dark page—a very dark one—in our history. Still the breaches of faith and trust and their aftermath are small by comparison to the disasters that will befall the legal profession and society once the barriers of moral responsibility now required of lawyers are reduced by easy stages to meaningless words.

To be realistic, we must expect some failures and scandals involving lawyers from time to time, just as there are misdeeds among the members of other professions, regardless of the action the legal profession takes to discipline itself. My overriding concern is the attitude of indifference exhibited in preserving the profession as one of trust and honor, not only by lawyers who have practiced at the bar for decades, but also by those who are entering the profession now.

We take an oath as we are admitted to the bar which itself is to impress us with our responsibilities. A model oath is printed at the conclusion of this essay. We become officers of the court which itself is to bring home to us the responsibilities we shoulder in the due administration of justice. Are these merely perfunctory procedures? Are these obligations lightly assumed and quickly forgotten? As Dean Lyman Patterson, dean of the Emory University School of Law, has so aptly put it in correspondence with me: "The private lawyer is, of course, in many respects a public official."

I know of no lawyer of fame at the bar I admired more than Charles Evans Hughes. While doing postgraduate law work in Washington, I heard this illustrious lawyer argue a case to the United States Supreme Court. I was so awed by his dignified manner, his clarity of presentation, and his overall advocacy, that the memory of that occasion has been deeply rooted in my recollections.

Truly there has been no greater, no nobler lawyer at the American bar. When he made his presidential address to the American Bar Association 2 September 1925, more than fifty years ago, he said:

> The first aid to the development of expertness in the administration of justice is in maintaining proper standards of legal education *and for admission to the bar*. There is no guarantee of liberty in any true sense in putting the community in bondage to the ignorant. The unlearned practitioner of medicine may deprive the unhappy subject of his life without any due process whatever. The chief losses of society are due to incompetence, and the charges of an ill-informed lawyer whatever they may be, are too high. It should be understood that there is no "unalienable right" of the untrained to practice law and there is no special need of multiplying lawyers at the expense of training. The first duty of Bar Associations in our states, cities and counties is to see that the *unfit as to either knowledge or character are not admitted to practice*. High standards of admission to the Bar will mean less ill-advised litigation *and few hardships for trustful clients*.

Several of the Watergate defendants who pleaded guilty to offenses that placed their licenses to practice law in jeopardy talked with me at length of the aftermath of their guilty pleas. Their concern was not the length of the imprisonment primarily, rather it was whether the license to practice law would be lost. Again the concern was not so much the use of the license in earning a livelihood, rather it was because for the first time they fully realized the real value of being a member of the legal profession—that while other ways of earning a living were open, the honor of being a member of the profession had a deep meaning and a worth beyond the dollars it could be used to earn. One is caused to wonder how many of the lawyers of today, along with those who are students of law, pause to evaluate the real intrinsic worth of the license to practice law.

So we come to the bottom line. What is the profession worth? What is its good name worth? What is it worth to the older generation of lawyers, and to the younger generation, and to the law students? And what will it be worth to future generations of lawyers? Is there any reason for devaluating it as an honorable profession? And finally, who are the caretakers of the profession's stature of honor; who will be the trustees of its good name?

My fifty years as a member of the bar have brought me certain deeply rooted convictions. One of them is that without ethics a lawyer may be the greatest artisan at the bar, the most skilled writer of briefs, the most literary and profound draftsman of instruments, the most persuasive and articulate advocate in the courtroom—yes, he may even be all of these. Yet if he does not invoke and practice the moral requisites of the profession, he dishonors it and fails in the trust reposed in him by his fellowman.[1]

OATH OF ADMISSION

The American Bar Association commends this form of oath for adoption by the proper authorities of all the States and Territories.

The general principles which should ever control the lawyer in the practice of his profession are clearly set forth in the following Oath of Admission to the Bar, formulated upon that in use in the State of Washington, and which conforms in its main outlines to the "duties" of Lawyers as defined by statutory enactments in that and many other States of the Union—duties which they are sworn on admission to obey and for the wilful violation of which disbarment is provided:

I DO SOLEMNLY SWEAR:

I will support the Constitution of the United States and the Constitution of the State of ....;

I will maintain the respect due to Courts of Justice and judicial officers;

I will not counsel or maintain any suit or proceeding which shall appear to me to be unjust, nor any defense except such as I believe to be honestly debatable under the law of the land;

I will employ for the purpose of maintaining the causes confided in me such means only as are consistent with truth and honor, and will never seek to mislead the Judge or jury by any artifice or false statement of fact or law;

I will maintain the confidence and preserve inviolate the secrets of my client, and will accept no compensation in connection with his business except from him or with his knowledge and approval;

I will abstain from all offensive personality, and advance no fact prejudicial to the honor or reputation of a party or witness, unless required by the justice of the cause with which I am charged;

I will never reject, from any consideration personal to myself, the cause of the defenseless or oppressed, or delay any man's cause for lucre or malice.

SO HELP ME GOD.

Honesty and Professional Ethics: Focus on Accounting

C. E. Graese, CPA

The distinctive characteristic of every true profession is its willingness to place its personal interest secondary to that of the public it serves. In exchange for assuming this responsibility, the public grants to it certain rights, privileges, and the prestige of professional status. Professional status is not self-bestowed, nor is it granted in perpetuity. Indeed a profession will continue to be recognized as such only so long as it continues to be responsive to the needs of the public it serves.

To help protect their status, most professions have voluntarily adopted formal codes of professional conduct or ethics which they enforce through various forms of self-regulation. Salutary as this may be, however, more than a code of ethics is required to justify the retention of professional status. Codes do not always focus adequately on the profession's responsibility to the public, sometimes over-emphasizing relationships among members of the profession, nor are they always enforced as diligently as they should be. On the other hand, professionals are often unjustly accused of failing to live up to proper ethical standards when their professional judgment does not turn out to be infallible or when a misunderstanding arises as to the responsibility the professional has assumed, or should have assumed. The accounting profession shares all of these characteristics with the other recognized professions. Yet in many ways it differs significantly. Therefore, a proper first step in focusing on honesty and professional ethics in accounting is to identify and explore these differences.

Most recognized professions, such as medicine or law, lay claim to a body of technical knowledge which is generally not shared with the laity, at least in its more advanced or technical concepts. Communication in the technical aspects of their bodies of knowledge is usually confined among fellow professionals. This is not true in accounting. Accounting is the language of business. Many individuals receive their formal education in accounting, but pursue their livelihood working as accounting employees of business, rather than engaging in professional practice. Although they have generally fulfilled all of the necessary educational requirements for becoming a professional accountant, they have chosen not to go the additional step of seeking to become licensed because they do not intend to practice publicly. Contrast this with the fields of law or medicine; few individuals complete the educational requirements necessary to enter those professions without taking the added step of becoming licensed. Indeed, there is little room to earn a livelihood with the technical knowledge they have gained, except as licensed practitioners. However, in most states it is possible to engage in some forms of public accounting practice without being licensed. For example, none of the "Income Tax Accountants" who hang out shingles each January are licensed Certified Public Accountants (CPA). Thus in focusing on professional ethics in accounting, it is necessary to draw a clear distinction between accountants practicing as licensed professionals and those who are employed as accountants in the broader sense of the term.

Closely related to the above difference is a second which deals with the nature of the service rendered. Again, contrasting accounting with law or medicine, one finds in the latter two fields the principal objective of the public in utilizing the professional service is to get the benefit of the professional's technical competence. But, in accounting, the client is frequently as competent as the professional, seeking primarily to add credibility to his financial statements in the eyes of third parties through the independence and objectivity of the professional accountant's opinion. This technical competence on the part of the client also enables him to form an opinion on the competence of the professional accountant. Much less is left to trust than, for example, in medicine.

This leads us to a third difference. In public accounting the ultimate beneficiary of the service rendered may be a third party or parties unknown to the professional accountant. As indicated above, the client who engages the accountant may have little direct need for the technical knowledge of the professional, but may require the accountant's service primarily to add credibility to his own financial statements in the eyes of third parties or the public. Because of this, the relationship between the accountant and his client becomes particularly important. The professional accountant must be totally independent of his client, both in fact and in appearance, if third parties are to rely on his objectivity. While professionals in the fields of medicine and law are not expected to lose their objectivity, the specifics of their relationship to their client are not significant. Indeed, they are expected to be direct advocates for their client's welfare, to assume a mutuality of interest with their clients. In contrast, in accounting there is a presumption that a dichotomy of interests or views may exist or develop between the third party beneficiary of the accountant's services and the client. Consequently the accountant cannot be viewed as an advocate for one if he is to remain credible to the other. This is, at times, a very narrow line, requiring a keen sense of balance. Thus the appearance, as well as the fact, of independence from his client is of vital interest to the professional accountant.

A fourth difference is the manner in which accounting is practiced professionally. Many accounting firms have, of necessity, become very large organizations. A single professional engagement may require several hundred professional personnel working simultaneously in various parts of the world. Legal and medical services, on the other hand, are generally rendered to a client in a single location and in a highly personal manner. To be sure, teams of physicians or lawyers may be involved in a single professional undertaking, but not on the scale which exists in the accounting profession. As a consequence, accounting firms range in size up to twenty thousand professionals per firm. Competence, integrity, and other matters of professional performance become matters of firm policy and practice, as well as personal characteristics.

The professional accounting firm also practices in a unique legal climate. It is highly susceptible to litigation for civil damages. As already mentioned, the very size of some of the accounting firms indicates that their aggregate resources are such as to make them worthwhile targets of litigation. More significantly, because the ultimate beneficiaries of their services are third parties who may number in the thousands on any one engagement, the exposure is significant. Additionally the federal securities laws in the United States are so written that it is not necessary to prove reliance on the work of a professional accountant in order to establish a legitimate basis for damages against the accountant. Indeed, when financial statements on which the public accountant has expressed an opinion turn out to be in error, the burden of proof shifts to the accountant to establish that his work was not negligent.

Finally, it is noteworthy that the role of the accountant is still very much in an early stage of evolution. Professional public accounting as we know it today is basically only forty years old. While CPAs have existed in the United States since the late 1890s, it was not until the passage of Federal Securities Laws in 1933 and 1934 that the role of the professional accountant as we know it today began to emerge. Consequently there is yet a great deal of misunderstanding between the professional accountant and the public as to the nature and extent of professional responsibilities assumed. More critically, these responsibilities are still very much in the process of growing, and as new roles are assumed, some difficulty is to be expected.

To focus properly on professional ethics in accounting, it will also be helpful to consider background information on the licensing, regulation and code of ethics of the accounting profession. As in most professions, licensing of accountants is accomplished by state boards in each of the fifty-four states and jurisdictions of the United States and its territories. While there are some minor variations in experience and educational requirements, the accounting profession is unique in that a single uniform written examination is utilized by all of the jurisdictions. This examination is prepared and graded by the American Institute of Certified Public Accountants (AICPA) on an anonymous basis, thereby achieving a high degree of uniformity in testing technical competence as a prerequisite to entrance into the profession. If an applicant is successful in passing these examinations, and meets other criteria, he is granted a professional license by the state to practice in its territory. Reciprocity between states does not require another examination because uniform examinations are used. The right to continue to practice is governed by state boards, who have the power to revoke or refuse to extend licenses to practice. In line with a recommendation by the AICPA, a growing number of states are requiring annual continuing professional education as a condition of retaining the license to practice.

The AICPA is the voluntary national professional organization. Each state also has a voluntary professional organization, most often referred to as a State Society. While many CPAs are members of both the Institute and one or more state societies, concurrent membership is not required. The AICPA promulgates standards of ethics and professional conduct as well as technical performance standards. In addition, it maintains significant research and professional education and development services for its members. Each of the state societies has a code of professional ethics which is identical, or similar, to AICPA's code. Both AICPA and the state societies maintain disciplinary machinery to sanction, suspend, or expel members who do not adhere to the Bylaws and Codes of Professional Ethics of their respective organizations. A unique joint disciplinary program has recently been adopted by the accounting profession under which the AICPA and most of the state societies have agreed to merge their disciplinary machinery into a single program. Not only will this avoid duplication, but it will achieve a higher degree of uniformity of disciplinary enforcement throughout the United States. Under this procedure, the results of a single hearing apply to the accountant's membership in the AICPA and each of the state societies to which he may belong. Although suspension or expulsion from the AICPA or state societies does not preclude continued practice, the possibility of such action and related publicity is a significant deterrent to the disregard of professional responsibilities. Further, the sanctions imposed may require attendance at professional development programs and, if sufficiently serious, could result in a referral to the state board for consideration of license revocation.

For further background, a brief discussion of AICPA's Code of Ethics will also be helpful. As previously stated, each of the state organizations has an identical or similar code. The accounting profession has always placed a great deal of emphasis on its Code of Ethics. Its structure and its content are somewhat unique, indicating this high level of concern. The Code was completely revised in 1973. Since that time there have been a number of revisions or additional interpretations of the rules. Basically, the Code of Professional Ethics consists of four categories of ethical standards. The first, Concepts of Professional Ethics, is a philosophical essay suggesting behavior which CPAs should strive for beyond the minimum level of acceptable conduct set forth in the Rules of Conduct. The second category, Rules of Conduct, consists of the enforceable ethical standards. The third category, Interpretations of Rules of Conduct, consists of interpretations by the AICPA's Professional Ethics Division providing guidelines as to the scope and application of the rules. Although all disciplinary actions must be brought under the Rules of Conduct, a member who departs from Interpretations has the burden of justifying such departure in a disciplinary hearing. A fourth category, Ethics Rulings, consists of rulings made by the AICPA's Professional Ethics Division, each of which summarizes the application of the Rules of Conduct and Interpretations to a particular set of factual circumstances. As in the case of Interpretations, members who depart from rulings in similar circumstances may be required to justify such departure in the event of a disciplinary hearing on charges brought under the Rules of Conduct.

For practical reasons, rules of conduct or professional codes of ethics, just as statutory laws, are generally written in the negative; that is, they define what is unethical or illegal rather than what is ethical or legal. It is generally not practicable to define the distinction in any other enforceable way. For this reason, rules of conduct seldom deal effectively with desirable levels of conduct; they speak only to the minimum level of acceptable conduct. The AICPA was very conscious of this and therefore in its latest restatement added a Concept of Professional Ethics section that sets forth the conduct towards which CPAs should strive in five broad concepts stated as "Affirmative Ethical Principles." They are as follows:

Independence, integrity, and objectivity. A certified public accountant should maintain his integrity and objectivity and, when engaged in the practice of public accounting, be independent of those he serves.

Competence and technical standards. A certified public accountant should observe the profession's technical standards and strive continually to improve his competence and the quality of his services.

Responsibilities to clients. A certified public accountant should be fair and candid with his clients and serve them to the best of his ability, with professional concern for their best interest, consistent with his responsibilities to the public.

Responsibilities to colleagues. A certified public accountant should conduct himself in a manner which will promote cooperation and good relations among members of the profession.

Other responsibilities and practices. A certified public accountant should conduct himself in a manner which will enhance the stature of the profession and its ability to serve the public.

With this background we can begin to focus more specifically on the level of professional ethics that actually exists in the accounting profession today. The accounting profession has certainly been severely criticized in recent years in many respects. If this criticism is valid, one has to conclude that the accounting profession has not adequately lived up to its responsibilities. The accounting profession, although admitting to areas where improvement should be made, believes that much of the criticism is not merited and that newspaper publicity has so over-emphasized the negative that a distorted picture has resulted. Just how valid is all this criticism?

Clearly the accounting profession is not alone; virtually every profession has been suffering recently from very severe criticism. At the root of much of this is the litigious environment which exists today. The vulnerability of the professional to adverse publicity and, therefore, his inclination to settle claims regardless of their merit, has become widely known. The existence of extensive malpractice insurance coverage as a financial resource from which to recover damages, the frequent inclination of juries to grant significant awards when insurance coverage is involved, and contingent legal fees—all have contributed to the present level of litigation. The rules permitting class-action suits have particularly complicated the lives of accountants. In this regard, the legal profession should reexamine the role it has played in creating or abetting the current litigious environment. No one can argue with responsible litigation that seeks proper compensation for damaged parties from those responsible for such damage. On the other hand, when damages sought bear little or no relationship to the professional services rendered, when suits are based on a performance standard of infallibility, or when financial resources are the basis for being included as defendants, such litigation is not responsible. It will, in the long run, significantly increase the cost of professional services or drive them out of existence. Our entire approach to malpractice litigation and insurance needs a thorough overhaul. The legal profession cannot use the role of advocacy on behalf of the client to avoid assessing the consequences of any action on the other parties directly involved and the public at large.

While all professions have recently been subject to considerable criticism, the accounting profession has had some particularly vocal critics who have received widespread media coverage. One reason may well be related to the nature of the accountant's practice. It is seldom of national interest if a doctor or lawyer is guilty of malpractice since, for the most part, the number of individuals directly affected is relatively small. On the other hand, if a major fraud is discovered in a large corporate enterprise, if that enterprise goes bankrupt, if it finds it necessary to restate previously issued financial statements, or if it is found to have made improper payments, it is usually of national interest and, therefore, reported by the financial, if not general, press. Invariably the questions are asked: "Where were the public accountants? Should they not have prevented this?" Since a significant percentage of the public feels these matters fall within the public accountants' responsibility, it follows that in their eyes such events must reflect negatively on the accounting profession. Incompetence, or, perhaps even more seriously, lack of integrity, is therefore automatically ascribed by them to the accountant involved. Unfortunately this is an oversimplistic analysis of the situation. If the patient dies, should the doctor be presumed guilty of malpractice? Ethical behavior rarely conforms to absolute values; for the most part it is heavily dependent on the relationship that exists between the parties involved. Intent and the exercise of due care must be considered. An act or the failure to act in one set of circumstances may be considered totally proper whereas in another set of circumstances such action would be totally unethical. Therefore, judgments cannot be rendered without a more specific insight into the underlying circumstances.

To the extent that the accountant has been a willing party to a fraud or deception there can be no question that such conduct is outside the bounds of professional ethics. To the extent that the accountant has failed to exercise reasonable care or competence in the application of technical standards in the assignment he undertook, there can be little question. However, the situation becomes much less clear if the professional has exercised his best judgment in the performance of his services and such judgment has subsequently been found less than infallible, or if there is a basic misunderstanding as to the nature of services to be performed or responsibility assumed. Should the doctor be found guilty of failing to detect a cancer if he was only asked to set a broken ankle? To be more precise, in the accounting field, if the accountant undertakes a test review of a set of financial statements to add a higher degree of credibility to them, but the third party who relies on them believes the accountant's responsibility was to guarantee the accuracy of such statements, any failure by the accountant to meet the third party public's expectations will undoubtedly be viewed as a failure of professional responsibility; whereas the professional will view the situation as outside the limits of his responsibility and a totally unwarranted assignment of blame. Such a gap is unacceptable both to the professional and to the public. Clearly the ability of the accounting profession to respond to the public's expectations depends not so much on policing basic competence, due care, or integrity, as it does on a better understanding, communication, and agreement as to the responsibilities assumed in a professional role. This need is probably more critical in the area of accounting than in any other profession. One reason this is so critical is because the ultimate beneficiary and user of the professional accountant's work, the third-party public, does not come in contact with, or deal directly with, the accountant. The results of the accountant's work are communicated to those who rely upon it through a relatively brief report, written in what must of necessity be somewhat technical language. While some of the third-party public may be familiar with the technical language of accounting and, therefore, have little difficulty in interpreting the accountant's report and accompanying financial statements, others of the public are less sophisticated, may totally misread the results, and may come to an entirely erroneous conclusion. Would we not expect similar problems if the doctor could only communicate his diagnosis and suggested treatment in a single one-way written communication?

Another reason why the need for better understanding is so critical can be paraphrased—is accounting an art or a science? Unfortunately, many people who are users of accounting data fail to realize that the determination of income or the value of an asset is not absolute, but, rather, is highly dependent on a large number of assumptions. Perhaps the most significant of these is whether the business will continue in operation as presently conducted, change its direction, or cease operation, all of which relate to the future. When the conduct of business or economic circumstances change, it may well be that previously issued financial statements no longer remain appropriate, even as they relate to the date they were issued, because the assumptions on which they were based are no longer appropriate. Unless the reader of financial statements realizes this, he is likely to misinterpret the amounts as absolute rather than conditional values and scream foul if the conditions do not hold.

Perhaps all of these are merely accountants' rationalizations that may or may not be applicable in any given situation. And, even if they are applicable, cannot, or should not, the accountant be doing more to find an acceptable solution?

In addition to following up on complaints received from the public or members of the profession, the AICPA monitors the financial press for the restatement of previously issued financial statements of any public company, any litigation involving a member, or any other acts involving a member. If the situation turns out to be one which involves a matter of ethics, or possible failure to live up to professional standards, an investigation file is opened. The AICPA has also established a program with federal government agencies for referral of any cases which may involve failure to comply with professional standards. Attempts to set up similar referral arrangements with banks and other financial institutions have been unproductive.

Disciplinary actions of the CPA profession are highly confidential. Investigations and findings are published only when a member is found guilty of an ethics violation by a duly constituted Trial Board. Consequently, statistics regarding complaints and findings on ethics are sparse. It is possible, however, to draw some conclusions from those that are available. During the fiscal years 1970 through 1974, the American Institute of CPAs opened 595 official investigations of AICPA members. Of the cases concluded in that period, approximately 20 percent resulted in suspension or expulsion from AICPA membership. Approximately 35 percent resulted in censures and approximately 45 percent resulted in a finding of not guilty. It is interesting to note that in spite of comprehensive monitoring procedures, relatively few cases involving outright dishonesty or loss of integrity have been discovered or reported. Some complaints have involved a lack of independence or of professional competence, and some have involved disputes between the client and the accountant regarding fees or other contractual differences, but by far the majority of the complaints have involved differences between two or more practitioners, typically in the area of encroachment upon another's practice or in solicitation of clients. These statistics, sketchy though they may be, lead me to several conclusions:

1. The number of complaints received by the AICPA is very small in comparison to the total membership, which exceeds one hundred thousand and encompasses the practice of several times that many of the members' professional staff. In part this is undoubtedly due to reluctance to file complaints, but it is also probably fair to conclude that relatively few, but highly publicized, cases are unduly affecting the public's view of the ethics of the accounting profession generally.

2. Professional accountants have an excellent record for basic integrity and honesty. Unlike competence, these traits can be judged by the laity as well as the professional. The absence of complaints is probably fairly reliable as an indicator of actual conditions.

3. Relatively few complaints are filed against CPAs relating to lack of technical competence. Most of the technical competence investigations are originated by the institute itself based on litigation or items reported in newspapers. No doubt there are many cases where accountants have been less proficient than they might have been, perhaps even some where the client has not recognized this, but it does not appear that lack of adequate technical competence is a serious problem in the accounting profession.

4. While matters of ethical conduct between professionals are the subject of most complaints, these matters, in my opinion, are of relatively low concern to the public. Obviously it is necessary to have harmonious relationships between professionals generally; certainly the public will not long retain confidence in a profession whose conduct amongst themselves is not at a high level. However, many of these complaints relate to matters such as publicity, indirect advertising, dual telephone listings, and recruiting brochures. I believe both the accounting profession and the public would benefit from a somewhat more liberal attitude in this area. Several recent interpretations have moved in this direction, but further reexamination is warranted.

All of this might suggest the state of professional ethics

within the accounting profession is very high and the profession deserves very high marks. Indeed, I believe this to be the case, at least in the sense of integrity, professional competence, and responsibility to their clients. However, a much broader ethical or professional issue emerges. Has the profession lived up to the broader responsibility that entitled it to professional status in the first instance? Has the profession been sufficiently responsive to the needs of the public it serves? I submit that in this area the accounting profession gets a much lower score.

For example, accountants have, for many years, been relatively content to let the public believe they possessed a comprehensive ability to uncover financial frauds or misappropriations. While, indeed, many such acts have been uncovered in the course of audits, both because of the test nature of an audit and the practical limits on what can be done to detect such acts on a timely basis, accountants have made it clear in their own literature that they do not assume responsibility for uncovering such acts; indeed, their typical engagement letter to a client will stipulate this in definite terms. Unfortunately, the general public, I believe, has felt accountants were providing them with assurance that such acts were not taking place within the entity being reported upon by the accountant. I believe the accounting profession must assume a significant share of the responsibility for not making the public more aware and better informed of the degree of responsibility the profession was prepared to assume and, indeed, was generally contracting to assume. While the audit limitations may have been perfectly clear to the management of the clients who engaged them, they were in many cases the very ones perpetrating the fraud.

Similarly, the accounting profession has failed to convey adequately to the public, who are the ultimate beneficiaries, that its opinion on financial statements does not mean that the business entity is financially sound, or is well managed, nor does it mean that statements are guaranteed to be reliable.

The point here is that neither the profession or the public is necessarily right in its view of the degree of responsibility the accounting profession can and should reasonably assume, or at what point the cost of additional assurance ceases to be justified economically. This is something that can and will evolve if both parties are in full communication. Failure lies in the gap that exists between the public's understanding of the auditors' assurance and the profession's knowledge of the inherent limitations of that assurance. Although it was admittedly heavily stimulated by the large number of law suits filed, the accounting profession, to its credit, has now set up a blue ribbon commission under the chairmanship of attorney Manuel Cohen, former chairman of the Securities and Exchange Commission. Its purpose is to investigate the gap between the public's expectation of the accounting profession and the role presently served as viewed by the profession itself. This study, when finalized, should help significantly to reduce the gap and point a way towards the elimination of many of the misunderstandings that have reflected so negatively on the accounting profession. Surely it must be considered a more professional approach than going on strike to protest malpractice insurance costs.

Accountants also must assume a major responsibility for having permitted their technical body of knowledge, the art of accounting, to become very obsolete. Most of the accounting principles in use today were developed in an environment free of inflation, or nearly so. Consequently, it is not surprising the accounting principles in existence today are, for the most part, not adequate to cope with the inflationary economy and, indeed, result in misleading financial statements, at least to the nonaccountant. Accountants have, to a large extent, shared the world's reaction to inflation: namely, that it is highly undesirable, but no one has been able to devise a good solution to it. It is one thing to control or eliminate inflation, but it is quite another to account for it. And, while other areas of accounting principles are also inadequate, quite clearly the most significant deficiencies arise from inflation. In expressing opinions, for too long the accounting profession has de-emphasized the words "presents fairly" and over-emphasized the words "in accordance with generally accepted accounting principles." Let me hasten to add that I believe "presents fairly" can only be interpreted on the basis of preestablished accounting principles, but I also believe that those principles must be kept up-to-date and be reasonably consistent with economic reality—otherwise it matters little how "fairly" the statements conform to the principles. Here again the accounting profession is responding. In virtually every major country it has projects under way today to revise accounting principles to better account for the effects of inflation. It will probably be several years before new accounting models will have been adequately tested and standardized and thus effective in financial reporting. However, it is now clear that a basic methodology is emerging and accounting reports will come far closer to reflecting economic reality than has been the case since inflation became a significant factor.

Accountants can also be criticized for not having dedicated more effort to standardizing and clarifying their principles and standards so 'that better communication with the public could be facilitated. A variety of alternative accounting principles exist today for accounting for the same or similar transactions; reporting formats are frequently confusing. Let me quickly add that responsibility does not rest solely with the professional accountant. Indeed, it is shared by underwriters, analysts, educators, corporate executives, government, and the public itself. Accounting is the language of all business, not just of professional accountants. No one element of the business community can enhance accounting principles without the cooperation and assistance of the other elements. The Financial Accounting Standards Board has been created to ensure that the establishment of accounting principles is based on input and, it is hoped, support from all of the segments of the business community. While it is only a few years old, it has made some notable strides toward achieving some of its goals. But, it is an organization still in its infancy and one that is still experiencing a great many growing pains. It continues to remain in desperate need of full support from all of the elements of the business community if, indeed, it is to meet its objectives.

The accounting profession has also not been alert to how all of the aforementioned shortcomings have been eroding public confidence in the profession. In the final analysis, it matters little if the public is not fully justified in its conclusions; the end result is just as damaging. Perhaps one of the boldest possible actions to restore full public confidence was taken recently when one of the so-called "Big 8" accounting firms engaged one of its competitor firms at a cost of over $500 thousand to make an audit of its professional practice procedures and controls and made public the findings. This "peer review" is now serving as an example for the AICPA in the adoption of an institute-sponsored peer-review program for multioffice accounting firms. I consider this program for monitoring the quality of professional practice to be clearly a most responsive step in meeting the public interest.

In summary, therefore, the level of integrity and honesty in the accounting profession is, in my opinion, extremely high, although the profession is rightfully deserving of criticism for failing to do a better job in being responsive to the broader needs of the public. Let me add that this criticism is not limited to the accounting profession alone. Most professions have, I believe, fallen into the trap of concentrating to such an extent on their technical competence and on the relationship between themselves and their clients individually, that their focus on the broader issue of responsiveness to the public, and society generally, has been dimmed. Thus the medical profession has indeed achieved many medical miracles, but has failed in providing an effective system for delivering the benefits of their science to the public at a reasonable cost. The legal profession, too, must share this general indictment. For example, the advent of no-fault insurance has demonstrated dramatically that the system of litigation that emerged in the automobile accident area served to siphon off a significant percentage of insurance premiums into legal fees for both sides merely to establish guilt, the cost of which, in the final analysis, was shared anyhow by both defendant and plaintiff through higher insurance premiums. Nor does the public generally have a high level of confidence in our total judicial and penal system. But it is not my purpose here to discuss the shortcomings of other professions. I allude to them simply to place my criticisms of the accounting profession in perspective.

One final observation. While I believe the accounting profession is now moving to correct these major deficiencies, progress is impeded to some extent by the litigious environment in which it operates. It is here that help from outside the profession is needed. A profession under constant attack of litigation must operate in a heavily defensive mode. This is not in the public interest since it stymies innovation and diverts a significant part of the profession's effort into defense mechanisms. No one would suggest that any professional who does not live up to the standards of his profession should be given safe harbor from litigation. But it is necessary to develop a clearer understanding among all parties concerned as to the extent of professional responsibility and to recognize that professional judgment carefully exercised does not mean infallibility. The sooner the public, the courts, and the accounting profession clarify these issues to their mutual satisfaction, the sooner the full effort of the profession can be dedicated to devising means of being more responsive to society at large.

Affirmative Ethical Principles

American Institute of Certified Public Accountants

Independence, integrity, and objectivity. A certified public accountant should maintain his integrity and objectivity and, when engaged in the practice of public accounting, be independent of those he serves.

Competence and technical standards. A certified public accountant should observe the profession's technical standards and strive continually to improve his competence and the quality of his services.

Responsibilities to clients. A certified public accountant should be fair and candid with his clients and serve them to the best of his ability, with professional concern for their best interest, consistent with his responsibilities to the public.

Responsibilities to colleagues. A certified public accountant should conduct himself in a manner which will promote cooperation and good relations among members of the profession.

Other responsibilities and practices. A certified public accountant should conduct himself in a manner which will enhance the stature of the profession and its ability to serve the public.

Ethics In Government Service

A Critical Look at Federal
Conflict of Interest Regulation

Andrew Kneier

An official in the Federal Maritime Commission recently held 589 shares of stock in a company regulated by the FMC. He was employed by this company before joining the FMC and had received $25 thousand a year from it over the last twelve years. The company also had maritime operations in the district where the official worked.[1]

The chairman of the Senate Finance Committee, an oil millionaire made richer by the oil depletion allowance, consistently used his committee chairmanship to uphold that tax preference. The depletion allowance was estimated to save oil companies over $2.7 billion annually. The senator has been quoted as saying this was "not a conflict of interest, but an identity of interests."

A former assistant secretary for Mineral Resources in the Department of Interior left the department in 1973 and is now vice president of Atlantic Richfield in charge of oil shale development. Before joining Interior, he was on the board of the American Mining Congress, the mining industry's main lobby in Washington.

A former chairman of the Civil Aeronautics Board (CAB) was treated to a golfing vacation in Bermuda by the United Aircraft Corporation.[2] At the time of this trip, United Aircraft was under special investigation by the CAB.

These examples indicate the kind of conflict of interest situations which can arise in federal service. Certainly the vast majority of federal officials and employees conscientiously avoid such conflicts. But many others do not. Whether it is through stock holdings, gratuities, employment with regulated companies, or other arrangements, these officials open themselves to conflicts between their private economic interests and the obligations of objective public service.

This essay is about conflicts of interest and what should be done to prevent them. First it discusses what a conflict of interest is, and how federal restrictions regarding them raise fundamental ethical issues about government. We will then turn to a critique of existing conflict of interest regulation. This critique seeks to demonstrate the inadequacy of existing restrictions in view of the types of conflicts which often arise. Further illustration of such conflicts will be given to make this point. Finally, the essay will outline various proposals for reform.

CONFLICTS AND ETHICS

The literature in this area presents different views as to what constitutes a conflict of interest. This is a difficult question, and has grown more difficult as government regulation of the private sector has increased. Some argue that whenever a public official has a personal interest in matters affected by his decisions, there exists at least a potential conflict of interest. But this could mean, if not further refined, that a senator's "personal interest" in clean air would create a conflict when voting on amendments to the Clean Air Act. It is somewhat ludicrous to call this a conflict of interest. What about a member of the House Ways and Means Committee, however, who saves hundreds of dollars in taxes every year by deducting the interest on his home mortgage—as do many other Americans —and who uses his position on the committee to uphold the tax provision allowing this deduction? Or what about a member of the Nuclear Regulatory Commission (NRC) who, under pressure from large utility companies and the White House, agrees to expedite the licensing of nuclear power plants?

As these cases suggest, we need to refine the notion of "personal interest" for a better understanding of what a conflict of interest means. To help do this, we should focus on two main kinds of personal interests: political interests and economic interests. The NRC official mentioned above would have a political interest in going along with the industry and the White House. If he refused, he could lose their support and incur their animosity. That could mean diminished political clout, which would jeopardize his ability to affect policy outcomes. Even his political career could be threatened, in which case his political interests begin to mesh with his economic interests.

The presence of political interests that influence votes and other decisions is evident most clearly on Capitol Hill. A legislator's need for private campaign contributions is the best example. There is an obvious political interest in getting reelected, for which most legislators need large amounts of campaign money. Most of this money is supplied by so-called "special interest groups."[3] If a legislator votes against the interests of those who have helped finance his campaign, there is a good chance he will not receive their financial support in future elections. Thus, he has a political interest in voting a certain way. Of course, most legislators receive campaign funds from diverse groups, which makes this game more complex. Moreover, their votes are influenced by political interests which have little to do with campaign financing, such as party loyalty, logrolling, and responsiveness to their particular constituencies.

In short, conflicts often arise between an official's political interest and the fair and unbiased execution of his duties. However, these conflicts are seldom regarded as "conflicts of interest" in a technical sense. Virtually all federal officials become involved in these kinds of conflicts, and it is impossible to eliminate them. Nevertheless, they involve real conflicts of interest in a lateral sense and have immense consequences on policy decisions and official behavior. And although they are part of "politics," it is important to devise ways of minimizing them. For example, the 1974 amendments to the Federal Election Campaign Act, that placed limits on campaign contributions and provided for limited public financing of presidential campaigns, was an important step toward diminishing the political incentives to respond favorably in office to those who give large campaign gifts.

Conflicts of interest are normally defined in terms of an official's private economic interests. Indeed, political and economic interests often intersect, as we have seen. Certainly a legislator's interest in getting reelected, for example, can be economic as well as political. To distinguish sharply between these two requires an impossible splitting of hairs. Interests which are political *in origin*, even though they may involve economic benefit as well, are not usually thought to create a "conflict of interest" for the official involved. Rather, most observers agree that a conflict of interest exists only when an official has a personal economic interest that might jeopardize his objectivity, and only when this interest is not an incidental by-product of overriding political factors. This is also the conception of "conflict of interest" that informs federal laws and regulations in this area.

As a working definition, then, we can accept that, developed by the Association of the Bar of the City of New York in 1960. The association defined "conflict of interest" as a clash between "two interests: one is the interest of the government official (and of the public) in the proper administration of his office; the other is the official's interest in his private economic affairs. A conflict of interest exists whenever these two interests clash, or appear to clash." As the association also noted:

> A conflict of interest does not necessarily presuppose that action by the official favoring one of these interests will be prejudiced to the other, nor that the official will in fact resolve the conflict to his own personal advantage rather than the government's. If a man is in a position of conflicting interests, he is subject to temptation however he resolves the issue. Regulation of conflicts of interest seeks to prevent situations of temptation from arising.[4]

This formulation raises two issues that warrant further comment. One is the nature of the interest with which one's economic concerns clash, or appear to clash, in conflict of interest situations. The other concerns the adequacy of government regulation dealing with such situations.

The association's definition refers to the public's interest in the "proper" administration of one's office. "Proper" is a normative term, and raises the question of what principles and values ought to inform the decision-making process. This question immediately opens endless philosophical debates that cannot be resolved here, if anywhere. But perhaps at least this much could be said: insofar as we are striving toward the ideal of representative democracy, there ought to be an equality of representation in the political process. The interests of everyone should be represented equally. Of course, the interests of everyone are not the same, so we are really talking about the proportional representation of diverse interest groups. Such representation is supposed to result, through compromise and balance, in government responsiveness to the general public interest.

Put differently: there is a general public interest in equality of representation in the decision-making process. This is the nature of the interest that stands in conflict with an official's private economic interest. The "conflict" is virtually inevitable. If an official can benefit economically from a certain decision, then his interest—and the interests of those who would share the possible economic gain—are disproportionately represented in deciding the issue. Equal representation therefore requires economic impartiality on the part of the official making the decision.

From this perspective, government regulation of conflicts of interest is a fundamental ethical issue because the principle of equality of representation is a fundamental norm for government. It is supposed to shape government structures and processes, thereby safeguarding and prompting the representativeness of government instructions. But how well is this norm actually translated into political realities? The answer is a very telling indication of what values and norms really make up the government ethic. It is also an indication of what ethical standards are being reinforced and strengthened. The process is cyclical. Not only are government rules and procedures shaped by operative values and norms, they also serve to perpetuate that ethic.

The point is this: the adequacy of government regulation of conflicts of interest is an important measure of the normative strength of "equality of representation" in the governmental process. An analysis of such regulation is therefore one measure of government ethics. The next section takes a critical look at government restrictions and procedures in this area.

CRITIQUE OF FEDERAL REGULATIONS

One analyst of conflict of interest law has identified five types of conflicts that federal laws and rules seek to regulate: self-dealing by a public official, discretionary transfer of economic value to a public official from a private source, post-employment assistance by former public officials to private parties dealing with the government, similar assistance by current public officials, and private gain derived from information acquired in an official capacity.[5] Here we will focus on just the first three areas and comment on enforcement procedures. These three areas cover the types of conflicts that occur most frequently. They involve stock holdings in companies affected by one's duties, receipt of gratuities, and postgovernment employment in regulated industries.

Stock Holdings

Over the last two years, the General Accounting Office (GAO) has investigated possible conflicts of interest in several executive agencies. By carefully reviewing both the financial statements and job responsibilities of agency employees, it has sought to determine whether these employees had stock holdings in companies affected by their duties. Its findings have been startling. In one agency after another, GAO investigators found numerous conflicts involving stock in regulated companies. For example:

—In the Federal Power Commission, nineteen officials owned securities in companies regulated by the commission. Seven of these officials were administrative law judges who write major regulatory decisions.[6]

—In the Food and Drug Administration, 159 officials had stock in companies affected by FDA regulations. Sixty-four of these officials had investments in companies directly affected by their duties.[7]

—In the United States Geological Survey, an agency in the Department of Interior, forty-two employees "showed financial interests that violated the Organic Act or raised conflict of interest possibilities."[8]

Such conflicts of interest also exist in Congress. A congressman from Florida, for example, has had a wide range of personal holdings directly related to his duties as chairman of the House Appropriations Subcommittee on Military Construction. In 1973 he advocated and voted for a $138 million Air Force contract to Fairchild Industries while owning a substantial block of stock in the contracting firm. He was also actively involved in obtaining a charter for the First Navy Bank at the Pensacola Naval Air Station, the first private bank ever allowed on a United States naval base and one in which he has major stockholdings.[9]

The financial reports filed by House members in 1975 indicate this is not an isolated example. The reports show that eighty-six representatives had financial interests in banks and other financial institutions and that forty-eight had holdings in the top one hundred defense contractors. The members of the tax-writing House Ways and Means Committee, taken together, own stock in three public utility companies, ten banks, and eight major oil and natural gas companies.

There are no effective rules prohibiting congressmen from voting on matters in which they have an economic interest. The Senate rules are totally silent on this issue. The House rules, however, contain an obscure provision requiring each member to vote on questions before the House "unless he has a direct personal or pecuniary interest in the event of such question." This rule has never been evoked to prevent a House member from voting on a matter in which he had a financial interest.

There are several restrictions that apply to executive branch employees, although they are poorly enforced and contain certain loopholes. Title 18 USC 208 forbids executive officials and employees from participating "personally and substantially" in matters in which they have a financial interest. Executive Order 11222, issued by President Lyndon Johnson in 1965, prohibits employees from having "direct or indirect financial interests that conflict substantially, or appear to conflict substantially, with their responsibilities and duties as Federal employees." The Civil Service Commission (CSC) has issued regulations spelling out specific rules and procedures for agencies to follow in complying with the Executive Order and Title 18. These rules also prohibit conflicting financial interests (5 CFR 735, 204). Finally, an agency's own conflict of interest regulations, which are usually modeled after the CSC rules and contain any additional restrictions established by legislation, prohibit financial interests in companies affected by one's duties.

All these prohibitions, however, contain various exemptions and modifications. There is no uniform, tightly-drawn, unequivocal ban on owning stock in companies affected by an employee's regulatory or contractual responsibilities. Instead, CSC regulations stipulate that if an employee does own such stock, the agency head can do one of four things: change the employee's assignment, require divestiture, apply disciplinary measures, or require disqualification from a decision (5 CFR 735, 107). None of this is done, of course, unless the employee reports the conflict. And maybe not even then. Some "prohibitions" can be waived if the supervisor determines that the financial interest "is not so substantial as to be deemed likely to affect the integrity" of the employee (18 USC 208 b). The agency can also issue blanket exemptions for certain kinds of interests.

In short, the existing restrictions contain loopholes, vary from one agency to the next, and—as will be discussed below—are not adequately enforced. These factors enable many executive employees, as the GAO has shown, to maintain stock holdings that directly conflict with their duties.

Receipt of Gratuities

The receipt of gifts, favors and honorariums from special-interest groups can place a public official in a conflict of interest. Those providing such gratuities usually have a stake in influencing the official's actions. The gratuity itself is of some economic value to the official. So, the acceptance of gratuities can create a conflict: on one side, there is the official's economic interest (as well as a feeling of "beholdenness") in deciding matters in accordance with the wishes of those who provided the gratuity; and on the other side, there is the public's interest in equality of representation in the decision-making process.

Several examples of this problem have been reported in the Washington press. The receipt of gratuities from special interests appears to be especially prominent in regulatory agencies. However, due to the secrecy involved, there is no thorough documentation of how widespread this practice actually is. Some recent examples include:

—Commissioners and staff members of the Securities and Exchange Commission have reportedly accepted convention trip expenses from trade associations of the industry they regulate. For example, the former chairman received reimbursement for travel and hotel expenses from the Securities Industry Association, an association of brokerage firms and investment bankers, on at least six occasions between 1973–75. This included two days at a convention at the Boca Raton resort community in Florida.[10]

—Several top Pentagon officials have reportedly accepted free vacations in company hunting lodges, trips on corporate jets and yachts, and other favors from some of the nation's largest defense contractors, including Northrop Corp., Lockheed Aircraft Corp., and Rockwell International. Forty officers were officially chided for accepting free liquor and accommodations at a Northrop hunting lodge in Maryland. These trips were provided during the company's successful quest for a jet-fighter contract.[11]

A recent study by the Brookings Institution on congressional ethics contains some startling revelations about accepting favors from special interests. The authors surveyed a random sample of fifty House members on their views on the propriety of various situations that might raise conflicts of interest, and on how prevalent such situations were in the House. Although the congressmen normally ranked the receipt of special favors from lobbyists as "probably unethical," several believed that "many" of their colleagues were guilty of this practice. Certain favors, however, were *not* considered improper by most of the respondents, who also believed their acceptance was rather widespread. These included the payment of entertainment cost and the use of company planes for personal travel.

The receipt of large honorariums from special interests was also thought to be fairly normal. One questionnaire item, for example, asked about a member who accepted a one-thousand-dollar honorarium from a group interested in upcoming legislation, while he was undecided how to vote on the issue. The respondents considered this at least "probably unethical," and yet fairly likely to be practiced.[12]

Other than the prohibitions against outright bribery, which apply to all federal employees (18 USC 201), members of Congress are under no restrictions concerning the acceptance of gratuities. There is a limit on honorariums, however. The 1974 amendments to the Federal Election Campaign Act forbids congressmen from accepting honorariums of over one thousand dollars each. Their cumulative total for one year cannot exceed $15 thousand.

Executive branch employees are subject to more stringent prohibitions. Executive Order 11222 states that "no employee shall solicit or accept, directly or indirectly, any gift, gratuity, favor, entertainment, loan, or any other thing of monetary value, from any person, corporation, or group [which is regulated by his agency or has interests that could be affected by his duties]" (Section 201). CSC regulations on employee conduct, and agency rules modeled after them, contain similar prohibitions.

The Civil Service Commission allows certain exceptions to these prohibitions. They permit the acceptance of gratuities from relatives and friends, loans from financial institutions, unsolicited advertising material of nominal value, and "food and refreshments of nominal value on infrequent occasions" (5 CFR 735, 202). This last exemption is the most open to abuse. Otherwise, the prohibitions on gratuities applying to executive personnel are, on paper at least, comprehensive and tightly-drawn.

The problem, of course, is inadequate enforcement. Employees and officials who receive gratuities do not have to report them, since most are prohibited in the first place. The

enforcement therefore relies on close scrutiny: agency supervisors are supposed to watch their employees, and CSC officials and Congress are supposed to watch agency heads. But
few officials or congressional committees are watching anyone
very carefully. Consequently, those who accept gifts and favors
from regulated interests—such as the SEC and Pentagon
officials cited above—usually get away with it. The prohibition
itself, of course, is somewhat self-enforcing. The fact that
gratuities are prohibited prevents most employees from
accepting them.

Postgovernment Employment

The opportunity of employment, after leaving an agency,
with companies who are affected by one's duties, or with law
firms representing them, can create conflicts of interest for
agency employees. This opportunity is very real, and many
officials have taken advantage of it. Former officials can be
valuable assets to industry because of their contacts and influence within their former agency. Once they leave, therefore,
high-paying jobs are often available with companies that were
affected by their involvement in regulatory or contractual decisions, or with these companies' law firms. But such opportunities usually depend on whether the official was a friend of
the industry, or the particular company, while in office. That's
where the conflict comes in. An official who has his eye on
employment in the industry has an economic interest in making decisions favorable to that industry or to a particular company. It has even been alleged that contracts or grants are
sometimes awarded as a quid pro quo for a lucrative postgovernment job.

There is little statistical data on how many former employees
of agencies have taken jobs in regulated industries. Most of
them do not have to disclose where they work once they leave
the agency. One notable exception is the requirement that
Pentagon officials report any employment with defense contractors for three years after leaving the department. In June
1975, the House Subcommittee on Oversight and Investigations sent questionnaires to nine regulatory agencies requesting, among other things, information on former officials who

took industry jobs. None of the agencies had the information, although a few were able to provide limited data on some of their former employees.

Nevertheless, numerous examples of postgovernment employment in regulated industries have been reported in recent years. A small sample is given here to indicate the nature of this problem.

—During a recent four-year period, over 1,400 Pentagon officials left the Department to take jobs with defense contractors. Four senior officials in the procurement agency for the Minuteman missile system, for example, were hired by Boeing, the prime contractor for the system.[13]

—Three top officials in the Nixon administration who helped develop and promote the plan to turn over to private industry the government's role in making atomic fuel are now executives in the Bechtel Corp., one of the firms to benefit from the new multibillion-dollar business. One of these former officials was secretary of the Treasury, one was former secretary of Health, Education, and Welfare, and the third was a general manager of the Atomic Energy Commission.[14]

—A former general counsel of the Food and Drug Administration left in May 1975 and is now working with a prestigious Washington law firm that represents food and drug companies.[15]

—A former head of the Environmental Protection Agency has set up his own law firm in Washington and is representing the polyvinyl chloride industry before EPA.[16]

—A former Transportation Secretary, who left the Ford cabinet in February 1975, is now a lobbyist for the Union Oil Company of California.[17]

—A former deputy assistant secretary in the Interior Department, who had also been an official in the Federal Power Commission, is now working for a Texas law firm representing oil and gas clients before the FPC.[18]

Similar cases have emerged in the Presidental Executive Interchange Program, through which business executives are temporarily placed in government posts. Their responsibilities often include matters affecting the company from which they came and to which they will return. In December 1975, a House small business subcommittee issued a report citing fifteen cases that involved this kind of conflict of interest. One case, for example, concerned a pesticides expert from Shell Oil Co. who was assigned to the EPA office responsible for developing pesticide regulations affecting industry. Another involved an executive from Litton Systems Inc. who worked with the Federal Administration helping design and develop new navigational systems. While he was there, Litton received a $34.5 million FAA contract for computer flight systems.

There are presently no restrictions whatsoever on where a former official or employee can work after leaving an agency. Former employees are prohibited only from representing clients on matters "in which [they] participated personally and substantially as an officer or employee" of the federal government (18 USC 207). However, this ban does not prohibit one from representing clients before his former agency on matters which arise after he leaves. As Roswell Perkins has pointed out:

> The most fundamental limitation on the postemployment ban is that it creates no bar whatsoever on immediate appearance before any government agency with respect to new matters. Any transaction involving the Government that comes up after the day the former employee leaves office cannot have been subject either to his personal participation or his official responsibility and therefore, as under present law, is outside the postemployment restriction. [19]

Enforcement and Disclosure

The enforcement of prohibitions on having financial interests that conflict with one's duties relies heavily on financial disclosure. The current disclosure system is inadequate on several counts. The information reported is minimal. The reports filed by executive employees are not made public. In many cases, they are not carefully reviewed by agency supervisors. When conflicts are spotted, remedial action is often slow and sometimes is never taken at all. And the reporting requirements do not cover all the agency employees they should.

House members are required to publicly disclose the names of companies doing substantial business with the government or regulated by the government in which they hold stock worth over five thousand dollars or from which they receive income of more than one thousand dollars. The value of these interests is not reported. Moreover, the value refers to holdings in one company, not the sum of holdings in a given industry. A member could therefore have several holdings in the same area just below the five-thousand-dollar level. This could add up to a substantial interest, and yet no disclosure would be required. They also have to report the source of income for services, capital gains, reimbursements, and honorariums, but not the amounts received in these categories. Senators have to disclose publicly only the amounts and source of honorariums over $300. Other information is filed with the Comptroller General, but it is kept confidential. It covers taxes, outside income, debts, gifts, and financial holdings of over $10 thousand.

In the executive branch, there is no public financial disclosure at all. Executive Order 11222 requires agency heads and Presidential appointees to file financial statements with the Civil Service Commission, and CSC regulations require other officials in policy-making positions to file with the head of their agency. The reports cover only the names of companies in which the person has a financial interest, creditors, and interests in real property. The value of stockholdings and other assets and the amount of income received from outside activities are not reported. All the financial statements are kept confidential.

The statements are supposed to be reviewed by agency "ethics counselors" for possible conflicts of interest. The General Accounting Office has found, however, that this review is often superficial at best. Most of the agencies it investigated had not developed adequate standards for determining conflicts, and those conducting the reviews often lacked the necessary expertise. The conflicts of interest it uncovered (mentioned earlier) all involved financial holdings listed on the employees' financial reports. These conflicts were not spotted by the agency supervisors who supposedly reviewed those statements.

The GAO also found that many employees who make decisions affecting regulated industries are not required to report their financial holdings. There is absolutely no check, therefore, on possible conflicts they may have. It found 1,400 such employees in the Department of Interior, 58 in the Civil Aeronautics Board, and 43 in the Federal Maritime Commission.[20] Moreover, those employees required to file sometimes don't. According to GAO, 203 officials in the Food and Drug Administration failed to file required financial statements in 1974. Of the 125 Federal Power Commission officials required to file in 1973, only 7 did.[21]

PROPOSALS FOR REFORM

This discussion has sought to show that existing restrictions and enforcement procedures are seriously deficient. They do not adequately check the kinds of conflicts of interest that arise in government service today. This is not merely a case of poorly drafted regulations or bureaucratic bungling. The problem is deeper than that. It is an indictment of governmental values and norms. Thus far, public officials have not implemented truly effective measures to safeguard the integrity of the governing process. The existing regulations and efforts to enforce them do not reflect a deep governmental commitment to equality of representation.

Such a commitment implies that steps should be taken to guarantee, so far as practical, that public officials not have an economic interest in matters affected by their duties. Here are some things that should be done:

Public Financial Disclosure

Officials in Congress and the executive branch should be required to publicly disclose their financial holdings and activities. Annual reports should be filed by all policy-making officials and employees, and should be available for public inspection upon request. The reports should cover sources and amounts of income, identity and value of stock holdings and other assets, identity and amount of liabilities, transactions in securities and commodities, and identity and value of all gifts, honorariums, services, and other things of value.

This would be the most effective way of deterring conflicts of interest in Congress and enforcing the executive branch prohibition on financial holdings that conflict with one's duties. Other measures have been tried, and they have obviously failed. The limited public disclosure required of congressmen has not been effective. Nor has the executive branch system of confidential financial reporting.

Ban of Gratuities

Members of Congress and their top staff should be subject to the same restrictions on receiving gratuities as are executive branch personnel. To enforce this restriction, officials in both branches should be required to publicly disclose, as noted above, any gratuity or honorarium received from a nonrelative. They also should be required to report all social contacts with certain outside parties, such as luncheons with representatives of interest groups, entertainment at industry conventions, and so forth.

Divestiture

All officials and employees in the executive branch should be required to divest themselves of all financial interests in any company affected by their duties. This should cover interests in companies affected by the official's participation in rule makings, contractual decisions, and other matters involving the exercise of his discretionary authority. Divestiture should be required prior to the official's participation in the matter in question.

This requirement would be uniform and unequivocal. As noted already, existing restrictions vary among agencies and many do not require outright divestiture of conflicting interests. Less effective measures are sometimes used.

Postemployment Restrictions

Executive branch officials should be prohibited from accepting employment, for a period of two years after leaving their agency, with any company that had been affected by their duties. Again, this ban should cover those companies which were affected by an official's participation in rule makings, contractual decisions, and other matters involving his discretionary authority. This prohibition could be set by legislation, or through a legally binding contract with the agency, the terms of which would ban certain employment after leaving. To help enforce this, former officials should be required to report to their agency their nongovernmental employment during the two-year period.

Former officials should also be prohibited from representing any party before their former agency in any legal, lobbying, or other professional capacity. This should apply to representation on any matter before the agency, not just matters in which the official was involved before leaving.

Enforcement Measures

The financial statements filed by executive branch employees should be carefully reviewed by a competent agency supervisor, such as a designated ethics counselor, within thirty days of the date filed. During this period, the supervisor should notify, in writing, each employee under his jurisdiction of the results of this review. This notification should instruct the employee to divest himself of any financial interests which conflict with his duties. These review notifications should be made available for public inspection upon request. Agency supervisors should issue an annual public report to the agency head summarizing their review findings and enforcement measures during the previous year.

The financial reports filed by congressmen should be reviewed within thirty days by the General Accounting Office. The GAO should then issue a public report on its findings. This report should note in particular any financial holdings or sources of outside income that may conflict with a congressman's committee assignments.

Some may protest that these measures would deter many highly qualified individuals from working for the government. For example, the financial disclosure requirements might be seen as an unwarranted invasion of privacy, or the limits on postgovernment employment may seem too restrictive. Consequently, it has been argued, many potential employees would choose to go elsewhere.

The experience in states that have strong financial disclosure laws indicates this is not a serious problem. Washington state, for example, has one of the broadest disclosure laws in the nation. Before it was adopted, opponents argued that massive resignations would result from its disclosure requirements. But this did not happen: out of 275 elected state officials, only one resignation has been attributed to the new law; and out of 378 county officials, there have been two resignations.[22] Similar results have come from California. That state's 1973 conflict of interest act, that covers over 7,500 state officials, was found by a United Press International survey to have prompted only fifty resignations.[23]

The supreme courts in Washington, California, Illinois, and Maryland have all upheld the constitutionality of financial disclosure requirements. As the Supreme Court of Washington stated in 1974:

> The right of the electorate to know most certainly is no less fundamental than the right of privacy. When the right of the people to be informed does not intrude upon intimate personal matters which are unrelated to fitness for public office, the candidate or officeholder may not complain that his own privacy is paramount to the interests of the people.[24]

It is true, however, that some individuals will shun government service due to strong conflict of interest laws. But this needs to be put in perspective. First, some of those who would find such laws unacceptable would not have made good public servants anyway. For example, a lot of people seem to take government jobs as a springboard into something more attractive in industry. Such individuals probably *should* be deterred from government employment. Second, working for the government involves a public trust. It is a special vocation. Those who enter it must be willing to abide by special rules that do not apply to work in the private sector. These rules are necessary to insure the objectivity of public servants and promote public confidence. Finally, from the government's point of view and that of the general public, the fact that some good people—such as experts from certain industries— may go elsewhere is the price we pay for strong policies on conflicts of interest and government integrity. There are trade-offs involved. On balance, though, it appears the public's interest is better served through measures that prevent government officials and employees from having private economic interests in the public issues they must decide.

How Labor Unions View
and Use Codes of Ethics

Kenneth Fiester

A dissertation on ethical practices in organized labor inevitably involves complexities and controversy to a greater degree, perhaps, than in other segments of American society.

The behavior of unions directly affects more individuals than the behavior of doctors and lawyers combined. Yet organized labor is not a relatively homogeneous body like organized medicine or the organized bar, which until recent years were virtual monoliths; on the contrary, its component parts are more heterogeneous than those of organized religion, with which it shares certain other characteristics as well.

The diversity of unions and their practices is only one obstacle to arriving at a balanced assessment of the whole. Another, even more troublesome, is the task of defining what areas of union performance should properly be measured by an ethical standard, if indeed any true standard exists. At this point, judgments rapidly proceed from objective to subjective and virtue rests with beauty in the eye of the beholder.

In an effort to clear a few patches of order in this tangle, let us arbitrarily but, I trust, reasonably set up four categories of union conduct:

1. Criminal acts by union officials and employees. This includes stealing from the union or from funds handled by the union; illicit dealings with fund trustees or with employers; acts of violence aimed at union dissidents or recalcitrant employers, and related offenses of the same nature but not including acts that take place during a strike management is trying to break.

2. Acts by union officers or policies by union organizations that deny or frustrate the democratic process. There is no need to offer a bill of particulars here: acceptable conduct requires not only honest elections, but proper notice to voters; reasonable eligibility standards for candidates; the secret ballot; full disclosure of financial affairs to members; strict limits on the right of a national union to impose a trusteeship over a local union, and so forth.

These are objective matters, readily determined by objective judgment, either by law or through the internal government of the union involved. They are disputed only on the evidence in a particular case. No one defends the cited acts in themselves.

3. Union policies and practices that govern wages, collateral benefits, and working conditions in the place of employment. Here we pass to the subjective. Union security—"compulsory membership," as it is often but wrongly called—comes in here; so do artificial limits on output and the manning rules that produce featherbedding. But less emotional issues are at least as important.

Is there an ethical consideration in union contract proposals that honestly reflect the aspirations of the union membership? To management, and often to others outside the union, the proposals may seem to be unreasonable. Are they therefore unethical?

To take the same point from another angle: Is it unethical for either party to force a bad bargain upon the other side—or is it merely unwise? To what extent, if any, is the labor movement concerned about the imposition of bad bargains by its constituent organizations?

4. Union activity in politics and public affairs. This is very largely subjective too, assuming the activities are legal. Does the union leadership recognize the possibility of an ethical

problem in attempting to mobilize members on behalf of candidates or issues with which some disagree?

Before proceeding to an examination of organized labor's position—or positions—in each of the four categories I so arbitrarily established above, I would like to strike a note of personal regret. Very few who read these pages will gain an understanding of organized labor's ethical standards, because very few will begin with any background whatever in the historical development of unions in America, or any appreciable knowledge of their structure, the way they function or the laws that govern them. Yet today's ethics reflect yesterday's experience, and can be seen clearly only in its light.

Therefore I will digress briefly at this point to offer an outrageously compressed and oversimplified history of American unionism, in the hope that it will make what follows it a bit more comprehensible.

One segment of today's labor movement traces its origins to the crafts—the building trades, the printing trades and, as time went on, the machinists and electricians. The first two can trace their spiritual heritage to colonial times and beyond; the indentured apprentice became a journeyman, and later, perhaps, a master craftsman who himself employed journeymen and indentured apprentices.

Initially a father taught his son the trade, its skills and its secrets. Later this process fell to the group—the guild, the union. The elders passed entry rights to their sons as the employer bequeathed his business to his progeny.

Outsiders could seldom break through. The craftsmen saw no reason to expand their ranks in a society beset by chronic insecurity and periodic financial panics. When extra workers were needed they could be placed through a system of work permits granted by the union for a fee; the craft itself would remain a little island of safety, among the last to be washed over by the waves of depression and among the first to emerge from them.

The employers, whose nephews, in-laws and younger sons were also admitted to the fraternity, had an interest in its preservation. All too often this led to very cozy relationships in the building trades. But beyond the actuality or the appearance of corruption, the closed society of the apprenticed trades, so understandable in human terms and certainly tolerable by nineteenth century standards, lingered far too long into the twentieth century. Among other things, it became a blatant instrument of racism; since there were no black fathers in the unions, there were no black sons in apprenticeship programs.

These apprenticeship terms were historically administered locally and the national organizations (then and now) had little or no authority over them. Thus it came about that in 1961, AFL-CIO President George Meany testified before a House labor subcommittee in support of a measure to outlaw racial discrimination in apprenticeship programs. Mr. Meany, a plumber by trade, had been sponsored as an apprentice by his father, also a plumber and the local union's business agent—a post that Mr. Meany succeeded to in time. But unlike many other products of the system, Mr. Meany knew it had to change.

A law was needed, Mr. Meany told the House committee, because neither the federation nor the national craft unions had the power to force a local union to change a policy which the local membership supported.

This point must be borne constantly in mind with respect to union ethics. Although, as we shall see, the AFL-CIO has since been endowed with broader authority over its affiliated unions in this area, it cannot effectively enforce that authority. Here as elsewhere, union organizations must suffer the handicaps of democracy.

One of the most respected unaligned authorities on labor relations, Dr. John T. Dunlop, made this point with great pungency in an address nearly twenty years before his service as secretary of labor.

"It is sheer demagoguery," he said, "to hold that we can have unions which are highly responsive to the rank and file and at the same time highly responsible and businesslike."

Dr. Dunlop was referring primarily to bargaining policy, which we will consider later, but the conflict between what the members want and what they ought to want arises in every context.

I do not agree that union democracy makes responsible

union leadership impossible; it just makes it vastly more difficult.

Besides the crafts, the pre-New Deal AFL included four major industrial unions. One, the Teamsters, was a functioning partner of the building trades; unlike most industrial unions it comprised an assortment of geographical baronies over which the national president, like a medieval British monarch, reigned but did not rule. Two were needle trades unions, social-democratic in their outlook, aggressively honest and democratic in practice. The fourth was the United Mine Workers, both reigned over and ruled by the imperious, unpredictable John L. Lewis.

The latter three unions and some smaller allies tried for years to induce the AFL to sanction industrial (one plant, one union) organization of workers in the giant steel, auto, electrical, and other manufacturing plants. But the crafts refused; they insisted that electrical work in a steel mill "belonged" to the electrical craftsmen, pipe installations to plumbers, and so on.

This hidebound attitude, characteristic of the AFL in that era, led to an explosion of protest in the form of the CIO. With Lewis at the helm and the resources of his union and one of the needle trades organizations as a nucleus, the CIO set up a swarm of committees that joined workers together according to place of employment rather than what they did there. Congress had ordained that "the encouragement of collective bargaining is the policy of the United States" (it still is), and established machinery to prevent employers from discouraging it. Workers by the millions flocked to the new unions.

There were more than structural differences involved. The CIO was an evangelical movement, too, calling not only for new unions that would achieve justice for the assembly-line captives in mass-production industries but also for a reordering of society for the betterment of the citizenry as a whole.

Reformers, radicals, academicians, and intellectuals in general were caught up in the fervor. The Communists were especially zealous; tireless, brave, and incorruptible, unhampered (until August 1939) by incompatible party doctrine, they rose to leadership in a number of unions and to posts of importance in many others and in the CIO itself. Only those CIO unions under social-democratic leadership, plus the Mine Workers, whose leadership began and ended with Mr. Lewis, escape some degree of Communist influence. Even the Stalin-Hitler pact, disillusioning to many intellectuals, hardly had time to be felt in the union halls before June 1941 and the following December submerged ideology again.

Meanwhile the AFL unions, after a period of shock, turned to industrial organization themselves. At first, and for many years to come, workers in factory units affiliated with old craft organizations were second-class union citizens in terms of voting power, as the craft members took care to keep control. Even worse off were workers herded into local unions that were little more than dues-collecting agencies. All too many employers like this much better than having to cope with negotiations, legitimate representation, and grievance procedure. All too many still do.

A truism among those of us who reported on union affairs for the dozen years starting around 1936 went like this: "The CIO has got the Communists and the AFL has got the crooks." Cynical and simplistic, it was close to the mark.

But changes were under way. Beginning in 1946 the non-Communist unions in the CIO stepped up their pressure against the party's influence at each annual convention. At the same time, Walter P. Reuther gradually overcame the Communist-oriented leadership of the United Auto Workers. In 1949 the CIO convention voted to expel its third largest affiliate, the United Electrical Workers (UE), for adhering to the Communist Party line in defiance of CIO policy; within a year ten other unions were ousted on the same grounds, the most notable being Harry Bridges's west coast longshoremen. In all, the CIO renounced about 20 percent of its membership.

Expulsion was the only available remedy after cajolery and appeals to the membership had failed. But here, in its first test, it proved to be less than a deadly weapon.

Six of the ousted unions were flimsy; some were quickly gobbled up by hungry rivals and others simply evaporated. Three were small but tough; all have negotiated honorable mergers with larger unions, after surviving for as long as twenty years. The UE, cut to less than one-third its size by the most intensive raiding attacks in labor history, is now respectable as well as viable; the west coast longshoremen have come through unscathed.

Meanwhile, George Meany had become AFL president in 1952. Among his first acts was to bring about the expulsion from the federation of the International Longshoremen's Association (ILA) on grounds of corruption. A rival union was chartered, and for the next four years—spanning the period of the AFL-CIO merger—vainly sought to win over the ILA members. In 1959, after several leadership overturns, the ILA asked and was granted reaffiliation under a probationary arrangement.

Thus at the time of merger each federation had attacked the major affliction of its affiliates by expulsion—drastically by the CIO, in one instance by the AFL. In each case the results accurately foresaw the limits of expulsion as an ultimate weapon by a labor federation against an offending affiliate.

Merger of the AFL and CIO took place in 1955. Almost immediately the new federation initiated investigations of four affiliated unions. A fifth was known by Mr. Meany to be dubious at best. The sixth—the Teamsters—was not formally challenged until after the disclosures before the McClellan Committee in 1957. What the committee uncovered was no great surprise to journalists but was a considerable shock to honest AFL leaders like Mr. Meany.

The first AFL-CIO convention after the merger, in 1957, had to face the corruption issue head-on. To the last moment there were many in the CIO wing who expected Mr. Meany and the old AFL leaders to avoid a confrontation. They were disappointed. With Mr. Meany taking the lead, the federation's largest affiliate, one with the most intimate ties to the building trades and, for that matter, to all unions whose ability to win a strike might depend upon halting deliveries and shipments, was cast out by the necessary two-thirds vote of delegates polled by roll-call. Also ejected were two smaller affiliates, whose constituent locals, after the offending national leaders were purged, have since been absorbed by appropriate AFL-CIO organizations. The other three were (necessarily with their concurrence) placed on probation under

AFL-CIO supervision, eventually being returned to respectability under new officers and new internal safeguards.

The nature of these safeguards was prescribed by the 1957 convention, which affirmed six codes of ethical practices adopted by the federation's executive council during the previous two years. The convention made observance of the codes mandatory on affiliates—the first time the proudly autonomous national unions had given any federation specific power to meddle in their internal affairs. (Comparable authority was subsequently given to the AFL-CIO in the areas of civil rights and interunion jurisdictional disputes.)

Here, in summary, are the six basic codes that are binding on all unions affiliated with the AFL-CIO:

Local union charters. Charters should be issued only to bona fide employee groups eligible for membership and within the jurisdiction of the issuing organization. They are not to be used as "hunting licenses" for catch-as-catch-can organizing. They must not be granted to any group that has been expelled for unethical practices by the AFL-CIO or an affiliate thereof. The charter of a local must be promptly withdrawn if it ceases to function.

Health and welfare funds. No full-time paid official of a union shall receive compensation of any kind from a health, welfare, or retirement program. No person acting as a union's representative in the establishment or administration of such programs shall have direct or indirect ties with outside agencies that do business with the programs (insurance carriers, brokers, and so forth). All programs must maintain complete records, subjected to an independent audit at least once a year and made available to the covered employees. An appeals procedure must be established for aggrieved claimants.

Racketeers, crooks, Communists, and Fascists. No person who constitutes a corrupt influence or represents or supports a Communist, Fascist, or totalitarian agency may hold elective or appointive office. This includes not only those convicted of a crime involving moral turpitude offensive to trade union morality, but anyone commonly known to be a crook or racketeer, convicted or not.

Investments and business interests of union officials. No responsible trade union official should have personal financial interests which conflict with his duties as a workers' representative, nor have a substantial business interest in any enterprise with which his union bargains collectively, nor in its competitors, suppliers, or customers. (The casual ownership of shares in a widely held corporation is exempted.) Kickbacks, under-the-table payments, gifts of more than nominal value or personal payments of any kind from an employer—except wages or salaries that may be earned for work as an employee—are forbidden.

Financial practices and proprietary activities of unions. In exhaustive detail too great for inclusion here, this code mandates a fishbowl operation in the handling of union funds, ranging from annual audits of local union accounts by each national union to a ban on loans to union officials. The text stresses that practices regarded as acceptable in the business world are not good enough for handling funds which belong to the members and must be used in their best interests.

Union democratic processes. Every union member has the equal right to free participation in union affairs, including the right to vote, run for office, and speak his mind. Union law must be fairly and uniformly applied, and an appeals procedure provided. A convention shall be the supreme governing body of a national union, held at least every four years; officers shall be elected either by delegates or by referendum, for specified terms of four years or less. Local unions are to meet periodically at a time and place known in advance by the membership. Local officers may be elected at a specified union meeting or by referendum, also for stated terms not to exceed four years. To insure the democratic, responsible, and honest conduct of subordinate bodies, the AFL-CIO and its affiliated national unions need the power to take disciplinary measures, including the power to establish trusteeships, but such powers should be used sparingly and trusteeships should be terminated promptly upon the elimination of their cause.

As the reader will recognize, application of these six codes effectively covers two of the four categories of union conduct I posed at the beginning—the two that are subject to objective assessment.

In practice, the codes mandated by the 1957 convention became the codes of every AFL-CIO affiliate. Although the convention encouraged member unions to go even further if they chose, few have done so.

The United Automobile Workers did create a public review board in 1957. It comprises seven "impartial persons of good repute" who hear the appeals of individual members or groups of members who feel their rights of union citizenship have been violated. The grievants must first exhaust the normal appeals procedure of the UAW. The board cannot entertain an appeal against a collective bargaining policy of the national union that has been approved by the membership. Only 345 formal appeals have been filed with the review board in eighteen years, although it has dealt with thousands of inquiries and informal protests.

It should be noted that while nearly every union constitution contains a lofty statement of principles and goals, the leadership of a typical union, from one generation to the next, felt their organization had no more need for a code of ethics than does the College of Cardinals. Most union leaders worthy of the name believe the labor movement is inherently a moral and ethical force. To a great many of them, the most shocking statement James R. Hoffa made during the McClellan investigation was that he and the Teamsters were in the "union business," which operated like any other enterprise.

The McClellan hearings were instrumental in another AFL-CIO action which accompanied the ethical codes but was separate from them. A union official who invokes the Fifth Amendment to avoid scrutiny into alleged corruption on his part will be removed from office unless he can satisfy a union investigation that the allegations are untrue.

Whether these AFL-CIO actions would have been rigorously enforced against any future misdeeds by affiliates will never be known for sure. In 1959 Congress passed the Landrum-Griffin Act, more formally the Labor-Management Reporting and Disclosure Act, preempting private jurisdiction over most internal administrative affairs of unions.

The AFL-CIO endorsed the Landrum-Griffin standards of union democracy and financial integrity, but bitterly opposed the scope of the bonding provisions and the extensive paper work required of even the smallest local union. It objected to the bill's clear assumption that the corrupt union leaders haled before the McClellan committee were typical and that organized labor was a moral cesspool (an assumption widely shared by the uninformed today). Thanks to astute work by then Senator John F. Kennedy in the House-Senate conference, the final measure modified the objectionable points, though the federation was not mollified.

The law applies to all labor organizations a standard of conduct very much like that of the AFL-CIO codes, with the added weapon of federal enforcement. Embezzlement of union funds is made a federal crime. The annual reports required of every union are open for inspection at field offices, and photostats can be ordered by phone or mail at a minimum charge. The Department of Labor's yearly account of experience under the act (and the original Welfare and Pension Plans Disclosure Act, which took effect some six years later) is a reasonable approximation of how much dirty work goes on in the tangible aspects of union operations.

The usefulness of all this is, or ought to be, beyond exaggeration. Solid statistical information is readily available to suspicious union members, in far greater detail than the act requires unions to make public through their periodicals, or by other means. The loser in a rigged election can obtain a remedy, not swiftly perhaps, but faster and more surely than would be likely otherwise. When crooks are uncovered by union auditors, their prosecution can be entrusted to the Department of Justice.

What is—or again, what ought to be—most important is that the law applies to unions beyond the reach of AFL-CIO sanctions. Three of those unions—the UAW, the UE, and the west coast longshoremen—are beyond reproach in the areas under discussion. A fourth, the Mine Workers, is emerging from a long, dark night of authoritarian and, ultimately, criminal control. But the largest union in America seems not to have altered in any particular the practices that caused its expulsion from the AFL-CIO in 1957, except perhaps for the worse; and in New York and other large cities, scores of imitators prey upon gullible workers and employers to extort money in the name of "unions" that in fact do not exist at all.

Before pursuing the latter point, let us see what the Landrum-Griffin experience has been.

The most recent Department of Labor report, covering fiscal 1974, recapitulated the record since the act was passed fifteen years earlier.

More than 50 thousand national and local unions are required to file reports with the department. In the beginning only about 30 thousand did so, mostly because the others didn't know how; a continuing educational program by the department, shrewdly run, has brought about virtually 100 percent compliance.

Over the fifteen years, 317 suits have been filed by the secretary of labor in election cases. Nearly all were resolved by reruns under the secretary's supervision. During this time at least 150 thousand, and more likely twice as many, elections were conducted by the 50 thousand reporting unions.

More than one thousand persons have been indicted for criminal violations of the act and less than eight hundred convicted. That's an average of fifty-three convictions a year, roughly one for each one thousand reporting unions. But in the important ripoffs, half a dozen culprits were often involved; the number of unions affected is closer to eight hundred a year, out of 50 thousand. Seventy-eight unions were sued for recalcitrant reporting; forty-nine for refusal to produce documents and four for violation of trusteeship regulations. The secretary was sued fifty-four times for implementing or not implementing the act in accordance with the plaintiff's interpretation of it.

The department reports also confirmed a long-standing AFL-CIO complaint that premiums charged by surety companies for the bonding of union officers, as required by the act, border on the extortionate. For the calendar years 1966–73, the companies collected some $22.5 million in earned premiums and disbursed barely over $3 million in direct losses.

The Landrum-Griffin experience does not, however, adequately indicate the abuses that still take place in unions that have little or no tradition of idealism or of genuine internal democracy. The largest bona fide union that fits this description is the Teamsters.

The almost incredible financial adventures of the Teamsters' Central States pension fund (which covers most of the country) have been graphically detailed by the *Wall Street Journal* and the Scripps-Howard newspapers, supplementing earlier disclosures in the Hoffa trials. Yet there has been an astonishing absence of public concern by Teamster members whose old-age security depends heavily upon the fund's solvency. This cannot be explained on the grounds that the fund's benefits are especially generous. The extravagant claims sometimes made for it are easy enough to expose; I have done so a number of times myself in helping AFL-CIO unions repel Teamster raids.

Compliance officers in the labor-management reports division are well aware that repeated revelations of Teamster affairs in the news media cast doubt upon the division's diligence in enforcing the law. Appearances were not improved by what appeared to be a continuing alliance between then President Richard M. Nixon and Frank Fitzsimmons, the Teamster president, nor by Mr. Nixon's first postresignation appearance as a golfing partner of Mr. Fitzsimmons on a course financed by one of the Teamster pension fund's losing investments. But division officials maintain that lack of manpower limits them to the investigation of complaints, which have failed to materialize.

Far from being abashed by their expulsion from the AFL-CIO or their unfavorable public image, the Teamsters more often than not take a "macho" stance. Their chief argument in organizing campaigns is their toughness. They seem to be dedicated not to the rights of man, but to the power of muscle. It is a commentary on the mores of the times that this swagger often proves effective. For example, the Teamsters wage and win more labor board elections among white collar workers than any other union—in some months, more than all the others combined. The units are small and defeats generally outnumber victories, but such a degree of interest in Teamster membership among educated employees is depressing in itself.

Perhaps I have devoted too much attention to the Teamsters, whose importance as a national political and economic force is minimal for an organization of that size. Unfortunately, Teamster ethical practices are too often looked upon as representative of unions as a whole.

Let me make two final observations that may help to differentiate the Teamsters Union from most others and put its vaunted power in perspective. First, only a handful of other unions control pension funds created by employer contributions. Where many small employers are under contract to one national union (as in trucking, the needle trades, shoes, textile dyers and finishers) the customary pattern is a regional fund, administered by trustees equally divided between union and management; both contributions and benefits are determined by collective bargaining. In mass-production industries like auto, steel, and electrical manufacturing the benefits are determined by collective bargaining, but the funds (usually one to a company) are wholly controlled by management. Some unions have sought to have the money invested in "socially useful" endeavors, but the corporations have resisted, probably to the benefit of actuarial soundness. Second, Teamster "muscle" has been notably ineffective in nontrucking enterprises, from aircraft to insurance to mattress manufacturing. In these and other industries, Teamster contracts are inferior to prevailing standards, and sometimes employer resistance has frustrated negotiations entirely.

Most other violators of basic union ethics—the standards of fiscal integrity and internal democracy—are found in the big cities, primarily in New York and Chicago. There are very practical difficulties involved in establishing fair wages and working conditions for mechanics, assistants, sweepers, and car-washers in, say, a thousand Manhattan garages employing as many as one hundred or fewer than ten. Unless there is an employers association empowered to deal for all or most of them, the most honorable union may well seem to be arbitrary; the corrupt union will be flexible at a price.

Moreover, in such circumstances the morality of unions tends to mirror that of management. To cite one historic and relatively innocent example: most fabrics stretch while going through the dyeing and finishing process; for generations the companies that performed this work under contract returned to the customer only the number of yards he delivered, keeping the remainder. It was hardly surprising that workers, in turn, stole a share of this illicit bonus, or that their union took account of it in dealing with the employers. The reforms that have curbed these practices over the last twenty-five years were initiated by the national union of which the dyers and finishers were a part.

Only the law can curb the outright rackets that proliferate in the center cities, preying on unlettered minority workers and on employers only a shade better informed. "Amalgamated Industrial Workers Local 1137" can be created by one unethical lawyer and four thugs, and through fraud, bribery, and intimidation become recognized bargaining agent in such circumstances. The employer, innocently or not, signs a contract that gives the workers very little, but calls for a union shop and dues checkoff. The workers see nothing more of their "union." Eventually one of them will complain to the authorities and the law will move in, but the racketeers will find a new target soon enough.

Abuses of this kind are outrageous but they cannot be laid at the door of organized labor. Essentially they are police-court cases, akin to the "protection" shakedowns that flourish in the same milieu. They survive because pusillanimous businessmen submit to real or imagined threats of violence which would evaporate in the face of determined resistance.

Despite the noted exceptions, the ethical practices of unions in the two objectively measurable categories I set up at the outset are equal to any and superior to most segments of American society, from bankers to veterinarians.

What, then, of the subjective categories? What about ethics at the bargaining table—the balance between what is right and what is possible?

Mythology to the contrary notwithstanding, only rarely can a union tilt this balance in a decisive way. Yes, in the crafts there were, and in some cases still are, limits on how many bricks a man can lay or how wide a brush a painter can use. As with membership restrictions, these limitations arose from economic fear; they have properly faded away at about the same speed as a national commitment to full employment has grown.

If I may inject a personal note, my engineering training

leads me to deplore artificial restrictions on productivity; I believe the elimination of poverty in this country and in the world can be achieved only through maximum application of man's technological genius, not through restraining it. We should seek to harness technology to the general good—an elusive goal whose attainment has thus far defied easy prescription.

At the same time I have little patience for those who look upon performance limits or featherbedding as monstrous evils. In the world in which I was reared, a very ethical one, "getting it while the getting's good" was sound business practice. In what way is this ethically superior to spreading the work through restricting output, if the bargaining circumstances permit? It can even be argued that because overmanning and under-producing are designed to benefit, not the employed workers but their jobless brethren, they have at least a tenuous claim to virtue rather than opprobrium.

However, the argument is hardly worth pursuing. In national terms the productivity that matters is what flows from the great mass-production industries. In those industries the diligence of individual workers is of little or no consequence. The pace of production is set by machines; the output per manhour depends upon how well the machines perform and how intensively they are utilized. An hour-long machine breakdown, or a temporary shortage of a component part, has more to do with the manhour productivity measurement than all the malingerers could muster in a month.

Because labor's critics rarely understand the nature of factory work, they often use manhour productivity statistics as a club to beat unions. During the deep recession of the early to mid-1970s, the United States figures were dreary compared to those from West Germany, Japan, and elsewhere, and there was much uninformed wailing about the decline of American labor. Starting in mid-1975 the figures turned upside down; there had been no decline in malingering, but a substantial increase in factory orders.

To return to bargaining policies and practices: there are circumstances that permit—or sometimes compel—a union to impose unendurable contract terms upon an employer. In many such cases the terms represent prevailing practice in the industry, trade, or occupation involved. The question, then, is whether the interests of the workers (or the public) are served by the survival of an enterprise that cannot meet generally accepted terms of employment for its employees. Mostly, a union would say no—with the hearty approval of competing employers who are paying standard rates.

There are other cases in which the pressure on an employer for uninterrupted production are so great that a strike would be disastrous. This sort of thing almost always involves a relatively small enterprise and a local union, rather than national or regional negotiations. The local union, pressed by members intent upon the main chance, may demand and get exorbitant benefits.

But for every such case there have been at least a thousand when unions have been forced to accept conditions that neither the members nor the leaders regarded as close to adequate, for the great weight of economic power still rests with the ownership. Moreover, there have been numerous instances when a national union has intervened to modify the excesses of a local. No mechanism exists for restraining excesses by an employer and there is no employer movement to create one.

Even so, organized labor in America has been far more sensitive than unions in other free nations to the survival point of employing enterprises. Unlike any other free labor movement, America's is not committed to an economic ideology; it is not dedicated to socialism, or to any form of Communism, or to any particular economic structure.

Leaders and members alike are inalterably devoted to a free *political* system, under which the economy can be tinkered with or even, if necessary, drastically altered if the people so choose. The absence of an economic ideology extends to capitalism, too; unions aren't against it, they just have no commitment to it. They take the economic system as it is and seek to do the best they can for the membership, and for wage-earners in general. This means a combination of hard bargaining and the welfare state.

As Dr. Dunlop and Derek Bok observed in their 1970 study (*Labor and the American Community*, Simon and Schuster) an intelligent evaluation of labor in America must "rightly perceive that unions are uncommitted to the profit system." This is the simple truth and any reader of AFL-CIO union periodicals and public statements can hardly deny it. Indeed, from my personal observations, the few staunch defenders of capitalism in labor's ranks are nearly always found in those organizations whose ethical practices are the most dubious.

None of this necessarily affects collective bargaining. Industries whose managements unreservedly accept the propriety and permanence of unions have achieved mature, stable, cooperative relationships—not guaranteed against strikes, but proof against truly destructive warfare. In these industries are found the highest wages and fringe benefits for workers, and the greatest degree of economic security; the fullest security for the union as an institution; and in general, the richest returns for the stockholders.

Unfortunately for the cause of labor-management stability and, in my view, for the national interest, most managements even now do not accept unions in the terms just described. This attitude simply confirms the conviction of workers and union leaders that the nature of management has not undergone much fundamental change since the nineteenth century. The conviction itself is based upon day-to-day experience, even in establishments where the union is accepted. The truth is that the typical factory is not a pleasant place for wage-earners no matter how effective a union they have. Since wages and fringe benefits are the only rewards for enduring their hours inside, workers invariably press for greater gains than possibly can be obtained. I know of no instance in which union officials sought more than the members wanted.

Arriving at a negotiated agreement acceptable to both sides is a demanding task. Both sides begin by taking positions from which they know they must retreat. Purists who deplore this are unrealistic. Management bargainers need to convince their stockholders that their firmness and skill staved off the union's extreme demands. Union bargainers need to convince their members that the proposed contract terms, while less than the original goals, are far better than management intended to grant.

There are no "right" answers that can be predetermined

either by computers or by less-material means. Management may sincerely believe that a certain benefit level involves too great a risk for stockholders; the union may just as sincerely believe that anything less would visit unreasonable hardship on the employees. A peaceful settlement is likely to be fair if neither side is really happy with it.

Thus the ethical content of free collective bargaining is largely a matter of genuine good faith. Sweet talk is no substitute, as in the case of the mammoth corporation which a generation ago declared its labor relations policy was "doing the right thing voluntarily." But management carefully retained for itself the definition of what was right, and the exclusive power to take voluntary action. Ultimately this pretentious policy was broken by a 101-day strike. Volumes could be written about other aspects of the fascinating process that is the essence of industrial democracy.

My fourth category dealt with union activity in politics and public affairs. It seems to me that there should be no problem with union activity on behalf of legislative issues that have been voted upon by delegated bodies like conventions or by membership referendum. But political candidacies and the collection of money for union distribution pose stickier problems.

A union member may wholeheartedly support a national health program, situs picketing, and public works jobs, but still prefer a moderate Republican to an all-out Democrat in his congressional district. But his local Committee on Political Education (COPE) has endorsed the Democrat; if he gives his voluntary two dollars that's where it will go.

When I was the unpaid president of a Newspaper Guild local almost forty years ago, this made me queasy. Yet no better system has developed that will help wage and salary workers to partially balance the enormous sums that business interests pour into the war chests of conservative candidates who oppose the legislative goals that workers support and, for the most part, seek to curb the effectiveness of their unions.

The AFL-CIO seriously regards its legislative operation as the "people's lobby," devoted in nine cases out of ten to causes that involve workers in general rather than union members in particular. The federal minimum wage, for instance, directly affects the earnings of only a handful of union members, and has an indirect impact on very few more. A national health-care system, its proponents believe, would increase the protection and reduce the direct costs of medical care for many union members, but since almost all of them enjoy far better and cheaper protection than other workers through their union contracts, they have far less to gain from it.

In its pursuit of what it regards as the best interests of all the people, the AFL-CIO has sometimes been accused of ignoring the imperatives of private enterprise. On the legislative level the accusation is true. The AFL-CIO's imperative is the general welfare of labor, not capital. With more confidence in America, perhaps, than the industrial and mercantile leaders, the AFL-CIO believes a free, democratic society is resilient enough to make any changes that are necessary to promote human progress and well-being.

Let me sum up.

There are many warts on the surface of the labor movement. They are far more visible, and even more painful, to those who believe unions are indispensable to a free society than to those who are indifferent or hostile.

Over the last two hundred years the struggle of American workers to achieve a measure of democracy in the workplace has produced both heroes and villains. The proportion compares favorably with the fields of politics, the professions, and most especially with business and industry.

Democracy and integrity are union essentials, but they can be lost if they are taken for granted.

Nothing has more gravely weakened the faith of workers in the institutions of government than the flagrant, unpunished violations of the labor relations law by corporations that still, forty years after the Wagner Act, refuse to accept the right of workers to organize and bargain collectively.

Differences between management and labor are inevitable in any free society, whether its economic mix is mostly weighted toward private enterprise, as in America, or toward socialism, as in Britain and Scandinavia. At best the differences will be accommodated after hard bargaining. At worst they will be accommodated after a strike. But there is no easy formula for resolving them, as those who were beguiled by the Moral Re-Armament flurry of the 1950s eventually discovered.

It is true that many of the intellectuals and academicians, who once ardently supported the labor movement and the CIO in particular, have turned critical now that unions have gained a measure of success. This was, in all probability, inevitable; as Irving Howe has written in another context, the result of nostalgia is "to set off the supposed best of one against the acknowledged worst of the other." Or as Bok and Dunlop concluded in their definitive volume six years ago, "The problems of unions are problems for all of us and, in our varying ways, we must surmount them together or not at all."

Part Four

Introduction to Commentaries and Codes

Arch N. Booth

*Former President, Chamber of Commerce
of the United States*

Is it possible to prevent business and the professions from sinking further and faster into the quicksand of government regulation? Is it possible to make a deliberate choice between further loss of freedom or of using voluntary action to raise the standard of ethics and morality in the commercial community?

The answer is that not only is it possible but it is now being done by numerous enlightened associations. There are excellent examples of successful voluntary efforts by trade and professional organizations that should inspire others to take the steps to choose between freedom and coercion.

The commentaries and the codes that follow are some of the brightest examples of what can be accomplished by taking the initiative through excellent professional leadership—through exercising patience, persistence, and the use of well-defined principles of procedure.

Today most association leadership and individual members are filled with concern and good intentions. But apprehension and strong positive emotions about right and wrong are of little help. They are a poor answer to the crying need for action.

Trade associations are in an ideal position to provide the essentials:

—a code of conduct or set of guidelines for those within the voluntary association;

—a process, a method, an arrangement of steps to be taken by the organization to encourage compliance and to discourage or penalize noncompliance;

—professional leadership to provide the planning, the procedures and, most important of all, the sustained action so vitally necessary.

Mrs. Virginia Knauer, special assistant to the president for Consumer Affairs has said that consumers need to know where to go with their complaints, and an independent third party they can trust to take their complaints to.

A trade association can be that "third party they can trust."

There are many other areas of action, aside from consumer relations, where conduct needs improvement—where associations can provide the procedures and the essential guidance—where strong leadership is needed to raise standards of ethics and morality through the process of evolving and growing.

Excellent results are being gained by associations through strong commitments, careful planning, competent professional staff work—all backed up by members who are patient, determined, and willing to start small and grow toward fully effective performance.

The examples presented here cover a wide range of problems and human relationships. They run from direct selling to broadcasting to purchasing management to football coaching and others. The procedures all follow basic patterns that can be applied almost without limit to groups choosing to accept the priceless opportunity of self-regulation instead of continued loss of freedom in our economic and social systems.

There is wide recognition of the fact that the vast majority of American commercial people are honest, ethical, and concerned about the public interest. There is equally wide concern about what General Hugh Johnson of NRA fame called, "the lunatic fringe," the small percentage of disreputable fly-by-night operators who care nothing about ethics or the disastrous consequence of their substandard actions. This part of the problem is being dealt with by constructive programs.

Neil H. Offen, Senior Vice President and Legal Counsel of the Direct Selling Association, tells in his commentary how their group started from step number one and developed one of the finest ethical programs in America to cope with both phases of the problem. He describes the process by which they provide service for members, nonmembers, and the buying public.

The initial step for the group, Mr. Offen says, "was to professionalize and upgrade its national trade association and devise a viable self-regulatory mechanism to assist consumers and legitimate companies in eliminating marketplace abuses."

Along with that move came the desire to take positive, constructive steps to improve the industry's relations with government and to give all possible help to consumers defrauded or abused.

Says Mr. Offen, "The seed for developing an effective self-regulatory mechanism was planted out of economic necessity and the desire of industry leaders to counter a negative image and speak out on behalf of a method of retailing that provides many people with income earning opportunities and consumers with quality products and services at fair prices."

Those words, with suitable variations, state the basic challenge troubling leaders in every line of commerce in America.

The methods the Direct Selling Association chose to meet the challenge that threatened them should stimulate thoughts and action by every trade or professional association leader as they seek usefulness, influence, and significance for themselves and their organizations in this period of crisis.

H. Jackson Pontius tells a similar story about the sixty-three-year effort in the National Association of Realtors® "to ensure honorable, faithful, and competent service to clients, customers, and other members of the public. They believed that through their collective efforts the ends of national policy and the general welfare could be served. . . . They had an awareness, too, that a voluntary commitment to peer review by knowledgeable, informed men and women sharing the same commitment had immeasurable advantages over resort to courts of law and equity."

Then Mr. Pontius writes, "Most of all, they recognized that

self-discipline in the interest of protecting the public was not inconsistent with the preservation of a competitive marketplace."

Consider one more example—the problems faced by football coaches facing the pressures involved in living up to their principles of conduct and at the same time having their teams win more games than they lose.

William W. Murray, Executive Director of the American Football Coaches Association, writes the fascinating story of how they developed a code of ethics and an enforcement procedure that have enabled coaches "to get the message" after being called to account for alleged breaches of good conduct.

The results—the benefits of this self-regulation have been outstanding proof of the validity of the procedures that can apply to other lines of professional or business activity and give the desperately needed ethical underpinning of our freedom.

Taking the initiative in raising the standards of morality and ethics within the professional and commercial community is a natural function for voluntary associations and is the most valuable kind of leadership they can give at a time when actions in both the private and public sectors are being questioned as never before.

The process requires skills of a highly professional nature. It quickly separates the strong from the weak.

The use of a code of ethics calls for an announced, deliberate commitment to certain responsibilities such as accurate and truthful representation of products and services, the use of a specific and understandable guarantee or warranty.

To be effective the code must provide for an orderly means of redress with prompt and certain follow-through to a definite conclusion.

Simplicity of language and procedures is the key to proper cooperation and understanding.

A commitment to take steps to raise the standard of ethics within a trade or professional group must be based upon a clear recognition of the basic problem to be dealt with.

One executive stated the choice facing every association: "Isn't it a lot better to mediate a complaint through your association than through a government agency? There are plenty of government agencies out there willing to do it for us, but the question of how far we are willing to go to regulate ourselves may be the key to dealing with increasing government encroachment. Therefore, we must apply ourselves to resolving legitimate consumer concerns voluntarily if remedies to those problems are not to be permanently imposed by legislative, regulatory, or other forms of coercive control."

Our choice is clear: we must take voluntary action to increase the number of people practicing honesty and ethics—or find our freedom repressed by centralized authority and coercive regulation.

Stockton Helffrich, Director of the Code Authority, National Association of Broadcasters, says ". . . freedoms can only be sustained through an exercise of the responsibilities that go with them."

Recently, in speaking about the new responsibilities for trade associations, James P. Low, president of the American Society of Association Executives, stated:

> Trade associations are experiencing their second evolution within a decade. A major shift of influence and responsibility came to associations a few years ago with the advent of issues that required businessmen to respond through a unified voice to issues concerning consumerism, environment, product safety, energy, and a host of others. These issues required trade associations and their chief executives to take a high profile as spokesmen and advocates for the industry.
>
> The second evolution has propelled the trade associations from the posture of external reaction to government to the internal monitoring of the industry itself. Trade associations are now working on this internal front. The association executives and elected leadership are taking dynamic action to self-police their industries through codes of ethics, standardization, product evaluation, and certification. More work must be done in the future. Most associations already have the necessary machinery, self-discipline, and confidence of their members to activate effective in-house programs to make their industries responsible for high ethical standards of conduct.

In view of Mr. Low's statement that trade associations are

now working on the task of internal monitoring, the essay appearing at the conclusion of this section authored by Earl Kintner, the distinguished Washington lawyer and former chairman of the Federal Trade Commission, should prove extremely valuable to association and industry executives. Attorney Kintner has long been recognized as an outstanding authority on regulatory law. His essay benefits not only from his established expertise in regulatory law, but includes observations from his special research related to the purposes of this volume.

The significant thing to be found in a study of these commentaries and codes is how thoroughly and earnestly so many associations have gone about the task of setting up codes and structures for enforcement. And more importantly, how effective even mild sanctions and reprimands can be if the leadership of an industry really inspires its members to live up to their code for their own good and for the public's good.

Commentary on Code of Ethics of Direct Selling Association

Neil H. Offen

Senior Vice President and Legal Counsel

How should an industry that has a large fringe element of disreputable fly-by-night operators go about taking effective action to counter the negative image that fringe group brings to it? The answer the direct selling industry came up with was to professionalize and upgrade its national trade association and devise a viable self-regulatory mechanism to assist both consumers and legitimate companies in eliminating marketplace abuses.

Formed in 1910, the association for the door-to-door method of marketing consumer products was headquartered until 1969 in the small town of Winona, Minnesota, with a total staff of two executives. During its first sixty years of life its raison d'etre could be described as that of fighting all government attempts to regulate it—attempts that were mostly at the municipal level.

Governmental control proposals markedly increased by the late sixties and were motivated in some instances by anticompetitive desires of local merchants, as well as by consumer abuses. The age of consumerism, however, had arrived. The industry itself was also experiencing internal change; it was growing at a tremendous rate. As a result, it became apparent to the top executives of leading firms that their association in Winona was not doing the job that needed to be done.

Accordingly, the decision was made to pay the price of professionalizing the staff and moving the association to Washington, D.C. J. Robert Brouse, a highly respected career association manager, was retained to handle this transition and to lead DSA in this building program. Along with this move came the desire to take positive, constructive steps to improve the industry's relations with government and to help consumers defrauded or abused by industry members. The seed for developing an effective self-regulatory mechanism was planted out of economic necessity and the desire of industry leaders to counter a negative image and speak out on behalf of a method of retailing that provided all Americans income opportunities and consumers quality products and services at fair prices.

Problems, however, arose almost immediately. Direct selling firms market their products through independent retailers (approximately three million persons today). Industry leaders prided themselves on being among the last bastions of free enterprise in America. Any attempt to implement a program of third-party controls, whether governmental or private, was feared and resented. Competition for salespeople is keen in the industry with proselytizing of sales forces a serious problem that furthered the threats inherent in acceptance of a code program. These problems were offset by the pressing need for the industry to take concerted, positive action and the commitment to proceed was made.

Legal counsel was next brought in to protect the newly vitalized association from potential liability in enforcing the code and to draft a code that could withstand legal challenges, yet do the job. Gerald E. Gilbert, a partner at the prestigious Washington law firm of Hogan and Hartson, was called in by Mr. Brouse. General Counsel Gilbert proceeded to research the entire area of private self-regulation efforts and relied on four main sources on which to base the DSA code and its procedures.

First, the Federal Trade Commission's pronouncements on codes and its actions against associations for going too far in this area were analyzed. Particular attention was paid to the dissenting opinion of former FTC Commissioner Phillip Elman in regard to the commission's analysis of the code of the Magazine Publishers Association, a group whose members produce products sold door-to-door and, therefore, an appropriate object for DSA observation. (Note: No magazine solicitation firms belonged to DSA.) Commissioner Elman's main objectives resulted from his comparison of public and private entities. He believed that when coercive powers are exercised by a government agency—especially powers to impose fines and penalties for violations of a standard of conduct—they are clearly defined by specific statutory provisions and are subject to judicial review. He feared these powers were awesome and might be too easily abused by private industry, no matter how well intentioned the industry association. Accordingly, DSA drafted its code without provisions for fines and other penalties, yet with enough teeth to be effective. These innovative "teeth" will be discussed subsequently.

Second, Mr. Gilbert reviewed various FTC advisory opinions and law review articles.

Third, various discussions with FTC officials, on an informal and unofficial basis, proved to be very helpful sources of information.

Fourth, the Administrative Procedure Act was used as a model for drafting the procedural safeguards into the enforcement aspects of the code.

The code, as finally drafted, recognized the obligations and moral and legal responsibilities of association members to consumers. It set forth the basic fair and ethical principles and practices to which DSA companies pledge their adherence. Annually, each member firm is asked twice to renew that pledge—once when it submits its dues payment and again at the annual meeting of the association. The code is meant to be a living document, subject to amendments which reflect changing times and circumstances. It is meant to lay a solid foundation in the areas of truthfulness, guarantees, terms of sale, and responsibility for the acts of a company's salespeople. DSA firms, for the purposes of the code, voluntarily accept responsibility for acts of employees and/or independent distributors falling within the purview of the code. This acceptance of responsibility for the conduct of independent retailers is an example of the industry going an extra mile to insure that the code is truly viable and not merely a token document that could easily be circumvented.

The DSA code of ethics is strictly a consumer protection code. The net effect of its implementation is to make restitution to consumers who have been mistreated and, thereby, make it more difficult for charlatans to deceive the public. Naturally, this results in improving the climate of business for legitimate merchants and helps promote competition in a fair and nondeceptive manner. Free and open competition is, therefore, fostered by the code and it is not used, as perhaps some codes are, as a subterfuge for price fixing or other anticompetitive acts or practices. In the same vein, DSA opposes occupational licensing concepts whenever encountered since the position of the association is that licensing chills competition, is ultimately inflationary, unduly subverts the free market and does not work to eliminate consumer abuses.

Since ease of entry into the industry is a hallmark of direct selling, the need for industry-wide ethical standards, backed up by a reliable third party, becomes pressing in this age of consumer suspicion of business. DSA firms offer income earning opportunities to all, regardless of race, education, financial position, religion, age, or sex. Direct selling is often used as a second income source and more than half of all direct sellers are women. For part time and career salespersons, direct selling is marked by individual freedom—the ability to work when, where, and how one desires. With all this freedom, so highly valued by corporation presidents and local salespersons alike, a code of ethics establishes necessary bounds.

How, then, did the industry fashion a code that works, yet does not violate the antitrust laws that severely limit actions industry members may take against each other? DSA's answer was to establish a position for an independent code administrator to be manned by a person of stature and impeccable credentials for competence and integrity. The administrator is mandated to conduct investigations into complaints filed under the code and follow due process safeguards devised by counsel. Upon reaching a decision against a member firm, the administrator *shall* advise appropriate state or federal authorities of the possible violation of law that has been committed and offer to cooperate with the authority in any feasible way toward the removal or correction of the violation for the mutual benefit of the public and the association. It is intended that such action by the administrator be highly publicized so that the governmental unit involved could not ignore the situation and would be hard pressed not to take remedial action. Since this code was established over five years ago, not one consumer complaint under our code has had to be referred to the government for action. Each complaint determined by the administrator to be valid has been quickly remedied by the company charged.

Two outstanding Washington attorneys have served as code administrator. The first, Clarence Lundquist, served as wage and price administrator of the Department of Labor under consecutive appointments by presidents Eisenhower, Kennedy, and Johnson with confirmation of each appointment by the United States Senate. The second and present administrator is former Alabama Congressman Kenneth Roberts. Appointed by the association's board of directors on an annual retainer, the administrator operates autonomously and exercises totally independent judgment on code issues brought before him. In commenting on the code, Roberts stated:

> The code represents the thinking of people in industry who believe they can approach the consumer with a new format that provides fairness, right to redress and satisfaction within the framework of a commercial relationship that is probably the oldest in the United States. It means that with proper attitude, industry can demonstrate that not only the customer is always right, but that it's better for the seller to voluntarily prove it than to be forced by the government to do so.

What are the key weaknesses of any ethics program, of our own code and what have we done to eliminate them? First and foremost, not enough consumers are aware of the existence of this self-regulatory mechanism. On the first anniversary of the code, DSA recorded a total of twenty-five complaints against member firms. Since these firms did well over two billion dollars in sales through millions of sales contracts, it was obvious that DSA wasn't getting its message to the public and that our member firms weren't helping it spread the word. (Today, industry sales volume is estimated at some six billion dollars per annum or some 2 percent of all retailing.)

Consequently, the association prepared and distributed a "Code Action Program" (CAP) for all our member companies. The CAP was intended to provide a guide on how to promote the code and outlined nine activities that could be undertaken. DSA Vice President of Communications Eileen Creamer O'Neill, who had responsibility for this program, provided actual letters, scripts, press releases, and similar items that the companies could reproduce as their own. She also produced a brochure, "DSA Opens the Door to Consumer Protection," which was published in quantity for internal distribution and for sale to member firms who then could imprint it with their own name, logo, address, and so forth and distribute it to the general public. The first million copies of the brochure were printed under a grant from Avon Products, Inc., and the first company subsequently to make purchases totaling a million copies for dissemination to prospective consumers was The Kirby Company.

At the same time, DSA recognized the need to conduct a public education campaign. Unfortunately, resources were, and still are, limited. (The total association budget at the time was around $300 thousand with top priority given to legal and legislative firefighting.) Accordingly, DSA selected a pilot project state, Wisconsin, to test methods of communicating with consumers about our assistance program. Radio and television public service announcements were prepared, press releases issued, and DSA staff and corporate executive appearances on talk shows arranged. We contacted state legislators, consumer protection groups, chambers of commerce, better business bureaus, extension home economists, and various civic groups. Our Wisconsin based companies were also recruited to play active roles in the project.

One of the lessons learned from the project has been that it takes continuing effort and a large amount of money to effectively communicate to the public. Another was that a few of our companies were actively promoting the code. The complaints we were receiving in increasing numbers against these companies were the result of their doing their job. These firms were not the bad apples of the industry, but rather, were ones trying to implement higher ethical standards among their sales forces. It would be ironic to condemn such firms because they had the courage to invite complaints.

A solution was needed to counter our own internal lack of capability to promote our self-regulation program. We were sure that the funds were available from industry sources and that we had to find a way to tap them. Consumer education activities seemed to be what were primarily needed. These activities, we thought, should not be limited to our own code program but should cover the direct selling industry as a method of retailing, provide tips on what consumers should be wary of in dealing with door-to-door salespersons, inform aggrieved consumers as to where they could go for assistance, and the like. Out of this recognition was born the Direct Selling Education Foundation, a nonprofit, public foundation dedicated to establishing, organizing, promoting, aiding, and engaging in exclusively public educational purposes, including awarding grants to further the cause of consumer and general public education through research, educational symposia and development and publication of educational materials. It is hoped the foundation's activities will assist, through a ripple effect if not directly, in acquainting the general public with the industry's code program. To date, over $500 thousand has been contributed to the foundation and it has, among other things, funded the publication of a consumer protection pamphlet entitled "Be Wise!" which contains tips on things to watch out for and how to deal with door-to-door sellers. Our code message is being transmitted but we have still to reach large numbers of the population.

Another problem we have run into is that we are effectively precluded from taking action against companies that do not belong to DSA due to antitrust law restrictions. Since the code program is voluntary, in the sense that membership in the association is voluntary, a company agrees to abide by the code without being permanently wed. If a firm does not belong to the association, thereby subscribing to obey our ethical standards, we have no jurisdiction to act against it. To do so might entail significant legal liability, although our motives may be pure. The present legal test is geared to analyzing the effect that our actions have on competition.

By way of additional background, DSA does not accredit its members nor provide product marketing research services, as do many other industry associations. Accordingly, the dangers of industry cooperative efforts resulting in antitrust actions are diminished. The common denominator between our member firms is that each markets products to be sold in the home. The product lines are as varied as can be imagined. Furthermore, we represent only a hundred or so corporations out of a total of several thousand firms in the industry—although our firms account for about 50 percent of total industry sales. Generally, our members are the best and most reputable companies in the industry, companies which effectively process consumer complaints themselves since they want satisfied customers. The worst offenders do not belong to DSA and, therefore, cannot be reached by our code. This inability to help in the most grievous cases brought to our attention is not only frustrating, but also endangers the effectiveness of the program. We fear that consumers may not understand the complexity of antitrust law and might blame DSA for holding out a promise of help and not being responsive to their needs.

One possible solution that I personally would like to explore is the creation of consumer redress funds. These funds, perhaps contributed jointly by industry and government, would be available to make restitution to consumers who had been harmed and have nowhere else to turn for satisfaction of their legitimate complaints. Funding could come from fines levied by the government in litigated cases or, perhaps, from voluntary industry contributions. The idea seems worth exploring. At the same time, steps should be taken to allow industry associations to assist consumers even if the complained-against party is not a member of the association. Equal treatment must be accorded such firms and due process safeguards must be met. The present inability to act against nonmembers, and the loophole that a company belonging to the association need merely quit to avoid our sanctions, must be altered. Reform of antitrust laws is required.

In the area of procedure, our original code was criticized for allowing too much time to elapse should the entire code process be utilized. Briefly, such a full utilization is outlined as follows:

Step 1

Complaint Received in Writing
Complaint Forwarded to Accused Party
Informal Investigation Begun

Step 2

Informal Hearing Called and Conducted
Administrator's Preliminary Decision Delivered

Step 3

Opportunity Provided for Company Rebuttal
Appeal for Special Ethics Committee Review Made

Step 4

Members to Special Ethics Committee Appointed
Positions by Administrator and Accused Company Submitted
Formal Hearing Date (minimum thirty days' notice) Selected
Formal Hearing Held and Decision Made

Step 5

Company Found Guilty and Fails to Satisy the Consumer upon Instruction of the Code Administrator
Association Requests Federal/State Authorities to Prosecute Member
Industry and Public Informed of Association Actions

The time elements required for each stage of the above process were substantially reduced as a result of criticism received from sources asked for comments, both within and outside the industry. However, several months could still elapse should a company take advantage of all the procedural safeguards in the code, with the consumer left without relief in the interim. The same situation, unfortunately, is true even if a consumer immediately seeks governmental assistance or files a private legal action. Our code approach, however, has been quite speedy in helping consumers. No code complaint has had to go to the formal hearing stage and the average time elapsed from receipt of complaint to final resolution is less than two weeks. I think this speaks well for our code administrator, our consumer ombudsman (a member of our staff whose job it is to assist the code administrator and be an internal consumer advocate) and their administrative support team. We are now satisfied that our code mechanism actually works quickly and effectively. Peer group pressure and the threat of public embarrassment (that is, a company's own trade association calling for its prosecution) seem to be the key elements for this success. It also is an indication that fining and expulsion are not essential ingredients for a successful code. Unfortunately, our major weaknesses still remain in that not enough consumers know of our program and our ethics program only applies to our member firms.

One problem that cannot be remedied by the association alone is government's unresponsiveness and/or inability to act. Should we ever have to go the full complaint mechanism route and request prosecution, will our efforts be negated should the local FTC regional director or the appropriate assistant state attorney general refuse to act? Our experience has been that there are conflicts between state and federal regulatory authorities with representatives of both groups claiming the other is inefficient and unresponsive to consumer needs. Industry could easily get caught in the middle of this conflict but industry could also act as a bridge between them and as a conduit for information and constructive suggestions. It is hoped that our self-regulation efforts will aid federal/state cooperation.

Establishment of DSA's code program has also brought about some originally unforeseen benefits and uses. Because we take an action, proconsumer legislative lobbying position in almost every state, DSA has established excellent lines of communication with state officials responsible for consumer protection activities. Our staff continually informs regulators and legislators about our code program and urges them to help us get the message across to consumers. As an example, the staff of the attorney general of Ohio contacted DSA to indicate that they were about to take action against one of our member firms, but thought they would give DSA a chance to invoke our code to settle the issue, thereby avoiding long and involved litigation. DSA contacted the company and it immediately agreed to make redress to a large group of aggrieved persons to the tune of some $60 thousand in refunds.

Another offshoot of our code promotional efforts has been the creation of our Zero Complaint Award. Developed by Stanley Home Products in cooperation with DSA, this award is given by a company to its sales managers who during the course of a year have no consumer complaints lodged against them or their sales units with either DSA, under our code of ethics, or with the company. The idea is for the field sales force to successfully handle consumer complaints on the scene, thereby keeping consumers happy and not bogging down the company or DSA with unnecessary complaint handling. At Stanley's first award ceremonies, over 25 percent of the company's 250 top managers did not have one complaint lodged against them. This represented over three million sales transactions, a truly remarkable accomplishment. The next year nearly 50 percent of Stanley dealers qualified. Every year new Stanley dealers vie to win the Zero Complaint Award, knowing that even one disgruntled customer can disqualify them. Competition is fierce and the company is quite pleased with the program, as are other DSA members who have since inaugurated it. Apparently, the customers of these award winners are pleased as well, and it all resulted from the existence of our code of ethics and the promotion of ethical conduct. Company recognition of high ethical standards serves as a source of motivation and makes good business sense as exemplified by this offshoot of our code.

Another unforeseen use of our code arose as the brainchild of W. Alan Luce, vice president of legal and consumer affairs of DSA. Mr. Luce's primary association responsibilities have been in the area of state and local governmental affairs, and his field experience is extensive. While DSA has constructive legislative positions in many areas, one concept we oppose, mentioned previously, is the attempt to license our company salespeople. All too often such licensing proposals are extremely burdensome and ineffective, as well as discriminatory. We are frequently told by licensing proponents that our member firms are not the targets of the proposal. Rest assured, we are promised, the authorities will not bother our people. The problem that arises is if a law is enacted, we feel an obligation to inform our members to instruct their people of its existence and to abide by it or challenge it in the courts.

What can, therefore, be done to help both the municipalities that feel a need for these measures and our firms? Mr. Luce, recognizing the potential of our code program, came up with a possible solution—a code of ethics exemption ordinance. Based on a general code program that provides an independent administrator (such as ours), sanctions that can be taken (such as ours), and the capability to respond in a short period of time (such as ours), Mr. Luce drafted a model ordinance amendment that could be attached to a municipal or state licensing law. If the proponents of legislation truly did not want to burden legitimate business, here was a constitutional way for them to exempt such firms. Control over the granting of the exemption based on a company or industry code of ethics program is left with the city. So far, Lansing, Michigan, Bloomington, Indiana, Prince Georges County, Maryland, and several smaller municipalities have adopted our code's alternative compliance concept. More will be coming. DSA still opposes licensing proposals, but if a community is intent on promulgating one, DSA member companies, through our code program, have a way to avoid the burdens that licensing entails.

If you are interested in creating a code program, the following are some tips that should be kept in mind.

1. Be clear on your objectives, and make sure of your constituent's support. It is important to get the commitment from the president of each company.
2. Set up a realistic timetable for developing and implementing your code.
3. Know the costs of running a code program, and be sure you have long-term as well as short-term funding.
4. Make sure to provide for changing the code to meet new situations and challenges. It should be a living document.
5. Gear your code to the problems faced by your industry or profession.

6. Be aware of the latest developments and trends in the area of self-regulation. Pay particular attention to FTC, Justice Department, and Congressional activities.
7. Make sure legal counsel is consulted and the code is legally defensible.
8. Get expert advice on how to promote the code and how to go about educating the public.
9. Watch your rhetoric. Don't promise more than you can deliver.
10. Write it as simply as possible. Avoid jargon and gobbledygook.
11. Be totally committed to being responsive and objective.
12. Select an independent administrator of unquestionable competence and integrity.
13. Be patient, maintain your perspective, and don't lose your sense of humor.

The benefits of adopting an effective code program become more and more apparent for us as time goes by. Our code has been amended to cover new areas of consumer abuse, to streamline procedures as we test them through actual operation and to reflect our continuing commitment to prove that our attempts at industry self-regulation are more than mere rhetoric. Our major problem is still to inform consumers of our existence and to win their trust as an industry association committed to helping them and thereby helping our own member companies. The standards enunciated in our code do not constitute the industry's minimal level of ethics. Rather, our code efforts are raising the industry's consciousness and setting higher goals for all to follow. By doing so the consuming public and the industry will be better served in the days ahead.

Code of Ethics and Regulations of the Direct Selling Association

Adopted 1970. Amended 1975.

PREAMBLE

The Direct Selling Association, recognizing that companies engaged in direct selling assume certain responsibilities toward consumers arising out of the personal-contact method of distribution of their products and services, hereby sets forth the basic fair and ethical principles and practices to which member companies of the association will continue to adhere in the conduct of their business.

I. Products or Services

The offer of products or services for sale by member companies of the Association shall be accurate and truthful as to price, grade, quality, make, value, performance, quantity, currency of model, and availability.

II. Guarantee

The terms of any guarantee offered by the seller in connection with the sale shall be furnished to the buyer in writing at the time of the sale or delivery and shall clearly state the nature and extent of said guarantee in a manner that fully conforms to the guaranty regulations promulgated by the Federal Trade Commission in accordance with Public Law 93-637. The manufacturer, distributor and/or seller shall fully and promptly perform in accordance with the terms of all guarantees offered to consumers.

III. Terms of Sale

A written order or receipt shall be delivered to the customer at the time of sale, which sets forth in language that is clear and free of ambiguity:

A. All the terms and conditions of sale, with specification of the total amount customer will be required to pay, including all interest, service charges and fees, and other costs and expenses;

B. The name and address of the salesperson or member of firm represented;

C. That the contract or negotiable instrument signed by the customer in connection with the sale may be sold or assigned by the seller to a third party, if such is the fact.

IV. Responsibility

In the event any consumer shall complain that the salesperson or representative offering for sale the products or service of a member company has engaged in any improper course of conduct pertaining to the sales presentation of its goods or services, the member company shall promptly investigate the complaint and shall take such steps as it may find appropriate and necessary under the circumstances to cause the redress of any wrongs which its investigation discloses to have been committed.

V. Deceptive or Unlawful Trade Practices

No member company of the Association shall engage in any deceptive or unlawful trade practice.

VI. Administration

A. Interpretation and Execution. The Board of Directors of the Direct Selling Association shall appoint a Code Administrator to serve, subject to the will of the Board, on an annual basis and will provide such Code Administrator with the authority necessary and proper to enable him to discharge the responsibilities entrusted to him in this Code. The Administrator will be responsible directly and solely to the Board. The Board of Directors will establish all regulations necessary to administer the provisions of this Code.

B. Code Administrator. The Administrator shall be a person of recognized integrity, knowledgeable in the industry, and of a stature that will command respect by the industry and from the public. He shall appoint a staff adequate and competent to assist him in the discharge of his duties. During his term of office, neither the Administrator nor any member of his staff shall be an officer, director, employee, or substantial stockholder in any member or affiliate of the DSA. The Administrator, in accordance with the regulations established by the Board of Directors as provided herein, shall hear and determine all charges against members subscribing hereto, affording such members or persons an opportunity to be heard fully. The Administrator shall have the power to originate any proceedings, and shall at all times have the full cooperation of all members.

C. Member Responsibility. Member companies will be considered responsible for Code violations by their solicitors and representatives where the Administrator finds, after considering all the facts, that a violation of the Code has occurred and the member has either authorized such practice found to be violative, condoned it, or in any other way supported it. A member shall be considered responsible for a Code violation by its solicitors or representatives, although it had no knowledge of such violations, if the Administrator finds that the member was grossly negligent by failing to establish procedures whereby the member would be kept informed of the activity of its solicitors and representatives. For purposes of this Code, in the interest of fostering consumer protection, companies shall voluntarily not raise the independent contractor status of salespersons distributing their products or services as a defense against code violation allegations and such action shall not be construed to be a waiver of the companies' right to raise such defense under any other circumstance.

D. Procedure. If it is determined by the Administrator or by a special ethics committee, in accordance with the regulations of this Code, that a violation of the Code has occurred, the Administrator may then consult with independent legal counsel to determine whether the facts that have been ascertained amount to a violation of state or Federal law. If the Administrator believes that such a violation has occurred, the Administrator may advise the appropriate Federal or local agency in any feasible way toward the removal or correction of such violation for the mutual benefit of the public and the Association.

E. Additional Functions of Administrator. The Administrator shall answer as promptly as possible all queries posed by members relating to the code and its application, and, when appropriate, may suggest, for consideration by the Board of Directors, new regulations, definitions, or other implementations to more fully give effect hereto.

The Administrator shall undertake through his office to maintain and improve all relations with better business bureaus and other organizations, both private and public, with a view toward improving the industry's relations with the public and receiving information from such organizations relating to the industry's sales activities.

F. Duties of members. The members subscribing to this Code recognize that its success will require diligence in creating an awareness among their employees and/or the independent retailers marketing the members' products or services of the members' obligations under the Code. No subscribing party shall in any way attempt to persuade, induce, or coerce another party to breach this Code, and the subscribers hereto agree that the inducing of the breach of this Code is considered a violation of the Code.

VII. Amendments

This Code may be amended by vote of two-thirds of the Board of Directors.

VIII. Amendments

Amendment 1. For the purpose of this Code, pyramid or endless chain schemes shall be considered consumer transactions actionable under this Code. The Code Administrator shall determine whether such pyramid or endless chain schemes constitute a violation of this Code in accordance with applicable Federal, state and/or local law or regulation.

REGULATIONS FOR ENFORCEMENT OF DSA CODE OF ETHICS

1. Receipt of Complaint

Upon receipt of a complaint that a member has violated the Code of Ethics, the Administrator shall request that the complaining party reduce the complaint to writing. If no written statement of the charges is received from the complaining party within ten days, no further action will be taken by the Administrator. Once a written complaint is received, the Administrator shall forward a copy of the complaint to the member against whom the charges have been made, with a notification that a preliminary investigation is being conducted and that the member will be informed of the results. During the investigation, the accused member may be asked to comment orally or in writing.

All notices and requests made in accordance with these regulations shall be provided by registered mail, return receipt requested, and the term "days," when used in connection with such notice and requests, shall encompass only business days.

2. Informal Investigation and Disposition Procedure

The Administrator, in his discretion, may call for an informal hearing, the purpose of which is to gather evidence, and take testimony surrounding a Code of Ethics complaint. Parties interested in the complaint shall be notified in writing of the date, time, and place of said hearing. Following the hearing, any evidence adduced shall be reduced to writing, and after due consideration, the Administrator shall communicate both the evidence and his decision thereon, if any, to the parties of interest. This preliminary decision shall not be binding upon any party involved with the complaint. Should any party be dissatisfied with the decision of the Administrator following an informal hearing, such dissatisfaction shall be forwarded to the Administrator in writing and the formal procedures under Sections 3 and 4 of the Regulations of the Code of Ethics will govern activity necessary to dispose of the complaint.

3. Post-Investigation Procedure

If, after his investigation, the Administrator believes the charges are unsupportable or frivolous, the Administrator shall terminate action on the charges. Such decision shall be made known to the member in question and to the complaining party who initiated the charges.

If, however, the Administrator believes after his investigation that a violation of the Code may have occurred and that further action should be taken, the Administrator shall so notify the accused member. The member shall have the opportunity to comment on the findings on or before the tenth day after notice is mailed.

After the accused member has submitted his comments to the Administrator, if the Administrator is satisfied that the facts revealed by his investigation are sufficiently rebutted or that the situation that formed the basis for the complaint has been corrected, he shall terminate action on the charges and shall notify the complaining and accused parties of his action. If the Administrator, however, is of the belief that the facts are not sufficiently rebutted or that the situation has not been corrected within fifteen days from the time he sent notice of his findings to the accused member, he shall so notify the accused member. Either the accused member or the Administrator shall have the right, within fifteen days from the date the accused member received notification of the Administrator's findings, to request a hearing by a special ethics committee. If the accused member makes the request for such a hearing, it must be in writing to the Administrator on or before the 15th day after the aforementioned notice from the Administrator is received.

4. Ethics Committee and Hearing Procedure

a. If a hearing is requested by an accused member, or if the Administrator desires to request one, the Administrator shall so notify the chairman of the Board of Directors, and the chairman shall immediately appoint a special ethics committee and name a chairman thereof to be comprised of five persons who are members of the Board of Directors, none of whom shall be a competitor of the accused member.

b. The chairman of the special ethics committee shall request the Administrator and the accused member to supply him within five days a brief outline of their respective positions concerning the pending allegations. Upon receipt of those outlines, the chairman shall disseminate the same to the members of his ethics committee, and within five days of the receipt of those outlines by the members, the chairman shall poll the members of his committee to determine whether a majority of the committee is in favor of terminating all further action by the Administrator concerning the charges or whether a hearing should be held. In the case of the former, the chairman shall notify the Administrator and the accused party of the committee's decision, and the Administrator shall in turn inform the complaining witness that no further action will be taken. If the committee decides that a hearing should be held, the chairman shall select a date for the hearing within twenty days of the time of the committee decision, unless more time is requested by the complaining witness or accused member on a showing of special need for the extension.

c. The accused member shall be given fifteen days' notice of the date of the hearing. At the hearing, the accused member shall have an opportunity to be represented by counsel and to refute the charges against him. He will also have an opportunity to hear the evidence and confront and cross-examine witnesses against him. He will further have the opportunity to present witnesses for his position, which witnesses also shall be subject to confrontation and cross-examination by the Administrator. All witnesses and the Administrator shall be subject to questioning by the members of the committee. The Administrator may be represented by counsel. A transcript will be made of the hearing at the request and expense of the accused member, or if the Administrator determines that a transcript is necessary to protect the integrity of the Association and/or the rights of the complaining witnesses. If a transcript is so requested, or if the Administrator determines that a record of the hearing is necessary, a tape recording of the hearing may be made in lieu of a transcript if all parties agree.

d. The decision by the ethics committee will be made upon a secret ballot after the committee has made an opportunity to discuss the charges and the evidence presented during the hearing. The violation or nonviolation of the Code will be detemined in all hearings by a majority vote of the ethics committee. The committee will determine either that no further action shall be taken or that the Administrator may proceed in accordance with the provisions of the Code.

e. The hearing shall be closed to all persons except the hearing committee, the Administrator, the charged member, and any necessary witnesses.

5. Action by the Association

If the Administrator or the special ethics committee has determined that a violation of the Code has taken place in accordance with the procedures provided in part 2 herein, the Administrator may then consult with independent legal counsel to determine whether the facts that have been ascertained amount to a violation of state or Federal law. If the Administrator believes that a violation of state or Federal law has occurred, he shall so notify the accused member by registered mail, return receipt requested, and after ten days following such notice the Administrator shall advise the appropriate Federal or local agency of his conclusion and offer to cooperate with such agency in any feasible way toward the removal or correction of such violation for the mutual benefit of the public and the Association.

6. Restrictions

a. At no time during the investigation or the hearing of charges against a member shall the Administrator or any member of a special ethics committee confer with anyone at any time concerning any alleged violation of the Code, except as provided herein and as may be necessary to conduct the investigation and hold a hearing. Any information ascertained during an investigation or hearing shall be treated as confidential except in cases where the accused member has been determined to have violated Code Section V or VIII. At no time during the investigation or the hearing of charges shall the Administrator or any member of a special ethics committee confer with a competitor of the member alleged to be in violation of the Code, except when it may be necessary to call a competitor as a witness to the facts, in which case the competitor shall be used only for the purpose of testifying as to the facts. At no time shall a competitor participate in the Administrator's or in a special ethics committee's disposition of a complaint.

b. Upon request by the Administrator to any member, all documents directly relating to an alleged violation shall be delivered to the Administrator. Any such information obtained by the Administrator shall be held in confidence in accord with the terms of these regulations and the Code. Whenever the Administrator, either by his own determination or pursuant to a decision by a special ethics committee, terminates an action which was begun under the Code, a record of the member accused shall be wiped clean and all documents, memoranda or other written material shall either be destroyed or returned, as may be deemed appropriate by the Administrator, except for those prosecutorial documents necessary for the filing of a complaint with a state or Federal agency. At no time during proceedings under these regulations or under the Code shall the Administrator or any member of a special ethics committee issue a press release concerning allegations or findings of a violation of the Code unless specifically authorized to do so by the Board of Directors. Further, the Administrator and members of special ethics committees shall at all times strive to keep such proceedings confidential and to avoid publicity concerning them, except as may be otherwise provided herein.

Commentary on Code of Ethics of Public Relations Society of America

Rea W. Smith

Executive Vice President

Public relations as a management function began to take form in the years immediately preceding and following World War I, emerging as a discipline distinct from advertising, journalism, sales, or marketing, albeit closely allied with all such activities which are now encompassed by the umbrella-term, "communications."

By 1935 there were several local and regional organizations of public relations practitioners that had developed the function beyond its original connotation of "publicity" into such areas as employee relations, shareholder relations, institutional advertising, and community and public affairs.

The explosion in communications technology that was a by-product of World War II created the need among corporations—both profit and nonprofit—to include public relations as a necessary, ongoing departmental function.

In the last half of the 1940s, demand for qualified people to staff public relations departments far exceeded the supply, principally because as yet there was little academic training available in this relatively new field. (New York University offered a public relations course in 1923, but the first break-through came in 1948 when Boston University established a school of public relations.) As a result, people from other disciplines—newswriting, advertising, sales, and so forth—moved into public relations, each taking an individualistic approach to the work and to the interpretation of what constituted ethical practice.

This diversity of background, educational preparation, and interpretation made it necessary to have a national organization that could develop consensus and, through seminars, conferences, and workshops, establish uniform standards that would form the body of knowledge for academic instruction.

In 1947 two large regional associations of public relations executives, one based in San Francisco and the other in New York City, merged to form the Public Relations Society of America (PRSA), the largest organization of public relations practitioners in the world. One of its first concerns was the development of an ethical code so that (1) its members would have behavioral guidelines, (2) managements would have a clear understanding of standards, and (3) professionals in public relations would be distinguished from shady promoters and ballyhoo advance men who, unfortunately, had been quick to appropriate the words "public relations" to describe their operations.

The first code document, like so many such initial attempts, set forth lofty aspirations and called for the ultimate in behavior. Adopted in 1952, it was soon found that the wording was too general for enforcement and of marginal value in meeting specific situations that arose in day-to-day practice. Three members were expelled under that early code, but in each instance it was the result of a finding of guilt in civil court.

A special committee was appointed in 1959 to revise the code, make its provisions more specific, and devise enforcement procedures. Working with the society's attorney, Francis K. Decker of Cabell, Medinger, Forsyth, and Decker (now Forsyth, Decker, Murray, and Broderick, New York City), the committee retained the essence of the original code as a preamble titled, "Declaration of Principles," and added sixteen paragraphs stipulating ethics in given situations. The document has withstood the test of time. An additional paragraph, number eight, was adopted in 1963, but otherwise the code is unchanged, even though periodically study committees have been appointed to review all its provisions.

The first case under the revised code was adjudicated in 1961. It tested and proved the soundness of the enforcement procedures. These are based upon judgment by peers, a six-member district judicial panel whose findings are subject to final review and decision by the society's board of directors. Having to do with unfair dealing of one member against another, the first case resulted in censure, the lesser of three penalties (censure, suspension, expulsion) that the organization's bylaws require be publicized to the entire membership. Warning, admonishment, or reprimand apply to minor infractions and need not be publicized.

Within a few years, it became apparent that one adjustment had to be made in the enforcement process. When the alleged violation was unfair dealing against another member or account piracy (encroachment), the injured member filed a charge with the district judicial panel of venue. But in cases where the alleged violation injured the public—in such circumstances as use of false fronts, dissemination of half truths, or attempts to bribe the press—the process for filing charges was fuzzy and somewhat impractical. Few individual members were willing to file charges and pay legal counsel fees to develop a case where they were not directly affected. Some sort of body akin to a grand jury had to serve the public interest in such situations, so a grievance board was established to investigate such cases and, where warranted, file and prosecute charges before a judicial panel. The grievance board retains its own attorney; the society's legal counsel advises the judicial panel so that there is no conflict of interest and the rights of all those involved are fully protected.

During the middle 1960s, official interpretations of the code were adopted to supplement and clarify code language. These interpretations were based primarily on actual cases and thus began to form a "body of law." Other interpretations were developed to explain how the code applied to specialized areas of practice, such as financial public relations, for which an interpretation was adopted after consultation with the SEC to make certain the wording conformed to SEC regulations.

Drafters of the code overcame several difficult problems, not the least of which was the desire to outlaw account piracy and job encroachment without infringing on individual freedoms or restraining competition, since the society had no wish to create an elitist monopoly. The solution was to require open competition for jobs or client accounts, calling for the incumbent to be made aware competition is taking place and to have equal opportunity to present his or her case. In the same vein, the drafters rejected a suggestion that advertising of public relations services be banned, although the committee, in making its report, stressed that such advertising should be professional in tone, reminding members that code paragraphs mandating truth, accuracy, and a concern for public welfare applied to all such advertising.

Another question before the drafters was how to define the ethics of relationships with media. In 1959 there was, as yet, no universally accepted code endorsed by journalists and press associations to use as a guideline. Obviously, corrupting channels of communication by attempting to bribe members of the press had to be outlawed. But in such matters as entertaining reporters, staging press parties, offering samples of products, or taking media representatives on travel junkets, the committee had to make decisions based upon what seemed to be general practice in the late 1950s. In the early 1970s several press organizations developed codes, in one instance through cooperative efforts with the society. In 1975 the society formed a special study committee to review the code, to make certain it has kept pace with development of the profession, as well as any legislation or court findings affecting ethics. Moreover, it was asked to insure that the code paragraphs and interpretations about media relationships conformed in all respects with the codes recently developed by journalistic organizations. It is incumbent upon any profession to respect and conform to the codes of behavior established by all other professions, especially insofar as interlocking relationships are concerned.

PRSA's code of ethics erupted solely from the desire of its members to establish enforceable rules of behavior as a standard of practice in the field. It did not come about as the result of external pressure, pending legal investigation, or a desire to establish exclusivity.

The society believed then, as it does now, that an enforceable code is far preferable to governmental regulation. The subject of state licensing of public relations practitioners has been discussed informally ever since the society was first formed. Formal studies were undertaken in the mid-60s and after extensive research, two white paper reports on the subject were prepared, one in 1968 and another in 1973. Each reached the same negative conclusion about licensing and was endorsed by the society's governing assembly of delegates, the voting representatives of each PRSA chapter.

The society neither advocates nor supports the premise of licensing for a variety of reasons. Foremost is the fact that any licensing of people engaged in a communication function offends the American tradition of freedom of speech and freedom of the press.

Many opponents of licensing believe there is already far too much unnecessary bureaucratic governmental regulation and attempts to regiment the public relations function fall within that category. Public relations people, like everyone else, are subject to the laws of libel and slander. If, they say, public relations people must be licensed because they prepare messages to the public, does it not then follow that for this same reason there must also be licensing of authors, newsmen, and even government officials?

Proponents of licensing believe it would protect the profession and the public from incompetent, shoddy opportunists who have neither the knowledge, nor the talent, nor the ethics required. But opponents are quick to respond that only if the licensing process were to include adequate testing and examination would this result ensue and, even then, the undesirable element might sidestep the law by the simple process of using words other than "public relations" as a designation for their work. Licensing without professional testing would be little more than revenue-producing for the state without in any way improving the profession.

The desire of a group of people in a specific calling to have the government police its ranks is not, in itself, adequate reason for legislation. There must be a clear element of public protection, as there is in the fields of medicine where health hazards exist. The work public relations people do in the area of public communication is always subject to editorial acceptance, rejection, or correction, as well as investigative reporting by the press.

To devise a code which sets forth the optimum behavioral goals of an industry or trade group in impressive language is comparatively easy. To establish one that is legally sound and capable of enforcement is a far different matter. The former may call for behavior of the highest order, but the latter may not. Few individuals are capable of the highest performance, day in and day out, and enforcement bodies are hard-pressed to decide what constitutes "highest" or "less than highest" behavior. Therefore, codes designed to be enforced must set attainable standards. They must also be consonant with good business practice so there is practical as well as moral motivation to adhere to the rules.

The society's enforcement process has a weakness which cannot easily be overcome. The association's jurisdiction extends only to its members and applies only to the conduct of the individual. The society has no authority over those outside its membership ranks and therefore cannot take action against a corporate entity, an institution, or a nonmember. It cannot, for instance, call to account a corporate president who authorizes an undercover slush fund for political contributions, or a controller who provides false financial information, or a corporate legal counsel who suppresses information the public has a right to know. Its only recourse is to investigate whether the public relations people employed by the same company are members and had knowledge of these acts and were either party to them or failed to take all possible action to stop them, in which case these members would be subject to penalty under the code.

Another problem of enforcement jurisdiction sometimes occurs when a member is under investigation by the grievance board or a charge against him has been filed with a judicial panel. The member may remove himself from society jurisdiction by resigning from the membership, thus bringing the society judicial process to a halt. However, under such circumstance, the society may and does run an item in its monthly newsletter to all members, stating that the member resigned while under investigation.

Time alone will correct this situation. The society grew from

500 members in 1948 to 7,500 in 1975, but the majority of people practicing public relations were still outside its ranks. At such time as a majority position is achieved, the code will be more widely applicable and greater stigma will be attached to nonmembership and nonconformance. This is not to say that nonmembers do not honor the code. Many do because they realize it is to their advantage to do so. Many heads of public relations departments who are members insist that all people they employ, whether members of the society or not, adhere to the code as a matter of corporate policy.

The society's code is a living, legally sound document of standards that insures professional integrity while, at the same time, not being so idealistic as to be incapable of application to daily practice. The code and its enforcement procedures recognize the difference between poor judgment and intentional violation so a practitioner need not fear harsh or unreasonable punishment for a momentary lapse into honest error. Responsibility is placed upon the individual for his or her conduct, and this responsibility includes severing connections with an employer or client who insists upon courses of action that violate the code.

The society is anxious to share the knowledge it has gained in twenty-five years of developing its code and exercising enforcement. Many national public relations associations in other countries have codes that are similar, in some cases identical. The society is ready and willing to share experience and information with organized groups in other fields as well.

On occasion the society has been criticized unfairly by members and outsiders alike for not acting swiftly enough, in their view, or for taking no action in circumstances where there is an appearance of guilt. Many times "appearance of guilt" is created through incomplete press accounts or by rumors that, upon investigation, are not supported by fact. The society's policy of confidentiality precludes issuance of a public statement if any aspect of a matter under society investigation is also the subject of pending court action. Any pronouncement in this situation would certainly be premature and probably prejudicial. For this reason many cases take a long time to reach final society decision because they must await final action by the courts.

The society has elected to conduct its judicial affairs dispassionately, in full accord with its established rules of procedure, accompanied by legal advice at every step of the process. It believes that code provisions and enforcement should not be modified to suit expediency or to mollify critics whose opinions rarely are based upon complete factual knowledge.

Code of Ethics and Interpretations
of the Public Relations
Society of America

Adopted 1959. Amended 1963.

Declaration of Principles

Members of the Public Relations Society of America acknowledge and publicly declare that the public relations profession in serving the legitimate interests of clients or employers is dedicated fundamentally to the goals of better mutual understanding and cooperation among the diverse individuals, groups, institutions and elements of our modern society.

In the performance of this mission, we pledge ourselves:

1. To conduct ourselves both privately and professionally in accord with the public welfare.

2. To be guided in all our activities by the generally accepted standards of truth, accuracy, fair dealing and good taste.

3. To support efforts designed to increase the proficiency of the profession by encouraging the continuous development of sound training and resourceful education in the practice of public relations.

4. To adhere faithfully to provisions of the duly adopted Code of Professional Standards for the Practice of Public Relations, a copy of which is in the possession of every member.

Code of Professional Standards for the Practice of Public Relations

This Code of Professional Standards for the Practice of Public Relations is adopted by the Public Relations Society of America to promote and maintain high standards of public service and conduct among its members in order that membership in the Society may be deemed a badge of ethical conduct; that Public Relations justly may be regarded as a profession; that the public may have increasing confidence in its integrity; and that the practice of Public Relations may best serve the public interest.

1. A member has a general duty of fair dealing towards his clients or employers, past and present, his fellow members and the general public.

2. A member shall conduct his professional life in accord with the public welfare.

3. A member has the affirmative duty of adhering to generally accepted standards of accuracy, truth and good taste.

4. A member shall not represent conflicting or competing interests without the express consent of those concerned, given after a full disclosure of the facts; nor shall he place himself in a position where his interest is or may be in conflict with his duty to his client, employer, another member or the public, without a full disclosure of such interests to all concerned.

5. A member shall safeguard the confidences of both present and former clients or employers and shall not accept retainers or employment which may involve the disclosure or use of these confidences to the disadvantage or prejudice of such clients or employers.

6. A member shall not engage in any practice which tends to corrupt the integrity of channels of public communication.

7. A member shall not intentionally disseminate false or misleading information and is obligated to use ordinary care to avoid dissemination of false or misleading information.

8. A member shall be prepared to identify to the public the source of any communication for which he is responsible, including the name of the client or employer on whose behalf the communication is made.

9. A member shall not make use of any individual or organization purporting to serve or represent some announced cause, or purporting to be independent or unbiased, but actually serving an undisclosed special or private interest of a member or his client or his employer.

10. A member shall not intentionally injure the professional reputation or practice of another member. However, if a member has evidence that another member has been guilty of unethical, illegal or unfair practices, including practices in violation of this Code, he should present the information to the proper authorities of the Society for action in accordance with the procedure set forth in Article XIII of the Bylaws.

11. A member shall not employ methods tending to be derogatory of another member's client or employer or of the products, business or services of such client or employer.

12. In performing services for a client or employer a member shall not accept fees, commissions or any other valuable consideration in connection with those services from anyone other than his client or employer without the express consent of his client or employer, given after a full disclosure of the facts.

13. A member shall not propose to a prospective client or employer that the amount of his fee or other compensation be contingent on or measured by the achievement of specified results; nor shall he enter into any fee agreement to the same effect.

14. A member shall not encroach upon the professional employment of another member. Where there are two engagements, both must be assured that there is no conflict between them.

15. A member shall, as soon as possible, sever his relations with any organization when he knows or should know that his continued employment would require him to conduct himself contrary to the principles of this Code.

16. A member called as a witness in a proceeding for the enforcement of this Code shall be bound to appear unless, for sufficient reason, he shall be excused by the panel hearing the same.

17. A member shall cooperate with fellow members in upholding and enforcing this Code.

OFFICIAL INTERPRETATIONS OF THE CODE

The following interpretations of Code paragraphs 6, 13 and 14 were adopted by the PRSA Board of Directors on November 6, 1966, and became effective that date.

Interpretation of Code Paragraph 6 which reads, "A member shall not engage in any practice which tends to corrupt the integrity of the channels of public communication."

1. Practices prohibited by this Code paragraph are those which tend to place representatives of media under obligation to the member or his company or his client, such as:

a. any form of payment or compensation to a media representative in order to obtain, and in exchange for which, preferential or guaranteed news or editorial coverage in the medium is promised, implied or delivered.

b. any retainer of a media employee which involves the use of his position as a media employee for the private purposes of the member or his client or employer where the circumstances of such retainer are not fully disclosed to and accepted by the media employer.

c. an agreement between a member and a media employee when such agreement includes a provision that the media employee will secure preferential or guaranteed coverage in the medium for the member, his firm or his client, or utilization by a member of such an agreement between his employer, his firm or his client and a media employee.

d. providing vacation trips to media representatives where no news assignment is involved.

e. any attempt by a member to lead his employer or client to believe that a member has obtained independent coverage for the employer or client in a medium over which the member has financial or editorial influence or control.

f. the use by a member of an investment made by the member, his firm or his client in a medium to obtain preferential or guaranteed coverage in the medium.

g. the use by a member of a loan of money made to a medium by the member, his firm or his client to obtain preferential or guaranteed coverage in the medium.

2. This Code paragraph does not prohibit entertaining media representatives at meals, cocktails or press parties, nor does it prohibit the bona fide press junket where media representatives are given an opportunity for on-the-spot viewing of a news event or product or service in which the media representative has a legitimate news interest, provided that independence of action is left to the media representative.

3. This Code paragraph does not prohibit the gift or loan of sample products or services to media representatives whose assignments indicate an interest in such products or services, if the sample products or services are manufactured, sold or rendered by the member's company or client and the sampling is a reasonable method of demonstrating the product or service.

4. This Code paragraph does not prohibit the giving of souvenirs or holiday gifts of nominal value as goodwill gestures to media representatives.

Interpretation of Code Paragraph 13 which reads, "A member shall not propose to a prospective client or employer that the amount of his fee or other compensation be contingent on or measured by the achievement of specified results; nor shall he enter into any fee agreement to the same effect."

1. This Code paragraph means that a member may take into consideration the following factors in determining compensation for his services:

a. the experience, judgment and skills required to handle the matter properly.

b. the characteristics and difficulty of the problems involved.

c. the time and labor required.

d. the effect on the member's employment by other clients or potential clients.

e. the customary or prevailing compensation for similar services.

f. the values involved in the matter and the benefits resulting to the client or employer from the services.

g. the duration and character of the employment, whether casual or for a continuing period.

h. the equipment or personnel investment required in order to perform the function.

2. This Code paragraph prohibits a member from entering into any agreement whereby the member's rate of compensation is determined or conditioned by the amount of newspaper or magazine lineage obtained for the member's company or client. This applies equally to radio and television coverage, or any form of exposure to a client's message. It applies further to any contingency fee based on increase in sales volume, increase in profit margins, increase in stock value or the attainment of specified political or legislative results. (See also paragraph 9, "Official Interpretation of the Code as it applies to Financial Public Relations.")

3. This Code paragraph means that a member may guarantee to produce certain materials, such as films, feature articles, scripts, news releases, etc., and promise that these will be of high quality or specific type; but any guarantee that such materials, once produced, shall achieve a specified minimum use by media outlets, in other than paid time or space, and failing which use the fee or compensation will be reduced, is a practice prohibited by this Code paragraph.

Interpretation of Code Paragraph 14 which reads, "A member shall not encroach upon the professional employment of another member. Where there are two engagements, both must be assured that there is no conflict between them."

1. This Code paragraph is not designed to curb the freedom of a member to seek employment or business for his counseling firm by all approved and legitimate means. However, it is interpreted to mean that a member shall not invade or infringe upon the counselor-client or employee-employer relationship of another member.

2. A member would not violate this Code paragraph by:

a. sending copies of his resume and examples of his work to potential employers even if the employers currently employ members of the Society.

b. advertising his or his firm's qualifications in any publication he deems suitable.

c. mailing copies of advertisements, circulars or booklets describing his or his firm's services, or copies of speeches or articles to potential clients, provided any such mailing is not one of solicitation and provided the mailing contains no derogatory comment about another member.

d. furnishing, upon specific request, factual information about his firm, its principals, personnel and types of services rendered, including names of clients, provided such information contains no proposals to a client of another member.

3. This Code paragraph prohibits a member from seeking individual professional employment by deprecating the character, ability or performance of another member.

4. This Code paragraph requires that a counselor member:

a. before soliciting a prospective client, make all reasonable attempts to determine whether the prospective client has an existing relationship with another counselor member who would be replaced, and, if so, make no contact until the incumbent has been notified that his replacement is being considered or that the employment of the incumbent has been terminated.

b. after making an initial contact with a prospective client and subsequently learning that a counselor member-client relationship exists of which he was unaware, shall at that point make no further overtures nor conduct any negotiations with the prospective client until the incumbent has been notified that his replacement is being considered or that the employment of the incumbent has been terminated.

5. Where a member is solicited by a prospective client to take over the functions currently performed by another member, he shall decline to consider the offer until the incumbent member has been advised that a replacement of his services is being considered. Upon specific request, the member may provide information of a factual nature about his firm and its services but shall make no proposals to the client of another member until he has determined that the incumbent has been notified of a possible change.

6. Where a member is solicited by a prospective client to perform functions separate from those currently performed for the same client by another member, it is the responsibility of the solicited member to determine that the incumbent member has been informed, since both must be assured that there is no conflict between the two functions.

An Official Interpretation of the PRSA Code of Professional Standards for the Practice of Public Relations as It Applies to Financial Public Relations

This interpretation of the Society Code as it applies to financial public relations practice was originally adopted in 1963 and amended in 1972 by action of the PRSA Board of Directors. "Financial public relations" is defined as "that area of public relations which relates to the dissemination of information that affects the understanding of stockholders and investors generally concerning the financial position and prospects of a company, and includes among its objectives the improvement of relations between corporations and their stockholders." The interpretation was prepared by the Society's Financial Relations Committee working with the Securities and Exchange Commission and with the advice of the Society's Legal Counsel. It is rooted directly in the Code with the full force of the Code behind it and a violation of any of the following points is subject to the same procedures and penalties as violation of the Code.

1. It is the responsibility of the PRSA member who practices financial public relations to be thoroughly familiar with and understand the rules and regulations of the SEC and the laws which it administers, as well as the other laws, rules and regulations affecting financial public relations—and to act in accordance with their letter and spirit. In carrying out this responsibility, the member shall also seek legal counsel, when appropriate, on matters concerning financial public relations.

2. The member shall adhere to the general policy of making full and timely disclosure of corporate information on behalf of his client or employer. The information disclosed shall be accurate, clear and understandable. The purpose of such disclosure is to provide the investing public with all material information affecting security values or influencing investment decisions. In complying with the duty of full and timely disclosure, the member shall present all material facts, including those adverse to the company. He shall exercise care to ascertain the facts and to disseminate only information which he believes to be accurate. He shall not knowingly omit information, the omission of which might make a release false or misleading. Under no circumstances shall the member participate in any activity designed to mislead, or manipulate the price of a company's securities.

3. The member shall publicly disclose or release information promptly so as to avoid the possibility of any use of the information by any insider or third party. To that end, the member shall make every effort to comply with the spirit and intent of the timely disclosure policies of the stock exchanges, NASD, and the Securities and Exchange Commission. Material information shall be made available to all on an equal basis.

4. The member shall not disclose confidential information the disclosure of which might be adverse to a valid corporate purpose or interest and whose disclosure is not required by the timely disclosure provisions of the law. During any such period of nondisclosure the member shall not directly or indirectly (a) communicate the confidential information to any other person or (b) buy or sell or in any other way deal in the company's securities where the confidential information may materially affect the market for the security when disclosed. Material information shall be disclosed publicly as soon as its confidential status has terminated or the requirement of timely disclosure take effect.

5. During the registration period a member shall not engage in practices designed to precondition the market for such securities. During registration the issuance of forecasts, projections, predictions about sales and earnings, or opinions concerning security values or other aspects of the future performance of the company, shall be in accordance with current SEC regulations and statements of policy. In the case of companies whose securities are publicly held, the normal flow of factual information to shareholders and the investing public shall continue during the registration period.

6. Where the member has any reason to doubt that projections have an adequate basis in fact, he shall satisfy himself as to the adequacy of the projections prior to disseminating them.

7. Acting in concert with client or employer, the member shall act promptly to correct false or misleading information or rumors concerning his client's or employer's securities or business whenever he has reason to believe such information or rumors are materially affecting investor attitudes.

8. The member shall not issue descriptive materials designed or written in such a fashion as to appear to be, contrary to fact, an independent third party endorsement or recommendation of a company or a security. Whenever the member issues material for a client or employer either in his own name or in the name of someone other than his client or employer, he shall disclose in large type and in a prominent position on the face of the material the source of such material and the existence of the issuer's client or employer relationship.

9. The member shall not use inside information for personal gain. However, this is not intended to prohibit the member from making bona fide investments in his company's or client's securities insofar as he can make such investments without the benefit of material inside information.

10. The member shall not accept compensation which would place him in a position of conflict with his duty to his client, employer or the investing public. Specifically, the member shall not accept a contingent fee nor shall he accept a stock option from his client or employer except as part of an overall plan for corporate employees, nor shall he accept securities as compensation at a price below market price.

11. The member shall act so as to maintain the integrity of channels of public communication. He shall not pay or permit to be paid to any publication or other communications medium any consideration in exchange for publicizing a company, except through clearly recognizable paid advertising.

12. The member shall in general be guided by the PRSA Declaration of Principles and the PRSA Code of Professional Standards for the Practice of Public Relations of which this Code is an official interpretation.

An Official Interpretation of the PRSA Code of Professional Standards for the Practice of Public Relations as It Applies to Political Public Relations

Adopted by the PRSA Board of Directors, April 3, 1974.

PREAMBLE

It is understood that in the practice of political public relations, the PRSA member will have something professional and substantial to offer his employer or client quite apart from the political dynamics of the client circumstance, and that he may serve his employer or client without having attributed to him the character, reputation or beliefs of those he serves.

DEFINITION

"Political Public Relations" is defined as those areas of public relations which relate to:

a. the counseling of political organizations, committees, candidates or potential candidates for public office; and groups constituted for the purpose of influencing the vote on any ballot issue;

b. the counseling of holders of public office;

c. the management, or direction, of a political campaign for or against a candidate for political office; or for or against a ballot issue to be determined by voter approval or rejection;

d. the practice of public relations on behalf of a client or an employer in connection with that client's or employer's relationships with any candidates or holders of public office with the purpose of influencing legislation or government regulation or treatment of a client or employer, regardless of whether the PRSA member is a recognized lobbyist;

e. the counseling of government bodies, or segments thereof, either domestic or foreign.

PRECEPTS

1. It is the responsibility of a PRSA member practicing political public relations, as defined above, to be conversant with the various statutes, local, state and federal, governing such activities and to adhere to them strictly. This includes, but is not limited to, the various local, state and federal laws, court decisions and official interpretations governing lobbying, political contributions, elections, libel, slander and the like. In carrying out this responsibility, the member shall seek appropriate counseling whenever necessary.

2. It is also the responsibility of a member to abide by PRSA's Code of Professional Standards and to heed especially, articles 4, 5, 6, 8, 9, 13 and 15.

3. A member shall represent his client or employer in good faith, and while partisan advocacy on behalf of a candidate or public issue may be expected, the member shall act in the public interest and exercise care in adhering to accepted standards of accuracy, truth and good taste.

4. A member shall not issue descriptive material or any advertising or publicity information or participate in the preparation or use thereof which is not signed by responsible persons or is false, misleading or un-labeled as to its source, and is obligated to use care to avoid dissemination of any such material.

5. A member has an obligation to his client to disclose what remuneration beyond his fee he expects to receive as a result of their relationship, such as commissions for media advertising, printing and the like, and should not accept such extra payment without his client's consent.

6. A member's compensation shall not be contingent on, or measured by, the achievement of specified results, nor shall the member improperly use his position to encourage additional future employment or compensation.

7. A member shall voluntarily disclose to his employer or client the identity of other employers or clients with whom he is currently associated and whose interests might be affected favorably or unfavorably by his political representation.

8. A member shall respect the confidentiality of information pertaining to his employer or client even after their relationship ceases.

RULES OF PROCEDURE FOR JUDICIAL PANELS

Adopted by the Board of Directors of the Society, November 18, 1965, and effective as of that date.

1. Every complaint against a member shall be in writing signed by the complaining party (hereinafter called the complainant) and shall set forth the facts constituting the complaint, plainly and in numbered paragraphs.

2. The complainant shall file nine copies of the complaint with the Chairman of the Panel having jurisdiction (see Section 6 of Article XIII of the Bylaws of the Society, printed in the Society's Register). The Chairman shall send copies of the complaint to members of the Panel, to the Society's counsel, to the Chairman of the Grievance Board and to the Headquarters Office of the Society.

3. In cases where the Grievance Board is not the complainant, the Chairman of the Panel shall acknowledge receipt of the complaint and inform the complainant that if the complaint is found by the Panel to be of sufficient importance and in proper form, the complainant will be expected to prosecute the complaint and a formal hearing will, in due course, be held at which the complainant will be expected to present evidence substantiating the facts set forth in the complaint, in accordance with the obligation imposed by paragraph 17 of the Code. However, the complainant may, on his written application and in the discretion of the Panel, be excused from prosecuting his complaint if the Panel finds that it would be appropriate for the Grievance Board to prosecute the matter. In the latter event, the Chairman of the Panel shall refer the complaint to the Grievance Board and advise the complainant that such action is being taken. The Grievance Board shall then be deemed the complainant and shall then be responsible for investigating the matter and prosecuting the complaint if warranted. Excuse from prosecuting the complaint, however, does not relieve the original complainant of his obligation to appear as a witness, in accordance with paragraph 16 of the Code, when required by the Panel.

4. If the Panel shall deem the complaint to be of sufficient importance and in proper form, the Chairman shall serve a copy of the complaint, together with a copy of these rules, upon the member complained of (hereinafter called the respondent). The foregoing sentence shall not apply to a complaint filed with the Panel by the Grievance Board. In the latter case, such complaint, together with a copy of these rules, shall be automatically served upon the member complained of, as above provided.

5. If the Panel shall determine that the complaint is not of sufficient importance or is not in proper form, the Chairman shall so advise the complainant who shall have the opportunity to file an amended complaint. The rules of procedure regarding complaints shall apply to amended complaints.

6. The respondent shall file with the Chairman of the Panel nine copies and shall serve on the complainant one copy of his written answer, signed by him within twenty days after service of the complaint. The answer shall reply to the complaint by referring to each numbered paragraph of the complaint by number, and each fact alleged by the complaint shall be (a) admitted, or (b) stated to be immaterial, with the reasons why, or (c) denied. The respondent may also include in his answer an affirmative statement of his position. The Chairman shall send copies of the answer to the members of the Panel, to the Society's counsel, to the Chairman of the Grievance Board and the Headquarters Office of the Society.

7. The complainant may within five days of the receipt of the answer, reply thereto by serving on the respondent one copy and filing with the Chairman of the Panel nine copies of a reply specifically replying to any new fact alleged in the answer. The Chairman shall send copies of the reply to members of the Panel, to the Society's counsel, to the Chairman of the Grievance Board and to the Headquarters Office of the Society.

8. If the respondent desires to make a counter-complaint, such counter-complaint shall be made in a separate document and the rules of procedure regarding complaints shall apply to the counter-complaint.

9. The Panel or its Chairman may, at any time in advance of the hearing, require either party to furnish a bill of particulars to the other party, eight copies thereof being filed with the Chairman of the Panel who shall send a copy to members of the Panel, to the Society's counsel and to the Headquarters Office of the Society.

10. After complainant's reply, or after the time to reply has expired, the matter shall be "at issue." When the matter is at issue, the Chairman of the Panel, upon his own motion or upon written request of either party, may direct the holding of pre-hearing depositions in accordance with the following rules:

a. Depositions may be taken of any party to the proceedings or of any person who appears to be a material witness.

b. The Chairman of the Panel shall designate a member of the Panel before whom the deposition is to take place.

c. The designated Panel member shall fix the time and place for the holding of the deposition, giving notice to the parties and to the other Panel members who may attend the deposition.

d. The taking of the deposition shall not be governed by the rules of evidence pertaining to court procedure. The designated Panel member shall decide all questions of evidence, subject to review at the hearing.

e. The designated Panel member shall have power to summon any member of the Society to appear at the deposition as a witness and to call for the production of documentary evidence.

f. The designated Panel member and the parties shall have the right to examine and cross-examine the witnesses and be represented by counsel.

g. The designated Panel member shall, at the expense of the Society, provide a public stenographer for the deposition. Copies of the transcript shall be distributed, at the expense of the Society, and prior to the hearing, to all members of the Panel, to the Society's Counsel and to the Executive Director of the Society, and if the Grievance Board has been notified of the pendency of the proceedings in accordance with paragraph 26, then the Chairman of the Grievance Board. Copies of the transcript for any other party shall be at the expense of the party.

h. When several depositions are taken in a proceeding, the same or different Panel members may be designated.

11. When the matter is at issue and the Panel or its Chairman have concluded that all appropriate depositions have been taken, the Panel or its Chairman shall set a time and place for hearing upon the complaint and shall give notice of the hearing to the parties.

12. At the hearing, the transcript of any depositions taken shall be placed in the record of the proceedings.

13. At the hearing the Panel shall not be bound by the rules of evidence pertaining to Court procedure, but shall decide all questions of evidence. The Panel may consider the past professional conduct of the respondent.

14. The Panel shall have power to summon any member of the Society to appear at the hearing as a witness and to call for the production of documentary evidence.

15. The Panel, the complainant and respondent shall have the right to call and examine and cross-examine witnesses and be represented by counsel.

16. The Panel Chairman shall, at the expense of the Society, provide a public stenographer for the hearing. Copies of the transcript shall be distributed, at the expense of the Society, to all members of the Panel, to the Society's counsel and to the Executive Director of the Society, and if the Grievance Board has been notified of the pendency of the proceedings in accordance with paragraph 26, then the Chairman of the Grievance Board. Copies of the transcript for any other party shall be at the expense of the party.

17. Personal attendance of a quorum of the Panel (four members) throughout the hearing is required. The Panel member or members designated to conduct pre-hearing depositions under paragraph 10 hereof need not form part of the quorum.

18. The Panel or its Chairman, where circumstances warrant, may accelerate limitations of time herein provided or grant extensions of time to the parties.

19. As promptly as possible after the hearing, the Panel, through its Chairman, shall make a written report to the President of the Society for submission to the Board of Directors of the Society and to the parties, setting forth its findings of fact, conclusions and recommendations with respect to disciplinary action or exoneration.

20. The complainant or respondent, not in default in appearing or answering, may file exceptions to the report within fifteen days from the date of mailing of a copy of such report to them. Such exceptions shall be filed with the President of the Society for submission to the Board of Directors and also with the other party and the Panel Chairman. The other party and the Panel Chairman may reply to such exceptions within ten days thereafter. Such replies shall be filed with the party excepting and with the President of the Society. Thereafter no further statements or exceptions shall be filed.

21. Exceptions shall state plainly and concisely the reasons why the party excepting asserts that the recommendations of the Panel should not be adopted by the Board.

22. Exceptions shall be based soley on the record before the Panel. No evidence not presented to the Panel will be received or considered. Oral argument before the Board of Directors will not be permitted. The matter shall be considered by the Board of Directors solely on the recommendation of the Panel, the record before the Panel, the exceptions if any, and the replies thereto.

23. The Panel may recommend disciplinary action against a member who as a party to a proceeding before the Panel shall, in the judgment of the Panel, be guilty of a violation of the Code (particularly paragraphs 3, 16 and 17 thereof) in his conduct during the proceeding including the hearing, provided that before the close of the hearing, the Panel shall give the member, if present, notice of the Panel's intention to recommend such disciplinary action and shall at such hearing give such member an opportunity to be heard with respect thereto.

24. The Panel may adopt additional rules of procedure not inconsistent with these rules. In the course of a proceeding, it may determine any points of procedure not covered by these rules.

25. The Society's counsel shall have the following duties and be governed by the following rules:

a. He shall advise the Panel, the Grievance Board, the parties to the proceedings, and their counsel, and the Board of Directors of the Society as to the application and interpretation of the Rules of Procedure.

b. At the hearing, he shall act as legal advisor to the Panel to assist it in the discharge of its duties.

c. He shall, subject to the Panel's control, direct the course of the hearing so that all concerned may have ample opportunity to present the material facts for the decision of the Panel. He shall, subject to the Panel's control, determine the order in which witnesses shall present their testimony and other matters of procedure.

d. He may participate in the questioning of witnesses for the purpose of clarifying the issues or the testimony of witnesses to assist the Panel in the discharge of its duties.

e. After the hearing, Counsel may attend the deliberations of the Panel and the Panel may call upon its legal advisor to submit for its consideration proposed findings, conclusions and recommendations as it might indicate.

f. The foregoing subdivisions of this paragraph 25 shall apply to pre-hearing depositions where applicable.

26. In a case where the Grievance Board is not a party, the Panel may, in its discretion, at any time in the proceedings notify the Grievance Board of the pendency of the proceedings and of all subsequent steps therein. Thereupon, the Grievance Board may, in its discretion, participate in any subsequent depositions and also at the hearing as if it were a party.

27. When these Rules require or authorize the service of papers they shall be served by certified or registered mail.

28. All documents sent pursuant to these Rules to the Headquarters Office of the Society shall be marked "Personal and Confidential, Attention Staff Assistant for Judicial Matters."

Rules of Procedure for Grievance Board

Adopted by the Board of Directors April 7, 1967 and effective as of that date.

(There are two main sources of complaints for Grievance Board considera-

tion—(1) *complaint from a member when he is not a directly aggrieved party, and* (2) *information from court proceedings or other events reported in public media.*)

1. Copies of source material of complaint, accompanied by an analysis by the Grievance Board Counsel, shall be sent to each member of the Grievance Board by the Grievance Board Chairman with a ballot opinion form to be returned to the Chairman within fifteen (15) days.

2. Investigation of complaints shall be conducted by Grievance Board Counsel as directed by the Grievance Board Chairman after the latter has received ballot opinions from Grievance Board members under Rule 1.

3. The Grievance Board Counsel shall prepare a report on his investigation and findings with a recommendation which shall be sent to all Grievance Board members by the Grievance Board Chairman.

4. Grievance Board members shall take action on the Grievance Board Counsel report filed in accordance with Rule 3, either at a meeting or by ballot, and decide:

a. to close case as being of insufficient importance to warrant filing charges with a judicial panel,

b. to ask Grievance Board Counsel for further specific investigation,

c. to hold case for further development (i.e. court cases), or

d. to file charges with the proper judicial panel of the Society.

5. If ballot vote is taken under Rule 4, Grievance Board members may have the option of asking that no action be taken until after the complaint has been discussed at a meeting of the Grievance Board, and if any Grievance Board member exercises this option, the Chairman shall call a meeting for this purpose.

6. A majority vote of the Grievance Board members present at a meeting or voting on a mail ballot shall be required under Rule 4d to file charges with a judicial panel of the Society.

7. Six members of the Grievance Board shall constitute a quorum for meetings or ballot voting.

8. In complaints where the Grievance Board votes to file charges, the Grievance Board Counsel shall prepare the complaint which shall then be filed by the Grievance Board Chairman with the proper judicial panel of the Society in accordance with Rules of Procedure for Panels as adopted by the PRSA Board of Directors, November 18, 1965.

9. In cases where the Grievance Board is the complainant in judicial proceedings before a judicial panel, the Grievance Board Chairman and the Grievance Board Counsel shall attend the hearing. The Chairman may designate another Grievance Board member to attend in his stead.

10. In all other procedures involved in a complaint before a judicial panel, including the filing of exceptions, the Grievance Board shall be governed by the Rules of Procedure for Panels adopted by the PRSA Board of Directors, November 18, 1965.

11. A quarterly status report of all pending cases before the Grievance Board shall be prepared by the Grievance Board Counsel and circulated by the Grievance Board Chairman to all members of the Grievance Board.

ARTICLE XIII. Code of Professional Standards

Section 1. Powers of the Assembly, Obligations of Members. The Assembly of the Society shall have power to adopt a Code of Professional Standards for the Practice of Public Relations, herein called, "the Code," and amendments thereto, either at its annual meeting or at a special meeting called for that purpose, after first receiving the report of the Board of Directors thereon. All members of the Society shall, by virtue of their membership therein, be bound by the Code as the same may be amended from time to time, and shall be obligated to comply with the procedures for the enforcement of the Code.

Section 2. Powers of the Board of Directors. The Board of Directors shall have power (a) to propose to the Assembly a Code of Professional Standards for the Practice of Public Relations; (b) to propose to the Assembly from time to time amendments to the Code when they may appear to be advisable; (c) to issue official interpretations of the Code and express its opinion regarding proper professional conduct; (d) to adopt Rules of Procedure for the enforcement of the Code and of these Bylaws and from time to time to amend the same; (e) to divide the United States into Judicial Districts and fix the boundaries thereof and from time to time to change the same; and (f) to warn, admonish or reprimand, or to censure, suspend or expel members either for violation of the Code or of these Bylaws or upon conviction of a crime as provided in Section 7 hereof.

The affirmative vote of two-thirds of the entire Board of Directors shall be requisite to take disciplinary action against a member.

If the Board of Directors does not adopt the recommendation of a Panel, as hereinafter provided, it may remand the proceedings to the Panel for further hearing and recommendation, or it may take independent disciplinary action based on the record of the proceedings before the Panel. Before taking such action, the Board shall give the member, the complainant, and the Panel reasonable opportunity to present their respective positions on such record.

Section 3. Judicial Panels. In connection with the enforcement of such Code, there shall be Judicial Panels consisting of six members each, one or more panels for each Judicial District formed pursuant to subdivision (d) of Section 2 hereof, the number of panels in each Judicial District to be determined by the Board of Directors. In Judicial Districts having more than one panel, the Board, by general rule or specific order in the particular case, may provide for the allocation of proceedings among the panels. Panel members shall be appointed by the President of the Society with the approval of the Board of Directors given at its Annual Meeting. To be eligible, a Panel Member shall be an Accredited or Active member in good standing of the Society and shall have his principal place of business in the Judicial District for which he is appointed. Panel Members shall be appointed for terms of three years and until their successors are appointed, and the terms of such members shall be so arranged that the terms of two Panel Members on each Panel shall expire each year. Appointments to Panels shall be subject to changes in the boundaries of Judicial Districts. The President of the Society shall have power to fill any vacancy on a Panel for the unexpired term.

Section 4. Organization of Panels. The President of the Society shall, at the Annual Meeting of the Board of Directors, appoint a Chairman and Vice Chairman of each Panel to serve for one year and until their successors are appointed. Each Panel shall meet at the call of the Chairman thereof at such time and place as he may designate in the call of the meeting. The Chairman shall call a meeting of the Panel at the request of two members thereof. The Vice Chairman shall, in the absence or disability of the Chairman, exercise the powers and perform the duties of the Chairman. The office of the Panel shall be the principal place of business of the Chairman of the Panel.

Four members of a Panel shall constitute a quorum for the transaction of business except that the Panel may conduct prehearing depositions in the presence of one or more members of the Panel under such rules as may be adopted by the Board of Directors. The affirmative vote of three members of the Panel or a majority of those present, whichever shall be the greater number, shall be required for a vote recommending disciplinary action.

A Panel Member who is either a complainant or respondent or otherwise directly involved in a proceeding before a Panel of which he is a member shall be disqualified from taking part in such proceeding as a Panel Member. In such event, the President of the Society shall have power to appoint a substitute Panel Member for the Panel Member so disqualified, to serve in such proceeding only.

Section 5. Powers of a Panel. Each Panel shall have power (a) to conduct disciplinary proceedings and to hear complaints relative to violations of the Code or of these Bylaws, upon complaint made by a member, or the Board of Directors or by the Grievance Board all in accordance with the Rules of Procedure adopted by the Board of Directors; (b) after a hearing upon such complaint, to make recommendations to the Board of Directors with respect to disciplinary action against a member for violation of the Code or of these Bylaws.

Section 6. Venue. Each Panel shall have independent jurisdiction to hear complaints against members having a place of business within the Judicial District, and also to hear complaints based on violations of the Code or of these Bylaws taking place within the Judicial District. Whenever venue is not determined by the foregoing sentence, the Board of Directors shall assign one of the Judicial Panels to hear the complaint and bring in a recommendation to the Board of Directors. A respondent named in a complaint may apply to the Board of Directors for a change of venue provided he makes application within fifteen (15) days of the service of a complaint upon him specifying the venue requested and the reasons for the change. Notice of the application shall be given to the complainant who shall have equal opportunity to submit his reasons in opposition to the change.

Section 7. Conviction of a Felony or Misdemeanor. The Board of Directors may, by a vote of a majority of the entire Board, suspend or expel any member who shall have been convicted of a felony or misdemeanor related to the conduct of his profession or involving moral turpitude. Before taking a vote on such suspension or expulsion, the Board of Directors shall give the member a hearing on reasonable notice or it may refer the matter to the Judicial Panel in the area in which the member has a place of business, for hearing and recommendation to the Board of Directors, in accordance with its rules. Proof of conviction shall be made by a duly authenticated copy of the order or judgment of the court or judge convicting the member.

Section 8. Suspension. If a member is suspended in accordance with the provisions of this Article, then during the period of his suspension (a) he shall not hold himself out to the public in any way as a member in good standing of the Society or of a Chapter, (b) he shall be removed from the mailing list of the Society, (c) he shall be required to pay dues, (d) he shall not be eligible to attend meetings, vote, or participate in any way in Society or chapter activities, (e) he shall forfeit his right to hold any National, District or Chapter office, directorship, or committee membership or to serve as a Delegate to the Assembly, (f) if Accredited, his Accreditation shall be suspended, (g) he shall be listed in the next issue of the Society's Bulletin as a suspended member, with the period of suspension.

No suspension shall continue for more than one year from the date of suspension.

Section 9. Suspension or Revocation of Accreditation. The Board of Directors may, by a vote of the majority of the entire Board, censure, suspend or expel any member whose Accreditation under Article XIV of these Bylaws shall have been suspended or revoked. Before taking a vote on such censure, suspension or expulsion, the Board of Directors shall give the member a hearing on reasonable notice or it may refer the matter to the Judicial Panel in the area in which the member has a place of business, for hearing and recommendation to the Board of Directors, in accordance with its rules.

Section 10. Grievance Board. There shall be a Grievance Board consisting of nine Accredited or Active members of the Society, three appointed each year by the President with the approval of the Board of Directors, each to serve for a term of three years. The Chairman of the Grievance Board shall be appointed each year by the President, with the approval of the Board of Directors.

It shall be the duty of the Grievance Board to make investigations regarding violation of the Code or of these Bylaws, to bring complaints before the appropriate Judicial Panel and to prosecute the same.

Section 11. Miscellaneous. All proceedings of the panel, the Grievance Board and of the Board of Directors under this Article shall be confidential and in closed sessions.

If a member resigns from membership in the Society while charges against him are pending before the Judicial Panel or before the Board of

Directors, the President of the Society or his representative designated by the Board of Directors are authorized to give notice of such fact to the membership and to make such public statements concerning the resignation and pending charges as they may deem appropriate.

In cases of warning, admonishment or reprimand, the Board of Directors may, in its discretion, cause notice of resolution of such disciplinary action against a member to be given to the members of the Society, and the President of the Society or his representative designated by the Board of Directors are authorized to make such public statements concerning such disciplinary action as they may deem proper.

The Board of Directors shall cause notice of a Resolution of Censure, Suspension or Expulsion to be given to members of the Society, and the President of the Society or his representative designated by the Board of Directors are authorized to make such public statements concerning any such resolution and the proceedings upon which it is based as they may deem appropriate.

Section 12. Definition. The term " disciplinary action" wherever used in these Bylaws shall be deemed to include warning, admonishment or reprimand, censure, suspension or expulsion.

Commentary on Television Code of Ethics of National Association of Broadcasters

Stockton Helffrich

Director, Code Authority

The Radio Code of the National Association of Broadcasters (NAB) and the Television Code which comprises a variation thereof are, respectively, in their twentieth and nineteenth editions as of June 1976. Because the one for television has in recent years attracted a generally wider attention, and been at the center of such controversy as surrounds considerations on the social impact of this comparative fledgling among the media, it is selected for the purposes of this publication.

THE ORIGIN AND OBJECTIVES OF A BROADCASTER'S CODE

The Television Code specifically came into being in 1952 because a need for it was recognized by thoughtful broadcasters. To a measurable degree it was then, as now, a crystallization of professional principles born out of broadcast experience and practice.

The "need" for a broadcast code itself deserves some attention. Candor must concede that the existence of the document, and the complex machinery required to implement it, flow out of a typically free enterprise mixture of ethics and reasonable self-interest. The observation is made in the belief not only that our traditional economic and political freedoms are in sync with our country's incredibly durable freedom of speech, but also that such freedoms can only be sustained through an exercise of the responsibilities that go with them.

The industry's *perceptions* at a management level of the *needs* as they are variously voiced are not automatically unanimous any more than are those of others within or without the industry who voice them. What is important is that out of the multiplicity of self or other challenges there tends to emerge in the broadcaster response a consensus of sorts, finding that certain criticisms indeed have some validity and therefore deserve being addressed through the code as a vehicle for orderly change.

CODE ADAPTABILITY TO CHANGE

Examples of ground-rule changes abound both in the Television Code language itself affecting matters of advertising *and* program content alike as well as in numerous separately publicized guidelines and interpretations expanding upon the more succinctly phrased of the code's advertising standards.

Changes evident in code standards and/or guidelines or interpretations derived from them cover, these days, not only special considerations affecting children in the audience (for example, in the advertising of toys, in premiums and offers, in promotions for snacks, candy, gum, and soft drinks), but also certain clearly significant concerns that have arisen in such categories of advertising as those promoting beers and wines; products for the symptomatic relief of arthritis and rheumatism; nonprescription medications; vegetable oils, margarines and related products; weight reduction products and services; chiropractic services; personal products; and so forth.

CODE ADMINISTRATION AND ENFORCEMENT

Regulations and procedures of the Television Code call for the establishment of a Television Code Review Board, the appointment of a Code Authority Director, and the appointment by the Director of Code Authority staff.

The Television Code Review Board is a nine-member body

of code-subscribing broadcasters responsible primarily for reviewing the work of the Code Authority and for recommending changes in, additions to, or deletions from the Television Code, subject to the approval of the NAB Television Board of Directors.

Six of the nine members are appointed by the president of the NAB, subject to the approval of the NAB Television Board of Directors. Each of the six members serves a two-year term and may be reappointed for another two-year term. These six members are operating television broadcasters holding management positions either at stations or in group operations. In making the appointments, due consideration is given to such factors as diversification of geographical location, market size, network affiliation, independent station, VHF or UHF status.

In addition to the aforementioned six Television Code Review Board members, each of the three television networks appoints a representative to serve on the board, subject to the approval of the president of the NAB and the NAB Television Board of Directors. Each network representative may serve a two-year term and be reappointed for an indeterminate number of additional two-year terms. The network representatives designated to serve on the Television Code Review Board are management level executives closely involved with the self-regulatory operation at the network.

Committees of the Television Code Review Board are appointed by the board chairman. The committees work with and are available to give guidance to the Code Authority on specific matters involving broadcast self-regulation. Currently, among key standing committees of the Television Code Review Board are an Alcoholic Beverage Advertising Committee, a Budget and Procedures Committee, a Children's Advertising Committee, a Comparative Advertising Committee, a Health Issues Committee, a Personal Products Advertising Committee, a Time Standards Committee, and a Tobacco Products Advertising Committee.

The Code Authority is a semiautonomous division of the NAB responsible in general for the interpretation, implementation, and enforcement of the standards contained in the Television Code as well as any guidelines and interpretations stemming therefrom. The Code Authority has offices in Washington, Hollywood, and New York.

The director of the Code Authority is appointed by the president of the NAB, subject to the approval of the NAB Television Board of Directors. The Code Authority has approximately three dozen full-time, salaried staffers.

In 1964, the Code Authority took steps to establish what is now known as its Medical and Science Advisory Panel. The idea of such a panel stemmed in part from a realization that expert professional opinion would be needed by the Code Authority in respect to many aspects of the work it performs. The panelists serve voluntarily and anonymously in order to minimize undue pressure inhibitory to their participation. They are consulted individually and represent specialities such as arthritis and rheumatism, analgesics, psychiatry, dermatology, internal medicine, dentistry, nutrition, hypnosis, and pediatrics.

Each Code Authority office includes among its responsibilities formal and informal review of television commercials to help assure their compliance with applicable Television Code standards, guidelines, and interpretations. All Code Authority offices engage in this commercial review activity with the preponderance thereof taking place in the New York and Hollywood code offices. The Washington code office for its part is particularly responsible for the Code Authority's quantitative monitoring program. Although the primary purpose of this procedure is to determine the compliance of code subscribers with Television Code time standards, the Code Authority also derives general commercial information from the activity which can lead to reviews of particular local/regional advertising.

When so designated by the Television Code Review Board the Code Authority serves a "central clearance" role for all commercials within designated categories of advertising. Currently, from storyboard stage through final film/tape, the Code Authority reviews all nationally advertised toy commercials, children's premiums/offer commercials, sanitary napkin/tampon/douche commercials, and commercials promoting vegetable oils/margarines and related products featuring claims involving cholesterol, saturated fats, and tied-in health issues.

Additionally, the Code Authority will review commercials, either prior to or after their production, when an advertiser or agency has a specific question regarding the compliance of a commercial with the code; when there is a difference of opinion among code subscribers regarding the status of the commercial under code standards; when any member of the public raises a bona fide question regarding the status of a commercial under code standards and seeks Code Authority evaluation of same; or when the Code Authority specifically requests review of advertising under code standards.

In the instance that the Code Authority staff is involved in the review of commercials, the screening procedures parallel those generally pursued on a day-in, day-out basis by code-subscribing networks or stations. This entails either the procedure involved in the review of commercials *prior* to their production or the procedure in the review of commercials *after* they have been produced (for example, when the Code Authority sporadically receives a complaint from outside groups or individuals, or on its own behalf initiates complaints concerning television advertising).

Regarding formal commercial reviews prior to production, the Code Authority generally receives an initial script/storyboard from the advertising agency handling the account. The audio and video of this material are reviewed to determine compliance with applicable Television Code standards, guidelines, or interpretations. Where obvious departures from code policies exist, the agency is so advised and asked to submit revised copy/video representations.

Should the proposed commercial contain a hard claim or claims, the Code Authority requests and receives the documentation on which same is based. No approval is given by the Code Authority until the documentation has been reviewed and found adequate to support the claim(s) and, when necessary, until product samples are examined.

When needed, opinions regarding the adequacy of documentation are sought from either individual Medical and Science Advisory Panel members and/or the NAB Research Department or other non-Medical and Science Advisory Panel consultants. Code Board committee members likewise are consulted for guidance when and as needed. Also, if necessary, meetings are held with the advertiser/agency involved to explore more deeply their rationales. The Code Authority's final position on a proposed commercial submitted for formal review is always detailed in a letter to the advertising agency/advertiser.

The procedures involved in the review of already-produced television commercials are identical to the procedures described above with the exception that Code Authority involvement begins with receipt of a completed film/tape rather than a proposed script/storyboard. Specific commercials are sometimes brought to the attention of the Television Code Review Board for review when the results of a Code Authority staff evaluation of a given commercial are appealed either by an advertiser or the agency for same that submitted the commercial to the Code Authority, or by a party challenging the status of an on-air commercial under Television Code standards and requesting a formal review by the Code Authority.

The above instances of the Code Authority's exercise of its sanctions option have, not too surprisingly, served for all practical purposes to minimize the actual need to utilize it. Rather, what instead has developed within the advertising community in cooperation with the Code Authority and code subscribers, is an advertiser appeals procedure particularly affecting any proposed advertising with which the Code Authority takes issue. Simultaneously, this appeals procedure serves the public interest while resolving, in a preventive way, the inevitable confrontations sometimes occasioned by interpretive differences between advertisers/agencies and broadcast media copy clearance staffers over the application of code standards.

Instituted late in 1972, these appeal procedures for advertisers/agencies basically codified then developed Code Authority practices. Because the appeal procedures are detailed in a somewhat lengthy document not readily condensed for reiteration here, they immediately follow the reprint of the Television Code included at the conclusion of this article.

As to the application of sanctions against code subscribers that have evidenced a pattern of continuing violation of Television Code standards, see "III. Subscribers, Section 4 'Sus-

pension of Subscription' " in the "Regulations and Procedures" section of the Television Code hereafter.

In the instance that the Code Authority under specified
Television Code requirements finds nonacceptable a proposed or on-air commercial and cannot resolve the issue with
the advertiser/agency involved, the Code Authority exercises a
censure (read "sanctions") option in the form of a publicly
released notice. This is generally featured in the Code Authority's monthly Code News.

This Code Authority option has been used for approximately two dozen such situations in a fifteen-year period commencing in 1961. The range of these notices covered categories
promoting products or services affecting weight reduction, the
relief of arthritic and rheumatic pain, antacid action, dandruff
control, antiseptic action, the treatment of cancer, the
treatment of stomach or duodenal ulcers, a local theatre's
motion picture, the ability to stop smoking cigarettes, beer
consumption, a polishing of wood, feminine personal
hygiene, battery reconditioning, and diuresis.

With the exception of a few of these designed exclusively
for radio airing, and some for both radio *and* television, most
of the notices were television related. The commercial involving an antiseptic or first aid product was designed to appeal
directly to children and yet as proposed would have promoted
it along lines clearly appealing to children despite a caution
on the product's label stating, in bold type, "Keep out of reach
of children."

AN APPRAISAL OF THE CODE AND ITS MECHANISMS, NOW AND FOR THE FUTURE

In an extolling of the code's obvious responses to public
interest-oriented issues which have arisen as the result of
broadcast advertising and programming practices, it nevertheless must inevitably be allowed that it may well occur to anyone, code-supporter or code-detractor, to inquire as to possible short-comings in the code and in the pronouncements
designed to implement it.

Following, therefore, are some thoughts both as to the

code's problem areas and as to possible approaches which could work to diminish them.

The television medium cannot be all things to all people even though, obviously, it offers many things to many people. The code in turn affecting the medium, and continuously evolving along with it, cannot and does not presume, or expect to be, all things to all people.

Therein lie inherent considerations which the code's detractors see at least as problems and at most as deficiencies. As criticisms these merit scrutiny simply because they so often flow from utopian expectations and thereby force upon the self-regulatory machinery time- and energy-wasting demands better funneled into getting on with one's job.

During the past few years demands upon all of us world wide, critics of broadcasting, and even certain broadcasters, have sometimes expected too much of regulation (self or governmental) and at the same time not credited regulation as it is, and as it improves, for even the most obvious of its real accomplishments. Actually established, ongoing and currently developing achievements of self-regulation are thus by some minimized, brushed off as inadequate, even denied as having any existence or, if recognized, are so taken for granted as not even to be considered worth applauding.

In the current climate of change, where all of us want improvement in those of our society's imperfections which most stand out, there is a prevailing temptation to malign and negate that which has been laboriously built. Further, there is a tendency to pursue, sometimes through unethical means, what amounts to presumptive demands upon broadcast self-regulation. Broadcast self-regulation is thus called upon to dictate through undemocratic fiats esoteric, subjective goals reflective of the kind of change which appears to suit advocates' expectations under the guise of meeting alleged needs of Everyman and Everywoman.

A reasoned responsiveness on the part of broadcasters to legitimate and considered expectations appears to comprise a sounder approach to these matters than a pressured acquiescence to arbitrary and ivory tower demands made without apparent regard to valid countervailing considerations.

Self-regulation generally and the code specifically are not set up to insulate viewers of any age from programs and products which find general audience acceptance. Rather, the code reflects an effort to determine *how* the promotion of various products or services is best handled as distinct from fulminating against the concept of revenue from advertisers to support the programming which is offered.

Additionally, the code—wisely, in many a broadcaster's view—makes haste slowly. It cannot move faster than the necessary fact gathering and due process permit.

Further, certain areas of consideration involve responsibilities in which the code can share but in which it cannot take over. The code cannot usurp the role of parents, the school and other established institutions which shape our values and culture. Nor, for that matter, can the code replace the continuing role of advocates for change who, on their own, assume the job of articulating what they believe needs doing, especially since many of these articulations fall outside the limits of the code.

There are, of course, mechanics of the code operation which might, if changed, serve to improve its effectiveness. Almost if not all of these potentialities involve greater budgetary support. They deserve attention against the day—and if—such greater budgetary leeway eventualizes.

First, more frequent meetings of the Television Code Review Board than a yearly two or three would be desirable assuming, of course, that a reasonable increase in their frequency could be accommodated by the hard-pressed board members and the staff. The chief value, from ad agencies' and other appellants' viewpoints, would be in the inherently greater speed for the resolution of such differences as they may have with broadcasters' self-regulatory policies.

Second, and tied in with the above, the board's subcommittee and appeals procedures should be further streamlined, if that is possible. Again, as above, this would help expedite the resolutions of differences between broadcasters and others.

Third, an increase in broadcaster/advertising seminars for the discussion of self-regulatory issues, as the participants perceive them, would be healthy. Agreements are often aided by a comparatively relaxed and informal forum for the airing of disagreements.

Fourth, it appears fair to suggest that the effectiveness of the code operations can be improved, and without budgetary strain (sic), by an intensification of top-level decisions within the advertising community determining and articulating the management wish and directive to staff to cooperate with broadcasters in the media self-regulatory effort. A prior determination by the advertiser that the broadcasters' self-regulatory mechanisms and precedents appear to be reasonable, and deserve being approached as such, could help improve upon and even diminish the more elementary of the give and take which develops.

THE CODE AS THE VEHICLE FOR ORDERLY CHANGE

The foregoing examination of the code mechanisms is intended to demonstrate the degree to which self-regulation can and does in the public interest influence changes in broadcasters', and broadcast advertisers', practices. Further, it is believed by most broadcasters and most advertisers that these self-regulatory procedures are innately and desirably flexible, as contrasted with an alternative expansion of statutory controls and regulations less responsive to the ever-shifting considerations brought about by the unrelenting change so characteristic of today's world.

THE PURPOSES SERVED BY THE CODE

The code, in sum, comprises an increasingly self-evident "answer" for the broadcasters on its roster. Subscription to it clearly means many things to many stations: a shared pursuit of professional standards; a continuing stress on broadcaster service in the public interest; the benefits of consensus attitudes on broadcast advertising and programming issues, reached as a result of broadcaster input based on experience; a systematic response by the broadcast industry to manifest needs, as they surface, including zeroing-in on key issues on a priority basis; a concentration on public interest-oriented concerns through the Code Authority apparatus (as contrasted with industry/business considerations handled by other NAB departments); the strength which derives from unity where every voice counts; a sharing of common experience which inevitably helps all to better chart a sound course.

Self-regulation, in brief, is a positive function. By striving to serve the public interest, it advances the reasonable self-interest of broadcasters. It creates reasonable standards based on experience. Lived up to, such self-imposed standards reduce broadcaster vulnerability to arbitrary outside criticism and to the potential overreaction of advocates and government bureaucracies to various issues. All of these positives for broadcasters in *their* responses to the mix of public interest and self-protective business interest equate with the reasonable expectations of those who make up our society.

In this respect, the code offers many positives to many people. Not all things to all people, but a decent response to the incredible range of expectations so remarkable about our pluralistic society.

Television Code of Ethics

of the

National Association of Broadcasters

Nineteenth Edition—1976*

PREAMBLE

Television is seen and heard in nearly every American home. These homes include children and adults of all ages, embrace all races and all varieties of philosophic or religious conviction and reach those of every educational background. Television broadcasters must take this pluralistic audience into account in programming their stations. They are obligated to bring their positive responsibility for professionalism and reasoned judgment to bear upon all those involved in the development, production and selection of programs.

The free, competitive American system of broadcasting which offers programs of entertainment, news, general information, education and culture is supported and made possible by revenues from advertising. While television broadcasters are responsible for the programming and advertising on their stations, the advertisers who use television to convey their commercial messages also have a responsibility to the viewing audience. Their advertising messages should be presented in an honest, responsible and tasteful manner. Advertisers should also support the endeavors of broadcasters to offer a diversity of programs that meet the needs and expectations of the total viewing audience.

The viewer also has a responsibility to help broadcasters serve the public. All viewers should make their criticisms and positive suggestions about programming and advertising known to the broadcast licensee. Parents particularly should oversee the viewing habits of their children, encouraging them to watch programs that will enrich their experience and broaden their intellectual horizons.

* Copyright 1976, National Association of Broadcasters

I. Principles Governing Program Content

It is in the interest of television as a vital medium to encourage programs that are innovative, reflect a high degree of creative skill, deal with significant moral and social issues and present challenging concepts and other subject matter that relate to the world in which the viewer lives.

Television programs should not only reflect the influence of the established institutions that shape our values and culture, but also expose the dynamics of social change which bear upon our lives.

To achieve these goals, television broadcasters should be conversant with the general and specific needs, interests and aspirations of all the segments of the communities they serve. They should affirmatively seek out responsible representatives of all parts of their communities so that they may structure a broad range of programs that will inform, enlighten, and entertain the total audience.

Broadcasters should also develop programs directed toward advancing the cultural and educational aspects of their communities.

To assure that broadcasters have the freedom to program fully and responsibly, none of the provisions of this Code should be construed as preventing or impeding broadcast of the broad range of material necessary to help broadcasters fulfill their obligations to operate in the public interest.

The challenge to the broadcaster is to determine how suitably to present the complexities of human behavior. For television, this requires exceptional awareness of considerations peculiar to the medium.

Accordingly, in selecting program subjects and themes, great care must be exercised to be sure that treatment and presentation are made in good faith and not for the purpose of sensationalism or to shock or exploit the audience or appeal to prurient interests or morbid curiosity.

Additionally, entertainment programming inappropriate for viewing by a general family audience should not be broadcast during the first hour of network entertainment programming in prime time and in the immediately preceding hour. In the occasional case when an entertainment program in this time period is deemed to be inappropriate for such an audience, advisories should be used to alert viewers. Advisories should also be used when programs in later prime time periods contain material that might be disturbing to significant segments of the audience.*

These advisories should be presented in audio and video form at the beginning of the program and when deemed appropriate at a later point in the program. Advisories should also be used responsibly in promotional material in advance of the program. When using an advisory, the broadcaster should attempt to notify publishers of television program listings.*

Special care should be taken with respect to the content and treatment of audience advisories so that they do not disserve their intended purpose by containing material that is promotional, sensational or exploitative. Promotional announcements for programs that include advisories should be

* Effective September 1975

scheduled on a basis consistent with the purpose of the advisory.* *(See Television Code Interpretation No. 5)*

II. Responsibility Toward Children

Broadcasters have a special responsibility to children. Programs designed primarily for children should take into account the range of interests and needs of children from instructional and cultural material to a wide variety of entertainment material. In their totality, programs should contribute to the sound, balanced development of children to help them achieve a sense of the world at large and informed adjustments to their society.

In the course of a child's development, numerous social factors and forces, including television, affect the ability of the child to make the transition to adult society.

The child's training and experience during the formative years should include positive sets of values which will allow the child to become a responsible adult, capable of coping with the challenges of maturity.

Children should also be exposed, at the appropriate times, to a reasonable range of the realities which exist in the world sufficient to help them make the transition to adulthood.

Because children are allowed to watch programs designed primarily for adults, broadcasters should take this practice into account in the presentation of material in such programs when children may constitute a substantial segment of the audience.

All the standards set forth in this section apply to both program and commercial material designed and intended for viewing by children.

III. Community Responsibility

1. Television broadcasters and their staffs occupy positions of unique responsibility in their communities and should conscientiously endeavor to be acquainted fully with the community's needs and characteristics in order better to serve the welfare of its citizens.

2. Requests for time for the placement of public service announcements or programs should be carefully reviewed with respect to the character and reputation of the group, campaign or organization involved, the public interest content of the message, and the manner of its presentation.

IV. Special Program Standards

1. Violence, physical or psychological, may only be projected in responsibly handled contexts, not used exploitatively. Programs involving violence should present the consequences of it to its victims and perpetrators.

Presentation of the details of violence should avoid the excessive, the gratuitous and the instructional.

* Effective September 1975

The use of violence for its own sake and the detailed dwelling upon brutality or physical agony, by sight or by sound, are not permissible.

The depiction of conflict, when presented in programs designed primarily for children, should be handled with sensitivity.

2. The treatment of criminal activities should always convey their social and human effects.

The presentation of techniques of crime in such detail as to be instructional or invite imitation shall be avoided.

3. Narcotic addiction shall not be presented except as a destructive habit. The use of illegal drugs or the abuse of legal drugs shall not be encouraged or shown as socially acceptable.

4. The use of gambling devices or scenes necessary to the development of plot or as appropriate background is acceptable only when presented with discretion and in moderation, and in a manner which would not excite interest in, or foster, betting nor be instructional in nature.

5. Telecasts of actual sports programs at which on-the-scene betting is permitted by law shall be presented in a manner in keeping with federal, state and local laws, and should concentrate on the subject as a public sporting event.

6. Special precautions must be taken to avoid demeaning or ridiculing members of the audience who suffer from physical or mental afflictions or deformities.

7. Special sensitivity is necessary in the use of material relating to sex, race, color, age, creed, religious functionaries or rites, or national or ethnic derivation.

8. Obscene, indecent or profane matter, as proscribed by law, is unacceptable.

9. The presentation of marriage, the family and similarly important human relationships, and material with sexual connotations, shall not be treated exploitatively or irresponsibly, but with sensitivity. Costuming and movements of all performers shall be handled in a similar fashion.

10. The use of liquor and the depiction of smoking in program content shall be de-emphasized. When shown, they should be consistent with plot and character development.

11. The creation of a state of hypnosis by act or detailed demonstration on camera is prohibited, and hypnosis as a form of "parlor game" antics to create humerous situations within a comedy setting is forbidden.

12. Program material pertaining to fortune-telling, occultism, astrology, phrenology, palm-reading, numerology, mind-reading, character-reading, and the like is unacceptable if it encourages people to regard such fields as providing commonly accepted appraisals of life.

13. Professional advice, diagnosis and treatment will be presented in conformity with law and recognized professional standards.

14. Any technique whereby an attempt is made to convey information to the viewer by transmitting messages below the threshold of normal awareness is not permitted.

15. The use of animals, consistent with plot and character delineation, shall be in conformity with accepted standards of humane treatment.

16. Quiz and similar programs that are presented as contests of knowledge, information, skill or luck must, in fact, be genuine contests; and the results must not be controlled by collusion with or between contestants, or by any other action which will favor one contestant against another.

17. The broadcaster shall be constantly alert to prevent inclusion of elements within a program dictated by factors other than the requirements of the program itself. The acceptance of cash payments or other considerations in return for including scenic properties, the choice and identification of prizes, the selection of music and other creative program elements and inclusion of any identification of commercial products or services, their trade names or advertising slogan within the program are prohibited except in accordance with Sections 317 and 508 of the Communications Act.

18. Contests may not constitute a lottery.

19. No program shall be presented in a manner which through artifice or simulation would mislead the audience as to any material fact. Each broadcaster must exercise reasonable judgment to determine whether a particular method of presentation would constitute a material deception, or would be accepted by the audience as normal theatrical illusion.

20. A television broadcaster should not present fictional events or other non-news material as authentic news telecasts or announcements, nor permit dramatizations in any program which would give the false impression that the dramatized material constitutes news.

21. The standards of this code covering program content are also understood to include, wherever applicable, the standards contained in the advertising section of the Code.

V. Treatment of News and Public Events

General

Television Code standards relating to the treatment of news and public events are, because of constitutional considerations, intended to be exhortatory. The standards set forth hereunder encourage high standards of professionalism in broadcast journalism. They are not to be interpreted as turning over to others the broadcaster's responsibility as to judgments necessary in news and public events programming.

News

1. A television station's news schedule should be adequate and well-balanced.

2. News reporting should be factual, fair and without bias.

3. A television broadcaster should exercise particular discrimination in the acceptance, placement and presentation of advertising in news programs so that such advertising should be clearly distinguishable from the news content.

4. At all times, pictorial and verbal material for both news and comment should conform to other sections of these standards, wherever such sections are reasonably applicable.

5. Good taste should prevail in the selection and handling of news: Morbid, sensational or alarming details not essential to the factual report, especially in connection with stories of crime or sex, should be avoided. News should be telecast in such a manner as to avoid panic and unnecessary alarm.

6. Commentary and analysis should be clearly identified as such.

7. Pictorial material should be chosen with care and not presented in a misleading manner.

8. All news interview programs should be governed by accepted standards of ethical journalism, under which the interviewer selects the questions to be asked. Where there is advance agreement materially restricting an important or newsworthy area of questioning, the interviewer will state on the program that such limitation has been agreed upon. Such disclosure should be made if the person being interviewed requires that questions be submitted in advance or participates in editing a recording of the interview prior to its use on the air.

9. A television broadcaster should exercise due care in the supervision of content, format, and presentation of newscasts originated by his/her station, and in the selection of newscasters, commentators, and analysts.

Public Events

1. A television broadcaster has an affirmative responsibility at all times to be informed of public events, and to provide coverage consonant with the ends of an informed and enlightened citizenry.

2. The treatment of such events by a television broadcaster should provide adequate and informed coverage.

VI. Controversial Public Issues

1. Television provides a valuable forum for the expression of responsible views on public issues of a controversial nature. The television broadcaster should seek out and develop with accountable individuals, groups and organizations, programs relating to controversial public issues of import to his/her fellow citizens; and to give fair representation to opposing sides of issues which materially affect the life or welfare of a substantial segment of the public.

2. Requests by individuals, groups or organizations for time to discuss their views on controversial public issues should be considered on the basis of their individual merits, and in the light of the contribution which the use requested would make to the public interest, and to a well-balanced program structure.

3. Programs devoted to the discussion of controversial public issues should be identified as such. They should not be presented in a manner which would mislead listeners or viewers to believe that the program is purely of an entertainment, news or other character.

4. Broadcasts in which stations express their own opinions about issues of general public interest should be clearly identified as editorials. They should be unmistakably identified as statements of station opinion and should be appropriately distinguished from news and other program material.

VII. Political Telecasts

1. Political telecasts should be clearly identified as such. They should not be presented by a television broadcaster in a manner which would mislead listeners or viewers to believe that the program is of any other character. (Ref.: Communications Act of 1934, as amended, Secs. 315 and 317, and FCC Rules and Regulations, Secs. 3.654, 3.657, 3.663, as discussed in NAB's "Political Broadcast Catechism & The Fairness Doctrine.")

VIII. Religious Programs

1. It is the responsibility of a television broadcaster to make available to the community appropriate opportunity for religious presentations.

2. Programs reach audiences of all creeds simultaneously. Therefore, both the advocates of broad or ecumenical religious precepts, and the exponents of specific doctrines, are urged to present their positions in a manner conducive to viewer enlightenment on the role of religion in society.

3. In the allocation of time for telecasts of religious programs the television station should use its best efforts to apportion such time fairly among responsible individuals, groups and organizations.

ADVERTISING STANDARDS

IX. General Advertising Standards

1. This Code establishes basic standards for all television broadcasting. The principles of acceptability and good taste within the Program Standards section govern the presentation of advertising where applicable. In addition, the Code establishes in this section special standards which apply to television advertising.

2. Commercial television broadcasters make their facilities available for the advertising of products and services and accept commercial presentations for such advertising. However, television broadcasters should, in recognition of their responsibility to the public, refuse the facilities of their stations to an advertiser where they have good reason to doubt the integrity of the advertiser, the truth of the advertising representations or the compliance of the advertiser with the spirit and purpose of all applicable legal requirements.

3. Identification of sponsorship must be made in all sponsored programs in accordance with the requirements of the Communications Act of 1934, as amended, and the Rules and Regulations of the Federal Communications Commission.

4. Representations which disregard normal safety precautions shall be avoided.

Children shall not be represented, except under proper adult supervision, as being in contact with or demonstrating a product recognized as potentially dangerous to them.

5. In consideration of the customs and attitudes of the communities served, each television broadcaster should refuse his/her facilities to the advertisement of products and services, or the use of advertising scripts, which the station has good reason to believe would be objectionable to a substantial and responsible segment of the community. These standards should be applied with judgment and flexibility, taking into consideration the characteristics of the medium, its home and family audience, and the form and content of the particular presentation.

6. The advertising of hard liquor (distilled spirits) is not acceptable.

7. The advertising of beer and wines is acceptable only when presented in the best of good taste and discretion, and is acceptable only subject to Federal and local laws (See Television Code Interpretation No. 4).

8. Advertising by institutions or enterprises which in their offers of instruction imply promises of employment or make exaggerated claims for the opportunities awaiting those who enroll for courses is generally unacceptable.

9. The advertising of firearms/ammunition is acceptable provided it promotes the product only as sporting equipment and conforms to recognized standards of safety as well as all applicable laws and regulations. Advertisements of firearms/ammunition by mail order are unacceptable. The advertising of fireworks is unacceptable.

10. The advertising of fortune-telling, occultism, astrology, phrenology, palm-reading, numerology, mind-reading, character-reading or subjects of a like nature is not permitted.

11. Because all products of a personal nature create special problems, acceptability of such products should be determined with especial emphasis on ethics and the canons of good taste. Such advertising of personal products as is accepted must be presented in a restrained and obviously inoffensive manner.

12. The advertising of tip sheets and other publications seeking to advertise for the purpose of giving odds or promoting betting is unacceptable.

The lawful advertising of government organizations which conduct legalized lotteries is acceptable provided such advertising does not unduly exhort the public to bet.

The advertising of private or governmental organizations which conduct legalized betting on sporting contests is acceptable provided such advertising is limited to institutional type announcements which do not exhort the public to bet.

13. An advertiser who markets more than one product should not be permitted to use advertising copy devoted to an acceptable product for purposes of publicizing the brand name or other identification of a product which is not acceptable.

14. "Bait-switch" advertising, whereby goods or services which the advertiser has no intention of selling are offered merely to lure the customer into purchasing higher-priced substitutes, is not acceptable.

15. Personal endorsements (testimonials) shall be genuine and reflect personal experience. They shall contain no statement that cannot be supported if presented in the advertiser's own words.

X. Presentation of Advertising

1. Advertising messages should be presented with courtesy and good taste; disturbing or annoying material should be avoided; every effort should be made to keep the advertising message in harmony with the content and general tone of the program in which it appears.

2. The role and capability of television to market sponsors' products are well recognized. In turn, this fact dictates that great care be exercised by the broadcaster to prevent the presentation of false, misleading or deceptive advertising. While it is entirely appropriate to present a product in a favorable light and atmosphere, the presentation must not, by copy or demonstration, involve a material deception as to the characteristics, performance or appearance of the product.

Broadcast advertisers are responsible for making available, at the request of the Code Authority, documentation adequate to support the validity and truthfulness of claims, demonstrations and testimonials contained in their commercial messages.

3. The broadcaster and the advertiser should exercise special caution with the content and presentation of television commercials placed in or near programs designed for children. Exploitation of children should be avoided. Commercials directed to children should in no way mislead as to the product's performance and usefulness.

Commercials, whether live, film or tape, within programs initially designed primarily for children under 12 years of age shall be clearly separated from program material by an appropriate device.

Trade name identification or other merchandising practices involving the gratuitous naming of products is discouraged in programs designed primarily for children.

Appeals involving matters of health which should be determined by physicians should not be directed primarily to children.

4. No children's program personality or cartoon character shall be utilized to deliver commercial messages within or adjacent to the programs in which such a personality or cartoon character regularly appears. This provision shall also apply to lead-ins to commercials when such lead-ins contain sell copy or imply endorsement of the product by program personalities or cartoon characters. (Effective September 1975.)

5. Appeals to help fictitious characters in television programs by purchasing the advertiser's product or service or sending for a premium should not be permitted, and such fictitious characters should not be introduced into the advertising message for such purposes.

6. Commercials for services or over-the-counter products involving health considerations are of intimate and far-reaching importance to the consumer. The following principles should apply to such advertising:

a. Physicians, dentists or nurses or actors representing physicians, dentists or nurses, shall not be employed directly or by implication. These restrictions also apply to persons professionally engaged in medical services (e.g. physical therapists, pharmacists, dental assistants, nurses' aides).

b. Visual representations of laboratory settings may be employed, provided they bear a direct relationship to bona fide research which has been conducted for the product or service. (See Television Code X, 11.) In such cases, laboratory technicians shall be identified as such and shall not be employed as spokespersons or in any other way speak on behalf of the product.

c. Institutional announcements not intended to sell a specific product or service to the consumer and public service announcements by nonprofit organizations may be presented by accredited physicians, dentists or nurses, subject to approval by the broadcaster. An accredited professional is one who has met required qualifications and has been licensed in his/her resident state.

7. Advertising should offer a product or service on its positive merits and refrain from discrediting, disparaging or unfairly attacking competitors, competing products, other industries, professions or institutions.

8. A sponsor's advertising messages should be confined within the framework of the sponsor's program structure. A television broadcaster should avoid the use of commercial announcements which are divorced from the program either by preceding the introduction of the program (as in the case of so-called "cow-catcher" announcements) or by following the apparent sign-off of the program (as in the case of so-called trailer or "hitch-hike" announcements). To this end, the program itself should be announced and clearly identified, both audio and video, before the sponsor's advertising material is first used, and should be signed off, both audio and video, after the sponsor's advertising material is last used.

9. Since advertising by television is a dynamic technique, a television broadcaster should keep under surveillance new advertising devices so that the spirit and purpose of these standards are fulfilled.

10. A charge for television time to churches and religious bodies is not recommended.

11. Reference to the results of bona fide research, surveys or tests relating to the product to be advertised shall not be presented in a manner so as to create an impression of fact beyond that established by the work that has been conducted.

XI. Advertising of Medical Products

1. The advertising of medical products presents considerations of intimate and far-reaching importance to consumers because of the direct bearing on their health.

2. Because of the personal nature of the advertising of medical products, claims that a product will effect a cure and the indiscriminate use of such words as "safe," "without risk," "harmless," or terms of similar meaning should not be accepted in the advertising of medical products on television stations.

3. A television broadcaster should not accept advertising material which in his/her opinion offensively describes or dramatizes distress or morbid situations involving ailments, by spoken word, sound or visual effects.

XII. Contests

1. Contents shall be conducted with fairness to all entrants, and shall comply with all pertinent laws and regulations. Care should be taken to avoid the concurrent use of the three elements which together constitute a lottery—prize, chance and consideration.

2. All contest details, including rules, eligibility requirements, opening and termination dates should be clearly and completely announced and/or shown, or easily accessible to the viewing public, and the winners' names should be released and prizes awarded as soon as possible after the close of the contest.

3. When advertising is accepted which requests contestants to submit items of product identification or other evidence of purchase of products, reasonable facsimiles thereof should be made acceptable unless the award is based upon skill and not upon chance.

4. All copy pertaining to any contest (except that which is required by law) associated with the exploitation or sale of the sponsor's product or service, and all references to prizes or gifts offered in such connection should be considered a part of and included in the total time allowances as herein provided. (*See Television Code, XIV.*)

XIII. Premiums and Offers

1. Full details of proposed offers should be required by the television broadcaster for investigation and approved before the first announcement of the offer is made to the public.

2. A final date for the termination of an offer should be announced as far in advance as possible.

3. Before accepting for telecast offers involving a monetary consideration, a television broadcaster should satisfy himself/herself as to the integrity of the advertiser and the advertiser's willingness to honor complaints indicating dissatisfaction with the premium by returning the monetary consideration.

4. There should be no misleading descriptions or visual representations of any premiums or gifts which would distort or enlarge their value in the minds of viewers.

5. Assurances should be obtained from the advertiser that premiums offered are not harmful to person or property.

6. Premiums should not be approved which appeal to superstition on the basis of "luck-bearing" powers or otherwise.

XIV. Time Standards for Non-Program Material*

In order that the time for non-program material and its placement shall best serve the viewer, the following standards are set forth in accordance with sound television practice:

1. Non-Program Material Definition:

Non-program material, in both prime time and all other time, includes billboards, commercials, promotional announcements and all credits in excess of 30 seconds per program, except in feature films. In no event should credits exceed 40 seconds per program. The 40-second limitation on credits shall not apply, however, in any situation governed by a contract entered into before October 1, 1971. Public service announcements and promotional announcements for the same program are excluded from this definition.

2. Allowable Time for Non-Program Material:

a. In prime time on network affiliated stations, non-program material shall not exceed nine minutes 30 seconds in any 60-minute period.

Prime time is a continuous period of not less than three consecutive hours per broadcast day as designated by the station between the hours of 6:00 PM and Midnight.

b. In all other time, non-program material shall not exceed 16 minutes in any 60-minute period.

c. Children's Programming Time—Defined as those hours other than prime time in which programs initially designed primarily for children under 12 years of age are scheduled.

Within this time period on Saturday and Sunday, non-program material shall not exceed 10 minutes in any 60-minute period after December 31, 1974 and nine minutes 30 seconds in any 60-minute period after December 31, 1975.

Within this time period on Monday through Friday, non-program material shall not exceed 14 minutes in any 60-minute period after December 31, 1974 and 12 minutes in any 60-minute period after December 31, 1975.

3. Program Interruptions:

a. Definition: A program interruption is any occurrence of non-program material within the main body of the program.

b. In prime time, the number of program interruptions shall not exceed two within any 30-minute program, or four within any 60-minute program.

* See Time Standards for Independent Stations, p. 333

Programs longer than 60 minutes shall be prorated at two interruptions per half-hour.

The number of interruptions in 60-minute variety shows shall not exceed five.

c. In all other time, the number of interruptions shall not exceed four within any 30-minute program period.

d. In children's weekend programming time, as above defined in 2c, the number of program interruptions shall not exceed two within any 30-minute program or four within any 60-minute program.

e. In both prime time and all other time, the following interruption standard shall apply within programs of 15 minutes or less in length:

5-minute program—1 interruption;

10-minute program—2 interruptions;

15-minute program—2 interruptions.

f. News, weather, sports and special events programs are exempt from the interruption standard because of the nature of such programs.

4. No more than four non-program material announcements shall be scheduled consecutively within programs, and no more than three non-program material announcements shall be scheduled consecutively during station breaks. The consecutive non-program material limitation shall not apply to a single sponsor who wishes to further reduce the number of interruptions in the program.

5. A multiple product announcement is one in which two or more products or services are presented within the framework of a single announcement. A multiple product announcement shall not be scheduled in a unit of time less than 60 seconds, except where integrated so as to appear to the viewer as a single message. A multiple product announcement shall be considered integrated and counted as a single announcement if:

a. the products or services are related and interwoven within the framework of the announcement (related products or services shall be defined as those having a common character, purpose and use); and

b. the voice(s), setting, background and continuity are used consistently throughout so as to appear to the viewer as a single message.

Multiple product announcements of 60 seconds in length or longer not meeting this definition of integration shall be counted as two or more announcements under this section of the Code. This provision shall not apply to retail or service establishments.

6. The use of billboards, in prime time and all other time, shall be confined to programs sponsored by a single or alternate week advertiser and shall be limited to products advertised in the program.

7. Reasonable and limited identification of prizes and donors' names where the presentation of contest awards or prizes is a necessary part of program content shall not be included as non-program material as defined above.

8. Programs presenting women's/men's service features, shopping guides, fashion shows, demonstrations and similar material provide a special service

to the public in which certain material normally classified as non-program is an informative and necessary part of the program content. Because of this, the time standards may be waived by the Code Authority to a reasonable extent on a case-by-case basis.

9. Gratuitous references in a program to a non-sponsor's product or service should be avoided except for normal guest identification.

10. Stationary backdrops or properties in television presentations showing the sponsor's name or product, the name of the sponsor's product, trademark or slogan should be used only incidentally and should not obtrude on program interest or entertainment.

Note: From time to time the Code Authority issues advertising guidelines and clarifications expanding on provisions of the Code. Among areas covered are acne, alcoholic beverages, arthritis and rheumatism remedies, bronchitis, comparative advertising, children's premiums and offers, children's TV advertising, disparagement, hallucinogens, hypnosis, lotteries, men-in-white, non-prescription medications, personal products, testimonials, time standards, toys, vegetable oils and margarines, and weight reducing products/services. Copies may be obtained from any NAB Code Authority office.

Time Standards for Independent Stations

1. Non-program elements shall be considered as all-inclusive, with the exception of required credits, legally required station identifications, and "bumpers." Promotion spots and public service announcements, as well as commercials, are to be considered non-program elements.

2. The allowed time for non-program elements, as defined above, shall not exceed seven minutes in a 30-minute period or multiples thereof in prime time (prime time is defined as any three contiguous hours between 6:00 PM and midnight, local time), or eight minutes in a 30-minute period or multiples thereof during all other times.

3. Where a station does not carry a commercial in a station break between programs, the number of program interruptions shall not exceed four within any 30-minute program, or seven within any 60-minute program, or 10 within any 90-minute program, or 13 in any 120-minute program. Stations which do carry commercials in station breaks between programs shall limit the number of program interruptions to three within any 30-minute program, or six within any 60-minute program, or nine within any 90-minute program, or 12 in any 120-minute program. News, weather, sports, and special events are exempted because of format.

4. Not more than four non-program material announcements as defined above shall be scheduled consecutively. An exception may be made only in the case of a program 60 minutes or more in length, when no more than seven non-program elements may be scheduled consecutively by stations who wish to reduce the number of program interruptions.

5. The conditions of paragraphs three and four shall not apply to live sports programs where the program format dictates and limits the number of program interruptions.

Interpretation No. 1

June 7, 1956, Revised June 9, 1958
"Pitch" Programs
The "pitchman" technique of advertising on television is inconsistent with good broadcast practice and generally damages the reputation of the industry and the advertising profession.

Sponsored program-length segments consisting substantially of continuous demonstrations or sales presentation, violate not only the time standards established in the Code but the broad philosophy of improvement implicit in the voluntary Code operation and are not acceptable.

Interpretation No. 2

June 7, 1956
Hollywood Film Promotion
The presentation of commentary or film excerpts from current theatrical releases in some instances may constitute commercial material under the Time Standards for Non-Program Material. Specifically, for example, when such presentation, directly or by inference, urges viewers to attend, it shall be counted against the commercial allowance for the program of which it is a part.

Interpretation No. 3

January 23, 1959
Prize Identification
Aural and/or visual prize identification of up to 10 seconds duration may be deemed "reasonable and limited" under the language of Paragraph 7 of the Time Standards for Non-Program Material. Where such identification is longer than 10 seconds, the entire announcement or visual presentation will be charged against the total commercial time for the program period.

Interpretation No. 4

March 4, 1965
Drinking on Camera
Paragraph 7, Section IX, General Advertising Standards, states that the "advertising of beer and wine is acceptable only when presented in the best of good taste and discretion." This requires that commercials involving beer and wine avoid any representation of on-camera drinking.

Interpretation No. 5

April 8, 1975

The scheduling provisions of Section I (Principles Governing Program Content) shall not apply to programs under contract to a station as of April 8, 1975, all episodes of which were then in existence, if such station is unable, despite reasonable good faith efforts, to edit such programs to make them appropriate for family viewing or to reschedule them so as not to occupy family viewing periods. This exception shall in no event apply after September 1, 1977. Any such programs excepted from scheduling provisions shall, of course, bear the required advisory notices. (Effective September 1975)

REGULATIONS AND PROCEDURES

The following Regulations and Procedures shall obtain as an integral part of the Television Code of the National Association of Broadcasters:

I. Name

The name of this Code shall be *The Television Code of the National Association of Broadcasters.**

II. Purpose of the Code

The purpose of this Code is cooperatively to maintain a level of television programming which gives full consideration to the educational, informational, cultural, economic, moral and entertainment needs of the American public to the end that more and more people will be better served.

III. Subscribers

Section 1. Eligibility

Any individual, firm or corporation which is engaged in the operation of a television broadcast station or network, or which holds a construction permit for a television broadcast station within the United States or its dependencies, shall, subject to the approval of the Television Board of Directors as hereinafter provided, be eligible to subscribe to the Television Code of the NAB to the extent of one subscription for each such station and/or network which it operates or for which it holds a construction permit; provided, that a non-television member of NAB shall not become

* By-Laws of the National Association of Broadcasters, Article VI, section 8, C: "Television Board. The Television Board is hereby authorized:—(4) to enact, amend and promulgate standards of practice or codes for its Television members, and to establish such methods to secure observance thereof as it may deem advisable:—."

eligible via Code subscription to receive any of the member services or to exercise any of the voting privileges of a member.

Section 2. Certification of Subscription

Upon subscribing to the Code, subject to the approval of the Television Board of Directors, there shall be granted forthwith to each such subscribing station authority to use the "NAB Television Seal of Good Practice," a copyrighted and registered seal to be provided in the form of a certificate, a slide and/or a film, signifying that the recipient thereof is a subscriber in good standing to the Television Code of the NAB. The seal and its significance shall be appropriately publicized by the NAB.

Section 3. Duration of Subscription

Subscription shall continue in full force and effect until thirty days after the first of the month following receipt of notice of written resignation. Subscription to the Code shall be effective from the date of application subject to the approval of the Television Board of Directors; provided, that the subscription of a television station going on the air for the first time shall, for the first six months of such subscription, be probationary, during which time its subscription can be summarily revoked by an affirmative two-thirds vote of the Television Board of Directors without the usual processes specified below.

Section 4. Suspension of Subscription

Any subscription, and/or the authority to utilize and show the above-noted seal, may be voided, revoked or temporarily suspended for television programming, including commercial copy, which, by theme, treatment or incident, in the judgment of the Television Board constitutes a continuing, willful or gross violation of any of the provisions of the Television Code, by an affirmative two-thirds vote of the Television Board of Directors at a regular or special meeting; provided, however, that the following conditions and procedures shall apply:

A. Preferring of Charges—Conditions

Precedent:
Prior to the preferring of charges to the Television Board of Directors concerning violation of the Code by a subscriber, the Television Code Review Board (hereinafter provided for) (1) Shall have appropriately, and in good time, informed and advised such subscriber of any and all complaints and information coming to the attention of the Television Code Review Board and relating to the programming of said subscriber. (2) Shall have reported to, and advised, said subscriber by analysis, interpretation, recommendation or otherwise, of the possibility of a violation or breach of the Television Code by the subscriber, and (3) Shall have served upon the subscriber, by Registered Mail a Notice of Intent to prefer charges, at least 20 days prior to the filing of any such charges with the Television Board of Directors. During this period the Television Code Review Board may, within

its sole discretion, reconsider its proposed action based upon such written reply as the subscriber may care to make, or upon such action as the subscriber may care to take program-wise, in conformance with the analysis, interpretation, or recommendation of the Television Code Review Board.

(i) Notice of Intent

The Notice of Intent shall include a statement of the grounds and reasons for the proposed charges, including appropriate references to the Television Code.

(ii) Time

In the event that the nature of the program in question is such that time is of the essence, the Television Code Review Board may prefer charges within less than the 20 days above specified, provided that a time certain in which reply may be made is included in its Notice of Intent, and provided that its reasons therefor must be specified in its statement of charges preferred.

B. *The Charges:*

The subscriber shall be advised in writing by Registered Mail of the charges preferred. The charges preferred by the Television Code Review Board to the Television Board of Directors shall include the grounds and reasons therefor, together with specific references to the Television Code. The charges shall contain a statement that the conditions precedent, herein before described, have been met.

C. *Hearing:*

The subscriber shall have the right to a hearing and may exercise same by filing an answer within 10 days of the date of such notification.

D. *Waiver:*

Failure to request a hearing shall be deemed a waiver to the subscriber's right thereto.

E. *Designation:*

If a hearing is requested by the subscriber, it shall be designated as promptly as possible and at such time and place as the Television Board may specify.

F. *Confidential Status:*

Hearings shall be closed; and all correspondence between a subscriber and the Television Code Review Board and/or the Television Board of Directors concerning specific programming shall be confidential; provided, however, that the confidential status of these procedures may be waived by a subscriber.

G. *Presentation: Representation:*

A subscriber against whom charges have been preferred and who has exercised his/her right to a hearing shall be entitled to effect presentation of his/her case personally, by agent, by attorney, or by deposition and interrogatory.

H. *Intervention:*

Upon request by the subscriber-respondent or the Television Code Review Board, the Television Board of Directors, in its discretion, may permit the intervention of one or more other subscribers as parties-in-interest.

I. *Transcript:*

A stenographic transcript record shall be taken and shall be certified by the Chairman of the Television Board of Directors to the office of the Secretary of the National Association of Broadcasters, where it shall be maintained. The transcript shall not be open to inspection unless otherwise provided by the party respondent in the proceeding.

J. *Television Code Review Board; Counsel:*

The Television Code Review Board may, at its discretion, utilize the services of an attorney from the staff of the NAB for the purpose of effecting its presentation in a hearing matter.

K. *Order of Procedure:*

At hearings the Television Code Review Board shall open and close.

L. *Cross-Examination:*

The right of cross-examination shall specifically obtain. Where procedure has been by deposition or interrogatory, the use of cross-interrogatories shall satisfy this right.

M. *Presentation:*

Oral and written evidence may be introduced by the subscriber and by the Television Code Review Board. Oral argument may be had at the hearing and written memoranda or briefs may be submitted by the subscriber and by the Television Code Review Board. The Television Board of Directors may admit such evidence as it deems relevant, material and competent, and may determine the nature and length of the oral argument and the written argument or briefs.

N. *Authority of Presiding Officer; of Television Board of Directors:*

The Presiding Officer shall rule upon all interlocutory matters, such as, but not limited to, the admissibility of evidence, the qualifications of witnesses, etc. On all other matters, authority to act shall be vested in a majority of the Television Board unless otherwise provided.

O. *Films, Transcriptions, etc.:*

Films, kinescopes, records, transcriptions, or other mechanical reproductions of television programs, properly identified, shall be accepted into evidence when relevant.

P. *Continuances and Extensions:*

Continuances and extension of any proceeding or for the time of filing or performing any act required or allowed to be done within a specific time may be granted upon request, for a good cause shown. The Board or the Presiding Officer may recess or adjourn a hearing for such time as may be deemed necessary, and may change the place thereof.

Q. *Findings and Conclusions:*

The Television Board of Directors shall decide the case as expeditiously as possible and shall notify the subscriber and the Television Code Review Board, in writing, of the decision. The decision of the Television Board of Directors shall contain findings of fact with conclusion, as well as the reasons or bases thereof. Findings of fact shall set out in detail and with particularity all basic evidentiary facts developed on the record (with appropriate citations to the transcript of record or exhibit relied on for each evidentiary fact) supporting the conclusion reached.

R. *Reconsiderations or Rehearing:*

A request for reconsideration or rehearing may be filed by parties to the hearing. Requests for reconsideration or rehearing shall state with particularity in what respect the decision or any matter determined therein is claimed to be unjust, unwarranted, or erroneous, and with respect to any finding of fact shall specify the pages of record relied on. If the existence of any newly discovered evidence is claimed, the request shall be accompanied by a verified statement of the facts together with the fact relied on to show that the party, with due diligence, could not have known or discovered such facts at the time of the hearing.

The request for rehearing may seek:

a. Reconsideration

b. Additional oral argument

c. Reopening of the proceedings

d. Amendment of any findings, or

e. Other relief.

S. *Time for Filing:*

Requests for reconsideration or rehearing shall be filed within 10 days after receipt by the respondent of the decision. Opposition thereto may be filed within five days after the filing request.

T. *Penalty, Suspension of:*

At the discretion of the Television Board, application of any penalty provided for in the decision may be suspended until the Board makes final disposition of the request for reconsideration or rehearing.

U. *Disqualification:*

Any member of the Television Board may disqualify himself/herself, or upon good cause shown by any interested party, may be disqualified by a majority vote of the Television Board.

Section 5. Additional Procedures

When necessary to the proper administration of the Code, additional rules of procedure will be established from time to time as authorized by the By-Laws of the NAB; in keeping therewith, special consideration shall be given to the procedures for receipt and processing of complaints and to necessary rules to be adopted from time to time, taking into account the source and nature of such complaints; such rules to include precautionary measures such as the posting of bonds to cover costs and expenses of processing same; and further provided that special consideration will be given to procedures insuring the confidential status of proceedings relating to Code observance.

Section 6. Amendment and Review

Because of the new and dynamic aspects inherent in television broadcast, the Television Code, as a living, flexible and continuing document, may be amended from time to time by the Television Board of Directors; provided that said Board is specifically charged with review and reconsideration of the entire Code, its appendices and procedures, at least once each year.

Section 7. Termination of Contracts

All subscribers on the air at the time of subscription to the Code shall be permitted that period prior to and including the earliest legal cancellation date to terminate any contracts, then outstanding, calling for program presentations which would not be in conformity with the Television Code, provided, however, that in no event shall such period be longer than 52 weeks.

IV. Affiliate Subscribers

Section 1. Eligibility

Any individual, firm or corporation, which is engaged in the production or distribution, lease, or sale of recorded programs for television presentation, subject to the approval of the Television Code Review Board as hereinafter provided, shall be eligible to become an affiliate subscriber to the Television Code of the NAB.

Section 2. Certification of Subscription

Upon becoming an affiliate subscriber to the Code, subject to the approval of the Television Code Review Board, there shall be granted forthwith to each such affiliate subscriber authority to use a copyrighted and registered seal and declaration, in a manner approved by the Television Code Review Board, identifying the individual firm or corporation as an affiliate subscriber to the Television Code of the NAB. Such authority shall not constitute formal clearance or approval by the Television Code Review Board of specific film programs or other recorded material.

Section 3. Duration of Affiliate Subscription

The affiliate subscription shall continue in full force and effect until 30 days after the first of the month following receipt of a written notice of resignation. The affiliate subscription of the Code shall be effective from the date of application subject to the approval of the Television Code Review Board.

Section 4. Suspension of Affiliate Subscription

Any affiliate subscription and the authority to utilize and show the above-noted seal may be voided, revoked, or temporarily suspended for the sale or distribution for television presentation of any film or other recorded material which by theme, treatment, or incident, in the judgment of the Television Code Review Board, constitutes a continuing, willful or gross violation of any of the provisions of the Television Code, by a majority vote of the Television Code Review Board at any regular or special meeting. The conditions and procedures applicable to subscribers shall not apply to affiliate subscribers.

Section 5. Representation of Affiliate Subscribers

Any affiliate subscriber or group of affiliate subscribers may authorize an individual or association to act for them in connection with their relations with the Television Code Review Board by filing a written notice of such representation with the Board. Such representation, however, in no way will limit the right of the Television Code Review Board to suspend individual affiliate subscribers in accordance with the provisions of Section 4.

V. Rates

Each Subscriber and affiliate subscriber shall pay "administrative" rates in accordance with such schedule, at such time, and under such conditions as may be determined from time to time by the Television Board (see Article VI, section 8, C. Television Board (3) and (4), By-Laws of the NAB); provided, that appropriate credit shall be afforded to a television member of the NAB against the regular dues paid to NAB.

VI. The Television Code Review Board

Section 1. Composition

There shall be a continuing committee entitled the Television Code Review Board to be composed of not more than nine members, all of whom shall be from subscribers to the Television Code. They shall be appointed by the President of NAB, subject to confirmation by the Television Board, and may include one member from each of the subscribing nationwide television networks. Members of the Television Board shall not be eligible to serve on the Review Board. Due consideration shall be given, in making the appoint-

342 THE ETHICAL BASIS OF ECONOMIC FREEDOM

ments to factors of diversification of geographical location, market size, company representation and network affiliation.

No person shall continue as a member of the Television Code Review Board if the station or entity he represents ceases to subscribe to the Television Code. In such case a vacancy occurs in the office immediately, and a successor may be appointed to serve out the unexpired term.

All terms shall be for two years, commencing at the close of the annual meeting of the membership following appointment.

A. *Limitation of Service:*

No person shall serve for more than two terms of two years each, consecutively, as a member of the Television Code Review Board; provided, however, this limitation shall not apply to network representatives.

Serving out the unexpired term of a former member shall not constitute a term within the meaning of this section.

B. *Meetings:*

The Television Code Review Board shall meet at least twice in each calendar year on a date to be determined by the Chairperson. The Chairperson, or the Code Authority Director, may, at any time, on at least five days written notice, call a special meeting of the Board.

C. *Quorum:*

For all purposes, a majority of the members of the Television Code Review Board shall constitute a quorum.

Section 2. *Authority and Responsibilities*

The Television Code Review Board is authorized and directed:

(1) To recommend to the Television Board of Directors amendments to the Television Code; (2) to consider, in its discretion, any appeal from any decision made by the Code Authority Director with respect to any matter which has arisen under the Code, and to suspend, reverse, or modify any such decision; (3) to prefer formal charges, looking toward the suspension or revocation of the authority to show the Code seal, to the Television Board of Directors concerning violations and breaches of the Television Code by a subscriber; (4) to be available to the Code Authority Director for consultation on any and all matters affecting the Television Code.

VII. Code Authority Director

Section 1. *Director*

There shall be a position designated as the Code Authority Director. This position shall be filled by appointment of the President of the NAB, subject to the approval of the Board of Directors.

Section 2. *Authority and Responsibilities*

The Code Authority Director is authorized and directed: (1) To maintain a continuing review of all programming and advertising material presented over television, especially that of subscribers to the Television Code of NAB; (2) to receive, screen and clear complaints concerning television programming; (3) to define and interpret words and phrases in the Television Code; (4) to develop and maintain appropriate liaison with governmental agencies and with responsible accountable organizations and institutions; (5) to inform, expeditiously and properly, a subscriber to the Television Code of complaints or commendations, as well as to advise all subscribers concerning the attitudes and desires program-wise of accountable organizations and institutions, and of the American public in general; (6) to review and monitor, if necessary, any certain series of programs, daily programming, or any other program presentations of a subscriber, as well as to request recorded material, or script and copy, with regard to any certain program presented by a subscriber; (7) to reach conclusions and make recommendations or prefer charges to the Television Code Review Board concerning violations and breaches of the Television Code by a subscriber; (8) to recommend to the Code Review Board amendments to the Television Code.

A. *Delegation of Powers and Responsibilities*

The Code Authority Director shall appoint such executive staff as is needed, consistent with resources, to carry out the above described functions, and may delegate to this staff such responsibilities as he/she may deem necessary.

APPEAL PROCEDURES FOR
ADVERTISERS/AGENCIES
FORMALIZED BY THE CODE AUTHORITY

The Code Authority has issued for the first time a set of appeal procedures which will apply to situations involving advertisers/agencies who take issue with evaluations rendered by any Code Authority office.

In general the procedures basically codify what has been Code Authority practice. Since they involve internal administration of the Codes, they are not intended to be included in the Radio and Television Codes under "Regulations and Procedures."

The Code Authority Appeal Procedures for advertisers/agencies state:

All disputes, controversies or questions as to the application of NAB Radio or Television Code standards, Code guidelines and/or interpretations thereof between an advertiser/advertising agency (hereinafter referred to as the appellant) and an NAB Code Authority editor with respect to any actual or planned commercial which the NAB Code Authority is evaluating shall be discussed and resolved according to the following procedure:

Step 1—Appeal to NAB Code Authority Regional Office

The dispute shall first be discussed with the NAB Code Authority editor handling the commercial involved in an attempt to effect a resolution thereof.

If the dispute is not resolved to the mutual satisfaction of the appellant and the NAB Code Authority editor, then the appellant may appeal the editor's evaluation to the Manager of the NAB Code Authority office involved in the review. The appellant may appeal to the Manager either in writing or orally his/her position on the issues involved.

If the dispute is not resolved to the mutual satisfaction of the appellant and the Code Authority Manager within five working days after receipt of the appeal, then the matter may be brought by the appellant to the attention of the NAB Code Authority Director's office.

Step 2—Appeal to NAB Code Authority Director's Office

If the appellant wishes to appeal the matter to the NAB Code Authority Director's office, he/she shall submit in writing to said office a "position paper" detailing why he/she takes exception to the specific ruling at issue. Within five working days following receipt of the appeal letter, the NAB Code Authority Director or a representative from said office shall either advise of a finding in favor of the appellant or, failing same, advise of a hearing date to discuss the merits of the appeal with the appellant.

If the matter is not resolved to the mutual satisfaction of the NAB Code Authority and the appellant, the appellant may then seek review of the issue by an appropriate subcommittee of the NAB Radio Code Board or NAB Television Code Review Board.

Step 3—Appeal to Subcommittees

If the appellant wishes to appeal the decision rendered by the NAB Code Authority Director's office, the appropriate NAB Radio Code Board or NAB Television Code Review Board subcommittee shall be convened for the purpose of reviewing this dispute upon condition that the appellant shall request such a review in writing by delivering to the NAB Code Authority Director five copies of a written statement of the claim, dispute or controversy to be considered including appellant's reasons for seeking review of the NAB Code Authority Director's decision. The NAB Code Authority Director shall arrange a meeting of the subcommittee as soon as possible but not longer than four weeks following receipt of the written request.

Should an appeal hearing be necessary, a majority of the subcommittee shall constitute a quorum and decisions of the subcommittee shall be rendered by majority vote.

Review procedures shall be informal and the appellant shall have the opportunity to produce evidence and witnesses on his/her own behalf. The subcommittee may direct the attendance of NAB Code Authority/NAB staff personnel at the meeting.

Decisions of the subcommittee shall be rendered in writing to the appellant as soon as possible after subcommittee review of the position/argument/material presented at the appeal meeting.

If the matter is not resolved to the satisfaction of the appellant, the appellant may then seek review of the issue by the full NAB Radio Code Board or the full NAB Television Code Review Board.

Step 4—Appeal to NAB Radio Code Board or NAB Television Code Review Board

Upon receipt by the NAB Code Authority Director of written notification of the intent of the appellant to seek a review of the subcommittee's decision, the NAB Radio Code Board or the NAB Television Code Review Board shall have the appeal item included on the agenda of its next regularly scheduled meeting provided said meeting follows by at least 10 working days the date of the written notification to the appellant of the subcommittee's decision on the matter.

The appeal to the NAB Radio Code Board or the NAB Television Code Review Board shall be handled either in writing or by a personal appearance of the appellant before the Board. Requests for personal appearances must be approved by the Chairman of the Board handling the appeal.

Whether the appeal to either Board is conducted in writing or through a personal appearance, appellant shall submit to the NAB Code Authority Director, no later than 10 working days before the date of the Board meeting, 50 copies of a written statement detailing appellant's position on the issue involved. (This written submission, together with any other material appellant may wish to provide to the Board, will be mailed to Board members by the NAB Code Authority prior to the meeting and also will be included in workbooks which are made available to Board members at the meeting.)

If a personal appearance is requested and approved, procedures at the Board meeting shall be informal and appellant shall have the opportunity to provide witnesses and evidence on his/her own behalf.

Decisions of the Board shall be rendered in writing as soon as possible after its review of the positions/arguments/material submitted/presented by appellant.

Although the NAB Code Authority believes it will be able to respond to routine appeals within the time spans outlined in the preceding steps, should new documentation/substantiation for copy claims be submitted by the appellant during any step of the appeal procedure, the NAB Code Authority reserves the right to extend the previously stated time limits in order to be able to undertake a complete analysis of the documentation/substantiation, including if necessary review of the material by consultants to the NAB Code Authority. Failure of the NAB Code Authority to act within the time limits set forth herein shall not be construed as a decision in favor of the appellant.

Commentary on Statement of Principles of American Society of Newspaper Editors

Mark Ethridge, Jr.

Chairman, Ethics Committee

So much is being made of the recent proliferation of codes of ethics that this, on behalf of the American Society of Newspaper Editors (ASNE), almost disqualifies as a disclaimer.

By definition, a code of ethics, or Canons of Journalism, as the 1923-vintage code of the ASNE called itself, implies some enforcement powers. Lawyers who violate their canons—and are caught—can have their licenses to practice suspended or revoked and can be thrown out of the club.

This is not true in the newspaper business. If Congress has no authority to enact any law abridging freedom of the press, certainly we cannot presume that authority. For good or evil, freedom of the press means precisely that, the freedom to publish a bad newspaper as well as a good one.

This was one of the first lessons the fledgling ASNE learned more than half a century ago. According to ASNE historians, the society was properly shocked when it discovered, in 1923, what was going on in Denver. There the Post, now an eminently respectable institution, was owned by ex-gambler Fred Bonfils and ex-barkeep Harry Tammen. Bonfils sought to blackmail oil magnate Harry Sinclair by publishing stories indicating massive corruption in what subsequently became known as the Teapot Dome scandal.

When Sinclair came through with half a million dollars for Bonfils, the published attacks ceased.

The ASNE anguished over the case, considered expelling Bonfils, and finally decided to do nothing because there was nothing it could do to enforce its code on the Denver Post. Besides, Bonfils resigned.

Critics at the time called it moral spinelessness. Even in 1947, the Hutchins Commission dismissed the ASNE and its code with these words: "Shortly after the code was adopted, a case of gross malpractice on the part of one of its members was reported. After the society had debated long and painfully, the case was dropped. This settled the function of the code."

In the sense of enforcement, the commission was probably correct. At least it taught our subcommittee of the ASNE Ethics Committee, appointed in 1974, not to attempt what was obviously impossible to accomplish.

Thus, in seeking to bring our standards of conduct up to date in 1974 and 1975, one of the first things we did was to recognize realities. We called it a Statement of Principles, hoping that it will be used "as a standard encouraging the highest ethical and professional performance."

With no enforcement powers among our eight hundred members or the approximately seventeen hundred daily newspapers in the United States, we could not hope to spell out every circumstance that might arise, every tough decision that some newspaper editor might have to face. The statement is therefore general.

Today, we feel, the American press is doing the best job in its history. We are less politically partisan, more objective, staffed with better-educated and better-trained personnel, and more dedicated to excellence and independence than ever before. That we are as a class more economically healthy than ever before plays no small role in our ability to do a better job.

The problem our committee faced, therefore, was not so much one of correcting evil and stopping abuses, but delineating clearly what the press must be constantly alert to do—

and not to do—to avoid the appearance of evil. In short, improving and shoring up our credibility, rather than advocating major changes in performance.

Reporters and editors these days are sufficiently well paid so they do not have to be bought and paid for. We were, then, not unduly concerned about the lavish junket, not to mention the outright bribe. What concerned us was the lesser junket, the sterling silver "favor" for attending a press conference, the loan of a new car for a vacation trip. Few reporters could be bought so cheaply, but we want to give the public, and our critics, no cause whatever for the jaundiced view.

At the same time, public events of the past few years had made us more conscious of our role as the watchdog for the public interest. Half a century ago, suggesting that the government would be less than honest with its citizens would have bordered on treason. And the 1923 code reflected that attitude.

"It is the unquestionable right (of the press)," said that document, "to discuss whatever is not explicitly forbidden by law, including the wisdom of any restrictive statute."

Had we of the press adhered closely to such a guideline in the last decade, the Pentagon Papers might still be state secrets, along with the cost overruns on the C5A cargo plane and the excesses of the CIA and FBI.

Our right and obligation to publish in such cases, without prior restraint, is a matter of principle to us and therefore, we felt, has a proper place in a statement of principles: "Journalists must be constantly alert to see that the public's business is conducted in public."

These are the major changes from the 1923 model code to the 1975 statement. Much else was changed, though mostly of a cosmetic or clarifying nature.

If our Statement of Principles adheres so closely to the 1923 formula, if it is so general as to afford wide latitude to individual newspapers, and if it is unenforceable in any case, why have one? Have we adopted a distinction without a difference?

Not to my mind, nor to the collective mind of the ASNE board. The Statement of Principles is more than that. We have not only brought it up to date, but more importantly, we have, through the many drafts, the winnowing process, and publications of drafts and the final version in our monthly Bulletin, focused attention on the principles.

It remains, though, only as good as those to whom it applies are willing to make it. Lacking teeth, it has, we hope, the force of moral suasion. We hope it will be used as a guide for individual newspapers and their staffs to draw up and live by their own sets of principles, tailored to the specifics of their operations in their communities.

Many newspapers have already done this, and we expect to see the trend continue.

Finally, we expect, this trend will benefit from fear or adverse publicity, through such organizations as the news councils, the growing tribe of newspaper ombudsmen, and the growing awareness on the part of the press that if we expect readers to trust us, we must be trustworthy.

Statement of Principles
of the American Society
# of Newspaper Editors

Adopted in 1975. Replaced Code adopted 1923.

PREAMBLE

The First Amendment, protecting freedom of expression from abridgment by any law, guarantees to the people through their press a constitutional right, and thereby places on newspaper people a particular responsibility.

Thus journalism demands of its practitioners not only industry ànd knowledge but also the pursuit of a standard of integrity proportionate to the journalist's singular obligation.

To this end the American Society of Newspaper Editors sets forth this Statement of Principles as a standard encouraging the highest ethical and professional performance.

ARTICLE I—Responsibility

The primary purpose of gathering and distributing news and opinion is to serve the general welfare by informing the people and enabling them to make judgments on the issues of the time. Newspapermen and women who abuse the power of their professional role for selfish motives or unworthy purposes are faithless to that public trust.

The American press was made free not just to inform or just to serve as a forum for debate but also to bring an independent scrutiny to bear on the forces of power in the society, including the conduct of official power at all levels of government.

ARTICLE II—Freedom of the Press

Freedom of the press belongs to the people. It must be defended against encroachment or assault from any quarter, public or private.

Journalists must be constantly alert to see that the public's business is conducted in public. They must be vigilant against all who would exploit the press for selfish purposes.

ARTICLE III—Independence

Journalists must avoid impropriety and the appearance of impropriety as well as any conflict of interest or the appearance of conflict. They should neither accept anything nor pursue any activity that might compromise or seem to compromise their integrity.

ARTICLE IV—Truth and Accuracy

Good faith with the reader is the foundation of good journalism. Every effort must be made to assure that the news content is accurate, free from bias and in context, and that all sides are presented fairly. Editorials, analytical articles and commentary should be held to the same standards of accuracy with respect to facts as news reports.

Significant errors of fact, as well as errors of omission, should be corrected promptly and prominently.

ARTICLE V—Impartiality

To be impartial does not require the press to be unquestioning or to refrain from editorial expression. Sound practice, however, demands a clear distinction for the reader between news reports and opinion. Articles that contain opinion or personal interpretation should be clearly identified.

ARTICLE VI—Fair Play

Journalists should respect the rights of people involved in the news, observe the common standards of decency and stand accountable to the public for the fairness and accuracy of their news reports.

Persons publicly accused should be given the earliest opportunity to respond.

Pledges of confidentiality to news sources must be honored at all costs, and therefore should not be given lightly. Unless there is clear and pressing need to maintain confidences, sources of information should be identified.

These principles are intended to preserve, protect and strengthen the bond of trust and respect between American journalists and the American people, a bond that is essential to sustain the grant of freedom entrusted to both by the nation's founders.

Commentary on Code of Ethics of National Association of Realtors®

H. Jackson Pontius

Executive Vice President

The Code of Ethics of the National Association of Realtors® celebrates its sixty-third birthday in this bicentennial year of 1976, having been adopted on 29 July 1913, at the sixth Annual Convention of the National Association of Real Estate Boards (Association's name changed in 1974 to National Association of Realtors®). The code was first adopted as "Rules of Conduct" to be recommended to real estate boards for voluntary adoption. Compliance with the code was made a condition of membership in the national association in 1924, and has remained so to date.

The Bylaws of the National Association, Article IV, Code of Ethics, state:

Section 1. Each Member Board shall adopt the Code of Ethics of the National Association as a part of its governing regulations for violation of which disciplinary action may be taken.

Section 2. Any Member Board which shall neglect or refuse to maintain and enforce the Code of Ethics with respect to the business activities of its members may, after due notice and opportunity for hearing, be expelled by the Board of Directors from membership in the National Association.

The establishment of a code of ethics recognizing high standards of business practice and professional conduct by real estate practitioners was a primary reason for the establishment of the national association in 1908. Men of integrity wanted to ensure honorable, faithful, and competent service to clients, customers, and other members of the public. They believed that through their collective efforts the ends of national policy and the general welfare could be served. The history of their early meetings clearly reflects the desire to avoid careless "horseback" or uninformed advice to those who relied upon them and to avoid the use of special knowledge to prey upon the unsuspecting and unsophisticated. They sought to make the broker recognize the truly fiduciary relationship he has with his client and to assure service of a professional quality in all respects. They had an awareness, too, that a voluntary commitment to peer review by knowledgeable, informed men and women sharing the same commitment had immeasurable advantages over resort to courts of law and equity. Most of all, they recognized that self-discipline in the interest of protecting the public was not inconsistent with the preservation of a competitive marketplace.

Author Pearl Jane Davies in her *History of Real Estate in America* records that Edward S. Judd, 1912 president of the national association, in accepting the presidency, "asked for a formal commitment by the voting body to a specific, written Code of Ethics. Himself a lawyer, he described the projected Code as 'similar to that of the American Bar Association' then recently approved and adopted by many local Bar Associations. 'A Committee on the Code of Ethics,' he announced, 'is expected to report at the next Convention for adoption and recommendation to all local Boards a definite Code of Ethics, a Code which shall be as the Ten Commandments to the real estate fraternity.'" Author Davies notes that the following year, on 29 July 1913, it was Judd who put the motion for the code, "The motion," he said, "is for the adoption of the Rules of Conduct and that a recommendation be sent to the local Boards that they be adopted as much as possible; and they be taken as the Code of Ethics of the National Association, and their adoption recommended everywhere as far as possible." The motion was carried by voice vote amidst applause. A delegate rose to say, "We have heard many important things here but nothing else is so important as the adoption of this resolution."

Thus, according to Pearl Davies, "The national real estate organization may claim to be the second trade or business group in the United States to follow examples of the professions of medicine, law, and engineering in formulating a Code of Ethics."

The first paragraph of that historic code for real estate practice, adopted in 1913, established the tone for the twenty-three separate ethical precepts which followed and for all subsequent versions of the code. It read: "The real estate agent should be absolutely honest, truthful, faithful and efficient. He should bear in mind that he is an employee—that his client is his employer and is entitled to the best service the real estate man can give—his information, talent, time, services, loyalty, confidence and fidelity."

The code of ethics of the national association has survived as a viable and relevant guide because it is a living document. As times have changed, new needs and insights have been recognized and, as the law has developed, the code has been amended. It has been amended twelve times since its adoption. These amendments all have reflected an interest in refining, on a continuing basis, the principles obligating Realtors® and Realtor®-Associates to the highest and best standards of personal and professional conduct in their practice of real estate. Such amendments have sought to simplify, clarify, and amplify the ethical principles established to preclude antisocial business practices, and to accommodate current legal, cultural, and national perspectives.

With all the amendments, however, the philosophical premise of the code has remained unchanged and is reflected in the preamble. That premise is that the interest of the nation and its citizens ". . . impose obligations (upon the Realtor®) beyond those of ordinary commerce. They impose *grave social responsibility* and a *patriotic duty* to which the Realtor® should *dedicate himself*, and *for which he should be diligent in preparing himself.* The Realtor®, therefore, is zealous to maintain and improve the standards of his calling and shares with his fellow Realtors® a common responsibility for its integrity and honor.

The term Realtor® has come to connote competency, fairness, and high integrity resulting from adherence to a lofty ideal of moral conduct in business relations. No inducement of profit and no instruction from clients can ever justify departure from this ideal."

Any code of ethics is meaningless unless it can be clearly understood by those who must live by it. To interpret and support the code, the Professional Standards Committee of the National Association has adopted standards of practice which are "interpretations" of the code. Such standards of practice are applications of ethical principles to specific conduct in specific circumstances as related to one or more articles of the code of ethics.

These standards of practice as well as the code and over 120 different numbered cases are set forth comprehensively in the publication of the national association, *Interpretations of the Code of Ethics*, sixth edition, January 1976.

The numbered case interpretations are of particular significance. These cases are intended to be used much like decisions in judicial proceedings. That is, they are specific and factual situations involving charges of alleged ethical violation by Realtors® and/or Realtor®-Associates and provide insight into the proper form of complaint, the procedures of a Board of Realtors® in processing the complaint to ensure due process, and the rationale of the peer judgment rendered in each case. These cases do not detail the specific sanction imposed. This is because any sanction must always fit the offense and must involve every consideration of justice, equity, and propriety. Because of this, a wide range of sanctions are available to vindicate violation of the code. Such sanctions include 1) a letter of censure, 2) suspension of membership for not more than one year, 3) expulsion from membership, 4) probation, and 5) conditional suspension or expulsion.

Acceptance of a code of ethics by the membership depends on its fair, reasonable, and impartial enforcement. Strict attention must be given to the requirements of due process. Acceptance of the code must never involve a sacrifice of the right to a fair and full hearing, of the right to an unbiased tribunal, of the right to counsel, or of any other procedural safeguard. Consistent with this concept, the national association has required each member board to establish a standing Professional Standards Committee and to establish appropriate professional standards procedures in its governing documents. The association provides and recommends to member boards the adoption of the *Code of Ethics and Arbitration Manual* of the national association, as reviewed and adapted by local legal counsel to conform to and comply with local law.

The Code of Ethics and Arbitration Manual contains "suggested provisions relating to enforcement of the Code of Ethics, disciplining of members and arbitration for inclusion in the Bylaws of local Boards of Realtors®." Part one, General Provisions, contains such things as definitions of terms, qualification for tribunal, and so forth. Part two, Membership Duties and their Enforcement, describes, among other things, duties of membership, power to take disciplinary action, nature of discipline, and deals with charges of alleged unethical conduct by members of the board and appropriate investigation and hearings. Part three deals with the arbitration of disputes (business disputes between Realtors® associated with different firms arising out of their relationship as Realtors®). Several forms that may be utilized in the professional standards proceedings are included. If this manual is not adopted, the board is nevertheless required to have local legal counsel review procedures as adopted and certify that his review assures the board's procedures accord due process and comply with the requirements of applicable law.

Since the adoption of the code of ethics for the national association in 1913, literally hundreds of thousands of disciplinary hearings and arbitration hearings have been conducted by Realtors® in the interest of protecting the public. The objective of such hearings in each case was to promote honesty, integrity, fairness, and competency, and to resolve controversies on the basis of the informed judgment of one's peers. The hearings have provided justice that has been both timely and economic. They have relieved overburdened civil courts and yet have resolved charges against Realtors® effectively and without the distortion and injury to reputation that so often attends litigation.

Article 15 of the code of ethics obligates Realtors® and

Realtor®-Associates to bring violations of the code to the board for resolution and to abide by the decision duly rendered, once all appeals have been exhausted. If a member refuses to accept a disciplinary decision after appeal, even then, before imposing the sanctions of expulsion or suspension, the board will, if there remains any doubt as to the legal propriety of the judgment, make such sanctions effective only upon entry of final judgment of competent jurisdiction in a suit by the board for declaratory judgment.

The code of ethics is the hallmark of the Realtor® and Realtor®-Associate. The public has come to recognize the unique and special protection this code affords. Clients and customers of Realtors® know that they have been given, by the code, an additional and effective source of protection. The Realtors®' code of ethics has never been more important or meaningful in the history of the association than it is today. The code adopted in 1913 was a prophecy of future concerns which only now are becoming recognized by the government: consumer protection, equal opportunity, the highest and best use of the land, professional education, and preservation of the environment.

As a viable, living, developing guide for Realtors®, the code will continue to provide the protection the public deserves and requires. The National Association of Realtors® and the respective state associations and member boards of Realtors® are committed and pledged to such protection.

The NATIONAL ASSOCIATION OF REALTORS® reserves exclusively unto itself the right to comment on and interpret the CODE and particular provisions thereof. For the NATIONAL ASSOCIATION's official interpretations of the CODE, see INTERPRETATIONS OF THE CODE OF ETHICS: NATIONAL ASSOCIATION OF REALTORS®

REALTOR®—is a registered collective membership mark which may be used by real estate professionals who are members of the NATIONAL ASSOCIATION OF REALTORS® and subscribe to its strict Code of Ethics.

Code of Ethics
of the
National Association of Realtors®

Adopted 1913. Amended 1974.

PREAMBLE

Under all is the land. Upon its wise utilization and widely allocated owner-ship depend the survival and growth of free institutions and of our civiliza-tion. The REALTOR® should recognize that the interests of the nation and its citizens require the highest and best use of the land and the widest dis-tribution of land ownership. They require the creation of adequate housing, the building of functioning cities, the development of productive indus-tries and farms, and the preservation of a healthful environment.

Such interests impose obligations beyond those of ordinary commerce. They impose grave social responsibility and a patriotic duty to which the REALTOR® should dedicate himself, and for which he should be diligent in preparing himself. The REALTOR®, therefore, is zealous to maintain and improve the standards of his calling and shares with his fellow-REALTORS® a common responsibility for its integrity and honor. The term REALTOR® has come to connote competency, fairness, and high integrity resulting from adherence to a lofty ideal of moral conduct in business rela-tions. No inducement of profit and no instruction from clients ever can justify departure from this ideal.

In the interpretation of his obligation, a REALTOR® can take no safer guide than that which has been handed down through the centuries, em-bodied in the Golden Rule, "Whatsoever ye would that men should do to you, do ye even so to them."

Accepting this standard as his own, every REALTOR® pledges himself to observe its spirit in all of his activities and to conduct his business in accordance with the tenets set forth below.

Article 1

The REALTOR® should keep himself informed on matters affecting real estate in his community, the state, and nation so that he may be able to contribute responsibly to public thinking on such matters.

Article 2

In justice to those who place their interests in his care, the REALTOR® should endeavour always to be informed regarding laws, proposed legislation, governmental regulations, public policies, and current market conditions in order to be in a position to advise his clients properly.

Article 3

It is the duty of the REALTOR® to protect the public against fraud, misrepresentation, and unethical practices in real estate transactions. He should endeavour to eliminate in his community any practices which could be damaging to the public or bring discredit to the real estate profession. The REALTOR® should assist the governmental agency charged with regulating the practices of brokers and salesmen in his state.

Article 4

The REALTOR® should seek no unfair advantage over other REALTORS® and should conduct his business so as to avoid controversies with other REALTORS®.

Article 5

In the best interests of society, of his associates, and his own business, the REALTOR® should willingly share with other REALTORS® the lessons of his experience and study for the benefit of the public, and should be loyal to the Board of REALTORS® of his community and active in its work.

Article 6

To prevent dissension and misunderstanding and to assure better service to the owner, the REALTOR® should urge the exclusive listing of property unless contrary to the best interest of the owner.

Article 7

In accepting employment as an agent, the REALTOR® pledges himself to protect and promote the interests of the client. This obligation of absolute fidelity to the client's interests is primary, but it does not relieve the REALTOR® of the obligation to treat fairly all parties to the transaction.

Article 8

The REALTOR® shall not accept compensation from more than one party, even if permitted by law, without the full knowledge of all parties to the transaction.

Article 9

The REALTOR® shall avoid exaggeration, misrepresentation, or concealment of pertinent facts. He has an affirmative obligation to discover adverse factors that a reasonably competent and diligent investigation would disclose.

Article 10

The REALTOR® shall not deny equal professional services to any person for reasons of race, creed, sex, or country of national origin. The REALTOR® shall not be a party to any plan or agreement to discriminate against a person or persons on the basis of race, creed, sex, or country of national origin.

Article 11

A REALTOR® is expected to provide a level of competent service in keeping with the Standards of Practice in those fields in which the REALTOR® customarily engages.

The REALTOR® shall not undertake to provide specialized professional services concerning a type of property or service that is outside his field of competence unless he engages the assistance of one who is competent on such types of property or service, or unless the facts are fully disclosed to the client. Any person engaged to provide such assistance shall be so identified to the client and his contribution to the assignment should be set forth.

The REALTOR® shall refer to the Standards of Practice of the National Association as to the degree of competence that a client has a right to expect the REALTOR® to possess, taking into consideration the complexity of the problem, the availability of expert assistance, and the opportunities for experience available to the REALTOR®.

Article 12

The REALTOR® shall not undertake to provide professional services concerning a property or its value where he has a present or contemplated interest unless such interest is specifically disclosed to all affected parties.

Article 13

The REALTOR® shall not acquire an interest in or buy for himself, any member of his immediate family, his firm or any member thereof, or any entity in which he has a substantial ownership interest, property listed with him, without making the true position known to the listing owner. In selling property owned by himself, or in which he has any interest, the REALTOR® shall reveal the facts of his ownership or interest to the purchaser.

Article 14

In the event of a controversy between REALTORS® associated with different firms, arising out of their relationship as REALTORS®, the REALTORS® shall submit the dispute to arbitration in accordance with the regulations of their board or boards rather than litigate the matter.

Article 15

If a REALTOR® is charged with unethical practice or is asked to present evidence in any disciplinary proceeding or investigation, he shall place all pertinent facts before the proper tribunal of the member board or affiliated institute, society, or council of which he is a member.

Article 16

When acting as agent, the REALTOR® shall not accept any commission, rebate, or profit on expenditures made for his principal owner, without the principal's knowledge and consent.

Article 17

The REALTOR® shall not engage in activities that constitute the unauthorized practice of law and shall recommend that legal counsel be obtained when the interest of any party to the transaction requires it.

Article 18

The REALTOR® shall keep in a special account in an appropriate financial institution, separated from his own funds, monies coming into his possession in trust for other persons, such as escrows, trust funds, clients' monies, and other like items.

Article 19

The REALTOR® shall be careful at all times to present a true picture in his advertising and representations to the public. He shall neither advertise without disclosing his name nor permit any person associated with him to use individual names or telephone numbers, unless such person's connection with the REALTOR® is obvious in the advertisement.

Article 20

The REALTOR®, for the protection of all parties, shall see that financial obligations and commitments regarding real estate transactions are in writing, expressing the exact agreement of the parties. A copy of each agreement shall be furnished to each party upon his signing such agreement.

Article 21

The REALTOR® shall not engage in any practice or take any action inconsistent with the agency of another REALTOR®.

Article 22

In the sale of property which is exclusively listed with a REALTOR®, the REALTOR® shall utilize the services of other brokers upon mutually agreed upon terms when it is in the best interests of the client.

Negotiations concerning property which is listed exclusively shall be carried on with the listing broker, not with the owner, except with the consent of the listing broker.

Article 23

The REALTOR® shall not publicly disparage the business practice of a competitor nor volunteer an opinion of a competitor's transaction. If his opinion is sought and if the REALTOR® deems it appropriate to respond, such opinion shall be rendered with strict professional integrity and courtesy.

Article 24

The REALTOR® shall not directly or indirectly solicit the services or affiliation of an employee or independent contractor in the organization of another REALTOR® without prior notice to said REALTOR®.

Where the word REALTOR® is used in this Code and Preamble, it shall be deemed to include REALTOR®-ASSOCIATE. Pronouns shall be considered to include REALTORS® and REALTOR®-ASSOCIATES of both genders.

The Code of Ethics was adopted in 1913. Amended at the Annual Convention in 1924, 1928, 1950, 1951, 1952, 1955, 1956, 1961, 1962, and 1974.

Commentary on
Code of Ethics of American
Football Coaches Association

William D. Murray

Executive Director

Football has been a prominent activity at colleges and universities since the first game was played more than a century ago. It has thrived because the institutions believe the sport provides a worthwhile educational experience for its participants and that it serves as a unifying force.

Over the years increasing pressures have evolved to maintain these objectives, but at the same time to have the institution's teams win more games than they lose. In some instances, where winning is traditional, the victories must outnumber the defeats by a large number to satisfy some followers.

Also, over the years there has been an increased tendency to stress the entertainment aspect of the sport because of competition for the gate-receipt dollar.

In addition, there has been little change from the general policy of requiring the sport to be self-sustaining and, in many cases, able to sustain all or most of the other athletic activities of the institution.

There also has been a growth of "booster" organizations with the primary purpose of raising funds for the support of athletic programs. This involves alumni and nonalumni, with the result that people outside the institution's administration often gain strong voices in the administration of the athletic programs.

All of the above developments place intense pressures on those who coach football. Few, if any, professional men on salary work with a greater threat to their job security.

Obviously this brings temptations to seek advantages over opposing teams and coaches. This creates a conflict with the basic aim of football: being a worthwhile educational experience for those who play.

To resolve this conflict—and even the most optimistic admit it cannot be resolved completely—the members of the American Football Coaches Association (AFCA) have adopted a code of ethics that attempts to guide a coach to the proper conduct of his profession.

The code was devised by the coaches themselves, with additional provisions or modifications being made as new situations developed over the years. It is administered by an Ethics Committee, whose membership is rotated by staggered appointments on a district basis.

Along with the AFCA Code of Ethics, coaches are required to observe the rules of their institution, of the conference to which the institution belongs and a national association— either the National Collegiate Athletic Association (NCAA) or the National Association of Intercollegiate Athletics (NAIA), or both.

There is also a code of conduct for coaches as part of the national rules of football.

Each year, from 15 to 25 percent of the head coaches in college football are either dismissed, resign under pressure, or do not have their contracts renewed. Almost always their assistant coaches lose their positions, too. The assistant coaches rarely have a contract of more than one-year's duration. Often they do not have a contract at all. This adds to the pressure of the head coach. It is not unusual for a football staff to work in close proximity for sixteen hours a day, seven days a week, from July to January. The head coach realizes that keeping his job has a direct effect on the livelihood of his assistants.

Efforts have been made to strengthen job security. After consultation with several university presidents, a set of guidelines for coaches' contracts was adopted by the AFCA and distributed to the administrative heads of those institutions that had football teams. The guidelines were for coaches in all sports.

Most of the university heads who responded were in sympathy with the guidelines and said they would adopt them or try to follow them as closely as possible. The major thrust of the guidelines was for some protection of coaches forty-five years of age or older and for salaries of all dismissed coaches to continue to the end of the school year, or until they obtained employment.

Job security, however, remains tenuous for many coaches.

Hence the temptation to seek advantages through nonobservance of regulatory provisions and the playing rules, and by ignoring the provisions of the code of ethics.

The football coach often is a prominent public figure who, in the public's eye, must be like Caesar's wife. Any slight misdeed in any manner becomes highly publicized. Despite this, such instances are remarkably few in view of the fact there are approximately 2,400 college coaches who are members of the AFCA and that approximately 3,000 college games are played each season.

AFCA would like to think its code of ethics is a strong instrument, even though its strongest penalty is suspension from the association. It has found over the years that coaches "get the message" after being called to account for alleged breaches of the code of ethics before a committee of fellow coaches.

After such appearances, there is no disclosure of the identity of the coaches involved, but there is a report to the AFCA membership about the nature of the charges and the action taken by the committee.

This has brought some criticism from the media that names and actions should be publicized. The AFCA, however, is convinced this would be unwise in that desired results are obtained without it and public disclosure then would create a situation where those charged with offenses would demand trials of a courtroom nature. This would be highly impracticable without making adherence to the code any greater than it is without it.

The enforcement procedure for those found guilty of violations involves four different penalties: a letter of reprimand; a letter of reprimand, with a copy going to the coach's president; a letter of reprimand and placement on AFCA probation; and a letter of reprimand and suspension from AFCA membership.

In the first five years of the code, the Ethics Committee was concerned mostly with establishing official AFCA positions on the type of cases brought before it and alerting the membership to the provisions of the code. Since 1958, penalties have been assessed. An average of five cases a year have been heard since then. The most severe penalty was probation, but in recent years that has been not deemed necessary.

It has been found that coaches appearing before the Ethics Committee have been cooperative and contrite. Judgment by one's peers is effective.

AFCS's code of ethics, like many others, has faults. One is brought about by the constant turnover of personnel in coaching. Some of the new people do not become aware of the code's provisions as soon as they should. Even coaches who have been in the profession for a number of years sometimes fail to review the code often enough.

All AFCA members receive a copy of the code each year. Every AFCA publication carries a reminder of the code and the importance of reviewing it at least once a year. In the AFCS Summer Manual an open letter from the AFCA president urges members to read and abide by the code. A greater effort in this area may be needed and will be studied.

In this area, there has been some thought about possible ways to require coaches to pass certain tests before they could obtain positions. The provisions of the code would be part of the examination. There are, however, many problems before such a testing program could be adopted on a national basis.

Another fault could be that some coaches are reluctant to report violations to the Ethics Committee. And, of course, not every college coach is a member of the association, even though the membership approximates 2,400.

The American Football Coaches Association was formed in 1922. It was not until 1953 that the membership adopted the code of ethics. It was created because, although there always had been certain understandings about what was right and what was wrong, no one had ever enumerated the accepted practices. Young men entering the profession had no way of knowing whether their actions conformed to accepted practices, and as they saw various members of the profession carry out their duties, they, in turn, accepted what was being done as being right.

The code was devised to get down in black and white the thinking of the majority of coaches as to what should be accepted practices—to bring the weight of opinion against those members of the coaching profession who were in violation. In some instances there were some prominent coaches whose actions indicated they felt they were a law unto themselves. They operated by "doing as they damned pleased" and dared anybody to do anything about it. A number of such coaches were brought before the Ethics Committee, with an excellent response resulting. There is, from time to time, an occasional lapse into unacceptable behavior that is brought to the attention of the Ethics Committee.

The coaches decided to take their problems into their own hands to establish the game on a solid basis. It did not take long to eliminate the feeling by some coaches that they were beyond the law.

The improvement in the situation was sudden enough to convince AFCA the code was workable and the enforcement procedures were effective.

Strangely enough, one motivation for the establishment of the code was that some coaches reported they had been ordered by their superiors in their institution to follow policies and practices contrary to the generally accepted proper conduct of coaches.

Over the years, a majority of the cases considered by the Ethics Committee involved either (a) violations for the rules for recruiting prospective football players or (b) public criticism of game officials.

Until just several years ago, the NCAA's enforcement procedures were based strictly on dealing with institutions. Coaches were not singled out individually. The NCAA, however, did turn over the names of coaches and their alleged violations to the AFCA Ethics Committee.

Now the NCAA enforcement also deals with coaches. Some penalties levied by the NCAA require an institution to dismiss a coach. This graver threat to the coaches, it is believed, will lessen the number of AFCA violations reported to the Ethics Committee. At its most recent meeting (1976) the Ethics Committee had only two cases to consider.

The fact that the NCAA now involves coaches more in its penalties has not brought any protests from AFCA members, the vast majority of whom are most anxious to have all rules and accepted practices followed as closely as possible.

The public criticism of game officials continues, but to a far lesser degree than before. Human nature being what it is, and with the outcome of key games playing such an important part in the job security of a large number of coaches, their silence in moments of great outrage requires the most stern self control. But progress in this area has been encouraging.

Not long ago a number of coaches had players feign injury to stop the game clock after their allowed timeouts had been exhausted. Some coaches devised ways to draw opponents offside. Some coaches had opponents' practice sessions scouted.

These are some of the things the Ethics Committee felt were deviations from the basic purpose of the game—making football a worthwhile educational experience for the young men who play. As a result, these practices have been almost eliminated.

Playing rules, and rules of the national organizations, conferences, and institutions, change constantly. With each change, there is the temptation to some coaches to discover loopholes and ways to evade the spirit of the rules.

The Ethics Committee, therefore, encounters new conditions and adopts new policies to control them. In 1973 the code was revised to include all of the committee's recommendations over the years, and any additional new policies will be added as they are adopted.

To make the Ethics Committee effective, a strong chairman is vital. The AFCA has been fortunate in this respect. In addition, no difficulty has been experienced in getting highly qualified coaches to serve on the committee.

A college football coach wants to enjoy the respect of his peers. If he strays from the accepted behavior designated by the code of ethics, he is held accountable by his peers. Hence the effectiveness of the code.

Code of Ethics of the American Football Coaches Association

Adopted 1952. Revised 1973.

PREAMBLE

The distinguishing characteristic of a profession is that its members are dedicated to rendering a service to humanity. Personal gain must be of lesser consideration. Those who select football coaching must understand the justification for football is that it provides spiritual and physical values for those who play it, and the game belongs, essentially, to the players.

The welfare of the game depends on how the coaches live up to the spirit and letter of ethical conduct and how coaches remain ever mindful of the high trust and confidence placed in them by their players and by the public.

Coaches unwilling or unable to comply with the principles of the Code of Ethics have no place in the profession.

Formation of a Code and procedures for its enforcement were approved unanimously by the American Football Coaches Association at the 29th annual meeting held in Cincinnati, Ohio, on January 10, 1952. Since then, additional provisions have been adopted and incorporated into the Code, the most complete revision being in 1973.

The committee on ethics that year presented the new revision to the American Football Coaches Association, and the Association unanimously approved the revised code on January 10, 1973, at the 50th annual meeting held in Chicago, Illinois.

This Code should be studied regularly by all coaches and its principles should always be followed. Violation of the Code should be reported to the Ethics Committee.

PURPOSE

The Code of Ethics has been developed to protect and promote the best interests of the game and the coaching profession. Its primary purpose is to clarify and distinguish ethical and approved professional practices from those which are detrimental. Its secondary purpose is to emphasize the purpose and value of football and to stress proper functions of coaches in relations to schools, players, and the public.

The ultimate success of the principles and standards of this Code depends on those for whom it has been established—the football coaches.

MEMBERSHIP

The Committee on Ethics shall consist of a chairman and eight members each representing one of the nine districts. Two members shall be appointed for four years, two for three years, two for two years, and two for one year. The ninth member shall be appointed for the proper amount of rotating years. New appointments shall be for four years. The committee shall meet each year on a date just prior to the Annual Meeting or at such other time as the chairman deems advisable, preferably at the American Football Coaches Association's All-America Game.

ENFORCEMENT

1. The Committee on Ethics is empowered to investigate any and all alleged violations of the Code. When an alleged violation is brought to the attention of the Committee on Ethics from any source, the method of proceeding with investigative action and requesting an appearance before the Committee shall be determined by a subcommittee consisting of the chairman, one at-large committee member and the committee district representative. Upon a decision to bring an alleged violation before the Ethics Committee, the member coach involved shall be notified thirty (30) days prior to the annual scheduled meeting date.

The member coach shall appear before the committee at the designated date and time. The Committee may request of the member coach that any official investigation data be forwarded to the committee. The member coach may submit to the committee any information relative to the alleged violation.

2. There is to be no acceptance of prima-facie evidence of a violation in any case. The member coach shall not be presumed in violation of the Code of Ethics because an institution has been found in violation of Article III of the National Collegiate Athletic Association or the conference rules and regulations to which that institution is a member. If the Committee on Ethics finds the member coach not in violation of the Code of Ethics, the committee shall write a letter to the member coaches, president and athletic director, detailing their findings.

3. If the Committee on Ethics finds the member coach in violation

of the Code of Ethics, it may elect one or more of the following courses of action:

a. A letter of reprimand.

b. A letter of reprimand with copies of the letter to the member coach's president and athletic director.

c. Place the member coach on a one year probation. Any violation of the Code of Ethics during the probationary period will result in immediate and indefinite suspension of membership.

d. Recommend to the President and ther Board of Trustees of the AFCA the suspension of membership for a period of one or more years.

After proper notification should member coach refuse to appear before the Committee on Ethics without cause, he shall be subject to immediate probation. Failure to appear at the subsequent annual meeting will result in a recommendation to the Board of Trustees for his indefinite suspension of membership from the Association.

4. The Board of Review shall act as an appeal board for members who have received disciplinary action from the Committee on Ethics. A member who wishes his case reviewed shall notify the chairman of the Board of Review, who shall then ask the Board of Review to meet for consideration of the appeal. The Board of Review will have final disposition of any case it has been asked to review.

The Board of Review shall consist of five members. Two past presidents, two trustees, and one active member who is not in either category. One is to be appointed for five years, one for four years, one for three years, one for two years, and one for one year. New appointments thereafter shall be for five years.

5. The entire proceedings are to be confidential. Exception: The findings of the Ethics Committee and the Board of Review on violations of the Code, may be announced to the membership at the annual meeting of the Association. However, names shall not be revealed.

Article One
RESPONSIBILITIES TO PLAYERS

1. In his relationship with players under his care, the coach should always be aware of the tremendous influence he wields for good or bad. Parents entrust their dearest possession to the coach's charge, and the coach, through his own example, must always be sure that the boys who have played under him are finer and more decent men for having done so. The coach should never place the value of a win above that of instilling the highest desirable ideals and character traits in his players. The safety and welfare of his players should always be uppermost in his mind, and they must never be sacrificed for any personal prestige or selfish glory.

2. In teaching the game of football, the coach must realize that there are certain rules designed to protect the player and provide common standards for determining a winner and a loser. Any attempts to beat these rules, to take unfair advantage of an opponent, or to teach deliberate unsportsman-like conduct, have no place in the game of football, nor has any coach guilty of such teaching any right to call himself a coach. The coach should set the example for winning without boasting and losing without bitterness. A coach who conducts himself according to these principles need have no fear of failure, for in the final analysis, the success of a coach can be measured in terms of the respect he has earned from his own players and from his opponents.

3. The diagnosis and treatment of injuries is a medical problem and should, under no circumstances, be considered a province of the coach. A coach's responsibility is to see that injured players are given prompt and competent medical attention and that the most minute detail of a physician's orders are carried out.

4. Under no circumstances should a coach authorize the use of drugs. Medicants, stimulants, or drugs should be used only when authorized and supervised by a physician.

5. A player's future should not be jeopardized by any circumvention of eligibility rules.

6. A coach should not make demands on his players that will interfere with the player's opportunities for achieving academic success.

Article Two
RESPONSIBILITY TO THE INSTITUTION

1. The function of the coach is to educate students through participation in the game of football. This primary and basic function must never be disregarded.

2. A coach shall conduct himself so as to maintain the principles, integrity, and dignity of his institution.

3. A coach should not exert pressure on faculty members to give players consideration they do not deserve.

4. A coach should not exert pressure on admissions office to admit players not qualified.

5. A coach should discuss his problems with his athletic director and/or faculty chairman in a friendly manner and then accept and support the decisions that have been reached.

6. Official student records and transcripts should never pass through the coach's office.

7. The coach should constantly be alert to see his program is being conducted and promoted properly. The coach should lend his experience and training to the governing body of the school's athletic program in the solution of a football problem. Where differences of opinion arise, and the council overrides the coach's judgment, discretion should be exercised in airing such differences outside the council meeting.

8. It is highly important that a coach support the administration in all policies, rules and regulations regarding football.

9. A coach's immediate superior, or superiors, should be notified immediately of a possible position transfer.

Article Three
RULES OF THE GAME

1. The Football Code which appears in the Official Football Rule Book shall be considered an integral part of this Code of Ethics and should be carefully read and observed.

2. Each coach should be acquainted thoroughly with the rules of the game. He is responsible for having the rules taught and interpreted for his players.

3. Both the letter and the spirit of the rules must be adhered to by the coaches.

4. To gain an advantage by circumvention or disregard for the rules brands a coach or player as unfit to be associated with football.

5. A coach is responsible for flagrant roughing tactics. He is responsible for illegal substitutions. He shall not permit faking of injuries in order to stop the clock. He shall not permit illegal shift with the intent of drawing an opponent offside.

6. A coach must remember always that IT IS NOT the purpose of football to hurt or injure an opponent by legal or illegal methods.

7. **Good Sportsmanship.** Habit formation is developed on the practice field. Where coaches permit, encourage or condone performance which is dangerous to an opponent, they are derelict in their responsibility to teach fair play and good sportsmanship. This aspect of coaching must be attacked just as vigorously as the teaching of offense and defense, and to the players it is more important than all the technical aspects of the game combined. Any coach who fails to stress this point, or who permits, encourages or defends the use of unsportsmanlike tactics shall be considered guilty of the most serious breach of football coaching ethics.

Article Four
OFFICIALS

1. No competitive contest can be played satisfactorily without impartial, competent officials. Officials must have the respect and support of coaches and players. On and off-the-record criticism of officials to players or to the public shall be considered unethical.

2. **Officials' Associations.** There should be a cooperative relationship between coaches and officials' associations, with frequent interchange of ideas and suggestions. Coaches should, whenever possible, accept invitations to attend officials' rules meetings. Similarly, coaches should extend officials invitations to discuss rules interpretations with their squads, and on occasion, to officials at scrimmages, for mutual benefits.

3. **Treatment of Officials.** On the day of a game officials should be treated in a courteous manner. They should be provided with a private

room in which to meet and dress for the game. Conferences between coaches and officials shall always be conducted according to procedures established by the governing Conference or Officials Association. In every respect the official Rule Book shall be followed in coach-official relationships, on the field and during and following a game. Any criticisms which the coach may have to make concerning officiating should be made in writing to the office which assigned the official to the game. For a coach to address, or permit anyone on his bench to address, uncomplimentary remarks to any official during the progress of a game, or to indulge in conduct which might incite players or spectators against the officials, is a violation of the rules of the game and must likewise be considered conduct unworthy of a member of the coaching profession.

4. Use of Movies in Checking Officials. It should be recognized that slow motion study of controversial decisions by officials is far different from on-the-spot decisions which must be made during the course of a game. To show critical plays to sport writers, sportscasters, alumni and the public, which may incite them to label officials as incompetents, must be considered unethical conduct.

Article Five
PUBLIC RELATIONS

1. Members of the news media should be treated with courtesy, honesty, and respect. Derogatory and misleading statements should be avoided. Direct questions should be answered honestly, or not at all. If good judgment indicates an honest answer would be prejudicial to the best interests of the game, ethical procedure demands that it not be answered. In such instances, "No comment" is justifiable.

2. Coaches should assume the responsibility of teaching their players how to conduct themselves in interviews in the best interests of football.

3. The Association recommends that the media be admitted to dressing rooms as soon as practicable after games.

4. Coaches should not stress injuries, disciplinary measures, academic difficulties, eligibility problems, and similar personal matters. Disciplinary problems should be a "family affair" to be solved between the coach and players. Scholastic eligibility is a province of the Dean's or Registrar's office. Injuries are essentially the province of the team's physician or trainer. No good purpose can be served by emphasizing such matters.

5. Coaches should avoid talking in public about unethical recruiting and use of illegal formations.

6. Any statements that tend to portray football in any light other than being part of the educational process is detrimental to the future of the profession.

7. Falsifying weights is a bad educational process.

8. Coaches should not predict game winners.

9. It shall be unethical for coaches to use alumni, booster, and quarterback club organizations in an attempt to defeat or obstruct institutional

athletic controls, or to encourage violation of established rules. It shall be unethical for coaches to make demands, financial or otherwise, upon such groups which are not in keeping with the letter and spirit of existing controls or in any other manner misuse such strength and power in violation of accepted rules and regulations.

10. Accepting money or goods for endorsement of any product or commodity not in keeping with the traditions of the coaching profession is unethical. It is the coach's responsibility to be certain the working and sense of any testimonial does not bring discredit. Endorsement, directly or indirectly by active members of the Association, of alcoholic beverages and/or tobacco products is unethical.

11. Solution of professional problems should be within the profession and not in the press. Newspaper columns and magazine articles over the signature of a coach are his responsibility exclusively.

Article Six
SCOUTING

1. It is unethical under any circumstances to scout any team by any means whatsoever, except in regularly scheduled games. The head coach shall be held responsible for all scouting. This includes the use of motion pictures.

2. It is unethical conduct to violate conference rules on the exchange of film.

3. Direct exchange of film is urged by the Association.

Article Seven
RECRUITING

1. All institutional, conference, and national regulatory body rules pertaining to recruiting shall be observed strictly.

2. It is a breach of ethics to recruit a player enrolled at another school (or to recruit a prospective freshman who has avowed his intention to enroll at another school and who has taken residence therein) for the purpose of participating in regularly organized fall practice.

3. A student-athlete should not be recruited during his participation in another sport so that he misses, or is late for, practices and games.

4. In discussing the advantages of his institution, the coach must confine his statements to an honest and forthright presentation of the facts. He shall refrain from making derogatory statements about other institutions and their officials.

5. It is unethical for any coach to make statements to any prospective student which cannot be fulfilled.

Article Eight
GAME DAY AND OTHER RESPONSIBILITIES

1. It is vitally important a coach's actions and behavior at all times bring credit to himself, his institution, and the game of football.

2. Before and after game, rival coaches should meet and exchange friendly greetings.

3. During a game a coach should be as inconspicuous as possible. Coaches are encouraged to demonstrate a friendly and kindly attitude toward their players. The attitude of coaches toward officials should be controlled and undemonstrative.

4. After game, visitors should not be permitted in team dressing room until coaches have completed their post-game responsibilities, including a careful check of player injuries.

5. Coaches should use their influence to upgrade levels of sportsmanship by rooting sections by working closely with cheerleaders and leaders of card sections.

6. A coach should do all he can to prevent scalping of tickets by players.

7. A coach shall not receive compensation from professional teams for talent scouting of or negotiation for his players.

Commentary on Code of Ethics of the International Association of Chiefs of Police

Glen D. King

Executive Director

The International Association of Chiefs of Police (IACP) was founded in 1893. In its constitution, a primary objective of the Association was stated: ". . . to bring about recruitment and training in the police profession of qualified persons and to encourage adherence of all police officers to high professional standards of performance and conduct." This mandate goes to the heart of police ethics.

Exacting ethical standards and a high degree of honesty are perhaps more essential for the police than for any other group in society. A police officer carries a lethal weapon and the authority to use it under certain circumstances. Because the police are entrusted with the enforcement of the fundamental rules that guide society's conduct, a police officer's violation of the law or corrupt failure to enforce it dishonors the law and the authority he represents.

Dishonesty within a police agency can, almost overnight, destroy respect and trust that has been built up over a period of years by honest government and police officials. Nothing undermines public confidence in the police and the process of criminal justice more than the illegal acts of officers. Support for the police in their work and the bringing about of crucial changes easily can be impaired by a belief that the police themselves are not taking every possible measure to eradicate corruption and unethical conduct.

And, since ethics relate to the positive internal forces of conscience that make our actions and deeds conform with the professional and/or socially acceptable mores of the environment in which we live and work, the development and implementation of a uniform code of ethics becomes absolutely essential to the proper control of a law enforcement agency. A perspective on that development and some of the measures taken toward implementation follow.

The original Law Enforcement Code of Ethics was the object of a three-year study by several police-related agencies. In 1956, a draft written by the Peace Officer's Research Association of California (PORAC) was presented in resolution form to the association's annual conference. PORAC had been working with the International Association of Chiefs of Police and the International Conference of Police Associations (ICPA) and the draft represented at least one hundred modifications of the original. The members of PORAC adopted the code on 1 October of that year. The code was then carried across the country by resolutions adopted in 1957 by the IACP, and the International Conference of Police Associations urged its adoption by each affiliated association in the tradition of its local autonomy.

Reasons why the code came into existence perhaps relate to a long felt need for intensive reforms by the police themselves. The problem of old-style domination of the police by political machines was especially abhorrent to professional-minded police officials. As a result, the effort to establish independent, professional law enforcement has made considerable headway over the past thirty years. This movement has not been without its own problems, however; the tradition of improper political interference is deep-rooted.

Further, civil service regulations in many jurisdictions have sometimes restricted reform attempts of honest police executives. In many cities, for example, it is extremely difficult to remove officers who have engaged in serious acts of misconduct.

It is obvious that improper political interference contributes to corruption. Patronage appointments lower the quality of personnel and encourage all officers to cooperate with politicians, even in improper circumstances. Although a man might withstand this temptation for himself, it may be futile for him to separate himself from the practices of superiors and partners.

Many steps have been taken towards implementation of the code and at least one state has legislated for its sanction. National, state, and local police associations have done a great deal to encourage police integrity. The code of ethics has been adopted by all major police associations and agencies throughout the nation. In California, state law requires that the code be administered as an oath to all police recruits training in the forty-five police academies certified by the State Commission on Peace Officers Standards.

The IACP pursues adherence to the code in several ways. Many of its publications carry the code and three training vehicles feature the code as a separate training aid for teaching ethics and police morality. The Professional Standards Division of IACP has developed the Professional Police Registry and Assessment Service for qualifying personnel of the police community. The IACP Resolutions Committee constantly strives to establish and maintain honest police leadership. Police agencies in states lacking enabling legislation are urged to include adherence to the code through departmental rules, regulations, and policies. And, by resolution, IACP has authored and adopted the Canons of Police Ethics as implementing principles for the code. The eleven articles of the canons appear with this article.

The code and canons offer the most universally adopted standards of behavior but there is no system yet for the profession to discipline its members on a national basis. IACP, with more than 10,500 police executive members, strives for individual acceptance by each state. Forty-four states have passed legislation for the minimum training of law enforcement practitioners. This leadership attitude by forward-thinking police officials and legislators provides the hope for universal adherence to the Law Enforcement Code of Ethics.

The day-to-day application of ethics considers the social role of the police officer. It has been said that morality cannot be legislated. And the officer who will not tolerate the misuse of authority in himself or other officers without the threat of punishment has properly identified his role in society. The police officer stands as guarantor of human rights and dignity. He or she is a member of the group that society has chosen to regulate and control its conduct. That responsibility cannot be taken lightly and its internationalization must be considered far above the control imposed by mere legal sanctions.

When a police officer's primary concern is the maximum possible service to mankind, society will fully realize the return on its investment. Without the active, heartfelt support of the citizens being served, no police agency will succeed.

Law Enforcement Code of Ethics of the International Association of Chiefs of Police

Adopted 1957.

AS A LAW ENFORCEMENT OFFICER, my fundamental duty is to serve mankind; to safeguard lives and property; to protect the innocent against deception, the weak against oppression or intimidation, and the peaceful against violence or disorder; and to respect the Constitutional rights of all men to liberty, equality and justice.

I WILL keep my private life unsullied as an example to all; maintain courageous calm in the face of danger, scorn or ridicule; develop self-restraint; and be constantly mindful of the welfare of others. Honest in thought and deed in both my personal and official life, I will be exemplary in obeying the laws of the land and the regulations of my department. Whatever I see or hear of a confidential nature or that is confided to me in my official capacity will be kept ever secret unless revelation is necessary in the performance of my duty.

I WILL never act officiously or permit personal feelings, prejudices, animosities or friendships to influence my decisions. With no compromise for crime and with relentless prosecution of criminals, I will enforce the law courteously and appropriately without fear or favor, malice or ill will, never employing unnecessary force or violence and never accepting gratuities.

I RECOGNIZE the badge of my office as a symbol of public faith, and I accept it as a public trust to be held so long as I am true to the ethics of the police service. I will constantly strive to achieve these objectives and ideals, dedicating myself before God to my chosen profession . . . law enforcement.

CANONS OF POLICE ETHICS

Article 1. Primary Responsibility of Job

The primary responsibility of the police service, and of the individual officer, is the protection of the people of the United States through the upholding of their laws; chief among these is the Constitution of the United States and its amendments. The law enforcement officer always represents the whole of the community and its legally expressed will and is never the arm of any political party or clique.

Article 2. Limitations of Authority

The first duty of a law enforcement officer, as upholder of the law, is to know its bounds upon him in enforcing it. Because he represents the legal will of the community, be it local, state or federal, he must be aware of the limitations and proscriptions which the people, through law have placed upon him. He must recognize the genius of the American system of government which gives to no man, groups of men, or institution, absolute power, and he must insure that he, as a prime defender of that system, does not pervert its character.

Article 3. Duty to Be Familiar with the Law and with Responsibilities of Self and Other Public Officials

The law enforcement officer shall assiduously apply himself to the study of the principles of the laws which he is sworn to uphold. He will make certain of his responsibilities in the particulars of their enforcement, seeking aid from his superiors in matters of technicality or principle when these are not clear to him; he will make special effort to fully understand his relationship to other public officials, including other law enforcement agencies, particularly on matters of jurisdiction, both geographically and substantively.

Article 4. Utilization of Proper Means to Gain Proper Ends

The law enforcement officer shall be mindful of his responsibility to pay strict heed to the selection of means in discharging the duties of his office. Violations of law or disregard for public safety and property on the part of an officer are intrinsically wrong; they are self-defeating in that they instill in the public mind a like disposition. The employment of illegal means, no matter how worthy the end, is certain to encourage disrespect for the law and its officers. If the law is to be honored, it must first be honored by those who enforce it.

Article 5. Cooperation with Public Officials in the Discharge of Their Authorized Duties

The law enforcement officer shall cooperate fully with other public officials in the discharge of authorized duties, regardless of party affiliation or personal prejudice. He shall be meticulous, however, in assuring himself of the propriety, under the law, of such actions and shall guard against the use of his office or person, whether knowingly or unknowingly, in any improper or illegal action. In any situation open to question, he shall seek authority from his superior officer, giving him a full report of the proposed service or action.

Article 6. Private Conduct

The law enforcement officer shall be mindful of his special identification by the public as an upholder of the law. Laxity of conduct or manner in private life, expressing either disrespect for the law or seeking to gain special privilege, cannot but reflect upon the police officer and the police service. The community and the service require that the law enforcement officer lead the life of a decent and honorable man. Following the career of a policeman gives no man special perquisites. It does give the satisfaction and pride of following and furthering an unbroken tradition of safeguarding the American republic. The officer who reflects upon this tradition will not degrade it. Rather, he will so conduct his private life that the public will regard him as an example of stability, fidelity, and morality.

Article 7. Conduct toward the Public

The law enforcement officer, mindful of his responsibility to the whole community, shall deal with individuals of the community in a manner calculated to instill respect for its laws and its police service. The law enforcement officer shall conduct his official life in a manner such as will inspire confidence and trust. Thus, he will be neither overbearing nor subservient, as no individual citizen has an obligation to stand in awe of him nor a right to command him. The officer will give service where he can, and require compliance with the law. He will do neither from personal preference or prejudice but rather as a duly appointed officer of the law discharging his sworn obligation.

Article 8. Conduct in Arresting and Dealing with Law Violators

The law enforcement officer shall use his powers of arrest strictly in accordance with the law and with due regard to the rights of the citizen concerned. His office gives him no right to prosecute the violator nor to mete out punishment for the offense. He shall, at all times, have a clear appreciation of his responsibilities and limitations regarding detention of the violator; he shall conduct himself in such a manner as will minimize the possibility of having to use force. To this end he shall cultivate a dedication to the service of the people and the equitable upholding of their laws whether in the handling of law violators or in dealing with the law-abiding.

Article 9.   Gifts and Favors

The law enforcement officer, representing government, bears the heavy responsibility of maintaining, in his own conduct, the honor and integrity of all government institutions. He shall, therefore, guard against placing himself in a position in which any person can expect special consideration or in which the public can reasonably assume that special consideration is being given. Thus, he should be firm in refusing gifts, favors, or gratuities, large or small, which can, in the public mind, be interpreted as capable of influencing his judgment in the discharge of his duties.

Article 10.   Presentation of Evidence

The law enforcement officer shall be concerned equally in the prosecution of the wrong-doer and the defense of the innocent. He shall ascertain what constitutes evidence and shall present such evidence impartially and without malice. In so doing, he will ignore social, political, and all other distinctions among the persons involved, strengthening the tradition of the reliability and integrity of an officer's word.

The law enforcement officer shall take special pains to increase his perception and skill of observation, mindful that in many situations his is the sole impartial testimony to the facts of a case.

Article 11.   Attitude toward Profession

The law enforcement officer shall regard the discharge of his duties as a public trust and recognize his responsibility as a public servant. By diligent study and sincere attention to self-improvement he shall strive to make the best possible application of science to the solution of crime and, in the field of human relationships, strive for effective leadership and public influence in matters affecting public safety. He shall appreciate the importance and responsibility of his office, and hold police work to be an honorable profession rendering valuable service to his community and his country.

Legal Limitations and Possibilities For Self-Enforcement of Codes of Ethics

Earl W. Kintner

The development of appropriate codes of ethics and adherence to their requirements can have substantial beneficial effects, both for the group observing the code and for the public at large. Nevertheless, the practical effects flowing from such codes must not unduly limit competition or unreasonably restrain trade or commerce or they will transgress the prohibitions of the antitrust laws.

This essay sets out the legal limitations upon permissible content of codes of conduct and the extent to which a group or organization that has developed a code of conduct may lawfully seek to enforce adherence to that code by private means. Collateral consideration is also given to the extent to which Congress might lawfully enlarge self-enforcement powers, consistent with the requirements of the Constitution.

In any discussion concerning the proper function and content of codes of ethics, it is important to emphasize at the outset that certain matters are not legally appropriate for inclusion in such codes. In general, it is not appropriate for competitors to seek uniformity in prices, terms, or conditions of sale or purchase of services, finished goods, or raw materials. Likewise, establishment of uniform hours of operation, uniform product or service specifications, or standardization of any other aspect of the group's business activities is inherently suspect under the antitrust laws. Most of the reported cases dealing with the legality of particular codes of conduct have involved factual situations in which one or more of these inappropriate activities has been an integral part of the code whose legality was challenged.

While concerted efforts to develop voluntary industry standards and/or objective testing procedures for certification of products or services have a vital role, such activities are measured against more stringent antitrust standards and should be developed separate and apart from any code establishing general ethical precepts designed to govern the general conduct of members of the group.

OVERVIEW OF THE ANTITRUST LAW

In general, the antitrust laws were established by Congress to protect and foster free and unfettered competition at all levels of the economy. In 1890, the Sherman Act was passed, declaring in simple language that "[e]very contract, combination . . . or conspiracy, in restraint of trade or commerce among the several States, or with foreign nations, is hereby declared to be illegal." Twenty-one years later, in *Standard Oil Co.* v. *United States*, 221 U.S. 1 (1911), the Supreme Court announced that the prohibitions of this language were to be applied under a "rule of reason" and that only those contracts, combinations, or conspiracies that are unreasonable are proscribed by the Sherman Act.

Except for certain types of commercial restraints that have been found so pernicious and destructive of competition as to foreclose any need to consider whether they might be reasonable, the rule of reason continues to be the applicable test of violation of the antitrust laws. Included within the types of practices which have been deemed so devoid of valid competitive purpose as to preclude the need for rule of reason consideration are agreements to fix prices, agreements to allocate among competitors geographic territories or customers, and the use of so-called "tying" contracts in which a buyer who wishes to purchase one commodity from a seller is required to purchase a second commodity he did not want.

Such practices are per se violations of the antitrust laws, foreclosing any judicial inquiries into either their purpose or effect —once existence of the practice is proven, judgment against the party using the practice follows as a matter of law.

Assuming that a proposed code of ethics does not contain any provisions which are per se violative of the antitrust laws, the provisions of the code as they affect the conduct of any trade or commerce will be tested under the rule of reason. It is imperative, therefore, that any provision whose inclusion in the code is proposed be carefully examined to determine that its effects on commerce—both direct and indirect—are reasonable.

ETHICAL PRECEPTS AND COMPETITIVE RESTRAINTS DISTINGUISHED

Ethical precepts are founded upon a general concern for attempting to do the right and proper thing in one's behavior towards others. Such general absolute concepts as honesty and fair dealing will almost always be embraced in the development of a code of ethics. Inclusion of these general precepts is totally appropriate and necessary if the code of ethics is to have any practical vitality.

Problems arise almost at once, however, when any group of competitors seeking to develop a code of ethics further attempts to subdivide the general ethical precepts into specific prohibitions against certain types of commercial practices the group would collectively like to see eliminated. For example, prohibitions against retail sales of commodities or services below cost may be proposed under the general rubric of elimination of unfair competition or preservation of fair competition among retail merchants dealing in those particular goods or services. It is readily apparent, however, that such purported ethical precepts are directed not at insuring honesty or fair dealing with the ultimate consumer, but rather impermissibly standardize and place a lower limit under the price structure the consumer will be charged. Such provisions are naked restraints upon competition and will not successfully withstand antitrust scrutiny.

When a group of competitors sits down together to consider

and develop a code of ethics for their industry, great care must be taken in distinguishing between ethical precepts and competitive restraints. While certain forms of competition may be clearly unfair or deceptive and have been held to be unlawful in decided cases, there are other forms of vigorous competitive activity that are not unfair, deceptive, or unlawful, and any combination or conspiracy to eliminate these practices is patently unlawful. As a rule of thumb, when the discussion turns to "cutthroat competition" and the like, careful legal review of any provisions dealing with such activities is absolutely mandated.

The following brief review of antitrust cases in which selective restraints on competition were held to violate the antitrust laws illustrates the need to distinguish ethics from competitive restraints and unequivocally establishes that the *good intentions* of the group selecting these unlawful restraints *are no defense to an antitrust prosecution*.

PROHIBITED ACTIVITIES

Provisions that directly or indirectly fix or standardize prices are the most vulnerable area under the antitrust laws. Regardless of the good intent of a particular provision, including the elimination of certain unequivocally unfair or deceptive practices, if the provision also has a direct effect upon the prices of goods or services it will not pass antitrust muster. *Standard Sanitary Manufacturing Co.* v. *United States*, 226 U.S. 220 (1912), is an early case establishing this principle. The Association of Sanitary Enameled Ware Manufacturers purchased the dominant patent under which such products were manufactured and then licensed all industry members on the condition they adhere to certain price schedules and not market "seconds."

Although such seconds were allegedly being palmed off on the public as first-quality goods and customers were being deceived thereby, the primary purpose of these activities was to enhance industry conditions and to eliminate price competition by withdrawing substandard products from the market. On review, the Supreme Court found that elimination of price competition between the companies and elimination of price competition through the marketing of lower-priced seconds was clearly anticompetitive, could not be justified, and was illegal, notwithstanding any possible beneficial effects to the industry flowing from the code.

In a later case, existence of an association code of ethics providing that, among other things "sugar should be sold only upon prices and terms publicly announced," was accepted by the Supreme Court as evidence of an illegal price agreement [*Sugar Institute* v. *United States*, 297 U.S. 553 (1936)]. Likewise, existence of an association purpose to maintain a multiple basing-point delivered-price system was accepted as part of the evidence establishing an unlawful price agreement in *FTC* v. *Cement Institute*, 333 U.S. 683 (1948).

To the same effect, the Federal Trade Commission (FTC) has issued a number of advisory opinions dealing with association codes and the legality of including certain provisions with indirect price-restricting consequences. For example, a wholesaler group's proposed resolution establishing uniform prices and terms to be paid to them for worn-out parts by parts rebuilders was refused approval in Advisory Opinion Digest No. 15. The following provisions have also been explicitly disapproved: establishment of uniform terms to govern dealing with commercial customers (AO 97); provisions calling for "fair and adequate profit levels" (AO 115); provisions seeking firm price quotations from suppliers (AO 137); provisions prohibiting sales below cost (AO 249); and prohibitions against the advertising of rates for performing services (AO 268).

Like price fixing provisions, group boycotts invariably receive harsh treatment under the antitrust laws. For example, the attempts of retail lumber dealers to eliminate direct retail sales by lumber wholesalers through the circulation among the trade of lists naming such direct selling wholesalers was declared to be a violation of the Sherman Act in *Eastern States Retail Lumber Dealers' Association* v. *United States*, 234 U.S. 600 (1914).

Even when a boycott is aimed at eliminating questionable competitive practices, it is unlikely to be held lawful under the antitrust laws. For example, in *Fashion Originators' Guild of America, Inc.* v. *FTC*, 312 U.S. 457 (1941), the Supreme Court upheld the commission's determination that an organized boycott established by fabric manufacturers in an attempt to eliminate so-called "style pirates" from the market was unlawful. The court's opinion clearly implies that the only legitimate source of protection for fabric designs must lie in the copyright and patent laws and it describes the guild as being:

> in reality an extra-governmental agency, which prescribes rules for the regulation and restraint of interstate commerce, and provides extra-judicial tribunals for determination and punishment of violations and this "trenches upon the power of the national legislature and violates the statute." [312 U.S. at 465.]

Two years later in *U.S.* v. *American Medical Association*, 317 U.S. 519 (1943), the Supreme Court, in ruling upon the AMA's efforts to boycott doctors who practiced for or consulted with a plan offering prepaid medical care, rejected the argument that such professional groups, which under state law have been given some authority to control aspects of professional practice, are thereby exempt from the strictures of the antitrust laws. In 1975, in *Goldfarb* v. *Virginia State Bar*, 421 U.S. 773 (1975), the Supreme Court reinforced this opinion by holding that there is no professional exemption available to a bar association seeking to justify its establishment of uniform minimum fee schedules.

THE BRIGHT SIDE: CODES OF ETHICS AND THE WELL-BEING OF SOCIETY

Virtually all of the unlawful practices outlined above are activities that do not properly belong in a code of ethics anyway. They are detailed here solely as a catalog of provisions that should be rigorously avoided in formulating a good and effective code of ethics. Inclusion of any one of these practices can later result in an otherwise exemplary code of conduct being used as evidence that your group conspired to violate the antitrust laws.

Now to the bright side. Codes of ethics can make a pre-eminent contribution to the well-being of society and can encourage a finer and more desirable quality of life for everyone. Nothing in a proper code of ethics or in its appropriate enforcement is inherently violative of either the antitrust laws, the general laws, or the mores of our society. In fact, it is questionable whether our democracy can continue to exist unless the behavior of its citizens is guided by proper ethical precepts.

For example, there are many types of business practices that have been ruled unlawful by the courts or the Federal Trade Commission, but neither the commission nor the Department of Justice has either the resources, manpower, or inclination to seek out each of these practices wherever it may be occurring in our economy. Here is the area where industry cooperation and a code of ethics can go a long way towards eliminating the more undesirable of these practices in any segment of industry. A good place to begin is in the area of advertising by establishing standards for honesty and full disclosure of material information concerning the industry's products. Far from imposing any restraint on trade, the elimination of false and misleading advertising has a strongly procompetitive effect—it insures that informed consumers will be enabled to make rational choices in their selection of goods or services.

Self-regulation of advertising practices is, in fact, an important function of many viable industry codes. Moreover, most of the situations in which either the FTC or Justice Department has approved self-government of an industry code has involved code provisions designed to eliminate deceptive practices in advertising or other representations made to consumers. For example, prior to the establishment of federal legislation limiting the broadcast advertising and other advertising of cigarettes, the industry had developed and received approval from the Justice Department of a comprehensive Cigarette Advertising Code, in which certain standards were laid down governing the content of cigarette advertising. Under the code, all cigarette advertising was required to be submitted to an independent administrator for advance clearance, and the code contained provisions requiring the payment of a sum of up to $100 thousand as liquidated damages for each violation of the code. A key element of this code was the strict limitation upon the promotion of cigarettes on school or college campuses and the prohibition against using free samples to solicit trade of persons under twenty-one years of age.

As a practical matter, the individual cigarette companies would have found it almost impossible to individually adhere to the code's standards without the assurance that their competitors would also follow the same standard. Similar codes dealing with program and film content have been established in the motion picture, radio, and television industry, permitting these industries as a whole to achieve higher standards than any one member of them could have achieved alone.

In this age of consumerism, no industry can with impunity ignore general industry practices that have a capacity to deceive or mislead consumers. With the increased budgets of the Justice Department and FTC and a growing militance among consumers who feel that they have been dealt with unfairly, chances are excellent that one or more companies in the industry will be selected and prosecuted to establish the illegality of these practices. Typically the government selects only one company and makes an example of it, since the cost of proceeding against all members in the industry would be prohibitive. Considering the severe competitive handicap that an adjudicated case can impose upon the company selected for enforcement activity, development, and adherence to appropriate industry advertising standards is a far more intelligent course, permitting each company's attention to be directed to enhancing its competitive position, rather than defending itself in a lawsuit.

Where certain practices within an industry are pernicious enough and enforcement activities alone have not been sufficient to eliminate harmful practices, Congress has occasionally acted by creating a new regulatory commission with plenary powers to impose uniform standards and requirements upon an industry. The enactment of federal legislation dealing with automobile safety in 1966 and legislation dealing with consumer product safety in 1972 can be directly traced to perceived shortcomings in the efforts of these industries to regulate themselves. Needless to say, these agencies and others like them have provided substantial additional burdens upon the industries affected and have greatly complicated the conduct of their businesses.

In 1967 a group of magazine publishers who were concerned

about certain abuses in the door-to-door sales of magazine subscriptions secured FTC approval for a self-regulatory program designed to identify salesmen guilty of deceptive practices and publicize their names to all subscription agencies employing such salesmen. (Advisory Opinion Digest No. 128.) In addition to identification of offending salesmen, the approved code also provided for penalties of up to five thousand dollars per violation to be imposed upon subscription agencies violating the provisions of the code. All enforcement activities were to be handled by an independent administrator retained to enforce the code's provisions. The commission expressed its judgment that such fines "will not operate anticompetitively or in a confiscatory manner but [will be] sufficient to constitute a deterrent." (Letter from Federal Trade Commission Secretary Joseph W. Shea to Earl W. Kintner, dated 22 May 1967.) Two further conditions imposed by the commission deserve note: first, the requirement that participation in the code by subscription agencies was to be on a completely voluntary basis; and second, that approval was granted for a three-year period subject to reconsideration by the commission at the end of that time. The plan expired in 1970 and no request was made to renew it, since the FTC had in the meantime issued formal complaints against a number of participants concerning alleged misrepresentations by salesmen in the sale of subscriptions.

No subsequent FTC advisory opinions concerning specific self-enforcement programs have been issued, but in 1969 and again in 1974 the commission issued advisory opinions recognizing the appropriateness of expulsion from association membership for those members refusing to adhere to code provisions modeled upon requirements imposed by law. In the first case, the FTC gave its explicit approval to the enforcement by an association of shippers' agents of code provisions requiring member compliance with the legal limitations imposed by the Interstate Commerce Act on the scope of permissible shipping activity. (Advisory Opinion Digest No. 373.) Under this code, repeated failure to comply would, subject to notice and an opportunity for a hearing, result in either a probationary period or expulsion of the offending member. The commission's opinion notes:

While the Code contains provisions restricting the business operations of members, it appears from the materials submitted that the purpose of these restrictions is to insure that members remain with the Act's limitations and respect the confidential agency status created in their dealings with shipper-customers. The purpose is also to encourage Association members voluntarily to refrain from unfair or deceptive practices. In this context there is a greater public interest in protecting shippers from dishonest shippers' agents than there is in condemning the minimal restraints that might result from application of the Code.

Undoubtedly, unreasonable and therefore unlawful restraints might result if an Association member is arbitrarily or improperly expelled from membership, but the Commission believes that there is ample public interest in effectively encouraging Association members to refrain from the clearly pernicious practices condemned by the Code. On the assumption that the Code will be administered in such a way as to promote this end, and not so as to place unreasonable restraint on the ability of members to do business, the provision permitting the Association to expel non-conforming members is approved.

Similarly, in 1974 the commission issued an unnumbered advisory opinion to the Constitution and Bylaws Modeling Association of America, International, concerning a revised draft of the association's constitution and bylaws. [*Trade Reg. Rep.* ¶20,549 (FTC 20 March 1974).] While declining to approve the specific language proposed by the requestor concerning the basis for dismissal of a member, the commission stated the following criterion for provisions dealing with expulsion: "Dismissal from membership should be allowed only for failure to comply with specific, non-discriminatory, objective criteria that adhere closely to the requirements of the law." The advisory opinion further suggested that any new language selected by the respondent could again be submitted to the commission for clearance as to its legality under section five of the Federal Trade Commission Act.

Given the existence of these prior approvals in specific situations, it appears clear that an industry code directed at the elimination of patently unlawful activities and limited in its scope to appropriate sanctions to correct these abuses will be permissible under the antitrust laws. Of course, great care must be taken in both the drafting of such codes and their enforcement since arbitrary or discriminatory application of otherwise lawful code provisions can constitute an independent violation of the antitrust laws. Moreover, where membership in the association or industry group is essential to commercial survival of a member firm, imposition of sanctions in the form of liquidated monetary damages is far preferable to use of dismissal or expulsion as a sanction. In fact, in such cases dismissal may not be a permissible alternative under the antitrust laws. Once again, good intention alone provides no defense to an antitrust challenge—it is imperative that codes of ethics and their enforcement methodologies receive careful legal review, including submission of proposed codes to the FTC for an advisory opinion in appropriate cases.

PROVISIONS FOR SELF-ENFORCEMENT UNDER FEDERAL AND STATE LAWS

While recent legislation has contained only limited grants to nongovernmental entities to regulate themselves, during the Great Depression in the early 1930s Congress enacted a great experiment in industry self-regulation. The National Industrial Recovery Act (NIRA), promulgated in 1933, authorized the president to approve "codes of fair competition for any trade or industry upon application from groups representing industry members." The only precondition established by this statute was that the president must make the following findings as to the proposed code:

(1) That such associations or groups impose no inequitable restrictions on admission to membership therein and are truly representative of such trades or industries or subdivisions thereof, and (2) that such Code or Codes are not designed to promote monopolies or eliminate or oppress small enterprises and will not operate to discriminate against them, and will tend to effectuate the policy of this title: Provided, that such Code or Codes shall not permit monopolies or monopolistic practices.
. . . The President may, as a condition of his approval of any such Code, impose such conditions . . . for the protection of consumers, competitors, employees and others, and in furtherance of the public interest, and may provide such exceptions to

and exemptions from the provisions of such Code as the President in his discretion deems necessary to effectuate the policy herein declared. [NIRA §3(a).]

Once such a code of fair competition has been approved by the president, any violation of the code was declared to be "an unfair method of competition in commerce within the meaning of the Federal Trade Commission Act as amended." A number of such codes were quickly developed, approved, and put into effect, including a "Live Poultry Code" applicable to New York City and the metropolitan area surrounding it.

In 1935, this code came before the Supreme Court on appeal by a New York City slaughter house from numerous convictions based upon violations of the code. [*A.L.A. Schechter Poultry Corp.* v. *United States*, 295 U.S. 495 (1935).] The Supreme Court first considered the government's argument that the provisions authorizing adoption of codes must be viewed in terms of the grave national crisis which existed. The court noted: "Extraordinary conditions may call for extraordinary remedies. But the argument necessarily stops short of an attempt to justify action which lies outside the sphere of constitutional authority. Extraordinary conditions do not create or enlarge constitutional power." [*295 U.S. at 528.*] The court noted further: ". . . the statutory plan is not simply one for voluntary effort. It does not seek merely to endow voluntary trade or industrial associations or groups with privileges or immunities. It involves the coercive exercise of the law making power. The codes of fair competition which the statute attempts to authorize are codes of laws." [*295 U.S. at 529.*] The court summed up the purpose of the NIRA as follows:

We think the conclusion is inescapable that the authority sought to be conferred by §3 was not merely to deal with "unfair competitive practices" which offend against existing law, and could be the subject of judicial condemnation without further legislation, or to create administrative machinery for the application of established principles of law to particular instances of violation. Rather, the purpose is clearly disclosed to authorize new and controlled prohibitions through codes of laws which would embrace what the formulators would propose, and what the President would approve, or prescribe, as wise and beneficial measures for the government of trades and industries in order to bring about their rehabilitation, correction, and development, according to the general declaration of policy in §1. [*295 U.S. at 535.*]

The court held the code provisions at issue to be invalid, both on the grounds that the attempted delegation of legislative power was unconstitutional and on the further grounds that all of the transactions involved occurred in intrastate commerce and had no direct effect on interstate commerce. [*295 U.S. at 551.*]

It is important to note that the *Schechter* case stands *not* for the proposition that self-enforcement of codes of ethics is unconstitutional, but rather that any attempt to delegate legislative authority to establish criminal codes to a private group is not permissible. At one point in its opinion, the court stated the question thus and gave the following answer:

> . . . [W]ould it be seriously contended that Congress could delegate its legislative authority to trade or industrial associations or groups so as to empower them to enact the laws they deem to be wise and beneficial for the rehabilitation and expansion of their trade or industries? Could trade or industrial associations or groups be constituted legislative bodies for that purpose because such associations or groups are familiar with the problems of their enterprises? . . . The answer is obvious. Such a delegation of legislative power is unknown to our law and is utterly inconsistent with the constitutional prerogatives and duties of Congress. [*295 U.S. at 537.*]

From this perspective, the *Schechter* case leaves open the issue of the extent to which a private organization may be empowered to enforce among its members provisions of substantive law through use of appropriate sanctions.

There are a number of federal regulatory statutes which authorize certain collective activities and provide limited antitrust exemptions for participation in such activities, such as the Interstate Commerce Act's express authorization of industry rate-making activities, subject to ICC approval. Even in those instances in which a regulatory statute has conveyed broad authority upon an industry to regulate its business activity, however, the industry typically remains subject to the general antitrust prohibitions against certain types of anticompetitive behavior. For example, in *Silver* v. *New York Stock Exchange*, 373 U.S. 341 (1963), the Supreme Court held that the power conferred under the Securities Exchange Act of 1934 did not extend to the Exchange's instructions to member firms to deny private wire connections to the nonmember plaintiff.

Similarly, the grant under state laws of extensive self-regulatory authority to the medical and legal professions has been held not to exempt a group boycott by doctors from antitrust challenge [*United States* v. *American Medical Association*, 317 U.S. 519 (1943)], and has recently been held not to exempt uniform minimum fee schedules from the prohibitions of the antitrust laws. [*Goldfarb* v. *Virginia State Bar*, 421 U.S. 773 (1975).] The particular activities challenged in each of these cases were, however, unequivocally anticompetitive and sought to regulate commercial transactions unrelated to the necessary regulation of the integrity and competence of members of the profession.

Aside from the two practices held unlawful by the Supreme Court, the general legality of the medical and legal professions' self-enforcement of codes for professional and ethical responsibility of their members has never been subject to serious challenge under the antitrust laws. Bearing in mind that the ultimate sanction used by each profession is the barring of unethical or incompetent doctors and lawyers from the practice of their professions, and that in most states, both admission to and expulsion from these professions is largely determined by members of the professions themselves, these are areas in which self-regulation has long been accepted.

CONCLUSION: THE NEED FOR CODES OF ETHICS

While the regulation of a society is based upon those fundamental values to which its members generally subscribe, there are two diametrically opposed means by which such values can be enforced. First, the values may be internalized by each member of the society and the moral suasion of the group employed to penalize deviations from these normative values, or second, the mores of the society may be transmuted into written law, with a formal enforcement methodology created to enforce that law.

The first system is obviously the more efficacious; it operates at all times and at all levels within the society and is capable of addressing virtually all significant deviations from accepted social norms. The legal approach, on the other hand, is based upon the assumption that a formal sanctioning entity, separate and apart from the rest of the society, is the best approach to insuring compliance to those general values that have been expressed in terms of legal requirements. Although laws must be based upon and must develop from the mores and social values of a society, under a system of laws primary jurisdiction for enforcement is, of course, invested in the governmental agencies that have been created to administer these laws.

Problems begin to arise, however, when society at large begins to rely solely upon the designated law enforcement agencies to protect and vindicate the values of the society. As noted earlier, the resources of any enforcement agency are finite and much too limited to permit the detection and sanctioning of every significant deviation from the law. At the present time, there is increasing recognition that the enforcement agencies alone under present laws cannot effectively reach all the behavior harmful to our society. One possible response to this deficiency is the creation of new and broader laws and new and more pervasive enforcement agencies to seek and eliminate such harmful practices.

This approach sets up a vicious circle: broader laws and broader enforcement will inevitably result in discovery of increasing numbers of violations, which in turn will engender even broader laws and still broader enforcement activities. The end result is authoritarianism—a society in which every significant activity is subject to direct governmental regulation. Such a result is, of course, antithetical to democratic principles.

What other alternatives exist for improving social conditions? There is only one viable alternative: a return to the fundamental principle that a society creates and enforces its own moral and ethical values through moral suasion and appropriate peer pressures. Codes of ethics have a preeminent role to play in any resurgence of self-regulation. Although historically a code of ethics has been a covenant among peers, modern codes require more; codes today also must be based upon integral consideration of the public interest.

Without formal codes of ethics, there is a very real danger that commercial intercourse will be smothered under the pressure of iron statutes—statutes which preclude the flexibility that is necessary if the laws are to be effective, just, and non-discriminatory. Just as undesirable advertising practices can largely be eliminated through their identification and prohibition under a code of ethical advertising practices, other deleterious practices can be identified, discredited, and made unpopular by a code of ethics supported by appropriate private sanctions.

Even without provisions for private sanctions, codes of ethics can identify and encourage good and desirable activities and can discourage undesirable activities by formally establishing a high standard against which each member of the industry may measure its performance. In this way, codes can stimulate the self-regulation and education of industry members and can serve to greatly minimize the need for further, pervasive governmental regulation which destroys individual freedoms, individual initiative, and the private enterprise system.

Present laws already permit extensive use of codes of ethics for beneficial social purposes and there appears to be growing recognition that private enforcement of codes of ethics is both necessary and appropriate in our democratic society.[1]

Part Five

Editor's Preview

Secretary of the Treasury Simon issues a strong challenge to all who wish to maintain and enlarge economic freedom in the United States. Anyone lukewarm about supporting our free enterprise system should read what Mr. Simon says; he'll be stimulated to battle for it. Not only is his essay informative and highly readable, but Mr. Simon does not allow his office or politics to dampen his directness.

A Challenge to
Free Enterprise

William E. Simon

If apologists for corporate corruption are to be taken at their word (a risky proposition at best), dishonesty is the best policy. Rigorous business ethics may be commendable from a moral point of view, they will tell you, but they interfere with the rough and tumble competition of the free market. The ethical businessman, according to advocates of corporate corner-cutting, is at an automatic competitive disadvantage; business ethics are a luxury, if not a liability.

Baloney. As Benjamin Franklin once sagely observed, "If the rascals knew the advantages of virtue, they would become honest men out of rascality." In the long run, honesty is not only the best business policy, but the *only* one compatible with a free market and open, honest competition. Corruption, whether it involves bribes to secure overseas government contracts, illegal contributions to political candidates here at home, or any other form of graft or payola, hampers the efficient functioning of the market place. It results in higher prices, lessened responsiveness to the consumer, and lower quality of goods and services. On these clear-cut, practical grounds, business corruption is *inefficient* and business ethics are efficient.

There are also overwhelming moral grounds for a strong

business ethic. History teaches us that no free society or free economy can long survive *without* an ethical base. It is only through a shared moral foundation—a set of binding ground rules for fair conduct—that free associations, be they social, diplomatic, or commercial, can flourish and endure. Far from being a luxury, a sound business ethic is essential to the preservation of free enterprise.

The real question facing the American business community today is not whether it can "afford" stronger ethical standards, but how much longer it can go on without them. Our entire way of life is held together by voluntary, society-wide bonds of mutual trust and respect. Once those bonds are broken—once public confidence falls too low (and every new opinion poll shows public confidence in both private and governmental institutions plummeting)—the whole social framework collapses and the result is either anarchy or authoritarianism. One way or the other, individual freedoms, including freedom in the marketplace, are inevitable casualties whether the blow falls gradually or all at once.

In our era, when the main political struggle is between controlled societies and free ones (and, on the economic front, between controlled economies and free ones), nothing is more vital to the survival of our economic way of life than a rigorous free enterprise ethic and business leaders with the courage and energy to stand up for it.

No one is more aware of this than the opponents of free enterprise. Advocates of a state-controlled economy, whether they are Communists, Fascists or democratic socialists, base their own position on an ethical view, though a mistaken one. Their economic philosophy is deliberately linked to a general philosophy of life for, to the "true believer," socialism and Marxism are not merely economic formulas, but all-embracing world views—a kind of temporal religion.

Their systems do not work as well as free enterprise but, like all religious devotees, they are willing to suffer and sacrifice for their beliefs. Instead of automatically weakening their faith, adversity may even fortify it as long as they *believe* and as long as they feel that their belief is anchored to something of moral worth.

Those of us on the side of economic freedom are not so

fortunate. The American free enterprise system has consistently outperformed Marxism and modified brands of socialism from the beginning, and continues to do so today. Any objective evaluation of economic performance clearly illustrates the United States' superior record in both economic output and the equitable distribution of economic benefits. In the past fifteen years alone, for example, the *real* personal disposable income of the average American has increased 50 percent!

Nevertheless, American free enterprise today is in serious danger of failing as a *belief*. The ethical and philosophic underpinnings of capitalism have not been thought out, articulated, and then disseminated to the millions of average citizens who enjoy the direct material benefits, and the indirect spiritual and political benefits our system provides. Nor is this lack of a perceivable moral anchor merely confined to the economic layman. It also afflicts many of the men and women who lead industry and business. Small wonder, then, that the man on the street has his doubts about the system.

Part of the reason is easy to understand. Until recently the very term "free enterprise" prompted a Pavlovian response. Almost everybody was for it, although many people who favored it might have had a hard time telling you what it meant. Even the Great Depression did not completely shake the American public's fundamental confidence in "free enterprise." Yet in a time of comparative prosperity, opinion polls show public confidence in the business community at low ebb. We must ask ourselves what has happened. Even more importantly, we must decide what we who believe in free enterprise should do to repair the damage.

The problem is a complex one and is not confined to business alone. Vietnam, Watergate, student unrest, shifting moral codes, the worst recession in a generation, and a number of other jarring cultural shocks have all combined to create a new climate of question and doubt. The same opinion samplings that show a decline of public confidence in business beginning in the turbulent 1960s, also show declines for the professions of religion, organized labor, government, and politics. It all adds up to a general malaise, a society-wide crisis of institutional confidence. For this very reason, no lasting progress can be made in building confidence in any one of these fields without affecting the others. For better or worse, they are all tied together.

There are, however, some specific symptoms and cures which apply particularly to the business community. Two of them, it seems to me, are uppermost. The first is the need for educating the general public to the social as well as economic benefits of the free enterprise system; the second is educating the business community itself to the relationship between good business and good citizenship: "ethicalizing" capitalism.

On the first score, it is ironic that at a time when Americans are enjoying such great abundance and such great opportunity so many of us have lost sight of the principles and institutions that have made our way of life possible. But the truth is as inescapable as it is unpleasant; somewhere along the line there has been a dangerous breakdown in communications. Too many Americans, especially those born into an affluent society that seemed to have no beginning and no end, no cause and no effect, have lost sight of, or have never been taught, the dynamics of prosperity in a free society and the interdependence of economic and other freedoms. Today, when nearly everyone takes the fruits of the free enterprise system for granted—the abundance, the opportunity for learning, travel, individual freedom, and general upward mobility —not everyone understands the basic economic facts of life that create all these benefits.

Inevitably, misunderstanding of the economic system has led to misdirection of the economy, as always must happen when long-term economic reality parts company with short-term political expediency. A classic example is the recent energy crisis and its aftermath, which I witnessed first hand. If the energy crisis proved anything it was that oil and politics don't mix. A political wrestling match was set into motion in which the president proposed one kind of legislation, then Congress reacted with another, the president vetoed, and so on, ad infinitum.

Meanwhile, oil prices and imports rose while production declined, and the oil cartel strengthened its grip.

Politicians wanted controlled prices and adequate supply at the same time. They ignored the simple truth that goods and services will be produced only so long as they can be sold at a reasonable profit. Their measures and half-measures were based on wishful thinking instead of the economic facts of life. As one commentator pointed out at the time: "No political compromises, no price rollbacks, no gradual decontrol, no $100 billion new federal bureaucracy can avoid the facts: if demand is greater than supply, then either we cut back on demand, increase supplies, or both. Let's separate politics and economics. Until we do, we will have both bad politics and bad economics. At a time like this, we can't afford *either*."[1]

Well, like it or not, politics and economics today are deeply interrelated. The only way for the business sector to get its side of the story across is to stand up and tell it itself. And the only way to get the public to *believe* it is to restore and strengthen public trust in the private sector by practicing high ethical standards that are both real and apparent.

Part, but not all, of the problem is a matter of image. Frequently, and especially to youthful idealists, those who support a state-dominated economic system are perceived as concerned, socially progressive men and women who "care"—in a nutshell, they are seen as the humane champions of the underdog. And, often enough, they really are the only ones who have effectively *communicated* their concern for social issues. It is the private sector which ultimately supplies new jobs and creates the material means for raising living standards, but the private sector seldom receives (and hardly ever clearly demonstrates its just claim to) credit from the man in the street.

Those who advocate strengthening the free enterprise system and who warn against injecting the government into every new economic and social problem that comes down the pike are seen as either outdated theorists or selfish opportunists concerned only with personal gain and preserving the status quo. To make matters worse, surface appearances often tend to confirm this impression, wrong though it is. Each new case of corporate graft, every new business scandal, further blackens the already tarnished image of the American business community. And when this happens, and the call for more government interference goes up, the innocent majority of businessmen suffer along with the guilty minority.

No one, then, has a stronger motive for stamping out unethical practices than the honest businessman, whether he runs the corner drugstore or a multibillion dollar conglomerate. Yet, through their own blind complacency many honest businessmen still either ignore the problem or respond to it with shallow clichés.

They can babble about the free enterprise system until they are blue in the face, but it still won't mean anything to those who do not understand the system behind the label, or those who have come to distrust the advocates of the system.

So one of our challenges is education—education of the public at large and greater self-understanding within the business community itself. One of the best ways to teach the pros and cons of any system is to compare it to the available alternatives. Most Americans never have been and, let us hope, never will be forced to experience first-hand what it means to live in a country where economic freedom has been destroyed or severely limited; yet, if our system is to survive, our people must have a valid standard for comparison on both material and moral grounds. This *can* be achieved through education but, so far, it has not been. Today, when considering the merits of the free enterprise system, most Americans simply do not have a valid standard for comparison.

They have never witnessed the long lines of workers and housewives who have to queue up for hours outside state-owned food and department stores in order to buy a poor selection of overpriced food staples and state-manufactured clothing and merchandise.

They do not realize what a miracle of variety, economy, and productive competition the average American shopping center would represent to most of the earth's people.

They have never asked themselves why a country like the Soviet Union, with some of the largest, richest tracts of grainland in the world, but with a government-owned and -run agricultural system, cannot even feed its own people without turning to American farmers who own their own land, make their own economic decisions, and feed not only their own people, but millions of others as well.

They have not had to suffer the loss of opportunity, the

social unrest, and economic instability of democratic countries like Italy, which has chosen to nationalize 47 percent of its industries, or Great Britain, where the postwar years of cradle-to-the-grave welfare and government stifling of private-sector initiative have led to economic stagnation and the demoralization and mass emigration of the productive middle class.

Too often they have been taught to distrust the very word profit and the profit motive that makes our prosperity possible, to somehow feel this system, that has done more to alleviate human suffering and privation than any other, is somehow cynical, selfish, and immoral.

And, of course, they have never lived in the countries where the seemingly unselfish and idealistic dream of a non-profit, propertyless society has turned into a nightmare reality —where the state and the state alone dictates what kind of education you will receive; whether you will be allowed to travel; what books you can read; what kind of job you have; what you will be paid, what merchandise you can buy with your earnings; where you will live; what medical treatment you will receive; what your children will be taught; and, ultimately, where you will be buried.

Only when economic freedom has already been destroyed is its vital relationship to personal freedom and opportunity vividly demonstrated. And when the process of erosion is gradual it can be likened to poisoning by hemlock; the numbness begins in the extremities and, by the time the victim realizes he is in danger, he is too weak and too far gone to do anything about it. As Alexander Hamilton warned so long ago, "Power over a man's substance amounts to power over his will." Unfortunately, however, economic freedom, like clean air, is something that most people do not really appreciate until it begins to run out—and then it is often too late.

Today we have reached a point where, although the free enterprise system works, and works better than any other economic system in effect anywhere in the world—feeding, clothing, and housing more people more humanely than any other while allowing them the enjoyment of our other basic freedoms —it is losing the semantic war to an alien philosophy of government control that somehow has managed to preserve an aura of idealism, altruism, and ethical soundness, at least when viewed without detailed knowledge and from a comfortable distance.

So the first part of the challenge for American capitalism is clear. We must get across the human side of capitalism, the fact that free enterprise has been and continues to be a force for human good and, in its correct application, an extension of much that is finest in our Judeo-Christian spiritual and ethical tradition.

This can be done very effectively, but not until American capitalism does some soul-searching and internal housecleaning of its own, until the business community becomes as concerned about corruption, bribes, and the need for ethical behavior as it is about turning a profit. Before we can sell the ethic of capitalism to the general public, we must be clear in our own minds about it; we must really believe in it and we must show that we really practice what we preach. Among other things, this means our being the first to denounce the few rotten apples in our midst. "The time to guard against corruption and tyranny is before they shall have gotten hold of us," Thomas Jefferson once wrote, and this eternal truth certainly applies to the American business community today. If we are to regain and hold lost public understanding and esteem, we, and not those who would destroy the capitalist system, must lead the way in wiping out abuses committed in its name.

This thought was uppermost in my mind when I testified on Capitol Hill in August 1975 concerning the revelations of widespread foreign bribery by the Lockheed Aircraft Corporation. At a time when it was benefiting from a government-guaranteed loan of $250 million provided by a consortium of American banks, Lockheed had been secretly paying out millions of dollars in graft to foreign officials. The revelation of this unethical conduct not only severely injured Lockheed's standing, but also greatly damaged America's international prestige and further weakened public confidence in all corporations—the innocent along with the guilty. I said then, and reemphasize now, that both government and the other members of the corporate community should unite in unequivocally condemning illegal or unethical activities by American businesses, whether at home or abroad.

In a recent *Newsweek* interview, a corporate executive lamented: "I've been coming to Washington for 30 years, and I used to love it. It's no fun now. It's an angry, humorless climate. I keep hoping the pendulum will swing back our way sometime. But it doesn't. It just doesn't." To my mind, the kind of passive, despairing attitude reflected in that statement is, if anything, more discouraging than any of the cases of corporate corruption involving Lockheed, Gulf, Exxon, and other firms that have lately come to light. Corruption can be detected and punished; defeatism within the ranks of the private sector—self-doubt and loss of the basic sense of ethical purpose underlying the balance sheets and the dividend checks—is a far more serious matter. The pendulum is never going to swing back if no one bothers to keep the clock wound, preferring to shrug and lay low in hopes of riding out the unpleasantness.

As long as many of America's executive suites house gutless wonders who are craving anonymity and are deathly afraid of "rocking the boat," the boat is going to keep on leaking and slowly sinking. Even more than the political sector, the private sector stands in desperate need of leaders who are statesmen of courage and principle.

The institutional cowardice of much of the private-sector hierarchy was painfully illustrated to me during the political battle over New York City. As the major spokesman within the administration for those who opposed a financial bail-out, I received repeated calls from many major business and investment executives congratulating me on my stand and urging me to "hang in there." But whenever I asked these summer soldiers to express their views in public testimony they ran like rabbits, spouting a thousand and one excuses for their cowardice, all of which added up to one: rather than risk temporary financial losses or a brief flurry of media criticism, they chose to turn their backs on their beliefs, and on those who dared to defend them in public.

What the private sector requires today is leaders who have deep convictions and will stand up for them; who will stop asking for government tariffs and subsidies as a substitute for good management; who will condemn the minority of corrupters in their midst instead of making excuses for them; and who will seek out the public limelight to state the case for ethical capitalism, instead of cowering in the shadows while the system comes under ever heavier attack.

Fortunately, not everyone is heading for cover. Some outstanding members of the business community are awake to the problem and are doing their best to warn others and stir them to positive action. In January 1976, A. W. Clausen, the president of Bank of America, blasted the "ethical blindness" of some American corporations and called for "strong and specific measures" to strengthen and cleanse the private sector from within. "If the market economy ever goes under," Mr. Clausen said, "our favorite villains—socialist economics and government regulators—won't be to blame; we will."

As a result of recent revelations, Mr. Clausen maintained, "Many of this nation's bluest of blue-chip corporations are perceived as operating on the assumption that payoffs, bribes, influence peddling, book-juggling, falsifications of records, and miscellaneous other hanky-panky are somehow a normal part and cost of doing business." Consequently, the American public is "rightfully skeptical of our practices and our preachings. To reverse this skepticism, we ourselves must initiate strong and specific measures" to demonstrate the good faith and good practice of American businessmen.

"Integrity," Mr. Clausen said, is not "some impractical notion dreamed up by naive do-gooders. Our integrity is the foundation for, the very basis of, our ability to do business."

How does Mr. Clausen propose to strengthen the ethical base of American capitalism? In the case of Bank of America, by developing a rigorous, formal code of business conduct—in other words, a codified set of ethics. Some business leaders, notably Irving Shapiro, chairman of the board of DuPont, go even further and advocate a new, uniform code of ethics to which all large corporations would subscribe, an admirable goal, if one that is not likely to be achieved in the immediate future, and definitely one we should all actively work toward realizing.

Even while some American corporations were being called to account for their use of bribery to stimulate foreign sales, many more were proving that the best way to compete abroad, as at home, is to sell a good product at a good price. The computer and data processing field, where the superiority of American technology is recognized worldwide, is a case in point, and Frank T. Cary, IBM's chairman, has put the question of domestic and overseas corruption in its proper perspective:

> When some businesses turn out shoddy products or engage in misleading advertising or ignore customer complaints, the public gets sour on business as a whole. When some executives . . . admit that they bribed foreign officials or illegally channeled corporate funds into political campaigns, the public believes this is standard business conduct. And when we read in the papers about corporate kickbacks and secret Swiss bank accounts, all business suffers.
>
> Some businessmen have tried to excuse themselves by saying that everybody does it. Well, everybody doesn't do it . . . The time has come for those of us in business to put our house in order . . . to restore the faith of Americans in the basic competence and purpose of business. And this requires a lot more than public-relations efforts.

Individually, this requires a new attitude of vigilance among honest businessmen and the willingness to pay as much attention to corporate responsibility as to corporate profits. Nothing is more efficient than honesty; those who break the law or abuse the basic moral code in the name of profit are doing more to make "profit" a dirty word than all of the critics of the free enterprise system put together. Both the legal and medical professions have long since recognized the need to ostracize peers who abuse their professional trust and thereby damage the standing of all of their colleagues; it is high time that the vast majority of honest American businessmen did as much.

Internationally, the United States government can help, and has already begun to do so by working through the Organization for Economic Cooperation in Paris for the adoption of an international code of ethics that could help curb bribery. Bribery, however, is a two-way street. The process requires willing corruptees as well as corrupters. The irony of most of the recent bribery and illegal contribution scandals is that, rather than involving unlawful or unethical practices between two or more corporations, they have involved joint lapses in conduct involving single corporations and American or foreign politicians or civil servants. Dealings with politicians and bureaucrats would seem to offer more opportunities and incentive for dishonesty than straight competition on the open market, a fact that says something about public as well as private sector moral standards. Old-fashioned consumer-oriented competition on the open market is apparently more resistant to corruption than the growing volume of corporate business without direct consumer involvement and in conditions of secrecy and convoluted bureaucratic red tape that makes keen competition more difficult and corner-cutting easier. Because of this it is tempting to rationalize unethical conduct overseas—tempting, but, as the *Wall Street Journal* pointed out in a commendable editorial of 27 February 1976, mistaken:

> It might be argued that Americans are the winners if Lockheed uses a bribe to beat out Dassault for a Saudi contract. At stake are United States aircraft industry jobs, economies of scale that reduce costs of military hardware bought by the United States itself, the maintenance of a production capability vital to United States defense and exports that are important to the soundness of the United States dollar.
>
> Such considerations salve the conscience of American businessmen who engage in bribery abroad. But at best they only represent an argument for an international attack on the problem. They have nothing to do with the fundamental morality.
>
> To argue that Americans should tolerate—because it might be in their own interests—the victimization of the people of Japan or Italy is to apply a dangerous double-standard. It is dangerous because the higher of two standards almost always sinks to the level of the lower one. It isn't long before the practices winked at abroad are used at home as well. It is dangerous also because it fails to recognize the essential interdependence of the market economics both in an economic and political sense.
>
> Ethical codes cannot, of course, revolutionize the mores of the world. But, when the United States becomes a nation with no standards to offer it will no longer be the leader of the non-socialist block. The ethic it must support to survive is the ethic of the free market and it is essential to the free market that governments enforce honest competition.

And herein, it seems to me, lies the heart of the matter of ethics. The whole point of free enterprise—of capitalism—is vigorous, honest competition. Every corner cut, every bribe placed, every little cheating move by a businessman in pursuit of quick plunder instead of honest profit, is an outright attack on the real free enterprise system. In the last analysis, good ethics actually do make good business because a vital free market, like any other voluntary association of individuals, can thrive only on mutual trust and voluntary cooperation. Just as you cannot maintain a home or a healthy society without a strong degree of shared respect and common values, you cannot maintain a healthy market without a strong degree of trust and a shared code of ethics (whether stated or implicit) among the participants.

"A good reputation," the old Roman proverb has it, "is more valuable than money." In his recently published memoirs, Mr. Stanley Marcus of Nieman-Marcus expressed the same thought another way: "There is never a good sale for Nieman-Marcus unless it's a good buy for the customer." The continuous struggle within capitalist ranks has always been between those enlightened businessmen who recognize this ethical but also utilitarian basis for sustained prosperity and those who lose sight of it in pursuit of the quick killing. The latter group is every bit as contemptible as the poacher who slaughters endangered species to sell a few fur coats, or the exploiter who plunders forests or destroys the environment for short-term returns at unacceptable long-term cost to us and to posterity. Such people are counterfeit capitalists, outlaws within the fold. They are modern Vandals who, unchecked, could damage or destroy a brilliant but delicate market system that has taken thousands of years to evolve and has rained more benefits on the human race than all of the utopian political and economic schemes ever dreamt of by social visionaries.

Two centuries ago, Adam Smith wrote the classic work that is still, in its broad philosophy at least, one of the most brilliant rationales for the free enterprise system ever written. In Book IV of *The Wealth of Nations*, Smith advocated a commercial system of what he termed "natural liberty," free of arbitrary preferences and restraints. "Every man,"

Smith said, "as long as he does not violate the laws of justice . . . [should be] left perfectly free to pursue his own interest his own way, and to bring both his industry and capital into competition with those of any other man, or order of men."

Business corruption, even when it is not in technical violation of what Smith called "the laws of justice," is an arbitrary restraint on open, honest competition. It is therefore unacceptable on both moral and practical grounds. At a time when the business community has been shorn of most of its traditional political leverage, in the face of a new public mood of angry questioning, and in a political atmosphere in which it is all too tempting for demagogues to blame American business for the whole litany of economic and social problems we face, the most valuable asset American capitalism retains is its reputation for providing honest value for money—in short, its good name.

In such a climate, developing and articulating a strong, clear American business ethic has become absolutely necessary to the survival of the free enterprise system. And just as each American citizen bears the awesome burden of meeting his civic obligations in a way that will preserve his heritage of political liberty for his children, each American businessman has a sacred duty to maintain a standard of behavior and a reputation for integrity that will preserve our economic liberties for generations of Americans yet unborn.

Essay Reference Notes

Note to *Introduction*

1. Dr. Clark's lectures, presented at the University of Bridgeport, Yale University, Columbia University, and Harvard University in the spring and fall of 1955, were sponsored by the Calvin K. Kazanjian Economic Foundation, Inc., of West Redding, Connecticut. Subsequently the lectures were published under the same title. We are deeply grateful to the Kazanjian Foundation for granting us permission to use the title and excerpts from Dr. Clark's lectures. We hope this book will be representative of both Dr. Clark's and the foundation's substantive contributions to economic freedom in America.

Note to *The Meaning of Ethics and Freedom*

1. Earl Warren, in remarks given 11 November 1962 at the Louis Marshall Award dinner of the Jewish Theological Seminary of America, Americana Hotel, New York City.

Notes to *Ethics in Evolutionary Perspective*

1. Any introductory textbook in general anthropology will supply such evidence; see, for example, Conrad Kottak, *Anthropology: The Exploration of Human Diversity* (New York: Random House, 1974).
2. Émile Durkheim, *De la Division du Travail Social* (Paris: Félix Alean, 1893).
3. Karl Marx, Verlag von Otto Meissner, (1867–1894.) *Capital: A Critique of Political Economy*. ed. Frederick Engles. vol. 3 (New York: International Pub-

lishers, 1967). Marx, is of course, not infallible, nor is any social theorist. For example, there are difficulties in directly applying certain of his analyses to America; we wish to stress, however, his enduring contribution to the general study of economy and society.

4. Portions of this work are translated and edited in *Max Weber: The Theory of Social and Economic Organization*, trans. A. M. Henderson and Talcott Parsons (Glencoe, Illinois: The Free Press, 1947).

5. Bronislaw Malinowski, *Argonauts of the Western Pacific* (New York: Dutton, 1961). Original 1922.

6. Raymond Firth, *Primitive Polynesian Economy*, second ed. (London: Routledge and Kegan Paul, 1965). Original 1946. D. W. Goodfellow, *Principles of Economic Sociology* (Philadelphia: Blakiston, 1939).

7. See, for example, George Dalton, "Theoretical Issues in Economic Anthropology." *Current Anthropology*, 10 (1969): 63–102. Paul Bohannon and George Dalton, *Markets in Africa* (Evanston: Northwestern University Press, 1962). Marshall D. Sahlins, *Stone Age Economies* (Chicago: Aldine, 1972).

8. Karl Polanyi, et al., eds., *Trade and Market in the Early Empires* (Glencoe, Illinois, The Free Press, 1957).

9. Edward E. Le Clair, Jr. and Harold K. Schneider, eds., *Economic Anthropology: Readings in Theory and Analysis* (New York: Holt, Rinehart and Winston, 1968).

10. Maurice Godelier, *Rationality and Irrationality in Economics*, trans. Brian Pearce (New York: Monthly Review Press, 1972). Claude Meillassoux, "From Reproduction to Production: A Marxist Approach to Economic Anthropology," *Economy and Society*, 1(1972):93–105.

11. See Scott Cook, "Economic Anthropology: Problems in Theory, Method and Analysis," in John J. Honigmann, ed., *Handbook of Social and Cultural Anthropology* (Chicago: Rand McNally, 1973) pp. 795–860.

12. This typology is elaborated in A. Thomas Kirsch and James L. Peacock, *The Human Direction: An Evolutionary Approach to Cultural Anthropology* (Englewood Cliffs, New Jersey: Prentice-Hall, 1973). See also James L. Peacock, *Consciousness and Change* (Oxford, England: Blackwell's, 1975).

13. Wallerstein makes this same point by saying that, in any particular historical epoch, there is only one world system. However, he distinguishes between the core, periphery, and semiperiphery of that system in order to deal with variations in economic forms. Immanuel Wallerstein, *The Modern World-System* (New York: Academic Press, 1974).

14. The terms "general" and "specific" evolution are more fully explained in Marshall D. Sahlins and Elman R. Service, eds., *Evolution and Culture* (Ann Arbor: University of Michigan Press, 1960).

15. An excellent recent exposition of reciprocity is J. van Baal, *Reciprocity and the Position of Women* (Assen, Amsterdam, Netherlands: Van Gorcum, 1975).

16. Marcel Mauss, *Essai sur le Don. Forme et Raison de l'Exchange dans les Societies Archaiques.* In *Année Sociologique*, nouv. serie I, pp. 30–186. *The Gift*, trans. T. Cunnison (London: Cohen and West, 1954).

17. Malinowski, *Argonauts of the Western Pacific*.

18. Claude Lévi-Strauss, *The Elementary Structures of Kinship*, second ed. (London: Eyre and Spottiswoode, 1969). First French edition, 1949.
19. Meillassoux, "From Reproduction to Production."
20. This principle of "redistribution" as opposed to "reciprocity" is developed in Polanyi et al., op. cit.
21. While Weber's thesis has been heavily criticized, many of these criticisms are misguided. For a brief summary and rebuttal, see Peacock, *The Human Direction*, pp. 75–77.
22. See Max Weber, *The Religion of China: Confucianism and Taoism*, trans. and ed. H. H. Gerth (Glencoe, Illinois: The Free Press, 1951).
23. On this modern trend, see Robert N. Bellah, "Religious Evolution," *American Sociological Review*, 29 (1964): 358–74.
24. Richard J. Barnet and Ronald E. Müller, *Global Reach: The Power of the Multinational Corporations.* (New York: Simon and Schuster, 1974).
25. I wish to acknowledge with gratitude the aid of James Wessman whose expertise in economic anthropology was indispensable in clarifying, elaborating, and adding certain sections of this essay. J.L.P.

Notes to *Adaptations and Maladaptions in Social Systems*

1. Jean Piaget, *Structuralism*, ed. and trans. Chaninah Maschler (London: Routledge and Kegan Paul, 1972).
2. Ascher and Hockett, "The Human Revolution," *Current Anthropology* 5(1964): 137; and Romer, *Men and the Vertebrates* (London: Penguin, 1954).
3. Gregory Bateson, *Steps to an Ecology of Mind* (New York: Ballantine Books, 1972).
4. Bateson, "The Role of Somatic Change in Evolution," *Evolution* 17(1963): 529–39; and Slobodkin, "Toward a Predictive Theory of Evolution," *Population Biology and Evolution.*
5. Bateson, "Somatic Change," *Evolution* 17(1963): 529–39; Frisancho, "Functional Adaptation to High Altitude Hypoxia," *Science* 187(1975): 313–19; and Slobodkin, "Toward a Predictive Theory," *Population Biology and Evolution.*
6. Kalmus, "Control Hierarchies," in *Regulation and Control of Living Systems*, ed. H. Kalmus; Miller, "Living Systems: Basic Concepts," 10(1965): 193–257; Miller, "Living Systems: Structure and Process," op. cit., pp. 337–79; Pattee, ed. *Hierarchy Theory* (International Library of Systems Theory and Philosophy, 1973); Powers, Clarke and McFarland, "A General Feedback Theory of Human Behavior," in *Communication and Culture*, ed. Alfred G. Smith (New York: Rinehart and Winston, 1966); Rappaport, "The Moral and Aesthetic Structure of Human Adaptation," *Coevolution Quarterly* 1(1974); Rappaport, "The Role of the Sacred in Human Evolution," *Annual Review of Ecology and Systematics*; and Simon, *The Sciences of the Artificial* (Cambridge: MIT Press, 1969).
7. Brookfield and Brown, *Struggle for Land* (Melbourne: Oxford University Press, 1963); Meggitt, *The Lineage System of the Mae Enga* (London: Oliver and Boyd, 1965); Meggitt, "Understanding Australian Aboriginal Society:

Kinship Systems or Cultural Categories," in *Kinship Studies in the Morgan Centennial Year*, ed. Priscilla Reining (Washington: The Anthropological Society of Washington, 1972); Ortiz, *The Tewa World* (Chicago: University of Chicago Press, 1970); Rappaport, *Pigs for the Ancestors* (New Haven: Yale University Press, 1968); and Sahlins, "The Segmentary Lineage: An Organization of Predatory Expansion," *American Anthropologist* 63(1961): 322–45.

8. Gordon Park, "Some Mechanical Concepts of Goals, Individuals, Consciousness and Symbolic Evolution," in *Wenner-Gren Symposium on the Effects of Conscious Purpose on Human Adaptation*, 1968.

9. Slobodkin, "Toward a Predictive Theory."

10. Hall and Fagen, "Definition of System," *General Systems Yearbook* 1(1956):19–28; and von Bertalanffy, *General System Theory* (New York: George Braziller, 1969).

11. Hall and Fagen, "Definition of System."

12. Marshall Sahlins, *The Tribesmen* (Englewood Cliffs: Prentice-Hall, 1967).

13. Rappaport, *Pigs for the Ancestors.*

14. Simon, *The Sciences of the Artificial.*

15. Simon, *The Sciences.*

16. I. J. Young and W. F. Rowley, "The Logic of Disease," *International Journal of Neuropsychiatry* (1967).

17. Flannery, "The Cultural Evolution of Civilizations," *Annual Review of Ecology and Systematics* 3(1972); and Rappaport, "Moral and Aesthetic Structure."

18. Geoffrey Vickers, "A Theory of Reflexive Consciousness," in *Wenner-Gren Conference on the Effects of Conscious Purpose on Human Adaptation*, 1968.

19. Roy A. Rappaport, "The Flow of Energy in an Agricultural Society," *Scientific American* 225(Sept. 1971): 116–32.

20. Flannery, "Cultural Evolution"; Rappaport, "Moral and Aesthetic Structure"; and idem, "The Role of the Sacred."

21. John Kenneth Galbraith, *The New Industrial State* (Boston: Houghton Mifflin, 1967).

22. Paul Tillich, *Dynamics of Faith* (New York: Harper and Row, 1957).

23. Denis de Rougemont, *La Part du Diable* (New York: Brentano's, 1944).

24. Lawrence Slobodkin and Roy A. Rappaport, "An Optimal Strategy of Evolution," *The Quarterly Review of Biology* 44(1974):181–200.

25. Ostwald, "The Modern Theory of Energetics," *The Monist* 17(1907):481–515; and White, *The Science of Culture* (New York: Farrar Straus, 1949).

26. Earl Cook, "The Flow of Energy in an Industrial Society," in *Energy and Power*, ed. Scientific American, pp. 83–94.

27. Rappaport, *Pigs for the Ancestors.*

28. Colin Turnbull, *The Forest People* (New York: Natural History Press, 1962).

29. Martin Buber, *I and Thou* (New York: Charles Scribner's Sons, new edition 1970).

30. Tillich, *Dynamics of Faith.*

31. Claude Levi-Strauss, *Totemism* (Boston: Beacon Press, 1962).

32. J. R. Searle, *Speech Acts: An Essay in the Philosophy of Language* (Cambridge: Cambridge University Press, 1969).

Notes to *Capitalist Enterprise and Bureaucracy*

1. Cf. Oxford English Dictionary: "The primary of the adjective free is dear . . . applied as the distinctive epithet of those members of the household who were connected by ties of kinship with the head, as opposed to the slaves. The converse process of sense-development appears in Latin *liberi* (children), literally the free members of the household."

2. L. Goldschmidt, *Handbuch des Handelsrechts,* (Erlangen, 1891), vol. 1, cited in Henry Higgs (ed.), *Palgrave's Dictionary of Political Economy,* (London, 1926), 2:577–82.

3. George Ridgeway, *Merchants of Peace* (New York, 1938).

4. Herbert Feus, *1933: Characters in Crisis* (Boston: Little, Brown Co., 1966), ch. 16–26.

5. Ibid., p. 342.

6. Cf. J. B. Condliffe, *The Commerce of Nations* (New York: W. W. Norton, 1950), p. 495.

7. For analysis of a trading system designed to maximize power rather than wealth, cf. Albert A. Hirschaman, *National Power and the Structure of Foreign Trade* (Berkeley: University of California Press, 1943).

8. Cf. Gottfried Haberler, *The Challenge to the Free Market Economy* (Washington, D.C.: The American Enterprise Institute for Public Policy, 1975).

9. J. J. Jusserand, *A Literary History of the English People* (London: T. Fisher Unwin, 1886), 2:5–6.

10. Helen Zimmern, *The Hansa Towns* (New York: G. P. Putnam's Sons, 1891). The Gothic word, Hansa, meant a society or group, and later a tax, or the entrance fee to the League.

11. R. H. Tawney, *Religion and the Rise of Capitalism* (London: John Murray, 1926), p. 212 seq. and pp. 319–20.

12. Ibid., p. 248.

13. Thomas Mun, *England's Treasure by Foreign Trade,* published in 1644 but probably written perhaps 30 years earlier.

14. J. M. Keynes, *The General Theory of Employment, Interest and Money* (London: Macmillan, 1936), ch. 23 "Notes on Mercantilism, the Usury Laws, Stamped Money and Theories of Under-consumption."

15. J. B. Condliffe, *The Commerce of Nations.*

16. Cf. G. H. Cuttridge, "Adam Smith on the American Revolution: An Unpublished Memorial," *American Hisitorical Review,* 38 (July 1933): 714–20; and Jacob Viner, *Guide to John Rae's "Life of Adam Smith"* (New York: Augustus M. Kelley, 1965), pp. 85–6 citing *The Wealth of Nations* (Cannan edition) 2:431 and 433.

17. Adam Smith, *An Inquiry into the Nature and Causes of the Wealth of Nations,* ed. by Edwin Cannan (London: Methuen & Co., reprinted 1961), 1:477.

18. Ibid., p. 478.

19. Ibid., 1:xlvi.

20. Ibid., 1:144.

21. Cf. Alfred Marshall, *Principles of Economics,* 9th (Variorum) edition (London: Macmillan, 1961), pp. 755–69.

22. Cf. Ross Terrill, *R. H. Tawney and His Times: Socialism as Fellowship* (Cambridge: Harvard University Press, 1973).

23. Donald T. Brash, "Problems and Prospects for the New Zealand Economy," Canterbury Chamber of Commerce Bulletin, no. 595 (November 10, 1975).

24. J. K. Galbraith, *The New Industrial State* (Boston: Houghton Mifflin Co., 1967), especially ch. 12, "Motivation in Perspective."

25. Between 1938 and 1974 the annual value of world exports rose from $23.5 to $753 billion, more than a thirty-fold increase.

26. *Federal Register,* Wednesday, November 26, 1975.

27. Department of the Treasury, U.S. Customs Service, "Headquarters Briefing Paper on the Generalized System of Preferences," (October 29, 1975).

28. Cf. *London Economist,* (May 10, 1975), p. 97.

29. *Areopagitica: A Speech of Mr. John Milton, for the Liberty of Unlicenc'd Printing: To the Parliament of England* (London, 1644; reprinted Westminster: Constable & Co., 1903).

30. Cf. e.g. Senator Warren G. Magnuson and Jean Carper, *The Dark Side of the Marketplace* (Englewood Cliffs, New Jersey: Prentice-Hall, 1968).

Notes to *Ethics and the Law Between Unequals*

1. Cf. J. B. Condliffe, *The Commerce of Nations* (New York: W. W. Norton, 1950), p. 32. A. B. Bozeman, *Politics and Culture in International History* (Princeton, N.J. 1960), p. 33.

2. R. S. Lopez and I. W. Raymond, *Medieval Trade in the Mediterranean World.* Illustrative Documents. Translated with Introductive Notes. (New York, 1955).

3. A. B. Bozeman, *Politics and Culture,* p. 402.

4. W. A. Bewes, *The Romance of the Law Merchant* (1923), p. 19.

5. R. C. Kelso, *International Law of Commerce* (1961), p. 23.

6. W. A. Bewes, *The Romance,* p. 22.

7. First published as "Die protestantische Ethik und der Geist des Kapitalismus," *Archiv für Sozialgeschichte,* vols. 20/21 (1904–05), reprinted in his *Gesammelte Aufsätze zur Religionssoziologie,* 2nd ed. (1922), and translated by Talcott Parsons as *The Protestant Ethic and the Spirit of Capitalism* (1930).

8. Cf. W. Fischer, *Drei Schweizer Pioniere der Industrie:* Johann Conrad Fischer (1773–1854), Johann Caspar Escher (1775–1859), Johann Georg Bodmer (1786–1864), in: *ibid., Wirtschaft und Gesellschaft im Zeitalter der Industrialisierung. Aufsätze—Studien-Vorträge* (1972), p. 434 (translated from the German by Gerald Strauss).

9. A. B. Bozeman, *The Future of Law in a Multicultural World* (1971), pp. 51 f.

10. Sir H. Jenkyns, *British Rule and Jurisdiction beyond the Seas* (1902), pp. 167 f.

11. V. K. Wellington Koo, *The Status of Aliens in China* (1912), p. 64. That this view was shared by other early Western writers on China is mentioned by W. L. Tung, *China and the Foreign Powers: The Impact of and Reaction to Unequal Treaties* (1970), p. 14, fn. 14.

12. J. K. Fairbank, *Trade and Diplomacy on the China Coast: The Opening of the Treaty Ports 1842–1854* (1953), p. 5.

13. P. S. Reinsch, *World Politics at the End of the Nineteenth Century as Influenced by the Oriental Situation* (1900), p. 189.

14. Ibid., p. 247.

15. Adam Smith, *An Inquiry into the Nature and Causes of the Wealth of Nations* (1776), book 4, ch. 3, part 2.

16. Ibid., book 4, ch. 2.

17. Cf. the interesting treatise by C. H. Alexandrowicz, *An Introduction to the History of the Law of Nations in the East Indies (16th, 17th and 18th centuries)* (1967).

18. B. H. Pandy, *The Introduction of English Law into India: The Career of Elijah Impey in Bengal, 1774–1783* (1967), p. 230.

Notes to *Codes for Transnational Enterprises*

1. See Organization for Economic Cooperation and Development, "Interim Report of the Industry Committee on International Companies," Paris, March 1974, pp. 20–22. This report includes also a review of restrictions and conditions imposed on foreign investment by a number of other countries.

2. See Thomas W. Allen, "Policies of ASEAN Countries Towards Direct Foreign Investment," in *SEADAG Papers,* (New York: The Asian Society, 1974); and Grupo Andino, "Regimen Comun de Tratamiento al Capital Extranjero," Lima, Peru, 1972 (also in U.S. Department of Commerce "Overseas Business Reports"). See also my *Decision-Criteria in Foreign Direct Investment in Latin-America,* (New York: Council of the Americas, 1974).

3. UNCTAD, Committee on Transfer of Technology, Intergovernmental Group of Experts on a Code of Conduct of Transfer of Technology, Geneva, May 5, 1975.

4. International Chamber of Commerce, *Guidelines for International Investment,* (Paris, November 29, 1972).

5. Pugwash Conference on Science and World Affairs, "Draft Code of Conduct on Transfer of Technology," in *World Development,* April–May (1974): 77–82; for comments on this and other codes see "Codes of Conduct for the

Transfer of Technology: A Critique," Fund for Multinational Management Education, New York, 1974. (The Pugwash Conference is a group of private citizens constituted to speak on science policy and is named for the place it first met in 1920.)
6. Caterpillar Tractor Co., "A Code for World Wide Business Conduct," Peoria, Ill., 1974.
7. See Don Wallace ed., *International Control of Foreign Investment*, (N.Y.: Praeger, 1974).
8. See Behrman, Boddewyn, and Kapoor, *International Business-Government Communication*, (Boston: Lexington Books, 1975).
9. For discussions of these criteria in the context of foreign investment and the new international economic order, see my monograph on *Conflicting Constraints on the Multinational Enterprise*, (New York: Fund for Multinational Management Education, 1974); and *Towards a New International Economic Order*, (Paris: The Atlantic Institute, 1974).

Note to *Honesty and Professional Ethics: Focus on Law*

1. I deeply appreciate the substantial contribution made to this essay by Professor Eugene L. Smith of the University of Houston College of Law. L. J.

Notes to *Ethics in Government Service*

1. U.S. General Accounting Report, *Improvements Needed in the Federal Maritime Commission's Financial Disclosure System for Employees*, 22 October 1975.
2. *Wall Street Journal*, 1 November, 1974.
3. Common Cause, *1972 Federal Campaign Finances: Interest Groups and Political Parties*, 3 volumes.
4. Association of the Bar of the City of New York, *Conflict of Interest and Federal Service*, (Harvard University Press, 1960), p. 3.
5. Roswell Perkins, "The New Federal Conflict of Interest Law," *Harvard Law Review*, 76 (April 1963): 1118–22.
6. U.S. General Accounting Office Report, *Need for Improving the Regulation of the Natural Gas Industry in Management of Internal Operations*, 15 December 1974.
7. U.S.General Accounting Report, *Financial Disclosure System for the Food and Drug Administration Needs Tightening*, 19 January 1976.
8. U.S. General Accounting Office Report, *Effectiveness of the Financial Disclosure System for Employees of the U.S. Geological Survey*, 3 March 1975.
9. *St. Petersburg Times*, 30 June 1975.
10. *The Washington Star*, 28 August 1974 and 18 December 1975.
11. *The Washington Post*, 23 October 1975 and *The Wall Street Journal*, 13 October 1975.
12. Edmund Beard and Stephen Horn, *Congressional Ethics, The View from the House*, (The Brookings Institution, 1975).

13. Leon Reed, *Military Maneuvers*, (Council on Economic Priorities, 1975).
14. *The Wall Street Journal*, 20 November 1975 and *The Los Angeles Times*, 16 November 1975.
15. *The Washington Star*, 11 September 1975.
16. *The New York Times*, 6 July 1975.
17. *The Congressional Quarterly*, 19 July 1975.
18. *American Public Gas Association Newsletter*, 18 July 1975.
19. Perkins, op. cit., p. 1155.
20. U.S. General Accounting Office reports, *Department of Interior Improves Its Financial Disclosure System for Employees* (2 December 1975), *Effectiveness of Financial Disclosure Systems for Civil Aeronautics Board Employees Needs Improvement* (16 September 1975), and report on the FMC, op. cit.
21. U.S. General Accounting Office reports on the FDA and FPC, op. cit.
22. Sam S. Reed, Assistant Secretary of State of the State of Washington, Testimony to be delivered to Alaskan legislators, 18 February 1974, pp. 2–3.
23. United Press International in *Los Angeles Times*, 4 January 1974.
24. Fritz vs. Gorton, 517 P 2d 911, at 925, (1974), appeal dismissed, 42 U.S.L.W. 3646.

Note to *Legal Limitations of Codes of Ethics*

1. I am indebted to my colleague, Robert W. Green, for his valued assistance in the preparation of this essay. E.W.K.

Note to *A Challenge to Free Enterprise*

1. C. Jackson Grayson, Jr. on *CBS Morning News*.

American Viewpoint, Inc. is a nonprofit, nonsectarian, nonpartisan, tax-exempt educational corporation. The editor and many of the contributors have donated their time and talent to produce this book. No royalties will be paid to anyone. All profits from its sale will be used by American Viewpoint, Inc. in its three-part campaign to extend economic and political freedom in America by strengthening its ethical underpinnings.

Briefly stated, American Viewpoint's goals are: 1) to extend economic and political freedom in America by promulgating the need for honesty and individual responsibility. We want to restigmatize dishonesty and make being honest socially and culturally "all right," or "smart," maybe even fashionable; 2) to encourage professional and trade associations to develop and implement codes of ethics and encourage corporate, labor, and government organizations to expand and enforce ethical policies; 3) to research, develop, and promulgate teaching materials on ethics for all levels of public school education. The publication and sale of this book is another step in the furtherance of these objectives.